THE AESTHETICS OF KINSHIP

❧

For more information about the series, please visit
www.bucknelluniversitypress.org.

THE AESTHETICS OF KINSHIP

Form and Family in the Long Eighteenth Century

Heidi Schlipphacke

BUCKNELL
UNIVERSITY PRESS

Lewisburg, Pennsylvania

Library of Congress Cataloging-in-Publication Data
Names: Schlipphacke, Heidi M., author.
Title: The aesthetics of kinship : form and family in the long
eighteenth century / Heidi Schlipphacke.
Description: Lewisburg : Bucknell University Press, [2023] | Series:
New studies in the age of Goethe | Includes bibliographical references and index.
Identifiers: LCCN 2022010611 | ISBN 9781684484539 (paperback) |
ISBN 9781684484546 (hardback) | ISBN 9781684484553 (epub) |
ISBN 9781684484577 (pdf)
Subjects: LCSH: Families in literature. | German literature—18th century—
History and criticism. | Families—Germany—Philosophy—History—18th century. |
Germany—Civilization—18th century. | Germany—Intellectual life—18th century.
Classification: LCC PT289 .S295 2023 | DDC 833/.6—dc23/eng/20220623
LC record available at https://lccn.loc.gov/2022010611

Bucknell University Press gratefully acknowledges the Goethe Society
of North America for their generous support of this project.

A British Cataloging-in-Publication record for this book is available from the British Library.

www.bucknelluniversitypress.org

Distributed worldwide by Rutgers University Press

Manufactured in the United States of America

For Imke

CONTENTS

ILLUSTRATIONS

ABBREVIATIONS

FA   Johann Wolfgang von Goethe. *Sämtliche Werke: Briefe, Tagebücher und Gespräche*. Frankfurter Ausgabe (Frankfurt edition). 40 volumes in 2 sections. Frankfurt am Main: Deutscher Klassiker Verlag.

WB   *Gotthold Ephraim Lessing: Werke und Briefe*, 12 vols. Frankfurt am Main: Deutscher Klassiker Verlag.

NA   Friedrich Schiller. *Werke und Briefe*. 12 volumes. Frankfurt am Main: Deutscher Klassiker Verlag.

THE AESTHETICS OF KINSHIP

Introduction

IN HIS 1798 essay on the Laocoön sculpture group depicting the Trojan priest and his two sons being attacked by snakes, Johann Wolfgang von Goethe expresses his preference for statuary groupings over sculptures that represent an individual figure:

> Aber in dem herrlichen Zirkel des mythischen Kunstkreises, in welchem diese einzelnen selbstständigen Naturen stehen und ruhen, gibt es kleinere Zirkel, wo die einzelnen Gestalten in Bezug auf andere gedacht und gearbeitet sind. Z.E. die neun Musen, mit ihrem Führer Apoll, ist jede für sich gedacht und ausgeführt, aber in dem ganzen mannigfaltigen Chor wird sie noch interessanter.

> [But within the glorious sphere of the mythical art world, where these self-contained beings reign in splendid isolation, there are also smaller spheres where figures are conceived and created in relation to others. For example, the nine Muses and their leader Apollo are conceived and created individually, yet each becomes more interesting if perceived as a member of a diverse group.][1]

Goethe's fascination does not affix to the closed and completed individual figure but instead to the sculptural constellation in which figures seem to encounter and respond to one another. What interests him the most is not the relational quality of these figures but the multifarious whole that is created through the assemblage[2] of diverse figures.

Goethe's interest in the aesthetic possibilities of statue groups mirrors his preference for ensemble over individual acting during his tenure as superintendent at the Weimar court theater from 1791 to 1817, when his actors were frequently part of "a moving *tableau*."[3] In his "Regeln für Schauspieler" ["Rules for Actors"] (1803), he writes that the central figure in the performance is not the individual actor representing the interiority of his character; rather, the stage, hall, actors, and spectators together create a social harmony: ". . . ein Ganzes . . . Das Theater ist als ein figurloses Tableau anzusehen, worin der Schauspieler die Staffage macht." [. . . a whole . . . The theater is to be considered a figureless tableau, in which the actor is the decoration.][4] This understanding of the theater as a *tableau* is a fascinating complement to Goethe's interest in statuary groupings. If the actor is the prop, then he is one part of the whole, signifying not as metaphor, as an indication of a deeper meaning hidden within, but rather as metonym, as meaningful only in a relational sense. In this way, it is the kinship groupings among the various figures on and off the stage that create legibility in a manner reminiscent both of pre- and postmodern notions of the individual. In each case—the statue groups and the acting ensemble—diverse elements collect to form a whole in a manner reflecting Goethe's morphology in which nature is viewed as a "Zusammenhang von vielen Elementen" [interrelation of numerous parts.][5] It is not the individual who emerges as central here, but instead an aesthetics of a heterogeneous whole.

Goethe is not alone among his contemporaries in privileging constellations over the individual. Indeed, we see numerous examples of aesthetic groupings of diverse figures in *tableaux* featured in novels and plays of the period, particularly in pre-Romantic literature. The bourgeois novels and dramas produced within the German territories were experiments in a new mode of literature and representation as German authors looked anxiously to England and France for literary models. Yet rather than representing the socialized modern individual within the circumscribed and nurturing space of the bourgeois family, *tableaux* in the German works frequently depict heterogeneous social groupings that include various mixtures of blood relations, distant kin, servants, political representatives, peasants, lovers and former lovers, and bureaucrats.

The *tableau* typically presents a framed narrative pause, picturing the interrelationality between the figures represented. In the many final *tableaux* in seminal bourgeois dramas and novels of the period, two scenarios feature prominently: the dead body surrounded by members of diverse ranks and social groups, and figures engaging in embraces and gestures of circumscription. Examples of the former are G. E. Lessing's drama *Miß Sara Sampson* (1755), Friedrich Schiller's play *Kabale und Liebe* (1784) [*Intrigue and Love*], and Goethe's epistolary novel *Die Leiden des jungen Werthers* (1774) [*The Sorrows of Young Werther*]. *Miß Sara Sampson*, often considered the first German bourgeois tragedy, presents a final *tableau* in which the corpse of the nobleman's daughter Sara is encircled by a diverse group of hand-wringing figures: her father, the father's recently liberated servant, and the servant of Sara's lover Mellefont. Mellefont's corpse lies adjacent to the group. No hero or modern individual emerges from the rubble. Even *Kabale und Liebe*, the play that Erich Auerbach considered the most politically relevant German literary work of the period, calling it "a first attempt to make an individual destiny echo the fullness of contemporary reality" (though he ultimately found it "desperately narrow"[6]), does not depict the victory of the rebellious son in the end. The stage directions in the final scene instead cue a curiously staged *tableau* comprised of "Ferdinand. Der Präsident. Wurm *und* Bediente, *welche alle voll Schrecken ins Zimmer stürzen, darauf* Miller *mit Volk und Gerichtsdienern, welche sich im Hintergrund sammeln.*" [Ferdinand. The President. Wurm and Servants, who, filled with horror, rush into the room, then Miller with a crowd of folk and court attendants which collects in the background.][7] This *tableau*, almost too large for a stage, includes the political representative of the state, the son of the President, the political bureaucrat, servants, the musician Miller, simple village people, and court employees, with no single figure rising out of the group to assert sovereignty. Goethe's *Werther* offers a similarly heterogeneous final *tableau*, in which Werther's dying body is surrounded by Lotte's fiancé Albert, a bailiff, and his two sons; in the end, craftsmen carry Werther's body out as the group exits. No sovereign individual emerges here, and the social constellation presents diversity in class, age, and function, if not gender. Scenes like these abound in German plays and novels of the period.

Tableaux presenting circumscribed heterogeneous groupings can be traced back to the first German family novel, C. F. Gellert's *Das Leben der schwedischen Gräfin von G**** (1747) [*The Life of the Swedish Countess of G****], in which a community of friends and kin expands and contracts in unpredictable ways. Scenes of embrace create frames around groupings of figures from diverse social and emotional contexts. The countess, believing her husband is dead, has married the bourgeois Herr R***; when the count returns, the three simply hug, creating a new community: "Der Graf kam auf uns zu, und wir umarmten uns alle drei zugleich." [The count approached us, and we all three embraced each other simultaneously.][8] The final *tableau* in Lessing's *Nathan der Weise* (1779) [*Nathan the Wise*] likewise collects a diverse group of figures (in terms of religion, age, and "blood") in a shared hug: "*Unter stummer Wiederholung allseitiger Umarmungen fällt der Vorhang.*" [The curtain falls while all present on stage repeatedly embrace in silence.][9] Here, again, the text highlights the *active* movement of all the figures ("*allseitiger*") as well as a temporality that repeats or slows the action in the *tableau*. In both cases, we have multiple figures ("alle drei," "allseitig") and a temporal slowing (simultaneity and repetition); the embrace is repeated as if in a temporal loop. In each case, the community is created through gestures rather than words, underscoring the importance of the framed grouping.[10]

We are accustomed to think of the latter half of the eighteenth century as the era of the birth of the autonomous, self-reflective individual. It is not Apollo and his muses or even Laocoön and his sons, but instead the seemingly isolated (male) hero of Sturm und Drang and the *Bildungsroman* unfolding and developing his inner self that has traditionally held the central role in the perception of the period,[11] one associated with the notion of radical semantic change.[12] As the narrative goes, the "modern" individual emerges in the context of a shift from a stratified, premodern, kinship-based society to what Niklas Luhmann characterizes as a functionally differentiated society in which individuals are no longer defined by their socially prescribed role; they must instead develop an "ego" in order to create a seemingly stable inner world within a modern system that of necessity renders them "socially displaced."[13] This subject, defined by the notion of an unfolding interior self,[14] rejects the entangled mesh of kinship ties and emerges as a sovereign individual.[15]

When we speak of the modern autonomous individual that purportedly rises out of the muck of kinship in the second half of the eighteenth century, we are immediately cued to look for the family; not the messy, extended version associated with the older term "Haus," but the vaunted "Kleinfamilie," the family of "daddy-mommy" (plus children to ensure property transfer and the reproduction of the family institution)—the family of psychoanalysis.[16] The modern sovereign subject doesn't simply emerge fully formed, "mündig" [politically mature], in the public sphere;[17] he (we are talking about a male figure) experiences the unfolding of his inner self within the refuge of the nuclear family. The dominant model for the formation of the modern individual relies on the simultaneous formation of the nuclear family; indeed, the tautological relationship of the two is likewise tethered to the emergence of a modern state and capitalist economy. As historians

David Warren Sabean and Simon Teuscher put it, "The history of the family is part of the history of the rise of the Western individual, cut loose from the responsibilities of kin, and cut out for the heroic task of building the self-generating economy."[18] In order for the idealized modern individual to be imagined as sovereign, he must always already be the product of the "walling off" of the nuclear family,[19] a social unit cut off from ties to kin and other extrafamilial networks.

We need the nuclear family to bolster the ideal of the autonomous individual, so much so that we see this family even when it isn't there: in pictures, in literature, in narrative. Ulrich Beck critiques the reliance on the "Kleinfamilie" [small or nuclear family] narrative within sociology of the past few decades as a tautological revival of a family form that is vanishing in modern culture. As Beck sarcastically writes, "Im Kern der Kernfamilie ist alles kerngesund!" [In the nucleus of the nuclear family everything is healthy!] This, despite the cultural landscape of "the pluralism of patchwork families," of "cohabitation, marriages without licenses, an exponential increase in single-person households, single-childcaring, single-moving, single-staying parents."[20] Indeed, recent statistics reveal that only around 24 percent of contemporary German households comprise the traditional "Kernfamilie"[21] [nuclear family] of mother, father, and children.[22] Yet the sustained focus on the typology of the nuclear family continues to produce data that reinforce this structure. As Eve Sedgwick puts it, the nuclear family signifier is so rigid that alternative family structures are not registered and have no power to budge ideology: "Now, the potency of any signifier is proven and increased, over and over, by how visibly and spectacularly it *fails* to be adequate by the various signifieds over which it is nonetheless seen to hold sway."[23] Rather than dooming it to oblivion, the failure of the nuclear family to adequately describe the multifarious social structures that determine people's lives shores up its function as the measure of all things.

Another way in which the nuclear (oedipal) family trope dominates epistemology and interpretation despite its elusiveness is via the discourse of "crisis." As the editors of the volume *Vor der Familie* [*Before the Family*] put it, "The crisis of the family is as old as the family itself."[24] They point to the idyllic space of harmony that characterizes the idealized family but that is nonetheless always in crisis in eighteenth-century German bourgeois literature.[25] Why, they ask, is the family form so resilient in the bourgeois tragedy when it is always in danger of crumbling under the weight of its limiting form?[26] In fact, it is precisely the discourse of crisis that bolsters the empty center of the nuclear family. Wilhelm Heinrich Riehl famously lamented the "demise of the family" in his reactionary *Die Familie* of 1855, written at a time when the nuclear family trope was arguably at its height in both historical and literary terms. In his history of the family concept, Dieter Schwab shows that the family trope was actually strengthened by the perceived crisis brought on by the weakening of the German family patriarch soon after his discursive emergence in light of the increased rights given to individual family members by civil laws.[27] The tautology of crisis results in the myopic focus on the largely fabricated form of the nuclear family.

A reversed take on the "family in crisis" reveals the irreplaceability of the nuclear family trope for modern thought. How, we might ask, can we understand the shift to modernity without the form of the "Kleinfamilie"? This social unit provides the sociopolitical context in miniature that produces the chain of signifiers of the modern: the "walled-off" family, the autonomous individual (the container of interiority), authenticity and truth, mimetic (transparent) representation, and the modern nation-state. Remove any one of these elements from the sequence and the teleology of modernity cracks. The social and the political meet at the hearth of the nuclear family.[28]

Hegel's family model, articulated most clearly in *Elements of the Philosophy of Right* (1821), rehearses the narrative of the family that gained ideological and discursive traction by the first third of the nineteenth century: the modern family is created and imagined via the process of the nuclear family's delinkage from larger kin structures. Hegel distills the elements of the modern family that mirror the social and political building blocks of modernity: new family (nuclear) separated from kin networks and hence "self-sufficient"; "blood" as a privileged connecting bond and signifier of "race"; ethical, monogamous love; and property, the linchpin of the modern family:

> When a marriage takes place, a *new family* is constituted, and this is *self-sufficient* for itself in relation to the *kinship groups* or houses from which it originated; its links with the latter are based on the natural blood relationship, but the new family is based on ethical love. The property of an individual is also therefore essentially connected with his marital relationship, and only more distantly connected with his kinship group or house.[29]

It is precisely control over property and inheritance that makes monogamous marriage necessary,[30] for the father's property should not be passed on to a "foreign" body.[31] Anything located outside the circumscribed nuclear family is of less value to its members than the bodies located within.

Hegel draws the outlines of the family idyll in a manner that narrows the frame and creates a privileged domestic space. This model has persisted despite countless political and social changes since the beginning of the nineteenth century. Indeed, post–World War II historians and sociologists reiterate this picture of the family in their narratives of the consolidation of the nuclear family. In *The Making of the Modern Family* (1975), an oft-cited work that was translated into German in 1977, Edward Shorter defines the nuclear family in terms that mirror Hegel's description of it as a discrete, closed, and intimate social unit:

> What really distinguishes the nuclear family—mother, father, and children—from other patterns of life in Western society is a special sense of solidarity that separates the domestic unit from the surrounding community. Its members feel that they have much more in common with one another than they do with anyone else on the outside—that they enjoy a privileged emotional climate they must protect from outside intrusion.[32]

The exclusive, inward-focused nuclear family is in need of protection from the threat of miscegenation from the external world. In a work that has likewise had an outsized influence on German thought, *The Family, Sex and Marriage in England 1500–1800* (1977), Lawrence Stone details the coeval rise of the individual with the nuclear family in the eighteenth century as a response to changing social, economic, and political conditions, such as the disintegration of the lordship system, the rise of the Protestant nation-state, and decreased mortality rates.[33] Whereas the sixteenth-century English family unit frequently included extended family members and was characterized by porous boundaries—"open to external influences"[34]—the "private nuclear family" that developed in the seventeenth and eighteenth centuries was "closed" and "walled off" from "either interference or support from the kin" and from the larger community.[35] Jürgen Habermas highlights the psychic and architectural interiority of this notion of the family after 1750: the "Court" of the aristocrats is replaced by small rooms for individuals to reflect the "Innerlichkeit bürgerlichen Familienlebens"[36] [the interiority of bourgeois family life], a space imagined as private and autonomous, one that represses its own economic origins.[37] It is not difficult to see how this potentially claustrophobic model would prompt Michel Foucault to call the nuclear family "'incestuous' from the start." On the one hand, the separation between public and private spheres enables the preservation of values associated with the family, in particular the emotionality that is banned from the modern public sphere. On the other hand, the narrowly imagined social grouping of the nuclear family fosters intense emotions, making it a volatile space for emotional and sexual feelings that complicates the status of this family as the ideal model of the modern nation-state.[38]

The nuclear family is imagined both as an apolitical unit, delinked from its larger social context, and as a microcosm of the nation-state. For Hegel the family is, on the one hand, an organic, prepolitical unit. Antigone stands for the household gods ("Penates"), whereas her brother Polyneices can leave the "immediate, elemental, and therefore strictly speaking, negative ethical life of the Family, in order to acquire and produce the ethical life that is conscious of itself and actual."[39] Gender roles are neatly mapped onto the household (female) and the political-ethical sphere (male). But on the other hand, the modern family in *Elements of the Philosophy of Right*—the monogamous couple and its children—stands as a dialectical precursor to Hegel's ideal state. In this sense, Hegel's family maps onto the flawed but curiously powerful analogy between the patriarchal family, in which the father holds absolute sovereignty, and the state, in which the sovereign functions like an all-powerful father.[40] By the first third of the nineteenth century, the nuclear family is metaphorically *both* political *and* apolitical, large *and* small.[41]

NARRATING THE FAMILY

As Sabean and Teuscher point out, "The old story of the rise of the nuclear family and the decline of the importance of kinship is not simply innocent."[42] What, we must ask, is gained by adhering to this story? And what is lost? Which figures take center stage, and which are relegated to the margins? There is no question that colonial/racialized fantasies and discourses have produced the dominant narrative that contrasts "primitive" kinship groups with the "civilized, cultured and modern" paternal family. Kinship is "coded as private, female, and primitive," a "residual category in the West's past."[43] The "individualizing project of modernity"[44] requires a tight frame that crops out those marginalized figures who provide the network and context for the narrative of sovereignty.

Adherence to the nuclear family narrative means that racially undesirable figures are brutally excised. Eugenicist fantasies of the nation produce a loss of racialized "family members" who are pushed to the margins of the nation. As Judith Butler points out, the reproduction of culture is the reproduction of race; the fantasy of the ideal nation is realized in the child.[45] Anxieties about miscegenation lie at the heart of the race-nation trope.[46] However, as Hegel emphasizes, kinship must not only be understood in terms of "bloodlines" but also in terms of property relations. Within the U.S.-American context, "blood" and property merge in the question of Black kinship; Butler quotes Saidiya Hartmann, who told her: "slavery is the ghost in the machine of kinship."[47] During the eighteenth century, colonial fantasies haunted the inhabitants of the German territories, who looked sideways to the lands won by their European neighbors.[48] Colonial envy and a new focus on genealogy, biology, and anthropology led German Enlightenment thinkers to circle around the topic of race,[49] a term that was first used in relation to humans in Immanuel Kant's 1775 essay "Von den verschiedenen Racen der Menschen" [On the Different Races of Humans].[50] As Susanne Zantop and Wendy Sutherland show, "race" becomes a metonym of "nation" as well as of family/genealogy and beauty. In Christian Ernst Wünsch's 1796 drawings of "German," "European," and "non-European" skulls and bodies, we see a slippage between race, nation, and beauty as non-European figures are depicted as physically and therefore morally inferior, and race becomes an aesthetic category.[51] The exclusion of racial others from the aesthetic project of the Enlightenment was fueled by, among other things, a desire for a national identity imagined along the lines of a circumscribed family unit.

The notion of race is notoriously slippery, and it cannot be neatly separated from class. It is predicated both upon fluid "blood" ties and the structures of exclusion and inclusion that are erected to control the threat of contamination from unwanted sources. Étienne Balibar makes a compelling argument for the slippage between race and class in the eighteenth century: as the bourgeoisie gains power in Europe, anxieties about class distinction are projected onto categories associated with race.[52] These anxieties are associated with the political frustrations of the middle class, and the nuclear family is discursively coded as bourgeois.[53] Of course, the encumbered development of a bourgeoisie in the eighteenth-century German states complicates this smooth narrative. Isabel Hull calls the use of the term "bourgeois" for the period anachronistic, "since neither capitalism nor capitalists characterized late-eighteenth century Germany."[54] Indeed, at the end of the century the bourgeois class represented less than 10 percent of the total population in the German states.[55] During this period the bourgeois family was more a cultural ideal than a norm, "future-oriented" and in many ways aspirational, just as the nation was.[56] But this cultural condition nevertheless provides ripe conditions for intersected anxieties about class and race, in particular in light of the eagerness of Germans to enter into European colonial competition.

If the erasure of racialized others from the family picture is one important loss associated with adherence to the nuclear family model, then why is this model utilized so frequently by critics of the Western history of racism and oppression, such as the early Frankfurt School theorists? The nuclear family not only represents a structure of exclusion; it also enables these theorists to analyze structures of oppression via a focus on the "Kleinfamilie," an irreplaceable cipher for the psychoanalytic, sociological, and philosophical (metaphorical) analysis of Nazism. The nuclear family is, in a word, a powerful heuristic tool for the critique of fascism.[57]

The early Frankfurt School theorists saw the family as the site where fascism is learned and reproduced. During the early days of Nazi rule, Horkheimer argued in "Autorität und Familie" [Authority and the Family] (1936) that the crisis of rational authority in the political sphere is mirrored in the abuses of authority within the nuclear family, and a version of this argument is retained in later writings by Horkheimer, Adorno, and Habermas.[58] The early Frankfurt School sees the Freudian nuclear family as the place where fascism emerges and grows, and this fascist, oedipal family persists as a dominant trope in the later writings of Horkheimer and Adorno as well as in anti-fascist thought in post-Nazi Germany and Austria.[59] As Claudia Jarzebowski points out, the notion of "Abstammung" [descent] needed to be discredited in Germany after 1945 not least because the family stood at the center of racist Nazi discourses.[60] In the post-fascist era the family has functioned as a central metaphor for the abuses of the Nazi period and for the relationship between Adolf Hitler and the German people. Psychologists Alexander and Margarete Mitscherlich and sociologist Klaus Theweleit link their analyses of the damaged psychological states and behaviors of Germans after 1945 to fixations on the (lost) Nazi father and the family,[61] and post-fascist literature reflects this fixation. In Ingeborg Bachmann's novel *Malina* (1971), the abusive Nazi father in the unnamed female narrator's dreams is a particularly poignant example among numerous literary and theoretical slippages between family, father, and fascism in the period. As Bachmann famously stated, "Fascism is the first thing in the relationship between a man and a woman."[62]

The nuclear family remains an indispensable trope for feminist critics within German studies who follow the early Frankfurt School in their use of the family as a critique of fascism. These critics have likewise revealed the blatant gender inequities that are built into the public-private split in which the domestic sphere both stands in for the patriarchal state *and* is feminized and de-politicized. Silvia Bovenschen's now canonical *Die imaginierte Weiblichkeit* (1979) critiques notions of Enlightenment progress by highlighting shifting conceptions of ideal femininity in the eighteenth century, when the female intellectual came to be perceived as "masculine" and, by the end of the century, femininity was naturalized and domesticated within the nuclear family.[63] Bovenschen's contemporary Karin Hausen shows that sex characteristics were mapped onto gender roles in the eighteenth century in order to reinforce patriarchal structures in the face of secularizing and Enlightenment trends. The more women pushed for emancipation, the more rigidly character differences between the sexes were postulated,[64] and these corresponded to domestic and political roles. It is the nuclear family, the bridge between the private, the social, and the political, that produces and reproduces modern gender inequities. Within contemporary literary criticism, studies on the literary father or mother or on questions of trauma and postmemory in German literature frequently return to the oedipal nuclear family as a privileged site of analysis.[65] Indeed, the plethora of German family novels and literary representations of the patriarchal family, particularly after World War II, invites us to read through an oedipal lens that guides our attention to the vertical power structures in which the patriarchal father stands in for the sovereign.[66]

Literary scholarship after Nazism, framed by the critique of fascism outlined above, has tended to view the family in eighteenth-century German literature as embedded within a realist aesthetic. As Gerhard Kaiser and Friedrich Kittler put it in their 1978 volume *Dichtung als Sozialisationsspiel* [Literature as a Game of Socialization], literature is a mimetic representation of the process of socialization.[67] Friedrich Kittler's essay in the collection focuses on the revisions Goethe made between the writing of *Wilhelm Meisters Theatralische Sendung* (1777–1785) [Wilhelm Meister's Theatrical Calling] and the completed *Wilhelm Meisters Lehrjahre* (1795–1796) as representative of the shift from the extended to the nuclear family in which the modern subject is socialized. For Kittler, all modern primary socialization takes place within the construct of the nuclear family as a process reinforced and reiterated through the "snowball effect" of writing, reading, and archiving life narratives.[68] However, as I have argued elsewhere, in highlighting the mimetic function of literary socialization Kittler overreads the centrality of the nuclear family in *Wilhelm Meisters Lehrjahre*, a novel that features multiple heterogeneous social constellations but few nuclear families.[69]

There is a larger critical project at the core of Kittler's groundbreaking interpretation of *Wilhelm Meister* that sheds light on his assumptions that the novel is mimetic. His essay contains the seeds of his *Aufschreibesysteme* [Discourse Networks] project, which posits the emergence of the modern interior subject via new media systems of documentation.[70] Kittler's project critiques the processes of instrumental reason that are at the core of German barbarism and fascism. Already employing the discourse of the early Frankfurt School critics of fascism in his *Wilhelm Meister* essay, Kittler links modern media systems to the history of "Gewalt" [violence or power]: "It is less the documents of a culture (as Benjamin assumed) than its techniques of documentation that are always also documents of barbarism."[71] This mode of critique is inclined to see post-1750 literature through the lens of realism. As Georg Lukács puts it, the realist (modern) novel that succeeded the baroque adventure novel should reflect the dialectical tension between the interior subject and the external, secular world.[72] It is precisely this mimetic function that makes the realist novel a viable tool for social and political critique. But Goethe's novels, even the one that at times approximates a realist aesthetic, *Wilhelm Meisters Lehrjahre*, frequently include nonmimetic aesthetic elements such as allegory and generic hybridity. In *Mimesis*, Erich Auerbach makes plain that Goethe's resistance to anything not "beautiful" takes German literature down a path more idiosyncratic than mimetic, a nonrealist aesthetic trend that makes German literature less politically relevant than English or French literature.[73] Auerbach identifies the underlying tensions of class struggle as the vital current of history and writes that Goethe's aversion to violence and extremes led him to turn away from the representation of seminal historical events he associated with "das Gemeine" [the vulgar].[74] Marxist critics understandably take issue with this mode of aesthetics. Lukács, too, expresses disappointment in the nonrealist turns taken in *Wilhelm Meisters Lehrjahre*, a novel he otherwise admires. He criticizes in particular the allegorical narrative of the Tower Society, which in his opinion destroys the novel's organicism, replacing depth with superficiality and superfluous ornamentation.[75] Indeed, Marxist and Frankfurt School criticism can do little with the premodern aesthetic forms that help shape German bourgeois literature.

If eighteenth-century bourgeois literature is not particularly mimetic, then its relationship to the history of the family form is not a dialectical one. A look at historiographical evidence suggests that the eighteenth-century German family form was shifting and messy. Over the past few decades, historians have shown that the early modern and eighteenth-century family likely did not follow the smooth line of development—from the extended family to the clear emergence of the nuclear family—that scholars like Shorter and Stone have proposed. Previously, post–World War II historians of the family tended to follow Otto Brunner's narrative of the eighteenth-century shift from the premodern "ganzes Haus" [whole household]—a combination of blood relatives, servants, and farm hands[76]—to the nuclear family unit that resulted from the functionalization of modern capitalist society and led to the severing of production and rationality (public, male) from consumption and emotion (private, female).[77] But in fact, the shift from "Haus" to "Häuslichkeit" (the "Haus" shrinking to father, mother, children)[78] was a dissonant affair. As Hull points out, family arrangements in the period were just as heterogeneous as the "socially, regionally, and religiously heterogeneous Enlighteners."[79] Discussions surrounding the 1791 production of the *Allgemeines Landrecht* ("General Code for the Prussian States," the first systematized and reformed legal code within an Enlightened absolutist German territory) reveal the fluidity of the term "Familie" at this time. "Gesinde" [farmhands and domestics], for example, are sometimes included as part of the family and sometimes not.[80] In-laws and step-relations belonged to the "Familie" just as much as blood relations did, and incest prohibitions reveal how blurred the outlines of the concept of the family were at the end of the century.[81] Indeed, it was not until 1788 that Krünitz's *Economic Encyclopedia* included the term "Familie" as a unit that referred "almost exclusively to 'married couples and their children'" and only occasionally included farmhands and domestics.[82] Historically speaking, the development of an exclusive nuclear family was gradual and not linear.[83]

Historians have highlighted the important role of horizontal kinship relations for members of the bourgeois and *Bildungsbürgertum* [educated bourgeoisie] classes from the middle of the eighteenth century into the twentieth.[84] They point to endogamous networks that retain and produce wealth and power. The "household-family framework" in the eighteenth century could "expand and contract" and was the site of "constant interaction with unrelated household members," creating networks of "family members, servants (especially those residing in the house) or lodgers and visitors of various types."[85] Sibling relationships were central to the preservation, health, and wealth of families, as they frequently helped forge alliances via in-laws.[86] As Lanzinger asserts, more intensive sibling relationships led to more cousin marriages as intimacy was experienced endogamously.[87] Davidoff argues that capitalist and industrial development was accompanied by more, not less, reliance on kin.[88] Indeed, endogamy is a powerful way to keep property within a group:[89] in this sense, *"kinship endogamy formed the nucleus of class endogamy."*[90] Or as Sabean and Teuscher put it, "Class differentiation went hand in hand with kin integration."[91]

These historians' focus on horizontal kinship structures offers a fruitful model for a nonteleological analysis of literary kinship structures. The object of this study is not historiography but the imaginative medium of literature, and yet the horizontal gaze is a productive way to think not only about aesthetic kinship groupings but also about the relationships between German authors and their counterparts across Europe at a time when the former looked longingly at the latter in order to imagine the future of a national German literature. Rather than retroactively applying the seductive narrative of the crystallization of the nuclear family in eighteenth-century literature, this book traces social groupings represented in literary works, without assuming that the "real" nuclear family can somehow be uncovered with the right amount of interpretation.[92] Indeed, focusing on constellational groupings instead of lineage, genealogy, and plot offers an alternative window onto representations of kinship. Whereas "kinship" ("Verwandtschaft") is a porous and malleable term, "family" is a far less flexible and more modern one. Yet the "family" (read bourgeois nuclear family) is the cornerstone of the smooth ideological construction that supports the metonym "nuclear family/ /interior subject/modern state" that is key for liberal and conservative political thought alike. The nuclear family is, in this sense, a unique placeholder bridging the social and the political, one that cannot be replaced by any other social form without creating radical crevices in Western political theory and philosophy and is furthermore invested with the ideological weight of modern notions of race, class, and gender. It is the linchpin between inside and outside, "walled off" yet dissolvable, as children leave to form their own nuclear families. In a word, the nuclear family is the ideal social trope for dialectical thought, and therein lies a good part of its allure. But the allure of recovering a literary picture of kinship that opens up paths for imagining alternative social constellations is similarly powerful, and that is the impetus for this book.

"FAMILY" VS. "KINSHIP"

The terms family ("Familie") and kinship ("Verwandtschaft"), although intricately linked, correspond to very different shapes of community. It is useful to consider the particular forms of "family" and "kinship" in terms articulated by Caroline Levine in *Forms: Whole, Rhythm, Hierarchy, Network*. Levine argues that formal analysis of literature offers important insights into social and political spheres. She proposes exploring forms in terms of their "affordances"; that is, "the particular constraints and possibilities that different forms afford," and which are portable across time and into new contexts: "No matter how different their historical and cultural circumstances, . . . bounded enclosures will always exclude, and rhyme will always repeat."[93] What is it, then, that the form of the family, always in the center and always in crisis, affords? As we have seen, discourses surrounding the family in the eighteenth century equate it with "nuclear family" and highlight its "walled-off" character. We have a shrinking household that solidifies in the form of the "Familie" = "Kleinfamilie" or "Kernfamilie" [nuclear family]. At this point, the notion of "blood" also becomes central to the concept.[94] Imagined as a "whole" that is closed, "Familie" affords circumscription as well as intimacy and inclusion in a select group whose members are permanently connected. The flip side of this mode of inclusion is, of course, claustrophobia, as there is no real escape from the family. An individual only leaves the family unit in order to create a new one that will be just as circumscribed and exclusive as the one left behind. Hence, the shape of the family is a circle whose circumference line re-forms after each break.

In contrast to the form of family/nuclear family, "kinship" affords less intimacy and security vis-à-vis one's place in the group. Kinship is a term that contains the concept of "family" within it but potentially includes far more individuals than those within the nuclear family.[95] Stone uses the term "porous" for the pre–nuclear family form of kinship.[96] Judith Butler uses this same term in her critique of the ideological linkages between "family" and the modern state, arguing that whereas a narrow concept of "family" is the basis for the modern definition of "human," it does not map onto lived kinship structures, because the latter "may well have more than one woman who operates as the mother, more than one man who operates as the father, or no mother or no father, with half-brothers who are also friends—this is a time in which kinship has become fragile, porous, and expansive."[97] Butler writes about the late twentieth century, but her description of kinship structures coalesces with those of many historians of kinship. The shape of kinship is not the closed circle; it is too fragile for even the semblance of clean circular lines. It is created in a given present and hence cannot hold any shape for long. It is expansive but also easily broken, subject to holes and blurred lines, producing a fragment of the circular family shape that is shot through with gaps and lines and is constantly shifting.[98]

Another quality associated with kinship groups is the privileging of proximity over blood. Zedler's *Grosses vollständiges Universal-Lexicon aller*

Wissenschafften und Künste [Large Complete Universal Lexicon of All Sciences and Arts] (1731–1754) highlights precisely this element of proximity in the entries under "Verwandt, oder Verwandte" [related or relations], defined at the outset as a relation between humans that creates community: "die mit einander auf eine oder die andere Weise einige Verbindlichkeit oder Gemeinschafft haben" [who have in some way a connection or community with one another].[99] Examples of these kinds of kinship relations include "Gesellschaffts, Handwercks, oder Innungs Genossen" [associates of societies, trades, or guilds] as well as "Schuldner und Gläubiger" [debtors and creditors]: "One says of a debtor that he is related to the creditor."[100] Kinship is imagined as a connection that creates a bond, and Zedler includes "Gemütsverwandt" [friendship][101] and "Geistliche Verwandtschafft" [spiritual relations including clerical relationships and godparents] as modes of kinship as well. Incest is defined in the Zedler entry in terms of proximity; intimate relations between those who live together ("die gemeiniglich beysammen wohnen") are "unnatural," regardless of blood ties, kin, and sex.[102] It is not nature that determines where incest begins and ends; rather, as Claude Lévi-Strauss put it, "the prohibition of incest merely affirms, in a field vital to the group's survival, the pre-eminence of the social over the natural, the collective over the individual, organization over the arbitrary."[103] Incest laws frequently change because their function is not to follow natural laws but to create a sense of order. Within kinship clans, Lévi-Strauss argues, "*A person cannot do just what he pleases*. The positive aspect of this prohibition is to initiate organization."[104]

If the prohibition that produces kinship ties, incest, is not based on nature, then we are thrown back to living relations that are not biologically given but are created and produced in real time; hence, we might add "assemblage" to the keyword "proximity" in order to delineate kinship. David Schneider defines kinship as "a kind of *doing*; one that does not reflect a prior structure but that can only be understood as enacted practice."[105] Franklin and McKinnon write that kinship is "self-consciously assembled from a multiplicity of possible bits and pieces."[106] Butler amends this definition by highlighting the temporal nature of kinship structures: "kinship is itself a kind of doing, a practice that enacts that assemblage of significations *as it takes place*."[107]

The porousness and dynamism of kinship afford it both flexibility and a threatening fluidity: Where is the line drawn between inside and outside? Not everyone can be a member of a particular kinship group, even if kinship structures tend to be larger and looser than ones that fall under the term "family." As Donna Haraway puts it, even if kin is a "wild category," "cuts" and "ties" are needed in order for certain bonds to be cemented and others to be loosened:

> Kin is a wild category that all sorts of people do their best to domesticate. Making kin as oddkin rather than, or at least in addition to, godkin and genealogical and biogenetic family troubles important matters, like to whom one is actually responsible. Who lives and who dies, and how, in this kinship rather than that one? What shape is this kinship, where and whom do its lines connect and disconnect, and so what? What must be cut and what must be tied if multispecies flourishing on earth, including human and other-than-human beings in kinship, are to have a chance?[108]

Even when delinked from clear biological and genealogical structures, kinship groups are subject to boundaries. Certain beings are members while others are excluded. If we think about the group within a frame, then certain figures will fall outside of this frame. Even if the incest taboo is, as Lévi-Strauss suggests, not a product of blood relations, it nevertheless creates conditions for insiders and outsiders, for endogamy and exogamy.

As Engelstein points out, the slippery boundaries of kinship relations reflect the anxiety about porous boundaries between epistemological binaries.[109] In what Eve Sedgwick calls the "avunculosuppressive move from 'kinship' to 'family,'" we are confronted with the binaries self/other, same/different.[110] Those individuals located in the vicinity of the center but outside of the fetishized nuclear unit, such as the aunts and uncles, are cut out of the family picture. Indeed, the concept of kinship itself connotes relation and resemblance, same and other, prompting Mark Turner to argue that kinship is a metaphor of metaphor:

> One way to understand the abstract notion of *metaphor* is in terms of what we know about *kinship*. Often, we think of two concepts as bearing a metaphoric relation because they resemble each other. We may understand the notion of *relation* and *resemblance* in terms of *kin relation* and *family resemblance*. So we may understand the abstract notion of *metaphor* by seeing that it stands in metaphoric relationship to kinship.[111]

Metaphors indicate similarity and difference simultaneously, and Turner's formulation underscores the relational force of kinship in contrast to the more ideologically laden term "family," which connotes resemblance. We could therefore extend Turner's point to call kinship not a metaphor but a metonym par excellence, a signifier that constantly points sideways to highlight relationality. Proximity becomes relation becomes resemblance as the kin group forms in time and space.

LITERATURE AND THE SOCIAL

This book approaches kinship in the manner outlined above, as a grouping in time and place that produces relational bonds. By attending to the social pictures/*tableaux* within eighteenth-century literature that offer freeze-frames of these groupings, I trace an aesthetics of kinship that is heterogeneous and nonnuclear. Literary criticism focused on the eighteenth-century family has historically been concerned with plot. Plot analysis invites an interpretive archeology that retraces presumed genealogies, cutting out figures perceived as irrelevant to the nuclear family narrative and tying together figures who may not be connected closely. In this book I turn the focus away from the ideologically loaded oedipal family plot and toward the shifting social groupings that are formed and represented in literature of the period.[112]

This book offers, in other words, a new point of reference for our literary gaze. Rather than tracing literary genealogies, I look at social constellations, attending to what resides within the frame. Indeed, we will look in vain for a freeze-frame of the nuclear family in eighteenth-century bourgeois drama and novels. We will instead see *tableaux* of heterogeneous groupings that call into question the social teleology of modernity normally viewed as the theoretical frame for literary analysis of the period. Whereas I describe this approach as a shift in the focal point, Sedgwick's call for an "avuncular angle" speaks to the ethics of my project. Sedgwick advocates for

> a more elastic, inclusive definition of "family," beginning with a relegitimation of the avunculate: an advocacy that would appeal backward to precapitalist models of kinship organization, or the supposed early-capitalist extended family, in order to project into the future a vision of "family" elastic enough to do justice to the depth and sometimes durability of nonmarital and/or nonprocreative bonds, same-sex bonds, nondyadic bonds, bonds not defined by genitality, "step"-bonds, adult sibling bonds, nonbiological bonds across generations, etc.[113]

Although Sedgwick is writing from and about the contemporary period, her emphasis on premodern family forms troubles a linear narrative of modernization in a manner akin to my own investigation of kinship aesthetics.

The eighteenth-century *tableau* emerged as an important feature of European drama most prominently in Denis Diderot's drama theory, which was anonymously translated by Lessing into German in 1760.[114] Diderot defines *tableau* within the French theater context as a device that frames familial domesticity, the thematic locus for the realist aesthetic aims of the new bourgeois domestic tragedy. More broadly conceived, the *tableau* functions as a formal device in theater and film allowing a "plastic and pictorial effect" to be achieved through a "freezing of the action."[115] The *tableau* often functions as "allegorical commentary";[116] upon its insertion into a play or film it stands on its own, gesturing toward the extradiegetic and the intermedial. The *tableau*, as a framed and cohesive whole within a larger work, introduces a medial shift and a pause, yielding a sense of stillness and slowness within the larger work as well as a moment of heightened intensity.[117]

The *tableau* is taken up by German authors of the period via the term "Gemälde" [painting]. This was Lessing's chosen German term for Diderot's *tableau* in his translation of the latter's plays and theoretical writings about the theater. Many a play of the time was described as a "Familiengemälde" [family portrait], but we need to look closely at what is meant here by "Familie." Lessing called C. F. Gellert's 1746 comedy *Die kranke Frau* [*The Sick Woman*] a "Familiengemälde, in which one feels that one is at home, each spectator believing he recognizes a cousin, an in-law, an aunt from his own relations ('Verwandtschaft')."[118] It is striking that Lessing's term "Familiengemälde" corresponds to the loose notions of "Verwandtschaft" of the period. The picture is domestic ("häuslich") and intimate, since every spectator can identify familiar characteristics in the figures represented. But this is not a nuclear family, and it is not solely made up of blood relations. We have not a father, mother, and child but a cousin, a brother-in-law, and an aunt. This picture, sans uncle, presents us with a salient image of the nonnuclear family that is so pervasive in literature of the period.[119]

The social *tableaux* in German bourgeois dramas and novels highlight neither an emerging sovereign individual nor the nuclear family that is ideologically linked to this figure. Even the novel most frequently cited as the first *Bildungsroman*, Goethe's *Wilhelm Meisters Lehrjahre* (1795–1796), ends not with a nuclear "Familiengemälde" but instead with a large, heterogeneous grouping of characters traversing categories of class, profession, age, and biological kinship that collects in one enclosed space (the estate of an uncle). A double wedding is planned, and the presumed socialized subject, Wilhelm, expresses surprise at the "Zufall" [coincidence] of his own luck rather than confidence in his own development into a sovereign subject.

The literary kinship *tableaux* within eighteenth-century bourgeois dramas and novels are characterized by porousness; yet these groupings are not without boundaries. Not just anyone can enter the space of the house of Gellert's countess, the uncle's estate in *Wilhelm Meisters Lehrjahre*, or the musician Miller's house in the closing scene of *Kabale und Liebe*. Large numbers of characters can be squeezed together in scenes that push the bounds of verisimilitude, like clowns piling into a Volkswagen beetle, but there are limits. The disappointed Lady Millford, reformed mistress of the Prince, is nowhere to be seen in the crowded Miller house at the end of *Kabale und Liebe*. There is seemingly no place for her in the future of this overpopulated little state. And members of Wilhelm's biological family, as well as his friend Werner, all representatives of Wilhelm's bourgeois origins, are excluded from the packed scene of unification at the end of *Wilhelm Meisters Lehrjahre*. These *tableaux* communities are surprisingly expansive, but they are not without their exclusions.

The representation of kinship in German literature of the period cannot be easily mapped onto a conservative-progressive divide, in particular with regard to social standing and class. On the one hand, heterogeneity is key: blood relations and sometimes even social rank do not delimit the connections between individual characters. Alliances and affinities might be formed in unexpected ways—through spontaneous adoption, intimate attachments between members of different ranks, or between future in-laws. Numerous *tableaux* feature servants, aristocrats, and bureaucrats representing a seemingly organic whole. But are these truly spaces of liberation from class constraints?[120] Curiously, the aristocrat retains a place within the majority of literary *tableaux* from the period. Habermas points to Wilhelm Meister's desire to emulate the subject position of the aristocrat;[121] indeed, Wilhelm's marriage to the aristocratic Natalie assuages his frequently articulated repulsion for his bourgeois status. One is in fact hard pressed to find any canonical German bourgeois dramas or novels from the second half of the eighteenth century in which the nobility is fully expelled. Even a rank-conscious Sturm und Drang play like Jakob M. R. Lenz's *Die Soldaten* [*The Soldiers*] (1776) places the critique of the social conditions that ruin young lower-class women into the mouths of aristocrats. In the bourgeois dramas and novels of the period, aristocrats never entirely leave the scene of the action.

The German bourgeois drama and novel emerged over the course of the eighteenth century, and there is a great deal of generic promiscuity in this literature. As Jane K. Brown maintains, the bourgeois drama and the epistolary novel were porous and borrowed liberally from one another.[122] Each genre is indebted to French and English models that preceded the German iterations, but the German bourgeois drama and novel are nevertheless distinct. For one, the German iterations of these genres only tenuously adhere to bourgeois realist aesthetics. In addition, the nuclear family, a trope normally seen as the building block of socialization that occurs within the bourgeois novel and as the central social unit within eighteenth-century bourgeois drama, is not clearly delineated in these German works. And both the German bourgeois drama and novel of the period integrate *tableaux* as well as other genres and media forms, thereby complicating clear genre and media distinctions.

THE AESTHETICS OF KINSHIP:
THE MATERIALITY OF INTERMEDIAL FORMS

By turning the focus away from narrative form and plot, I look to the aesthetics and semiotics of kinship—defined as a porous but not unlimited social grouping—embedded within nonnarrative aesthetic forms, including the *tableau*, the letter, the portrait, props, and the *tableau vivant*. What picture of the family/kinship emerges through a focus on these intermedial forms within literary texts? Although each of them can be linked to plot, these forms can also be analyzed as moments of temporal slowing in which the forms themselves interrupt the process of storytelling.

Kinship and the family are not simply ideological concepts (though they are surely this); they also stand in an intimate relationship to aesthetic form. Indeed, nuclear family and monogamous marriage models adhere to structures of interiority, depth (verticality), the nonvisible, and truth (understood as a secret, linking it to depth); alternatively, nonnuclear kinship constellations are conceptually and aesthetically linked to flatness, surface (horizontality), the visible (immediately legible), and materiality. Aesthetic forms that foreground interiority and depth (the domain of the nuclear family) include letters, diaries, intimate dialogue, and the monologue; aesthetic forms that tend to foreground surface/materiality (the domain of the extended and queer family) include allegory, tableaux, props, and *tableaux vivants*. Hence, the aesthetic forms adhering to kinship constellations offer a window onto the conflicts inherent in eighteenth-century sociopolitical shifts, shifts that are often assumed to be smooth and monolithic.

As intermedial forms, the *tableau*, the letter, the portrait, props, and the *tableau vivant* highlight collisions and moments of overlap between genres and media. The *tableau* offers a framed picture of a social grouping in a moment of heightened intensity; *tableaux* of this kind appear in dramas and novels of the period, frequently, though not always, at the end. The *tableau* mediates between painting and narratives of various kinds, always necessitating a pause in the movement of the plot. The other intermedial forms at the center of this study, such as the portrait, function similarly in plays and dramas of the latter half of the eighteenth century, bridging the divide between various forms of media and genre. As intermedial elements, they often function in unexpected ways; for example, the letter, generally interpreted as the sign of interiority par excellence in the period, acts intermedially not as a signifier of the interior self but as an artificial plot-shifting device that calls attention to itself—a *coup de théâtre* generally derided as a clumsy baroque theater technique.[123]

When we attend to the function of aesthetic forms as nonnarrative, intermedial signifiers, we become aware of other nonnarrative formal elements. We experience a slowing and interruption within the narrative and we are thrown out of the teleological pull of the family/oedipal saga. Indeed, intermedial forms call attention to their own materiality through the interruptions they introduce into the narrative process. We might think of intermedial forms as breaking the fourth wall, as inviting us to consider the work done by the medium itself. Eric Méchoulan and Angela Carr call attention to the "materiality effect" of intermediality,[124] and John Guillory argues that "it is much easier to see what a medium does—the possibilities inherent in the material form of an art—when the same expressive or communicative contents are transposed from one medium to another. Remediation makes the medium as such *visible*."[125]

A shift of the lens *away* from narrative and *toward* nonnarrative aesthetic form gives us the opportunity to dwell upon and *see* the kinship constellations represented in literature. A conscious turn away from dominant psychological, sociological, and literary theories of the history of the family does not negate their importance; yet any entrenched narrative, such as that of the rise and dominance of the triad of nuclear family, interior subject, and imagined nation in the eighteenth century—with all of the ideological baggage it entails—is ripe territory for alternative approaches. Reflections on "surface reading" practices as well as Eve Sedgwick's notion of "paranoid" vs. "reparative" reading offer productive methodological cues for the exercise of reading with one eye closed to narrative. "Paranoid reading" assumes there is always a hidden truth to be uncovered in the text, whereas "reparative reading" is a metonymic form of reading that creates connections.[126] The notion of "surface reading" surely takes its cue from Sedgwick's formulation, as "symptomatic reading" allies with paranoia. "Symptomatic reading" is spurred by Marxist and psychoanalytic criticism for which the most important aspect of a text is that which is repressed, and interpretations should therefore seek "a latent meaning behind a manifest one."[127] Emily Apter and Elaine Freedgood point to the "hypersymptomatic reading" of Marxist, psychoanalytic, and deconstructive rhetorical analysis. Just as the psychoanalyst works with the field of condensation and displacement that is the manifest layer of any dream text, so does the Marxist critic unmask "the superstructural symptom as a mode of praxis."[128] For the symptomatic critic, according to Best and Marcus, domination is always masked and in need of being uncovered.[129]

The privileging of depth over surface shapes our modern epistemology. What is hidden is true, and what appears to the eye is surely in need of depth interpretation.[130] These reflections are relevant not only for the ways we read literature but also for how we read the literary family: methods of depth reading map cleanly onto both the vertical nuclear family structure—always oedipal and partially repressed—and the modern interior subject that emerges from it. In the analytical context of German literature of the period beginning in 1750, a reading practice that does not take for granted a depth/truth/oedipal epistemology is needed to pull apart the smooth structural parallels between the nuclear family model and critical method.

The triad of nuclear family, autonomous subject, and nation that defines modern sociality is dependent upon the emergence of interiority as the defining mode of subjectivity beginning in the modern period. Individuals in a premodern extended kinship group are distinguished by their roles and hence not by their own uniqueness; in contrast, the individual in the nuclear family is imagined as an interior subject. The former are characterized by a lack of depth, whereas the latter holds their truth under the surface. In *The Persistence of Allegory*, a work that is key for my argument here, Jane K. Brown calls into question a linear and sudden progression from premodern modes of identity to the modern, interior one, pointing out that we retroactively and incorrectly read interiority into literature that gestures toward older literary traditions and modes of subjectivity: "Although the great neoclassical commentaries on Aristotle shifted his focus from plot to character, the first appearance of an interiorized self in drama is unclear, because we as post-Rousseauist critics have such a well-developed sense of the interior subject that we tend to see it even where it has not been intentionally represented."[131]

We see depth everywhere, even where it isn't. We are cued into the "modernness" of the eighteenth century and read accordingly, retroactively modernizing both the subject and the family as portrayed in literature of this century.

Queer theory has forcefully analyzed this ideological pull of interiority. As Judith Butler pointed out in her early work, the ideology of interiority is linked to a "construction of coherence" that conceals differences that do not map along a clear sex-gender binary.[132] Moe Meyers productively defines "queer" as "an ontological challenge that displaces bourgeois notions of the Self as unique, abiding, and continuous while substituting instead a concept of the Self as performative, improvisational, discontinuous, and processually constituted by repetitive and stylized acts."[133] Queerness is a critique of the "depth model of identity"[134] created by the bourgeoisie, an interior identity that is, as Foucault points out in *Discipline and Punish*, marked on the body by a dominant culture.[135] Queer theory reveals the ideological function both of depth psychology and autonomous subjectivity and of the reduction of kinship to the circumscribed, vertical nuclear family.

The surface-depth dichotomy, in which surface is considered to be of secondary value in the modern period, is mirrored aesthetically in eighteenth- and early nineteenth-century discussions about the priority of the idea (the invisible, the internal) over the material. Hegel's lectures on aesthetics from the 1820s crystallize this preference for the imaginative/ spiritual/intellectual over materiality when he writes in the *Lectures on Aesthetics* that sculpture embodies the sensuous beauty of nature in its "corporeal externality presented in terms of heavy matter" that forecloses sculpture's engagement with the spirit.[136] Hence, whereas sculpture and the material correspond to the past, painting and, even more so, poetry, as Lessing also proposed in his *Laocoön, oder die Grenzen der Malerei und Poesie* (1766) [*Laocoön: An Essay on the Limits of Painting and Poetry*], correspond to the modern, the imaginative, and the less "plastic" that characterizes "inner life" ("die innere Lebendigkeit").[137]

Eighteenth- and early nineteenth-century discourses about aesthetic value have correlates in the discourses about kinship/family and the modern subject. The modern arts correspond to a notion of subjectivity that is interior, complex, and unique, one that is animated by the imagination, the invisible soul, and the ideal. The older, "heavy" arts correspond to a premodern notion of subjectivity characterized by materiality, sensuousness, and a lack of interiority and depth. The premodern individual would be legible through the roles they are assigned within a preestablished order, whereas the modern interior subject is unique, always carrying a secret that reveals one's complex truth. This interior subject is, of course, the one who inhabits the modern bourgeois nuclear family, itself representing a dialectic of interiority and exteriority.

The concepts of the "modern" and newness are key here. Brown shows us that the aesthetic shift from allegory to mimesis, just like the transition to the interior subject, is not smooth but halting and gradual.[138] If mimesis is modern, allegory corresponds to an older mode of representation and conception of the self: "Indeed, allegory is characterized not by its abstraction but by its concreteness, by making ideas material in sometimes disturbing ways."[139] While there is no clear one-to-one relationship between the concept and the allegorical representation, this is not an aesthetics of depth. Hence, aesthetics and notions of subjectivity ally in the history of aesthetic judgment. As Brown points out, allegory became outmoded as "visibility became equated with superficiality."[140]

I utilize in this book a concept of allegory that emerges from early modern drama, as laid out above, one that purports to be a concrete representation, though modern interpreters are always aware of the gap between the concept and its representation. Eighteenth-century thinkers saw allegory simply as a representational image, "bildlich, figürlich überhaupt" [pictorial, in any way figural],[141] but by the beginning of the nineteenth century, allegory became denigrated in favor of the more organic and translucent notion of the symbol. Samuel Taylor Coleridge highlighted this distinction early in the nineteenth century as "mechanic" form (allegory) vs. "organic" form (symbol);[142] we might also think of this distinction as one between whole (allegory) and part or synecdoche (symbol).[143] The symbol is part and, hence, a cousin to the Romantic fragment that contains within it infinite signifying possibilities ("unendlich wirksam und unerreichbar" [endlessly effective and unreachable], as Goethe puts it),[144] whereas allegory is, as Coleridge writes, a figure in which "the parts combine to form a consistent whole."[145] Hegel's rejection of allegory in his *Lectures on Aesthetics* is informed by Coleridge's and the Romantics' critique of allegory's "thinness,"[146] its lack of "inner life."[147] Allegory flattens the dichotomy between interior and exterior and is hence not a suitable mode of representation in Hegel's Romantic and final stage of aesthetics. Allegory stands, nevertheless, in the eighteenth century and into the present, as an aesthetic marker of the return of the repressed and of the nonlinear nature of experienced time.

These considerations of the historicity of aesthetic and social development present us with a chicken-egg problem. We might ask here: What is the temporality of structural historical change? Does a "Bruch" [caesura] occur at midnight on December 31, 1749, shortly after Goethe's birth?[148] Or are we looking at a gradual process of shifting perceptions and realities? Or does the story get told retroactively? These questions are important for scholars of literature precisely because we read literary works in the context of periods and epochs.[149] In terms of the trope of kinship, it is clear that the tale of interiority, both subjective and aesthetic, goes hand in hand with the story of the family. A less linear reflection on these linked tropes invites new insights into literature's intervention into imagined realities.

Literature is representation, but even mimetic art cannot succeed in depicting transparently. Denis Diderot conceived of the dramatic *tableau* as a representation of "naturalness," with the actors forgetting they were on the stage. But this is an impossible feat even in Diderot's *tableau*, which is always focused on the idealized interior family sphere. German literature of the long eighteenth century does not follow Diderot's naturalist aesthetic program but instead stages in dramas and novels a complex assemblage of overlapping representations of sociality and kinship. This is where literature diverges from non-imaginative works. Kant, Hippel, and Hegel can write about the ideal case of the family in their theoretical and philosophical works, but the literary works of the period present a much more fraught and ultimately more interesting picture of the family via an intermedial aesthetics of kinship.

My book investigates the questions laid out here over the course of seven chapters. Chapter 1 discusses the comparative cultural context of bourgeois drama in eighteenth-century England, France, and Germany, exploring the particular ways in which realism and the notions "bourgeois/bürgerlich" and domesticity/"Häuslichkeit" translate into the German-speaking realms. Chapter 2 offers a comparative reading of Diderot and Lessing, exploring Lessing's appropriation of Diderot's dramatic *tableau* into his own dramas that depict heterogeneous social constellations not present in Diderot's plays. Chapter 3 focuses on *tableaux* in a variety of German bourgeois dramas of the period, which reveal the representation of diverse and complex kinship groups. Chapter 4 analyzes the nonnarrative functions of letters, props, and portraits in a number of German dramas and highlights their importance as metonymic signifiers of kin groupings. Chapter 5 examines Lessing's *Nathan der Weise*, highlighting the signifying function of props for an understanding of kinship structures in the play. Chapter 6 provides an overview and analysis of the German bourgeois novel form vis-à-vis English and French models and explores the literary kinship *tableaux* represented in these novels. In Chapter 7, I turn to the *tableau vivant* in the novel that represents the latest chronological point in the book, Goethe's *Wahlverwandtschaften* (1809), exploring the complex social constellations represented via the *tableau vivant* form. In the book's conclusion I reflect on the continued slippages in contemporary discourse between family, kinship, and "household" ("Haushalt") and return to the potential alternative pasts and futures that present themselves to us if we look beyond the discursive and ideological hegemony of the "family."

In pointing to the epistemological vulnerabilities in the genealogy and inherent teleology of the discourse on family and kinship, a fixation on organicism likewise comes under scrutiny. Indeed, the model of *Bildung*, bringing together all of these terms in an ideal notion of modern development, is in need of renewed critical inquiry. If the kinship constellations are assemblages rather than circumscribed, organic wholes, then this fact surely affects our understandings of modern subjectivity and of modern social and political spheres. As Butler argues in her interpretation of Sophocles's *Antigone*, kinship is the sphere that conditions the possibility of politics.[150] Shifting the lens on kinship structures will affect both the working of symbolic knowledge forms and our understanding of social and political spheres.

Put another way, what would our narrative of the present be if we had told the story of the development of the family, individual, and nation differently? The dialectic of the Enlightenment is dependent upon the smooth mapping of the autonomous individual onto patriarchy, nation, and fascism, and all of these concepts themselves rest upon a circumscribed definition of the family as nuclear family, the microcosm from which everything else emerges. Indeed, the nuclear family is the ideal dialectical kinship model, as Hegel so clearly saw. Perhaps the exercise of temporarily dispensing with dialectical analytical methods has the potential to break apart some of the tightly woven ideological bulwarks of our understanding of European modernity. And the imaginative art of literature is precisely the place where we can fruitfully engage in this practice. Indeed, an alternative picture of social constellations in eighteenth-century literary works, ones that have long stood as indices for our understanding of family and subjectivity, can open up retroactively alternative futures located within the modern beginnings of the German imaginary.

CHAPTER ONE

Middle Class/Bourgeois/Bürger

The Idiosyncrasies of
German Dramatic Realism

IN *Laocoön, oder die Grenzen der Malerei und Poesie* (1766), Lessing sets out to distinguish the semiotics of poetry from those of painting, but this seemingly straightforward project is complicated from the beginning. We need only look to the resilience of the *tableau* within German Enlightenment dramas and novels to see a vibrantly intermedial semiotics within the literature of the period. The *tableau* integrates a static and painterly quality into bourgeois drama that harks back to the theater history of wandering acting troupes and pantomime. Indeed, Lessing's theoretical polemics aside, eighteenth-century literature continues the early modern tradition of intermingling text and image, a tradition celebrated by the Swiss philologians Johann Jakob Bodmer and Johann Jakob Breitinger as an ideal painterly mode of poetics. And this tradition of semiotic hybridity lives on in eighteenth-century bourgeois dramas and novels via the *tableau*. As August Langen puts it, Lessing's treatise thus represented "only the theoretical overcoming, but by no means the end in practice" of literature inflected with visual media.[1]

Tableaux abound in eighteenth-century dramas and were often cued by precise stage directions that called for embraces or kisses, for one character to fall to one knee before another, or for other gestures of generosity, forgiveness, or regret—ideally ones that would prompt the characters to weep and thereby elicit tears from the audience in response.[2] Characters would be grouped together and choreographed to re-create familiar paintings or scenarios that could serve as the subject for a painting. In this sense, the *tableau* and the *tableau vivant* tend to merge. Diderot's own famous concluding *tableaux* from his two dramas *The Natural Son* (1757) and *The Father of the*

Family (1758) depict groupings of family members and their betrothed inching closer and closer to one another to create a communal circle. In Lessing's concluding *tableau* from *Nathan der Weise*, the principals, representing estranged blood and adoptive kin, similarly collect in a group hug. The dramatic *tableau* is used not only by Lessing but also by Goethe, by popular authors of the *Rührstück* [popular sentimental play] such as August von Kotzebue and August Wilhelm Iffland, and by Schiller. In Schiller's *Die Jungfrau von Orleans* [The Maid of Orleans] the cast is instructed, "alle stehen lange in sprachloser Rührung" [all stand for a long time speechless and emotionally moved],[3] and in *Wilhelm Tell* the directions stipulate, "Alle stehen gerührt" [all stand emotionally moved].[4] Indeed, Schiller's *tableaux* complicate the popular perception that his works resisted Lessing's reception aesthetics of *Mitleid* [empathy] in favor of a more politically relevant realism.

The abovementioned examples from German dramas remind us that, contrary to Diderot's *tableaux*, eighteenth-century German dramatic *tableaux* did not frame the modern nuclear family but instead heterogeneous social constellations. *Tableaux* produced groupings of characters in postures that indicated not just stillness but also multiple future potentialities. The positioning of the character of Nathan in the concluding *tableau* of Lessing's play is ambiguous. Does he get pulled in as an honorary member of the group of hugging blood relatives, this group itself consisting of unexpected kin relations that expand the nuclear family? Or does he step to the side of the stage, watching the proceedings as an outsider and thereby signaling a potential interruption of the shrinking circle of newly formed kin?

In "What is Epic Theater?," Walter Benjamin highlights the relationship between the theatrical *tableau* and interruption, giving the example of a stranger observing the domestic scene of a *tableau* to illustrate his point:

> The most primitive example: a family scene:
> Suddenly a stranger enters. The wife was just about to grab a pillow in order to throw it at the daughter; the father was just about to open the window in order to call a policeman. In this moment the stranger appears in the door. "Tableau," as one called it around 1900. This means: the stranger stumbles into this scene: wrinkled bedding, open window, neglected furniture.[5]

Benjamin's choice of the term "primitive" to connote the family *tableau* is telling: the *tableau* is represented in its most basic form, as domestic and familial, even unenlightened. The *tableau* pictures, as in Diderot, the domestic scene of the nuclear family, but here it is both circumscribed and in the process of "dis-aggregating."[6] The figure of the stranger both interrupts the domestic *tableau* and provides the vantage point from which the scene can be observed. With-out the stranger the family is not perceived as a whole, even if that whole is on the verge of fragmenting. The domestic *tableau* is thus coded as both "primitive"/closed and as a site of porous heterogeneity.

Benjamin's "primitive" *tableau* is a degraded twentieth-century picture of the eighteenth-century *tableau*. In his theoretical work on drama, French playwright Louis Sébastien Mercier sketches the ideal *tableau* of bourgeois life in a structurally similar manner. Here, again, a domestic scene is inter-rupted by an outsider:

> Invite yourself congenially to be a guest at the home of an honor-able bourgeois, whose innocent and humble daughter smiles at you full of joy. Here you will observe authentic, soft, open, manifold manners; here you see the painting of bourgeois life, just as Rich-ardson and Fielding saw it. . . . Here you might see this dandy appear as a fine deceiver who has the intention of conning the good old man or of seducing his daughter. This is the moment, take your palette and let the chips fall as they may.[7]

The *tableau* of idealized bourgeois domestic life pictures the innocent (vir-ginal) daughter and the upright father, while the mother, as in so many bour-geois tragedies, is missing from the scene. Mercier writes that this *tableau* is modeled after similar ones created by the English novelists Fielding and, especially, Richardson, but the scene is also an homage to his teacher Diderot, whose theorization of the dramatic *tableau* shaped Mercier's use of the concept.

Very interestingly, this *tableau* features two figures who are not mem-bers of the family dyad: the intruder and the observer ("you"), an uninvited guest and an implied invited guest. The domestic *tableau*, conceived as a closed unit, is only relevant when functioning as a spectacle that belies its theatricality. The intruder threatens to seduce the daughter and remove her from the scene, and the observer is invited (we do not know by whom) to take a voyeuristic position. We see here, as in Benjamin's *tableau*, an ideal always in the process of dissolution, the ubiquitous "family in crisis." The naturalness of the family *tableau* is revealed to be a self-conscious represen-tation directed to the outside world.

DOMESTIC/*HÄUSLICH*/*BÜRGERLICH*

In literary and cultural theory, discourses around the eighteenth-century *tableau* connect it to domesticity (*Häuslichkeit*) and the bourgeois milieu. Even when we are not technically dealing with bourgeois characters, as in many seminal German dramas from the period, the *tableau* cues us to bourgeois values. And bourgeois values, as framed within the *tableau*, are domestic, a concept patronizingly called *häuslich* [domestic]. As Erich Auerbach points out in *Mimesis*, his seminal study on literary realism, the characters in Lessing's *Minna von Barnhelm* do not represent the middle class, but they nevertheless behave as if they were living "in einem bürgerlich-häuslichen Rahmen" [in a bourgeois-domestic frame].[8] Peter Szondi "rescues" Mercier's *tableau* from an apolitical interpretation by reading it as a *tableau* of *civil* and not simply *familial* life; thus, Szondi sees the crisis represented by the intruder as introducing political relevance into an otherwise unimportant domestic scene.

A derogatory association of *bürgerlich* with *häuslich* colors the reception of eighteenth-century German bourgeois drama, reflecting a broadly shared belief in the apolitical quality of the family. In his lectures on aesthetics, Hegel denigrates the "narrowness" associated with *Häuslichkeit* [domesticity], pointing in particular to *Rührstücke* [sentimental plays] by August Wilhelm Iffland and August von Kotzebue as culprits in the devaluation of drama. The *Rührstück* that gained popularity toward the end of the eighteenth century was perceived as a sign and symptom of the increasing turn inward of the bourgeois family and an intensification of Lessing's reception aesthetics based on the emotional response of the spectator.[9] For Hegel, all drama should strive toward a dialectical reconciliation (his forced interpretation of the reconciliation between Antigone and Creon is a case in point). German "plays and dramas," as Hegel calls them, are simply too subjective in scope for his concerns; the reconciliation offered in the plays by Kotzebue and Iffland is too individual and trivial with its focus on "das Rührende im Kreise des bürgerlichen Lebens und des Familienkreises" [the emotionally moving element in the sphere of bourgeois life and the family].[10] Hegel associates what he sees as the rigid moral outlook and trivial resolutions of these plays with the perceived narrowness of the environments being represented within them.

Schiller himself mimics this critique of popular bourgeois dramas and *Rührstücke* in his *Xenien* poem "Shakespeares Schatten" (1797) [Shakespeare's Shadow]:

Also sieht man bei euch den leichten Tanz der Thalia
Neben dem ernsten Gang, welchen Melpomene geht?
Keines von beiden! Uns kann nur das Christlich-Moralische rühren,
Und was recht populär, häuslich und bürgerlich ist.

[Can one see from where you are the light dance of Thalia
Next to the earnest gait of Melpomene?
Neither of them! Only the Christian and moral can move us,
And whatever is truly popular, domestic, and bourgeois.]

. . . Woher nehmt ihr denn aber das große gigantische Schicksal,
Welches den Menschen erhebt, wenn es den Menschen zermalmt?

[But where, though, do you gather the great giant fate,
Which raises humans when it crushes them?]

Das sind Grillen! Uns selbst und unsere guten Bekannten,
Unsern Jammer und Not suchen und finden wir hier.

[Those are whims! Ourselves and our good acquaintances,
Our lament and plight are what we look for and find here.]

Aber das habt ihr ja alles bequemer und besser zu Hause;
Warum entliehet ihr euch, wenn ihr euch selber nur sucht?

[But you have all of that more comfortably and better at home;
Why do you lend yourselves out, when you are only looking for
    yourselves?][11]

In the fourth line of the poem, Schiller has added the term "populär" to
"häuslich" [domestic] and "bürgerlich" [bourgeois], connecting all terms
via "rühren," the catalyzing verb for Lessing's reception aesthetics focused on
Mitleid. By the time Schiller wrote the *Xenien*, he and Goethe had turned
away from a theater of mimesis and moral betterment, embracing instead
an aesthetics of performance in their work at the Weimar Court Theater.[12]
Whereas Lessing sees the bourgeois drama as having the potential to improve
the course of human lives across the spectrum, Schiller situates it squarely
within the camp of the trivial. The author of "Die Schaubühne als eine moralische Anstalt betrachtet" [The Theater as a Moral Institution] looks cyni-

cally at the educational function of compassion here, demoting the emotions produced within the bourgeois play to the narcissistic love of the self. The condescending tone Schiller takes here is nevertheless indicative of the post-Lessing critical conflation of the concepts domesticity/family/ *bürgerlich* with a lack of political and aesthetic relevance.[13]

BOURGEOIS/*BÜRGER*/MIDDLE CLASS

The bourgeois milieu resides at the heart of the bourgeois tragedy genre in its iterations within the three intersecting European literary spaces of the period: France, Germany, and England.[14] Even the notion of "bourgeois" or "middle class" has unique connotations in each geographic location.[15] Scholars trying to define and analyze the bourgeois tragedy mode consistently draw connections between the iterations of the genre as it develops in the eighteenth century in England, France, and the German-speaking territories. A common line is drawn from Lillo's *The London Merchant* (England, 1731) to Diderot's *tragédies domestiques* [domestic tragedies]—the bourgeois *The Natural Son* (1757) and *The Father of the Family* (1758)—including Lessing's *Miß Sara Sampson* (1755) and *Emilia Galotti* (1772) and frequently ending with Schiller's *Kabale und Liebe* (1784).[16]

The bourgeois tragedy is a dramatic genre that is self-consciously interested in social betterment through the representation of, as Lessing put it, characters that are "von gleichem Schrot und Korne" [of the same grist and grain] as the bourgeois audience.[17] This is a value shared by eighteenth-century writers and theorists of bourgeois tragedy in England, France, and Germany.[18] Beyond this shared interest, however, the quite radical differences of cultural context and aesthetic concerns among these geographic spaces mean that terminology cannot be assumed to signify the same way across locales.

During the eighteenth century the German world looked westward to England and France in all its literary endeavors. Indeed, eighteenth-century Germans were far more eager to translate English and French works into German than their neighbors were to translate German literature into English and French. Diderot could not read German, but Lessing translated Diderot's plays and theoretical works on drama into German in 1760.[19] Lessing and his contemporaries were keenly aware of Lillo, Moore, and Diderot, frequently translating them and writing German adaptations of their famous plays, and Lessing's *Sara* is a clear homage to Lillo, featuring English characters and a seductress named Marwood. In comparative discussions about the bourgeois tragedy, German literature functions as the "and also" country (*they too* had a bourgeois tragedy that is assumed to have followed the

demarcation lines drawn by the English and the French!). But this genealogy is anything but smooth, particularly in light of the differing economic
and social conditions of these diverse cultural spaces.

The merchant class around 1750 was substantially more developed in
England than in France or Germany, and it is thus unsurprising that French
and German domestic dramas were less concerned with economic and social
conflict. Indeed, scholars of British bourgeois tragedy point out again and
again that capitalism is at the heart of Lillo's play—a moralistic tale of a
young merchant's downfall at the hands of a greedy and avenging seductress/
harlot named Millwood. Lisa A. Freeman shows that Millwood functions
as a scapegoat to represent the ugly truth of modern capitalism and empire
that have come to replace orthodox mercantilism in England.[20] For Tom
McCall, tears, the most valuable commodity of bourgeois tragedy aesthetics, are always linked to capital in the domestic tragedy. Characters who
weep are, without exception, attached in some way to property, and our
sympathy is channeled via tears toward a community of "good" merchants.[21]
But McCall's use of *Miß Sara Sampson* in his discussion of the tears produced
by the English bourgeois tragedy misreads Lessing's play through the lens
of British drama history.[22] *Mitleid* is, of course, central to Lessing's first
German bourgeois tragedy, but it is not cultivated on behalf of good capitalist characters. Sara's value is not a product of her wealth. Her exchange
value is, of course, heightened by her connection to the sentimental father,
Sir William; and Sir William is a figure holding relative wealth. But this
wealth is not at the core of Sara's allure for Mellefont; indeed, she has given
it up by running away with him. Although all of the figures in *Miß Sara
Sampson* have adequate access to wealth, capitalism is not the source of the
many tears shed by the sentimental father, his servant, and Sara herself.
The eighteenth-century German imaginary is far less focused on the moral
dangers of capitalism than on the abstract bourgeois values that Sara and
her father represent.

In his *Begriffsgeschichten* [History of Concepts], Reinhart Koselleck
shows that the concept of *bürgerliche Gesellschaft* [bourgeois society] has very
different connotations in its English, French, and German variations. The
term, he points out, corresponds to the concepts *société civile* and *civil society*, which are both translated from the Latin as modern variations of the
Roman *societas civilis*, a concept indebted to the Greek *koinonia politike*.[23]
In this sense, there is a continuity to the concept of *civil society* that predates
our modern notions of the middle class. With regard to the Enlightenment
uses of the terms *bürgerlich* and *Bürger*, Koselleck points to John Locke who

locates *work* as the necessary condition for *property*, and *property* as the necessary condition for political rights.[24] German uses of these terms differ, however, from the English and French uses.

In the 1731–1754 *Großes vollständiges Universal-Lexicon* [Large Complete Universal-Lexicon], Zedler links the German term *Bürger* to *Burg* [castle] and *Stadtbürger* [citizen of a city].[25] Koselleck highlights how the *Bürgerschaft* [bourgeois] in this period is apolitical, and "not critical of the state."[26] Initially, *Bürger* were *Stadtbürger*, and prior to the nineteenth century we cannot talk about a "bürgerliche Gesellschaft" [bourgeois society] in the modern sense (a space located between family and the state, as Koselleck describes it).[27] In comparative terms, German coined only one term, *Bürger*, corresponding to the French Enlightenment *bourgeois* and *citoyen*, and *Bürger* connotes a group with no geographical center and almost no political power, one unable to coalesce revolutionary forces. The term, as Koselleck shows, had so many different connotations and rights associated with it that it could not be mobilized for political action: "Just as there was no geographic center in 1848 in which the revolution could have condensed, there was likewise no semantic kernel around which the demands of the new *Bürger* could crystallize."[28] Even by the middle of the nineteenth century the German concept *Bürgertum* connoted a self-identity with a harmonizing function: "This group saw itself in the role of mediator between opposites."[29]

The German *Bürger* becomes more explicitly linked to the English concept of the "middle class" through the lens of national identity. As Koselleck argues, the self-conscious identity of the middle classes in England, France, and Germany become more streamlined as "*national* middle classes" in the wake of German unification in 1871.[30] The uneven development of the German concept of *Bürger* vis-à-vis Germany's neighbors is important for a number of reasons. For one, it helps us weed out some of the assumptions we bring to the genre of the bourgeois tragedy based on our transnational and transtemporal conceptions of the connotations associated with *bürgerlich*. In addition, it reminds us that the bourgeois tragedy is not simply a representative literary genre corresponding to an emerging economic and social middle class. Instead, we are called upon to de-link the eighteenth-century semantics of the term *bürgerlich* from Marxist assumptions about the relationship between the nuclear family, literature, and ideology.

In his lectures on the bourgeois tragedy, Peter Szondi likewise highlights the apolitical connotations of *bürgerlich* in the bourgeois tragedy genre up until Schiller's *Kabale und Liebe*, pointing out that "the word 'bürgerlich' does not so much refer to a social class designation as to a name for the private and the domestic ("das Häusliche") within the German genre sig-nification."[31] Jürgen Habermas distinguishes between the *Haus* of the nobility, one in which the spouses rarely met (instead preferring to live in different "hotels"), and the new patriarchal bourgeois family that embodies intimacy within a house characterized by its small rooms and fetishization of privacy.[32] Here again, *häuslich* refers derogatorily to the narrowness associ-ated with the nuclear family sphere and a space of apolitical passivity. This circumscribed familial home is the location for both of Diderot's *dramas serieux*, but interestingly it is not the location of the closing scenes of Lillo's *The London Merchant*. The final scenes of Lillo's play take place in the prison where Barnwell is awaiting his execution and seeking forgiveness. We have left behind the safe space of the home of his uncle, the virtuous merchant Thorowgood, and repentance and forgiveness are enacted within the institu-tional walls of the prison. Hence, the world of *The London Merchant* is not limited to the sphere that can properly be called bourgeois or the private sphere. Within Lessing's homage to Lillo, *Miß Sara Sampson*, as in all of his later plays, the primary locale is likewise not the domestic, private space of the family. Instead, the play's events take place at inns (the one where Sara and her entourage live as well as the one where Marwood resides): these are liminal spaces that are neither exclusively intimate nor exclusively public.

BOURGEOIS REALISM AND SHAME

At the center of dominant twentieth- and twenty-first-century discussions of the German bourgeois drama is the Marxist question of political message. Does *Emilia Galotti* present a narrative of rebellion that opens up critical views on despotism and unequal class structures? If so, then the play is seen as aesthetically valuable; if not, then the moral hedging the play performs overrides its other aesthetic or social characteristics. Of course, Lessing very consciously wrote an adaptation of Livy's *Virginius* story that offered a con-densed representation of human suffering without explicit reference to the vagaries of the political state: "A state is a much too abstract concept for our sentiments [Empfindungen]."[33] And "sentiments," as we know, are at the heart of Lessing's theater project.

In his lectures on the bourgeois tragedy, Szondi contrasts an aesthetics of compassion (the "Mitleid" of Lessing's reception aesthetics) and the politi-cal. For Szondi, the German bourgeois tragedy is not political (i.e., not concerned with class struggle) but is instead focused on sentimentality, which is the affective tenor at what he sees as the heart of the bourgeois tragedy, the bourgeois family: that sentimentality, in which humans, joined together as a bourgeois nuclear family, don't dare to confront their conflicts but rather choke in tears and excessive emotion ["Rührung"].[34] The members of the nuclear family, shut up together in the private sphere, cannot and will not act. Instead, they cry, and the spectators follow suit: tears replace blood, diluting action and representing, for Szondi, political passivity.[35]

Georg Lukács's Marxist sociological analysis of the bourgeois tragedy was influential for Szondi and other scholars concerned with the intersections between bourgeois drama, realism, and the political. For Lukács drama is always social and therefore poses the vital contradictions that face all humans in a given epoch. In his 1914 essay on the sociology of modern drama, he proposes that the bourgeois drama was predicated upon class difference: "The bourgeois drama is the first that grew out of a conscious class struggle; the first whose goal it was to give expression to the manner of feeling and thought of a class that is struggling for freedom and power and to give expression to its relationship to the other classes."[36] In Lukács's Hegelian reading, bourgeois drama is, at its best, a dialectical representation of class struggle, which, for him as well as for Auerbach and Szondi, is the vital conflict at the heart of realist aesthetics.

At the crux of what for Lukács is problematic about bourgeois drama is the demeaned quality of the "bourgeois milieu" at its center:[37] "The thematic material of bourgeois drama is *trivial* [my italics], because it is all too near to us; the natural pathos of its living men is nondramatic and its most subtle values are lost when heightened into drama."[38] Here we have the problem that already plagued the Dutch genre painters, and later Flaubert, as they turned to a mode of mimesis in their artistic renderings; that is, the shameful feelings associated with representing not the sublime but "das Vorübergende und Gleichgültige" [the transitory and indifferent].[39] We know that Flaubert fretted that his Emma Bovary was too lowly of a subject and not worthy of him. Lukács points to the shame associated with representing that which we understand primarily in terms of purposiveness and reproduction: the domestic, interior—and hence feminized—realm of bourgeois life. Indeed, the milieu of bourgeois drama always already embodies this shame vis-à-vis the degraded subject of realism.[40] Literary criticism after Kant's *Kritik der Urteilskraft* [*Critique of Judgment*] (1790)—after, that is, the theory of autonomous art—and in the wake of Hegel, Marx, and Freud cringes in light of the lowly subject of the nuclear family that is presumed to reside always at the center of things.

Lukács's engagement with bourgeois drama brings to the fore the collision between tragedy and realism in a post-sacral world, a collision that stages an uncomfortable encounter between the sublime and the trivial. Indeed, Lukács points out that the new bourgeois drama writhes under the shame of its own triviality at the same time as it is concerned with the most "vital" elements of life.[41] Valiantly invested in the personality of the individual, that element that cannot be consumed by a rationalized and quantified world, bourgeois drama is both debased and potentially sublime; hence, both aesthetics and ethics and the corresponding concepts of form and content are irreconcilable in the modern age.[42] In a post-Enlightenment age, one in which "ethics cease to be given, the ethical knotting within the drama—thus, its aesthetics—has to be created." Whereas there had been a "spontaneous unity of ethics and aesthetics" in the "old" drama, the new drama is still seeking the form to represent the modern tragic.[43] Without the solid ethical ground that had been provided to us in a sacral world, aesthetics mimics the shakiness of ethics. Aesthetic form struggles to reconcile with the "trivial" thematic of the family, yet it is, Lukács asserts, in dialectical form that we will find the ethical and even ontological crises of our epoch revealed.

Lukács's reflections pave the way for discourses of "failure" that surround the genre of the bourgeois tragedy. British literary critics have highlighted the ways in which the English bourgeois tragedy has been perceived as having "failed."[44] The term "failure" is less pronounced in the scholarly reception of the German bourgeois tragedy, but the frequent critique leveled at this genre for its perceived retreat from political relevance nevertheless points in that direction. Auerbach calls German bourgeois tragedy pivotal for European literature's shift to a realist representation of social and economic life, pointing to the sole example of Schiller's *Kabale und Liebe*. However, after calling *Kabale und Liebe* an early revolutionary work in the history of literature, he shows us exactly how the play ultimately fails in its task of representing historical truth.

Auerbach highlights the ways in which the political and social particularities that inhered in the German states created the environment for the birth of modern realism. Due to the survival of a "Christian-creatural mixing of styles" through the seventeenth century and to a strong resistance to French classicism and the rigidity of the "Ständeklausel" [estates clause], "the evolution of middle-class realism assumed exceptionally vigorous forms . . . works were produced that were at once sentimental, narrowly middle-class, realistic and revolutionary."[45] Auerbach does not consider any of Lessing's major plays to have successfully apprehended and represented the political conditions of the time.[46] It is the Sturm und Drang writers, and particularly Schiller in the bourgeois tragedy *Kabale und Liebe*, who initiate the connection of "sentimental middle-class realism with idealistic politics and concern for human rights."[47] *Kabale und Liebe* attempts to comprehend its political context in a way that, for Auerbach, no European play had done before, combining the political with the familiar milieu in a realist manner that renders "the fullness of contemporary reality."[48]

Having located *Kabale und Liebe* as a revolutionary literary marker in the development of modern realism, Auerbach deconstructs his own claim via the collision laid out by Lukács between the degraded topos of the domestic sphere and the sublime ambitions of tragedy. Auerbach focuses on the weakness of the bourgeois tragedy genre: "It was a genre wedded to the personal, the domestic, the touching and the sentimental, and it could not relinquish them. And this, through the tone and level of style which it implied, was unfavorable to a broadening of the social setting and the inclusion of general political and social problems."[49] The milieu presumed to be at the center of the action of the bourgeois tragedy—the domestic space of the middle-class nuclear family—is, once again, the downfall of the genre. The development of literary realism is predicated upon the shift from high tragedy to the real, political conditions of capitalist exploitation. Yet the middle-class milieu is too narrow and sentimental. For Auerbach, the details presented by Schiller are too isolated and not linked to larger cultural forces. Representations are caricatured; the duke and his court have no political function outside of the sadistic abuse of their subjects: "We hear and sense practically nothing of inner problems, historical complications, the function of the ruling class, the causes of its moral decline, nor of practical conditions in the principality. This is not realism, it is melodrama."[50] Because of its indulgence in melodrama, Auerbach calls *Kabale und Liebe* "a fairly bad play."[51] Although he praises Schiller's "homogenous and natural" representation of the musician Miller, he nevertheless describes the world of the play as "desperately narrow, both spatially and ethically. A petty-bourgeois parlor; a duchy so small that (as we are repeatedly told) it is only an hour's drive to the border; and class dictation of propriety and ethics in its most unnatural and pernicious form."[52] Along these lines, Auerbach's critique of Schiller's play mimics Schiller's own *Xenien* poem in which domesticity begets claustrophobia.

Schiller's play, considered by Auerbach to be both revolutionary and an artistic failure, initiates German literature's turn "away from realism in the sense of a concrete portrayal of contemporary political and economic conditions, with its forceful mixing of styles."[53] For Auerbach, as for Lukács, realism is a dialectical mode of representation that embraces not only the political but also art, economy, and material and intellectual culture in order to grasp what is both unique and prevailing about a particular place and time. But *Kabale und Liebe*'s tentative steps toward a Hegelian literary realism are interrupted before they can find a path forward. The potential for a mixing of styles is replaced by a return to a static separation of styles that does not reflect the dynamism of the present but instead artificially preserves boundaries between forms and ideas (i.e., the boundary between the sensual and the ideal in German classicism).[54] Indeed, Auerbach sees Goethe as largely to blame for the anti-realist turn taken by German literature; Goethe's tastes are simply too attuned to the beautiful and too resistant to destruction to allow him to represent political and social turmoil in a manner that would subordinate the perfection of form to the messy class struggles of contemporary content. Auerbach seems to accuse Goethe, whom he nonetheless admires, of resisting something akin to the truth of "dissonance" that inheres to Adorno's aesthetics after Auschwitz.

LITERATURE WITHOUT A CENTER

The fragmented and fractured quality of the Germanic territories in the second half of the eighteenth century, Auerbach argues, does not produce a dynamically cohesive realism:

> The social picture was *heterogeneous*, the general life was conducted in the confused setting of a host of "historical territories," unities which had come into existence through dynastic and political contingencies. In each of them the oppressive and at times choking atmosphere was counterbalanced by a certain pious submission and the sense of a historical solidity, all of which was more conducive to speculation, introspection, contemplation, and the development of local idiosyncrasies than to coming to grips with the practical and the real in a spirit of determination and with an awareness of greater contexts and more extensive territories.[55]

For Auerbach, the prenational context provided the ground for a mode of thinking and representation that was at once too small (the tiny principality in Schiller's *Kabale und Liebe*) and too universal and abstract (the ideal symbols and concepts that dominate German classicism), and therefore lacked the visible germs of concrete futurity that would suture the particular and the universal.

Auerbach names Goethe as a pivotal figure in the split between the particular and the general that he sees as characterizing the period and resulting in abstraction and idiosyncrasy. Goethe was acutely aware of the glaring lack of a central cultural community within the conglomeration of territories that made up Germany, a center "where authors might congregate and, in their several domains, develop in one common manner and in one common direction." Such authors were "born in scattered places, subject to most different forms of education, generally left only to themselves and the impressions of very different conditions."[56] In this sense, as Norbert Elias shows, the status of the German intelligentsia in the mid-eighteenth century was radically different from that of its French and English counterparts, and this difference is inevitably reflected in the literary and cultural products of the period. Goethe complained to Eckermann in 1827 that German writers of his time "lead in essence an isolated and impoverished life!"[57] Without a global center like Paris where artists and intellectuals can meet on a daily basis, he observes, German authors toil in isolation, which is why Germans are less likely to produce mature art at a young age.[58]

The lack of a central "good society," as Elias calls it, was a product of both the "fragmentation of the German territory into a multiplicity of sovereign states" and the "extreme isolation of large parts of the nobility from the German middle class."[59] Elias argues that this is one of the reasons why the attacks by the bourgeois intelligentsia on the courtly upper class were waged almost entirely outside the political sphere, and why those attacks were directed predominantly against the conduct of the upper class, and against general human characteristics like "'superficiality,' 'outward politeness,' 'insecurity,' and so on."[60] Without a centralizing national identity, eighteenth-century German literature was bound to produce a stylistically diverse and idiosyncratic body of works. Eckermann quotes Goethe as having said, "We Germans are from yesterday," and this concept of a temporal lag offers another window onto the idiosyncratic path taken by German bourgeois literature.[61]

Marxist and literary-sociological analyses of German drama lament the shortcomings of eighteenth-century German realist aesthetics and offer crucial insights into the corresponding "failure" of German bourgeois drama of the period to dialectically reconcile history, ethics, and aesthetics. In other words, the narrow focus on the Miller household and duchy in Schiller's play cannot be reconciled with the sublime aims of tragedy. Here, again, it is clear that these analyses are predicated on the assumption that the bourgeois drama in question places the nuclear family at its center, an assumption this book calls into question. As I show in chapters 2 and 3, the metonymic linkages between the concepts of *bourgeois*, *domestic*, *realism*, and *nuclear family* are far looser within German drama than they are within English and French drama of the period, thereby rendering German bourgeois drama stylistically and generically unique. What is more, the intermedial quality of the ubiquitous *tableau* opens up possibilities for the representation of real and imagined social constellations that exceed or fall short of modern expectations for dialectical sublation. If we do not fall prey to a myopic focus on a largely imagined claustrophobic and narrow (*häuslich*) nuclear family, then the social heterogeneity of the dramatic *tableaux* can open insights into the political and aesthetic significance of the history of social forms that trace an alternative genealogy of sociality. Suddenly, the encounter staged between bourgeois tragedy and the *tableau* must be conceived not as a contradiction between the sublime aesthetic aim of tragedy's action, as Aristotle defined it,[62] and the degraded, bourgeois content of the domestic (its stillness and entrapment always coded as feminine). Instead, each dramatic *tableau* offers a new heterogeneous grouping that, as we will see, utilizes the suspension of action to open tragic and non-tragic potentialities for the individual figures and various subgroups pictured therein.

❧❧❧

CHAPTER TWO

Tableau/Tableau Vivant
German-French Dramatic Encounters

DENIS DIDEROT'S WRITINGS on drama famously served as the catalyst for Lessing's own dramatic aesthetics. Yet the cultural translation of these aesthetics from France to prenational Germany resulted in formal deviations, particularly in the case of Diderot's *tableau*. If we defer to Lessing's own view on this cross-cultural encounter, we might be tempted to overread Diderot's direct influence on Lessing's works. Lessing wrote in 1781 that "without Diderot's model and teachings" his "Geschmack" [taste] "would have taken on a wholly different direction. Maybe a more singular one: but surely not one with which my understanding would have been more content."[1] This statement appears in the preface to Lessing's own translation of Diderot's works on the theater, which he originally published anonymously in 1760.[2] We are left to muse here about the direction Lessing's work might have taken had he not encountered Diderot's writings, but we would be led astray were we to assume Diderot's unmediated influence on Lessing's theater aesthetics and, by extension, on German bourgeois drama. A case in point is the dramatic *tableau*.

Two of the central formal concepts in Diderot's theoretical writings on drama are his idea of the "fourth wall" and the *tableau*. The fourth wall is an imaginary barrier that separates the actors from the spectators, an aesthetic device that contributes to the suspension of disbelief that is crucial for modern, post-Enlightenment theater. The dramatic device of the *tableau* freezes the action of the play, presenting an intensified image of emotional pathos. Diderot's examples of the *tableau* focus, without exception, on an organic image of domestic authenticity, a picture of the "natural" family. An ideal play for Diderot would consist almost entirely of a series of

tableaux. The *tableau* is an intermedial aesthetic device that integrates the
semiotics of painting with those of theater, of action. Diderot famously
wanted to emphasize the image over words, believing that the spectator's
emotional response would be more intense if the semiotics of the frozen
action were to render speech superfluous.

Lessing does not engage explicitly in any sustained way with the concepts of the fourth wall and the *tableau* (a term he translated as "Gemälde"
[painting]), but he utilizes both in his plays. In particular, the notion of the
fourth wall allies with Lessing's interest in a reception aesthetics that advocates for the spectator's intense emotional engagement with the theatrical
characters. Lessing's reception of the concept of the *tableau* is, however, more
difficult to parse. Indeed, in practice he integrated into his plays scenes that
clearly indicate a slowing of time for pictorial and emotional effect.[3] For
instance, scholars frequently refer to the ending scene of familial reconciliation and religious tolerance in *Nathan der Weise* (1779) as a *tableau*,[4] a scene
that cites Diderot's ending *tableau* in *The Natural Son* in interesting ways.
The final moments in *Emilia Galotti* (1772), which depict the killing of Emilia
in a citation of Livy's Virginia narrative, have likewise been linked to the
tableau, as Virginia was among the most popular themes for paintings in
the second half of the eighteenth century.[5] *Tableaux* in Lessing's plays and
in those written by his contemporaries frequently picture people embracing
or gathering and are often cued by stage directions that stipulate a slowing
of the action and the suspension of speech. The stage directions at the close of
Nathan der Weise indicate not only multiple and repeated embraces but also
the absence of speech that Diderot prescribed for the *tableau*: "*Unter stummer Wiederholung allseitiger Umarmungen fällt der Vorhang*" [The curtain falls
while all present on stage repeatedly embrace in silence].[6] This and other
examples suggest that Lessing and his contemporaries were cognizant of the
new aesthetics linked to Diderot's concept of the theatrical *tableau*.

Despite his deep familiarity with Diderot's writings on drama, Lessing nevertheless does not write explicitly about the *tableau*. This fact is particularly intriguing given that Lessing's use of the device in his plays deviates
in important ways from Diderot's guidelines. Whereas Diderot's *tableaux*
were meant to represent natural, domestic groupings consisting of members
of a bourgeois nuclear family, Lessing's *tableaux* offer a picture of social constellations that eschews the bourgeois family idyll. Instead, these *tableaux*
present groupings of figures embodying a variety of familial and social roles,
bringing together fathers and daughters as well as extended family members, servants, political figures, functionaries, and village communities in

constellations that mix allegory and realism. Indeed, a closer look at the *tableau*'s travels from France to the German-speaking states reveals a surprisingly complex and chaotic picture of the literary family form, a form that serves as the linchpin for our understanding of the development of the modern subject and nation.

LESSING READS DIDEROT

Lessing viewed Diderot as a kindred spirit who was critical of what both writers perceived as the rigidity of the French neoclassical dramatic tradition, and who was eager to usher in a new, emotionally engaging and pedagogical theater for the nation. In the 1781 preface to *Das Theater des Herrn Diderot* [The Theater of Mr. Diderot], Lessing asserts: "Diderot seems to have had in fact far more influence on the German theater than on the theater of his own people."[7] Indeed, Diderot's play *The Father of the Family* was highly popular on the German stage and influenced every important German dramatic work written between 1767 and 1774.[8] Whereas the German translation of *The Natural Son* received a mixed reception in Germany (as in France, where neither of Diderot's plays were well regarded by his contemporaries),[9] *The Father of the Family* (*Der Hausvater*) was one of the most popular plays performed in the German-speaking states during the two decades after its translation into German in 1759.[10] Numerous German plays with similar narratives and subjects were written during the years following the introduction of Diderot's dramas into the German-speaking world, culminating in Otto Heinrich von Gemmingen-Hornberg's popular play *Der deutsche Hausvater oder die Familie: Ein Schauspiel* [The German Father of the Family or the Family: A Play] in 1780. For Mortier, it is Lessing's translation of Diderot's play and his accompanying theoretical works that were decisive for Diderot's influence in the German-speaking world.

Mortier makes the convincing case that Lessing translated and then utilized Diderot for polemical purposes. Diderot's critical stance vis-à-vis French theater's love affair with neoclassicism fueled Lessing's critique of the dominance of French neoclassicism in the German theater world, an arena dominated by Johann Christoph Gottsched.[11] Shortly before publishing his translation of Diderot's theater works, Lessing wrote his eighty-first *Literaturbrief* [letter on literature] (February 9, 1760), in which Diderot's critique of the French stage, spoken from within France, serves as the springboard for Lessing's own savage attack on the German theater: "This is how a Frenchman speaks! And what a jump from the Frenchman to the German! The French still have at least a stage; where the German barely has shacks ('Buden')."[12]

Lessing not only felt allied with Diderot vis-à-vis French classicism, but he likewise borrowed liberally from Diderot's drama theory.[13] Diderot's central concept of the fourth wall was clearly a catalyst for Lessing's reception aesthetics. The idea of the fourth wall emerges implicitly in Diderot's introduction to the "Conversations on *The Natural Son*." Here we learn that the play *The Natural Son* is only performed annually for and by family members who have personally experienced the story. The "I" (presumably Diderot) who engages in conversation about the drama with the main character, Dorval, hides while the family performs the play, thus experiencing it as a fully unselfconscious event on the part of the players. This frame for the performance rehearses the notion of the fourth wall that Diderot describes in *On Dramatic Poetry*: "One thinks about the spectator as little while writing as while performing, as if no one were there. One should imagine a large wall at the extreme edge of the stage where the theater's ground level is divided. One performs as if the curtain had been closed."[14] The players should perform as if there were, in fact, no audience at all. In his *Hamburgische Dramaturgie* Lessing subsequently cites at length from Diderot's erotic novel *Les bijoux indiscrets* (1748), in which the sultan's mistress advocates for a new theater that would offer unmediated emotional access to the characters and events represented so that "the constantly deceived spectator believes he is present amidst the action."[15] The fourth wall produces the "Täuschung" [deception] that results in an emotional engagement at once intense and pedagogically useful.

The reception aesthetics associated with Diderot's notion of the *tableau* mirror those of the fourth wall. Diderot compares the shock experienced by the spectator within this new theater world to that produced by an earthquake shaking the walls of a house.[16] For Diderot it is not words but impressions that should threaten to topple the spectator's emotional walls. As Günther Heeg and Helmut Schneider remind us in their discussions of Diderot and the German theater, the reorganization of spectatorship in the middle of the eighteenth century was radical. The removal from the stage of the banquette (*Bankette*), that in the *Comédie Française* seated groups of spectators on either side of the stage, opened possibilities for the theater of the fourth wall, allowing the spectators to experience the "Bühnenbild als Tableau" [theater image as *tableau*][17] and inviting new conceptions of "an imaginary social body."[18] Previous forms of theater had invited an active physical relationship between the spectators and the actors, an arrangement that was interrupted by the new theater architecture. As Heeg points out, the stage itself in the French classical theater highlighted its own theatricality. The French classical theater included multiple areas whose divisions were visible, thereby undercutting the harmonizing and closed image of the fourth wall.[19] Hence, Diderot's fourth wall theater and *tableau* aesthetics offered a radically new way of experiencing theatrical representation.

Whereas the aesthetic concept of the fourth wall clearly resonated with Lessing's interest in enhancing the emotional experience of the spectator, it seems that the *tableau* could not be adapted as easily by Lessing and his German contemporaries. Even Lessing's rendering of Diderot's term *tableau* as "Gemälde" underscores the conceptual and semiotic changes suffered by the concept in its travels eastward.

THE *TABLEAU* AND VERISIMILITUDE

We might think about Diderot's ideas of the new domestic drama and its central feature, the *tableau*, with the aid of one of his favorite painters, Jean-Baptiste Greuze. In the *Salons* Diderot wrote about the paintings that were exhibited at the Louvre for mass consumption between 1759 and 1783. Famously one of the first in his generation to appreciate genre painting over the more popular historical style, Diderot wrote enthusiastically about Greuze's *L'Accordée de Village* [The Village Betrothal] of 1761, a painting depicting precisely the kind of domestic scene of harmony that interested Diderot.

The painting was originally exhibited in 1761 with the title "A Marriage, and the instant in which the father of the bride hands over the dowry to his son-in-law" and was viewed by "unprecedented," "rapturous crowds" that made approaching the painting difficult and contributed to making it a "public work to an extent that no previous French painting had been."[20] As the longer title makes clear, the painting depicts a family gathering at which the father is handing over the dowry to the future son-in-law. The painting features not only the father of the bride and the future groom but also the mother of the bride, the bride's siblings, a number of household servants, the notary, and animals—including a chicken and some baby chicks. With minimal décor, the painting brings to life the individual members of the family *tableau* in a manner that was perceived to be highly natural. Here we have not the Rococo representation of historical and mythical figures or the aristocracy but an ideal grouping of middle-class family members.[21] As Emma Barker points out, the painting reconciles "virtue with prosperity"[22] (as the father is a rich, landowning farmer) and offers a "utopian vision of an enlightenment social order."[23]

Greuze's *L'Accordée de Village* served as the model for the first documented *tableau vivant* performance, which took place as a sort of intermission

fig. 2.1. Jean-Baptiste Greuze, *Betrothal in the Village*, 1761, oil on canvas, Musée du Louvre, Paris, France. Photo Credit: Scala/Art Resource, NY.

at the Théâtre Italien in Paris in 1761.[24] The play, *Les Noces d'Arlequin*, was written in response to Greuze's popular painting such that the presentation of the *tableau vivant* as an interruption served as both an introduction of stillness into the play and a bringing to life of the stillness represented in Greuze's painting. Indeed, the intermedial art form of the *tableau vivant* hovers like a ghost around Greuze's painting. As Barker points out, the style of the painting evoked a "startling frontality and immediacy," yielding a new reception experience in which viewers tended to believe in the realness of the picture in front of them.[25] What Michael Fried calls the "radical intelligibility" of anti-Rococo art is pictured here.[26] As Barker shows, the "striking pictorial innovations" of the painting enhanced the verisimilitude of its subject matter, mimicking the grouping of bodies in a theater *tableau*.

> The shallow space and statuesque figures style endow the painting with an unparalleled sense of physical presence. It is devoid of the picturesque disorder of traditional genre scenes and the space is

defined by strong vertical and horizontal lines formed by the wall and cupboard door and the shelf above. Against this austere backdrop, the figures stand out with a force that makes their formal grouping instantly legible. . . . The overall effect is arresting.[27]

The figures are grouped together in Greuze's painting like live actors on a stage, free of the complex landscapes and scenery of historical paintings. The family grouping in *L'Accordée de Village* almost jumps out of the canvas, blurring the lines between painting and theater in a manner reminiscent of the *tableau vivant*. The arrested effect of the painting rehearses the temporality of a "Dialektik im Stillstand" [dialectical image], as the line between past and present, and between two-dimensional and three-dimensional, is obscured.[28]

In Diderot's view, painting should represent a natural unity that is easily readable. Greuze's painting offered the beholder precisely this kind of naive harmony.[29] In contrast, Diderot found allegory to be, as Fried puts it, "cold, obscure and uninteresting."[30] Diderot's theory of the dramatic *tableau*, developed in his idiosyncratic "Conversations on *The Natural Son*," reiterates his aesthetics of painting and emerges as the ideal form for the "domestic bourgeois tragedy." *The Natural Son* plot circles around a "natural" (biological but not legally recognized) son whose affections for his beloved and for his best friend lead him to sacrifice both romance and his fortune, only to receive in the end an exponential return on his investment through the return of his biological father (presumed dead), who now recognizes his son, increases the family fortune, and arranges the young people in appropriate (not incestuous) pairings for future prosperity.

The *tableau*, as defined in "Conversations on *The Natural Son*," is tied to the problem of verisimilitude. Dorval, the hero of *The Natural Son*, engages with the narrator in a discussion about the theater. Here, yet again, we have a situation of the "real" colliding with representation, of verisimilitude *almost* closing the gap between history and fiction, between life and art. Dorval explains that the events of the plot should be linked in such a way "that a sensible observer can always see a reason for them which satisfies him."[31] The concept of naturalness is key here, in contrast to the contrived coup de théâtre.[32] And what is not contrived is natural. Like the "natural" son, a product of the most natural act in the world, the "natural" scene, according to Dorval, is almost devoid of plot; it is, in fact, a *tableau*: "An arrangement of these characters on stage, so natural and so true that, faithfully rendered by a painter, it would please me on a canvas, is a tableau."[33]

The fourth scene in act 2 of *The Natural Son* is, we learn, a *tableau*: "What a fine tableau, for I think it is one, is made by Clairville leaning on his friend's breast as though this were the only refuge left to him."[34] The scene is not "artificial" or "contrived,"[35] like dramatic scenes in which characters "stand in a circle, separated, at a certain distance from one another, and in a symmetrical pattern." Instead, the *tableau* is precisely a scene from "which one could make a tolerable composition for a painting." As Dorval puts it in the "Conversations," "My own view is that if a dramatic work were well made and well performed, the stage would offer the spectator as many real tableaux as the action would contain moments suitable for a painting."[36] But what sort of painting would fulfill the requirements of verisimilitude and nature—that is, of a situation and mode of representation that creates the conditions for identification and direct affective response? Surely Greuze's *L'Accordée de Village* serves as a fruitful model for the kinds of scenes Dorval imagines for his theater. Here we have the focus on the figures themselves, seemingly so real as to transform into a *tableau vivant* before our eyes, representing a scene of intense emotion but one that has emerged naturally from what came before it.

Dorval proposes that an ideal *tableau* pictures a "natural situation" as a domestic incident. He describes a scene he presumably witnessed in which a wife unknowingly sent her husband to her parents' home, where he was killed by his brother-in-law:

> The dead man was lying on a bed. His naked legs hung over its side. His disheveled wife was on the floor beside him. She was holding her husband's feet, and she said as she broke down in tears, tears which drew more from everyone present: "Alas! when I sent you here, I did not think that these feet were taking you to your death." Do you imagine a woman from another class would have said anything more moving? No. The same situation would have inspired the same words. Her mind would have been absorbed in that moment; and what the artist must look for is what anyone would have said in the same circumstances; what nobody will hear without immediately recognizing it in themselves.[37]

According to Dorval, this *tableau* scene is as moving as that of Clytemnestra, queen of Argos, mourning her daughter. Importantly, Dorval describes the scene of the grieving wife as if it were part of a play, including stage directions for the actors who could stylize a *tableau*: "His naked legs hung over its side. His disheveled wife was on the floor beside him." Dorval sees the *tableau* as both organically generated and as something an artist would have composed.

WHOLE, PART, FRAME

Michael Fried points out that Diderot's notion of the *tableau* is indebted to discussions begun by Anthony Ashley Cooper, Earl of Shaftesbury, earlier in the eighteenth century. Shaftesbury develops a conception of the *tableau* in his essay "A Notion of the Historical Draught or Tablature of the Judgment of Hercules" (1712):

> Before we enter on the examination of our historical sketch, it may be proper to remark, that by the word Tablature (for which we have yet no name in English, besides the general one of picture) we denote, according to the original word Tabula, a work not only distinct from a mere portraiture, but from all those wilder sorts of painting which are in a manner absolute and independent (i.e. not subject to the demand for unity); such as the paintings in fresco upon the walls, the ceilings, the staircases, the cupolas, and other remarkable places either of churches or palaces.[38]

The *tableau* is therefore not a work that depicts multiple scenarios and temporalities, because the *demand for unity* is key. In his posthumously published *Second Characters, or the Language of Forms*, Shaftesbury posits that the "tablature" is a work that displays a harmonious whole: "a single piece, comprehended in one view, and formed according to one single intelligence, meaning, or design; which constitutes a real whole, by a mutual and necessary relation of its parts, the same as of the members in a natural body."[39] The *tableau* is, for Shaftesbury as for Diderot, a single organic whole, like a "natural body."

Inscribed within Diderot's notion of the *tableau* is an awareness of its unfinished, fleeting nature. It is a transitory moment, cut from a larger body and therefore, of necessity, lacking.[40] As Helmut Schneider reminds us, the *tableau* is predicated upon the tropes of loss and separation.[41] The opening *tableau* of *Le Père de Famille* presents an absence: the son is away, and no one knows where he is. And the play is itself, we learn, based on the story of the family who performs it every year since the death of their real father, Lysimond. The actor who performs Lysimond in the drama can, to be sure, never replace the lost father.

Roland Barthes emphasizes the necessarily fragmented, fetishized nature of the framed unity that characterizes Diderot's concept of the *tableau*. He quotes the following from Diderot's *Encyclopédie* article "Composition," which very clearly refers to Shaftesbury's metaphors of the body and organicism:

> Diderot: A well-composed picture (*tableau*) is a whole contained under a single point of view, in which the parts work together to one end and form by their mutual correspondence a unity as real as that of the members of the body of an animal; so that a piece of painting made up of a large number of figures thrown at random on to the canvas, with neither proportion, intelligence nor unity, no more deserves to be called a *true composition* than scattered studies of legs, nose and eyes on the same cartoon deserve to be called a *portrait* or even a *human figure*.[42]

Barthes further writes, "Thus is the body expressly introduced into the idea of the tableau, but it is the whole body that is so introduced—the organs, grouped together and as though held in cohesion by the magnetic power of the segmentation, function in the name of a transcendence, that of the *figure*, which receives the full fetishistic load and becomes the sublime substitute of meaning: it is this meaning that is fetishized."[43]

Barthes reminds us here that the unity of the *tableau* is artificially produced and created through the process of "cutting out" everything that surrounds it. Diderot's

> tableau (pictorial, theatrical, literary) is a pure cut-out segment with clearly defined edges, irreversible and incorruptible; everything that surrounds it is banished into nothingness, remains unnamed, while everything that it admits within its field is promoted into essence, into light, into view.[44]

The "essence" of the *tableau* is manufactured in a process of excision that we might even call brutal. The "light" that emerges is a displacement of the truth of the fetish. As Freud defines it, the fetish represents the delicate balance between the disavowal and representation of castration. Castration stands for a vulnerability, a lack of completion. The fetish works to mask and disavow this vulnerability and restore a sense of wholeness and power to the subject.[45]

What, then, is the function of the *tableau* as both an imagined whole and a partial object, cut out from the larger context in which it is embedded? The notion of cutting out reminds us of the frame, the parameters of a painting that cannot easily be reproduced in the theater. The theater *tableau* is, of course, difficult to clearly distinguish from the *tableau vivant* that similarly brings together diverse media, including painting, theater, and even sculpture. Although the *tableau vivant* performance of the Greuze painting in *Les Noces d'Arlequin* was not presented within a frame per se, seventeenth-century dramatic performances often included *tableaux vivants* of allegorical figures that were literally circumscribed by large frames.[46] Alexandra Tacke points to the fascination with frames ("Rahmungsmanie") at the dawn of the Enlightenment, associating it with the eighteenth-century desire to see and analyze everything possible: "Mirrors, paintings, ceiling frescos, fireplaces, windows and niches are similarly framed and divided by plaster or ostentatious gold frames" throughout the period leading up to the Enlightenment.[47] We know from Goethe and others who witnessed Emma Hamilton performing her famous "attitudes" that Lord Hamilton would hold up a large frame to capture her individual poses as unified, organic *tableaux*. Hence, when Barthes refers to the "cutting out" quality of Diderot's *tableau*, he is reminding us of the (invisible) frame, the "fourth wall," as Diderot described it.

Barthes uses the concept of the "perfect instant" to discuss Diderot's *tableau*, one that, as he himself points out, is reminiscent of the "pregnant moment" in Lessing's *Laocoön* (1767) that crystallizes the semiotic rules of painting. Barthes describes the "pregnant moment" as both "totally concrete and totally abstract," an instant that is "artificial, a hieroglyph in which can be read at a single glance the present, the past and the future: that is, the historical meaning of the represented action."[48] As Barthes describes it, Diderot's *tableau* and Lessing's "pregnant moment" are both constructed to connote multiple temporalities and potentialities. Hence, the frozen moment is bursting with multiplicity, recalling Diderot's understanding of Greuze's *L'Accordée de Village* as offering varied strands of narrative potentiality.

As Lacan posits in his "Mirror Stage" essay, our notion of wholeness and completeness is based on a misreading and misunderstanding. One could put it differently: the mirror stage is the moment at which the individual sees themself for the first time as a bounded subject, and this moment is of necessity not just visual but *framed*. The mirror both enframes us and gives us a false sense of wholeness; indeed, without the frame, there is no "wholeness." The desire for the phallus is the desire to believe in the wholeness of the framed image of the self or an Other.[49] Indeed, within a secular, post-Enlightenment age the frame itself *necessitates* that we perceive the enframed object as whole and vital, lest we be stranded in a sea of partial objects.

A reflection on the *tableau* and related notion of the "pregnant moment" invites comparisons to Gilles Deleuze's analysis of the "movement image" in cinema. The *tableau* is precisely the attempt to freeze the ideal moment, or what Deleuze calls the "privileged instant."[50] Deleuze connects this moment to a premodern conception of time and movement. "Privileged instances" reflect the Ancients' notion of movement as "the regulated transition from one form to another, that is, an order of *poses* or privileged instants, as in a dance." In contrast, "the modern scientific revolution has consisted in relating movement not to privileged instants, but to any-instant-whatever."[51] "Any-instant-whatevers" can be understood as "not Euclidean but Cartesian," as Deleuze puts it—as measuring out equal cuts of time in the post–scientific revolution world.[52] Deleuze compares the "any-instant-whatever" to the snapshot, and the privileged image to the long-exposure photo.[53] Indeed, "Any-instant-whatevers" mirror Walter Benjamin's notion of a "homogene[n] und leere[n] Zeit" [homogenous and empty time],[54] the privileged experience of time of a disenchanted modernity.

But Deleuze contends that "privileged instants," the "pregnant moments" about which Lessing wrote, are not anathema to modernity. The difference between premodern and modern "privileged instants" are that the Moderns are aware, we might say, of the frame, the cut that makes the "privileged instant"—a notion of the Whole—possible. Even the father of cinematic montage, Sergei Eisenstein, imagined these instants as compositions, as something "pathetic" and "organic," as Deleuze puts it.[55] So how do we conceive of the notion of organicism in a post-Enlightenment age?

The shifting architecture of the theater in the eighteenth century can be mapped onto the rise of secularism and modern conceptions of the sublime. Günther Heeg likens this shift to the emergence of a theater aesthetics of the *tableau*. The earlier theater of the *Tragédie classique* offers the spectator a depth view of the events taking place, as the spectator can observe the space in front of the stage as well as the various parts of the stage, taking in, as it were, the whole world that the theater represents. In contrast, the theater of the *tableau* is a flat line between spectator and stage; the spectator is consequently shut out from a view of all aspects of represented life that are contained within the classical theater. The spectators are invited to imagine that the image presented to them contains within it the sublime, a transcendental element that in the older stage productions was represented materially in the set as the heavens. The *tableau* represses the representational field of God and hence becomes itself both sublime[56] and a fetish.

The earthquake that Diderot describes as profoundly shaking up the lives of the spectators in the new mode of theater represents precisely the shift from a premodern, not-yet-secular stage world to a secular one in which sublimity takes the place of God. The horrified realization that one lives in a godless world, that the *tableau* might, just like an "any-instant-whatever," simply reflect an arbitrary cut within a larger, incomprehensible universe of images, is banished from the moral and aesthetic world of the *tableau*. The crisis of representation that stems from the process of secularization gives birth to the modern notion of the sublime. Diderot's *tableaux* engage in what we might call the work of the sublime fetish, the representation both of the sublime and that affect which always attends the modern sublime, the "Horror vacui."[57] But scholars often resist seeing Diderot's *tableaux* as sublime in light of his choice to focus on the banal object of the domestic family, an object generally seen as unfit for an aesthetics of sublime pathos and one that instead signifies sentimentality.[58] We must remember, though, that Diderot wanted his *tableaux* to represent the domestic sphere not as profane and inferior but as a space embodying the full pathos of existence. The pathos felt by a simple woman upon the death of her husband is no less profound than the queen Clytemnestra's pain at the loss of her daughter. Hence, for Diderot the family scene is not simply a site of sentimentality but is precisely the appropriate subject for the *tableau*. In Diderot's theory, the *tableau* of the bourgeois nuclear family embodies both a link to a transcendent sphere (death) and an awareness of the fleeting nature of the enframed Now.

THE FAMILY *TABLEAU*

In Diderot's dramatic works and drama theory, the nuclear family is the privileged, "natural" site of the *tableau*.[59] Indeed, all examples of *tableaux* in "Conversations" refer to scenes of trauma in the nuclear family. The *tableau* is meant to frame this "naturalness," to compose it and then to obscure the visibility of the frame, the cut.[60] The spectators are supposed to view the action as if they are unaware of the existence of the stage, absorbed in the world being presented to them. In this way, the "naturalness" of the *tableau* presentation is experienced by the audience. Indeed, Diderot was also interested in the architecture of the stage, introducing the idea that rooms could be recreated on the stage to enhance the realism of the performance and to invite audience members to forget they were watching a play "by turning the stage into a private home."[61]

The action in Diderot's *Le Fils naturel* presents couplings between two sets of siblings, Dorval and Rosalie and Clairville and Constance, that occur exclusively within the family home.[62] It is precisely the return of the father, Lysimond, to the domestic sphere that provides a resolution to the conflicts between these four principals. The tensions between Clairville and Dorval are relieved when the father reveals that Rosalie and Dorval are siblings, thereby introducing the incest taboo into their relationship and restoring the previous pairings of Rosalie and Clairville as well as Dorval and Constance. Indeed, the incestuous love between Dorval and Rosalie could be seen as a product of the play's claustrophobic setting, in which the characters exchange their discourses of love and renunciation while cooped up in the house. The father's return saves the community from its impending implosion, yet he likewise cements their relationships with one another by hindering Dorval's departure. The ending *tableau* of the play resembles Greuze's *L'Accordée de Village*, as all of the principals and "toute la maison" [the entire house] gather together around old Lysimond to be blessed and married off. The final line is spoken by the father, who reiterates the circularity of the claustrophobic family by referring to future generations who will reproduce the very same *tableau*: "Lysimond: I wish that God, who blesses children through their father and fathers through their children, will give you children who love you the same way you have loved me."[63]

The circular logic of the bourgeois nuclear family mimics the logic of the *tableau*. The triad God-father-children to which Lysimond refers while surrounded by his offspring is assured of its own permanence and immovability thanks to the reciprocal nature of these relationships, while movement, as Deleuze reminds us, is anathema to wholeness: "Movement only occurs if the whole is neither given nor giveable. As soon as a whole is given to one in the eternal order of forms or poses, or in the set of any-instant-whatevers, then either time is no more than the image of eternity, or it is the consequence of the set; there is no longer room for real movement."[64] Whether in the premodern logic of forms or poses or the modern one of sets and any-instant-whatevers, movement threatens the whole, just as it threatens the integrity of the *tableau*. Hence, the inclusion of only children, their potential spouses, and the father (as well as a few servants who provide a "frame" for the family) in *The Natural Son*, a play that is set in one house (and seemingly in one room),[65] assures the least amount of *movement* so that an almost perfectly still *tableau* is formed.[66]

The action in *The Father of the Family* likewise takes place entirely in the family house, and the players are the father and his children (represented as biological children, a young man adopted into the family as a child, and a niece). Here too, servants and an uncle function to frame the nuclear family unit, but the final scene offers a powerful *tableau* of the father surrounded by his biological and adoptive offspring.

> *He unites his four children and he says*: A beautiful wife and a virtu-
> ous husband are two of the most inspiring beings in nature. Offer
> this spectacle to the world twice in the same day. My children, may
> heaven bless you as I do. (*He raises his hands as they bow their heads
> to receive his benediction.*)[67]

As in *The Natural Son*, the father rhetorically creates a unity between God, himself, and the children while physically uniting the group and ensuring its future. In the final moments of the play he pulls his children closer to him multiple times so that the audience can enjoy these arrested moments of wholeness, repeating the line "Come my children" four times in the final scene. As Szondi puts it, "It is as if time wanted to stop, just as in the image."[68]

The theater of sentimentality is one in which the father stands symboli-cally at the center. In his *Salons* piece on Greuze's *L'Accordée de Village*, Diderot writes that the father of the family is the only one who speaks.[69] The focus here is on the father in his function as *Hausvater*. For Diderot, the bourgeois drama is not concerned primarily with *characters* but rather with the functions that particular *conditions* create for individuals in their prescribed roles:

> i: So you would want to see the characters of the man of letters,
>   the philosopher, the trader, the judge, the lawyer, the politi-
>   cian, the citizen, the magistrate, the financier, the great
>   noble, the intendant.
> DORVAL: Add to that all the family relationships: father, husband,
>   sister, brothers. The head of the family! What a subject, in an
>   age such as ours when it seems no one has the least idea what it
>   means to be a father![70]

Whereas the speaker "I" lists functional roles that include not only bour-geois figures but also aristocratic ones, Dorval focuses on familial ones: "father, husband, sister, brothers," lingering in the end on the head of the family, the *Hausvater*. Szondi argues that although Diderot puts forth the concept of *conditions*, he is really only interested in the bourgeois father, as he repeats the phrase "le père de famille" [father of the family] three times in this short passage.[71]

The bourgeois father is at the center of Diderot's interest in *conditions* and *relations*, and it is noteworthy that all of the members of the traditional bourgeois nuclear family are named except for the mother.[72] The mother's absence heightens the intensity of the father's emotional force for the family in both of Diderot's plays, as the repeated tears and embraces of Diderot's fathers have the effect of slowing the plot. It is, nevertheless, curious that Dorval provides a note of nostalgia with his lament that one no longer has any idea what a "father of the family" is. Why this nostalgia for a role and function that has just emerged on the stage and in the social sphere?[73] The father, it seems, arrives on the stage already anxious about the stability of his role.

Read from this vantage point, the sentimental father's insistence on keeping everyone in the house and pulling them closer together is desperate and, ultimately, claustrophobic. The family picture that the father helps create by bringing the members of the group closer together both unites them within the invisible frame of the *tableau* and likewise radically limits their future possibilities. Indeed, the flip side of the sentimental family might be precisely the circumscribed family picture that the father insists on. If wholeness is going to be produced, it means no one can ever leave. Szondi suggests that the crisis depicted at the opening of the play, the absence of the son, is a modern one. In sixteenth- and seventeenth-century tragedies, fathers wonder about the whereabouts of their sons because they fear an oedipal revolt, not, as Szondi writes, because the family is not whole without the son.[74] Here again, we have the crisis of the fragment that the *tableau* is meant to address.

All manner of argument is used to keep everyone in the house—in the *tableau*, so to speak. When the daughter Cecile threatens to go to a convent rather than marry, the father calls it a betrayal of society, for motherhood is how women provide the world with "worthy citizens."[75] A similarly compelling moment of persuasion is the father's performance of the role of the sentimental father in response to his son's threat to leave: "You don't want me to die of a broken heart," he pleads, vowing to follow his son wherever he goes. "Where could you go that I wouldn't follow? No matter where, I will follow you, I will reclaim my son."[76]

The father rejects the role of the tyrant prescribed to him by his brother-in-law, the Commander, who tells him he must act as master of his house. But tyranny returns in the guise of the sentimental goal of keeping the family together. There is no outside of the house—not in the play, nor in the future world of the members of the family. In *The Father of the Family*, the outside world/society perverts the natural, and in the end the father's house is the only safe place left. In the play's final scene, the sentimental father reminds his "children" that any fragmentation of the family picture will lead to danger: "Don't you see? You couldn't distance yourselves from me without losing your way."[77]

LESSING'S DYNAMIC *TABLEAUX*

Diderot's linkage of the domestic nuclear family and organicism reflects the larger French Enlightenment context, one in which the concept of nation is not aspirational, as it is in the German context. Prerevolutionary, Enlightenment France was a place where not only Diderot but figures like Rousseau consistently utilized a metaphor of the "natural" nuclear family as an allegory for the modern nation. The Germans were, as we know, great fans of Rousseau and of Diderot. But whereas the French could conceive of an ideal nation as an improved form of the structure already uniting them, the Germans had to picture "Germany" both as a revitalization of a "Germanic" past along the lines imagined by Johann Gottfried Herder and as a future utopian body that would unite the divided principalities of the German-speaking areas. In other words, in contrast to the French imagined ideal state, the concept of a German nation could not easily be imagined as an organic body.

Helmut Schneider describes a shift in the middle of the eighteenth century from an older notion of community characterized by an individual body's "intense physical exchange with its environment and other bodies" to a newer, more abstract one based on notions such as the nation or a republic in which the boundaries between bodies become fixed.[78] As Albrecht Koschorke argues, the notion of "sympathy," a kind of spiritual connection between souls, takes the place of the former "physical transaction," imagined along the lines of contagion, infection, and transfusion. For Koschorke, literacy replaces physical intimacy, producing an abstract and mediated conception of a human social body.[79] The purpose of the *tableau* is, as Heeg puts it, the creation of a social body out of the communion of the spectators.[80] In this sense the theater of the *tableau* mediates a sympathetic experience of community within theater itself. But what do we do if the social body itself is not unified in a manner that easily lends itself to a theory of abstract sympathy? What if, as in the case of the German states, there is no clear, unified whole and, indeed, no revolutionary momentum to speak of between the middle class and the feudal structures that persist in the individual principalities? What notion of community is called forth by the *tableau* in this case?

The bourgeois nuclear family is central to the German conception of nation in the Enlightenment and beyond, but the conceptual link between organicism and nation is, of necessity, weaker in the prenational German context. As we have seen, Hegel's ideal state is predicated upon the nuclear family and monogamous marriage as its structural precursors.[81] Kant likewise ends his narrative of a model education with the marriage of the ideal citizen who will produce future ideal citizens,[82] recalling Diderot's Father of the family who reminds his daughter that her purpose is marriage and the production of "worthy citizens."[83]

The gap between the imagined, "natural" family/state of Diderot's plays and the actual sociopolitical structure of multiple loosely connected German-speaking states is reflected in German plays in the form of a semiotics that reveals its own seams in a pastiche-like manner. Whereas, in the French context, Diderot's model plays are able to circumscribe the domestic, nuclear family and link the *tableau* intrinsically with the family, the aesthetic device of the *tableau* in German drama presents heterogeneous social constellations that invariably extend beyond the nuclear family and the future spouses of the offspring, suturing the feudal extended family and the bourgeois nuclear family.

Diderot's attempt to stave off the precarity of the outside modern world via the domestic *tableau* is not an option in Lessing's social and aesthetic context. His plays show that Lessing's time has not yet successfully transitioned to a modern mode of representation.[84] Court society may have deteriorated in the German principalities but, as Eyck and Arens write, "it has not yet been replaced by modern social forms."[85] Indeed, the *tableaux* in Lessing's plays depict social groupings that are both courtly and bourgeois, allegorical and familial.

There are no protected domestic spaces within Lessing's dramas: both *Miß Sara Sampson* (1755) and *Minna von Barnhelm* (1767) are set not in domestic spaces but at inns.[86] The final scenario in *Miß Sara Sampson* includes Sir William, Mellefont, the dead Sara, and Waitwell, William's servant, whom William has just raised to equal status.[87] The sentimental father begs to physically embrace the libertine Mellefont, who seduced his dead daughter, and to call him "my son."[88] Mellefont resists with a reference to Sara's murderer, the Medea figure Marwood:

Nicht so, Sir! Diese Heilige [Sara] befahl mehr, als die menschli-
che Natur vermag! Sie können mein Vater nicht sein.—Sehen Sie,
Sir, *Indem er den Dolch aus dem Busen ʒieht*, dieses ist der Dolch,
den Marwood heute auf mich zückte."[89]

[Not like this, Sir! This saint (Sara) demanded more than human
nature is capable of! You cannot be my father.—Look, Sir, *as he
draws the dagger from his breast*, this is the dagger that Marwood
pointed at me today.]

Whereas Sir William speaks the transparent language of the forgiving father
of Diderot's *Father of the Family*, Mellefont is aware of the colliding discourses and modes of representation at play: the discourse of the organic,
natural family confronts that of allegory. As Brown shows, the mimetic
quality of the play, its depiction of characters who exhibit bourgeois values,
is complicated by the relics of allegorical, "cosmic drama."[90] Sara represents the Christian allegory of the martyr. It is therefore telling that Mellefont is only willing to take on the role of "son" once he has stabbed himself
with Marwood's dagger, performing the role of martyr left behind by Sara.
The clash of these representational systems does not produce a synthesis or
harmony. The *tableau* of Sir William embracing the dying Mellefont is, in
this sense, a picture of incongruity, not harmony, a pietà sutured onto an
awkward performance of bourgeois sentimentality.

The father-daughter scene in *Emilia Galotti* (1772), the center of a poetics of compassion, similarly takes place in the Prince's *Lustschloß* [pleasure
palace] and not in the domestic family home. This is an in-between space,
neither fully public nor fully private, insofar as the Prince signifies courtly
representation even when he cannot be seen.[91] The *tableau* here is, again,
an incongruent picture of competing discourses and roles. Emilia has convinced her father Odoardo to stab her—to save her virtue, as the discourse
goes[92]—and the *tableau* features a father laying his dead daughter on the
ground as the Prince and his adviser ("devil") blame Odoardo and each
other.[93] The domestic scene of presumed protected virtue takes place not at
home but in a space of danger, and the competing discursive and representational modes provide for a *tableau* that is anything but organic. Particularly important here is the intertext with Livy's story of the murder of
Virginia and the many paintings of the scene available to the imaginations
of the spectators. Hence, we might argue along with Neil Flax that the play's

final *tableau* is a kind of *tableau vivant*, a performance of one of the many artistic renderings of the death of Virginia. Yet the problem with the *tableau vivant* is that the bodies are always eventually betrayed by their materiality; movement, the destroyer of absorption and the reminder of the cut—the frame—is always a danger in the *tableau vivant*. At the very end of the play, we see the corpse of Emilia and three male figures[94] who stand between prescribed courtly roles that they can no longer perform and a vague future notion of subjectivity that includes both modern "Menschen" [humans] and allegorical "Teufel" [devils].[95] In the end, the Prince proclaims, "Gott! Gott!—Ist es, zum Unglücke so mancher, nicht genug, daß Fürsten Menschen sind: Müssen sich auch noch Teufel in ihren Freund verstellen?"[96] [God! God! Is it not enough for the misfortune of some that Princes are humans: Must devils also mask themselves as their friend?]

As a reimagined adaptation of *The Natural Son* (as an early prose draft of the play makes clear),[97] *Nathan der Weise* (1779) likewise engages in a domestic drama mode: the love between the siblings is reminiscent of the attraction between Dorval and his sister in Diderot's play. Diderot resolves this crisis through an elegant double marriage at the end of the play, in which one of the siblings marries the sister of the other. In the early draft, Lessing opened the possibility for a double wedding between Sittah and the Templar and Saladin and Recha. However, the crisscrossing biological connections of the final version excluded this more traditional option for a happy ending. Peter Demetz has called the final *tableau* of the play a "sterile tableau," recalling the critique of the *tableau* as lacking in tension and, hence, boring.[98] The concluding *tableau* depicts what Helmut Schneider has called a "Menschheitsfamilie" [family of humanity] in which the future is not imagined as biological but as humanist.[99] As mentioned earlier in this chapter, the figures join on the stage in a group embrace, *"Unter stummer Wiederholung allseitiger Umarmungen fällt der Vorhang."* [The curtain falls while all present on stage repeatedly embrace in silence.][100] The stage directions suggest repetition ("stumme Wiederholung") and intensity, as if the actors should wordlessly and repeatedly hug one another in a loop, creating a *tableau* that incorporates the most minimal movement in order to preemptively address the impending crisis of movement and precarity. Taking place in Saladin's palace, the scene combines domestic bliss with courtly excess, as servants bring goods onto the stage.[101] Whereas the impending marriages at the end of Diderot's dramas promise dynamism while foreclosing it in the final claustrophobic *tableaux*, the concluding *tableau* in *Nathan der Weise* represents a seeming dead end, from the perspective of a heteronormatively coded futurity. This grouping of presumably organically linked characters (with the exception of Nathan) will generate neither a marriage nor a biological future. But the multiple potential futures that can be imagined between the various members of the *tableau* introduce a dynamism into Lessing's *tableau* that is absent in Diderot's more traditional one.

A focus on Lessing's *tableaux* of complex social constellations offers an intriguing counterimage not only to the French *tableau* of domestic harmony but also to the bourgeois nuclear family. At the moment when movement pauses—the pregnant moment, so to speak—we are not presented with organic familial harmony but instead with a multitude of roles, social classes, and discourses that reveal incongruencies and cracks in both the mirror and the frame. The repercussions for such a semiotics of the theater *tableau* point both to conceptions of the form of the nation and that of the modern subject, intimately tied as they are to the idea of the family.

In light of Lessing's dynamic engagement with multiple social forms in his theoretical writings on drama and in his plays, it is not surprising that he did not discuss the *tableau* in any sustained way in his writings. As Saße argues, Lessing is deeply interested in *Handlung* in a manner not central to Diderot's theater aesthetics.[102] The dynamism of experiences at the core of Lessing's plays mirrors the comparatively unharmonious prenational space within which Lessing attempted to create his new ideal theater. The freeze-frame that the *tableau* represents is hence far less static in Lessing's plays than in Diderot's, providing a window onto social constellations that are anything but organically circumscribed. As Carl Niekerk points out, Lessing's plays are potentially much more radical in their dynamic openness than we often assume in light of his common ascription to the Moderate Enlightenment.[103] Just as the action in his plays is dynamic and open, so too the *tableaux* in his dramas are complex semiotic hybrids that can barely maintain a pause, tending rather to the never-quite-still temporality of the *tableaux vivant*. The representational crisis at the heart of any notion of naturalness or organicism is reflected in the tendency for *tableaux* to slip, as Günther Heeg puts it, into the realm of too much or too little.[104] In Lessing's *tableaux* the social constellations represented generally tend to the "too much" side of the equation—picturing too many social and familial configurations. Indeed, Lessing's *tableaux* remind us, rather, of the patchwork, expansive nature of the German "Haus" in Lessing's time, a "Haus" whose walls of privacy had not yet been erected as a domesticating, "natural" frame.

CHAPTER THREE

The German Dramatic *Tableau* beyond Lessing

LESSING'S DRAMATIC *tableaux* are of a piece with the many similarly heterogeneous *tableaux* in German tragedies and *Rührstücke* from the second half of the eighteenth century. Many of these plays cannot be neatly categorized as bourgeois tragedies, but they nevertheless engage themes, semiotic modes, and moods characteristic of the genre. Often but not exclusively constituting *Schlußtableaux* [concluding *tableaux*], these scenes feature characters grouped together as if posing for a painting or portrait. Far from mirroring the idealized natural nuclear family (sans mother) of Diderot's *tableaux*, German dramatic *tableaux* of the period restage the complexity of social and class/rank relations in the German-speaking states during the latter half of the eighteenth century, revealing the overlaps and collisions between at least two social and aesthetic systems—the old, feudal one and the new, bourgeois one. The old system was still very much operant in the period, and the new was emerging in symbolic and economic, but not overtly political, ways. Hence, the German *tableaux* represent sociality as a heterogeneous system of figures often not in harmony with one another. The *tableau*'s frame cannot hide the seams between diverse social groups, and therefore the picture becomes one that eschews the implied depth of the interior family and concomitant subject, offering instead a textured surface of varied social groupings.

The notion of literary genre was likewise undergoing mutations during the period; the bourgeois tragedy is both everywhere and nowhere in German literature of the eighteenth century, borrowed from French and English models that themselves cannot easily be categorized as bourgeois tragedies. German bourgeois drama is indebted to the French *comedie lar-*

moyante, referred to by the Germans as the *weinerliches* [tearful] or *rührendes Lustspiel* [emotionally moving comedy], which was taken up by Christian Fürchtegott Gellert in his *Die zärtlichen Schwestern* [The Affectionate Sisters] (1747).[1] Indeed, we might think of Diderot's bourgeois dramas as representative of this generic hybrid, since they end with implied, imminent marriages.[2] Lessing himself takes great liberties with genre categorizations in his plays. Winfried Woesler reminds us how laughter and "Rührung" are central to all of Lessing's plays, including those characterized as tragedies, such as *Emilia Galotti* (particularly in its comedic scenes featuring the servants Angelo and Pirro or the *Kupplerin* [matchmaker] theme associated with Claudia Galotti).[3] These plays engage in a highly flexible mixing of genres that may reveal a process of searching for a properly German dramatic genre; or, conversely, the flexibility of genre may coincide with the heterogenous geographic and political scene within which the authors are writing.

In "The Law of Genre," Jacques Derrida articulates the inherent contradictions in the notion of genre, particularly in light of the word's etymological connection to terms like *genus* and *gender*. The law of genre is stated thus: "Genres are not to be mixed. . . . As soon as a genre announces itself, one must respect a norm, one must not cross a line of demarcation, one must not risk impurity, anomaly, or monstrosity."[4] Derrida shows how the law of genre circles around the notion of exemplarity, which is always in danger of becoming "contaminated" or "impure." Genre is the construction of a system of categorization that engenders a process of naturalizing so that, as in the case of the gender binary, a kind of natural system is created predicated on a neat distinction between nature and history.

Exemplarity's fragility is apparent in any single representative of a genre that is expected to represent the "naturalness" of form, but there is a particularly egregious gap between genre and organicism in German bourgeois dramas of the latter half of the eighteenth century, which are themselves ostensibly concerned with the representation of an organic domesticity.[5] As Stefano Castelvecchi points out, "Some notion of 'familial' groupings has often proved a useful tool for thinking about genres," noting that genres can be imagined as a series of resemblances, similar to the way in which Wittgenstein theorized relations between languages as "Familienähnlichkeiten" [family resemblances].[6] Conflicted notions of genre, in particular vis-à-vis emerging bourgeois genres in the eighteenth century, therefore reveal the aesthetics of kinship to be at the heart of the matter. The family stands at the locus of eighteenth-century notions of organicism. Herder contrasts the "natural" body of the family with the constructed state, writing that "das ewige Werk Natur" [the eternal work of Nature] plants the seeds of humanity in humans, nurturing and educating them along the way.[7] But if theory was able to utilize the construct of the family as a signifier for organic wholeness and purity, dramatic literature represented this social body very differently in practice. The heterogeneous and uncircumscribed form of the family as it is captured in the dramatic *tableaux* that frame it underscores both the instability of genre and the lack of conceptual cohesion in the social spheres of the period.

Tableaux in eighteenth-century German bourgeois plays represent both the "serious"/canonical and the "trivial." As we have seen, the family is linked to tears, to the domestic, bourgeois sphere, and to triviality, whether in works considered to be aesthetically and politically important or in those deemed derivative and therefore trivial. Schiller's self-categorized bourgeois tragedy *Kabale und Liebe* (1784) offers *tableaux* that, interestingly, are no more or less bourgeois than those in classicist historical dramas that follow a bourgeois tragedy mode, such as *Die Jungfrau von Orleans* [*The Maid of Orleans*] (1801) and *Wilhelm Tell* (1804). Goethe's early plays *Clavigo* (1774) and *Stella* (1775) likewise are not in any strict sense bourgeois tragedies, but they betray elements of the bourgeois tragedy such as family and class/rank, and *Clavigo* has frequently been compared to the bourgeois tragedy *Emilia Galotti*.[8] "Trivial" dramas that are associated with the hybrid genre of the *Rührstück* include Otto Heinrich von Gemmingen-Hornberg's *Der deutsche Hausvater oder die Familie* [The German Father of the House or the Family] (1780), a popular play that attempted to recreate Diderot's *The Father of the Family* as a fully German work, and August von Kotzebue's *Menschenhaß und Reue* [Misanthropy and Regret] (1790) and *La Peyrouse* (1798), the latter of which constitutes a retelling of Goethe's *Stella* that takes place in the South Seas.

The *tableaux* featured in the plays discussed in this chapter often feature a cluttered mise-en-scène, with noble figures invariably squeezing into the bourgeois-inflected picture. Why are so many figures frequently squished into one scene? And why, in so many plays of the period, must at least one unambiguous representative of the aristocracy join the grouping? The generic crisis of bourgeois tragedy—the collision of two seemingly unreconcilable concepts (the bourgeois and the tragic)—is revealed in the image of the cluttered, heterogeneous dramatic *tableau*. The bourgeois milieu is judged too "narrow" to transmit the grand, even sublime, emotions that tragedy demands. Hence, aristocratic figures are included as signifiers for tragedy, sometimes gratuitously, even when they are not central to the plot.

We might think of these figures as bridge signifiers: they lend a grandness to the scene that might otherwise be missing and that renders them allegorical. They connote, not as developed characters but simply through costume and rank, the sublime potentiality of tragedy. Indeed, the inclusion of aristocratic bridge figures within these *tableaux* likely reveals their bourgeois authors' deep-seated insecurity about their own socioeconomic milieu.

THE ANXIOUS MISE-EN-SCÈNE OF CLUTTER

Schiller's *Kabale und Liebe* begins with a *tableau* of petit bourgeois domesticity worthy of the Dutch masters.[9] The scene is set in the sitting room of the musician Miller: *"Miller steht eben vom Sessel auf und stellt seine Violoncell auf die Seite. An einem Tisch sitzt Frau Millerin noch im Nachgewand und trinkt ihren Kaffee."* [Miller is just getting up from his chair and is putting his cello aside. Mrs. Miller, still in her nightgown, is sitting at a table drinking her coffee.][10] The scene recalls Johann Georg Wille's 1765 engraving entitled *Die väterliche Ermahnung* [The Paternal Admonition] (1765), itself copied from Gerard ter Borch's *The Gallant Conversation* (1653).[11] The image was well known in Schiller's time and famously features as a model for one of the *tableau vivant* performances in Goethe's *Die Wahlverwandtschaften*, a topic I discuss in detail in chapter 7. The tawdriness indicated by Schiller's Frau Millerin wearing her nightgown and slurping her coffee (*"Frau schlürft eine Tasse aus"*) [Wife slurps from a cup.][12] echoes the simple domestic environment in Wille's etching: the bed, the dresser, two simple chairs, books, and some objects related to personal hygiene on the little table on the left-hand side of the painting. The mother drinks her wine as Wille's father lectures his daughter. As scholars have shown, ter Borch's original painting presents a scene in which a young gallant is procuring a daughter from a mother, or even a prostitute from a madam,[13] but Wille's title (*"Die väterliche Ermahnung"*) [Paternal Admonition] transports the scene to a bourgeois family setting. Schiller's opening *tableau* also recalls the opening scene of Diderot's *Father of the Family* in which the father laments the absence of his son. In *Kabale und Liebe*, the daughter is absent while the father frets about potentially losing her to the shameful fate of seduction—Luise is being wooed at court by Ferdinand, the son of the President. The diverging significations of the two images, ter Borch's painting and Wille's engraving/interpretation of it, combine in Schiller's opening scene as Miller frets about the selling of his daughter to the court: *"Das Blutgeld meiner Tochter?"* [The blood money of my daughter?][14] Schiller's opening scene situates Miller both as the father of Wille's "väterliche Ermahnung," attempting to keep his daughter close to home, and as spectator in the scene of procurement in ter Borch's painting, as he watches his wife sell his daughter for her beauty.

Whereas Diderot's *Father of the Family* presents an opening *tableau* that mirrors Diderot's desire for a simple and transparent stage and *tableau*, Schiller's opening *tableau* already points to the imperfect superimposition of old onto new (ter Borch and Wille), of representative court semiotics and bourgeois family semiotics. The names of the characters likewise reflect this overlapping semiotics. Schiller nods to Lillo's *The London Merchant* when he names the musician Miller and the Prince's mistress Lady Milford. Not only does he use English names here (although many of the other names are Germanic: Luise, Wurm, Präsident von Walter), but the monikers Miller and Milford recall Lillo's seductress/villain Millwood. As with the Wille/ter Borch intertext, a kind of superimposition takes place between Miller and Milford via the figure of Lillo's Millwood. As the villainess of Lillo's play who, as Lisa Freeman argues, takes on the role of the scapegoat for the ills of rampant capitalism,[15] it is intriguing that both Lady Milford, the figure in *Kabale und Liebe* who should serve as Millwood's counterpart but who proves virtuous in the end, and Miller, the petit bourgeois musician who should represent that source of bourgeois virtue, are tied etymologically to the villain of Lillo's play, a figure representing sexual lust and greed. What do Lady Milford and Miller have in common? Each, it seems, is linked to Millwood via the tropes of money and sexuality: Miller is fixated on capital and lured by the money offered to him by Luise's suitors,[16] and Lady Milford is beholden to the Prince for her lifestyle, selling her beauty much like Miller is tempted to have his daughter do. The overlapping roles and signifiers transform what should be a simple bourgeois setting into an intertextual palimpsest.

The closing *tableau* of Schiller's only explicitly titled "bürgerliches Trauerspiel" [bourgeois tragedy] again depicts a community so diverse and large that it can barely fit into the picture.[17] The stage directions for the last scene are as follows: "Ferdinand. Der Präsident. Wurm und Bediente, *welche alle voll Schrecken ins Zimmer stürzen, darauf* Miller *mit* Volk *und* Gerichtsdienern, *welche sich im Hintergrund sammeln*" [Ferdinand. The President. Wurm and Servants, who, filled with horror, rush into the room, then Miller with a crowd of folk and court attendants, which collects in the background].[18] What picture is presented here? The spectator is confronted with so many figures that the extras need to line up at the back of the stage. What frame can contain so many horrified figures without collapsing under their weight? The scene resembles an allegorical collection of figures at the end of a morality play. What are the "Volk" [folk] doing here in the Miller sitting room? How can so many people fit into this humble room? It is as if the milieu has suddenly exploded and Schiller has given up on mimesis, choosing instead to offer a hybrid form of representation in which allegory and mimesis collide and overlap. Important and middling representatives of court bureaucracy are present, as well as the bourgeois father, a variety of servants (not desired in Diderot's ideal bourgeois drama scenes, as we recall), and, again, "Volk." The entire principality gathers in the narrow Miller sitting room, reminding us of Schiller's own trivializing gesture toward the bourgeois dramatic milieu in *Xenien*. "Volk" represents the inhabitants of the small principality, and we would normally think of this signifier as a mimetic one. But since we have heretofore had no access to something called *Volk*, the term takes on an allegorical note, as if a figure were standing in front of the audience bearing the word "Volk" on a sign. Allegorical signifiers are immediately trumped out; Ferdinand calls the dead Luise (who has drunk poisoned lemonade) "eine Heilige" [a saint].[19] The President calls his secretary Wurm "Satan,"[20] and Wurm responds with an invitation to dance away to hell with the President: "Arm und Arm mit dir zum Blutgerüst! Arm in Arm mit dir zur Hölle! Es soll mich kitzeln, Bube, mit dir verdammt zu sein!" [Arm and arm with you to the blood scaffolding! Arm in Arm with you to hell! It will tickle me, knave, to be condemned together with you!][21]

As in the case of *Miß Sara Sampson* and *Emilia Galotti*, the final scene in *Kabale und Liebe* occurs around the dead body of the daughter, in this case Luise. Male figures representing various classes and roles dance and gesticulate around Luise's corpse, blaming one another for the tragedy and pointing to a higher power in their attempts to exonerate themselves. When Ferdinand blames his father for Luise's death, the President turns to the heavens, *"eine schrecklicke Bewegung des Arms gegen den Himmel*: Von mir nicht, von mir nicht, Richter der Welt—fodre diese Seelen von diesem! *Er geht auf Wurm ʒu.*" [a horrible movement of the arm toward Heaven: Not from me, not from me, judge of the world—claim these souls from this one! He approaches Wurm.][22] His act of gesturing to heaven and to a higher power while simultaneously blaming his secretary is reminiscent of the Prince's gesture of powerlessness and blame at the end of *Emilia Galotti*, as the latter turns to Marinetti and then upward in his desperation to avoid culpability for Emilia's death. Miller initially lies with his head in his dead daughter's lap before leaping up, throwing the money given him by Ferdinand (and which he had previously fetishized) onto the floor, and running out of the room. This means we are left with a final *tableau* in which Ferdinand dies and seems to forgive his father, and in which the *Gerichtsdiener* [bailiff] as well as the representatives of the "Volk" join Ferdinand's father around Ferdinand's corpse. One short scene thus contains a bourgeois tragedy scenario of an innocent bourgeois daughter dying and causing deep remorse and pain to her father (the mother never appears in the scene), allegorical signifiers of Heaven, Hell, and Wealth (gold), and a father-son oedipal scenario between members of the second class (lower-level aristocrats who serve the Prince) playing out before inhabitants of the principality ("Volk") and the representatives of the court.

Schiller's *Don Carlos, Infant von Spanien* (1787) serves as another example of this kind of multi-layered collision between bourgeois family semiotics and those stemming from earlier aesthetic traditions. Schiller famously called the play a "Familiengemälde in einem fürstlichen Hauße" [Family *tableau* in a prince's house.][23] The work's final scene and concluding *tableau* brings Carlos together with Elisabeth, his beloved, who has been forced to marry Carlos's father, the king of Spain, as well as the king himself, accompanied by the grand inquisitor and his representatives.[24] We are confronted with a family *tableau* that reiterates the bourgeois family trajectory, as Carlos's beloved/stepmother faints, mirroring the concluding *tableaux* from earlier plays in which the innocent female figure lies prostrate while male figures in various roles bicker over who is responsible for her death.[25] As the king enters the scene with his ecclesiastical entourage, the scene of modern intimacy between Carlos and Elisabeth collides with the allegorical semiotics at play in the physical representations of the king and the Catholic church. Just as Carlos is shifting between discourses of intimacy with Elisabeth—from lover to friend to mother—he is confronted by his father the king and the church sovereigns. As the king appears, Elisabeth "*fällt ohnmächtig nieder*" [*faints*]; and Carlos "*eilt auf sie zu und empfängt sie mit den Armen*" [*rushes towards her and takes her in his arms*], asking, "Ist sie todt? O Himmel und Erde!" [Is she dead? O Heaven and Earth!][26] In response, the king/father says to the grand inquisitor: "Kardinal! Ich habe das Meinige getan. Tun Sie das Ihre!" [Cardinal! I have done my part. Now do yours!][27] The central moment of pathos in the bourgeois tragedy, in which the motionless female body is embraced by a remorseful male figure, is rehearsed in front of a father who is anything but sentimental. The latter, split between the roles of father and king, turns to the grand inquisitor in a call to action, reiterating the appeal to a higher power that we saw with Odoardo and the Prince in *Emilia Galotti*.[28] The inclusion of the grand inquisitor and his representatives in this *tableau* marks it, as was the case with the concluding *tableau* in *Kabale und Liebe*, as a scene of allegorical representation. The intimate discourse between Carlos and Elisabeth, centering on the idealized homosocial friendship between Carlos and the murdered Posa, is sutured to the allegorical scene of political and ecclesiastical power. Indeed, the king/father speaks immediately after Carlos takes off the mask he was wearing to hide his identity, signifying metonymically the scene's clash of representational systems—between modern depth transparency and premodern surface representation. As was the case in *Miß Sara Sampson* and *Emilia Galotti*, these systems are not reconciled in the final *tableau*. Again, we are not presented with a concluding *tableau* that circumscribes the family, a grouping that would align with the modern discourse of intimacy in the scene. Not only the king/father but also the allegorical extras help produce a pastiche *tableau* in which the seams between old and modern, the allegorical and the familial, are laid bare.

Despite his shift to a classicist aesthetics in his later dramas, Schiller's historical plays nevertheless retain a thread of the bourgeois tragedy narrative focused on the father-daughter relationship. Two plays from this period illustrate these seemingly competing interests and semiotics, *Die Jungfrau von Orleans* (1801) and *Wilhelm Tell* (1804). *Tableaux* abound in both works, cued by stage directions such as *"Alle stehen gerührt"* [All stand emotionally moved], in the famous scene in *Wilhelm Tell* after Tell spears the apple with the arrow and saves his son,[29] or *"Alle stehen lange in sprachloser Rührung"* [all stand for a long time speechless and emotionally moved], in the concluding *tableau* in *Die Jungfrau von Orleans*. In the latter play, multiple kings, a consort, and soldiers stand together in a representative fashion around the dead body of the innocent Johanna against a background in which *"Der Himmel [ist] von einem rosigen Schein beleuchtet"* [The heavens are lit by a rosy hue].[30] In each case, the language of "Rührung" that so irritates Schiller and, later, Hegel in their critique of the narrowness of the German bourgeois drama is central to the effect of the *tableau*.

Both plays feature frequent embraces that cue the *tableaux*. For example, in Act 3, scene 3 of *Die Jungfrau von Orleans*, the King of France, the Duke of Burgundy, and Karl embrace multiple times, combining the representative semiotics of the court (falling to the knee) and the "natural" embrace of the bourgeois family. The scene begins with the duke kneeling before the king, *"und in dem Augenblick, wo er sich auf ein Knie will niederlassen, empfängt ihn der König in seinen Armen"* [and in the moment in which he wants to fall to one knee, the king receives him in his arms].[31] This kind of transparent sentimentality is repeated throughout the scene. The king's mistress Agnes Sorel is moved to tears by the beautiful gift Burgund gives her: *"Agnes Sorel, in Tränen ausbrechend, tritt auf die Seite, auch der König bekämpft eine große Bewegung, alle Umstehende blicken gerührt auf beide Fürsten."* [Agnes Sorel, bursting into tears, steps aside; the king, too, struggles with great agitation; all who surround them gaze, emotionally moved, at the two princes.][32] The tears of sentimentality are contagious, and the entire grouping is, as the stage directions indicate, *"gerührt"* [moved]. The stage directions that follow present multiple embraces that are motivated by the previous ones in a manner similar to a game of dominoes:

> BURGUND *nachdem er alle der Reihe nach angesehen, wirft er sich in die Arme des Königs:* O mein König!
> *In demselben Augenblick eilen die drei burgundischen Ritter auf Dunois, La Hire und den Erzbischof zu und umarmen einander. Beide Fürsten liegen eine Zeitlang einander sprachlos in den Armen.*

> Euch konnt ich hassen! Euch konnt ich entsagen![33]

> [BURGUND *after having looked at everyone one by one, throws himself into the arms of the king:* O my king!
> *At the same moment the three Burgundian knights rush to Dunois, La Hire, and the archbishop and embrace one another. Both princes remain for a while speechless in each other's arms.*
> That I should have hated you! That I should have renounced you!]

The multiple embraces combined with the language of sentimentality ("hassen! . . . entsagen!") offer a *tableau* that is overcoded as a scene brimming with the sentimental (bourgeois) affect that Lessing's reception aesthetics linked to the education of humankind. We are, however, likewise confronted with the *tableau* in excess: How many weeping, embracing nobles can we keep track of in this cluttered scene? The elements of Diderot's *tableau* are present—the privileging of gesture over words, the framing of naturalness—but, again, there are simply too many elements squished into one scene.

Die Jungfrau von Orleans offers collisions between allegorical and mimetic/bourgeois family aesthetics by linking sentimental *tableaux* with traditionally allegorical figures (such as the king) and by embedding a bourgeois tragedy narrative within the play's plot. In Act 4, scene 9, Johanna's sisters come to see her, and she expresses her desire to return to her father's "home,"[34] a space of safety that is only threatened by the imminence of marriage: "Johanna *schnell:* Kommt, laßt uns fliehen! Ich geh mit euch, ich kehre in unser Dorf, in Vaters Schoß zurück." [Johanna, quickly: Come, let us flee! I will go with you all, I am returning to our village, back to Father's lap.][35] We know from earlier bourgeois tragedies that the daughter can only return as a corpse. The bourgeois tragedy narrative collides, then, with the semiotics of allegory: Johanna is frequently called "Angel"[36] and Burgund at one point calls her "Circe,"[37] a central figure in allegorical drama.[38] Schiller's *Die Jungfrau von Orleans* therefore presents the historical drama as a hybrid form that joins the overlapping and sometimes colliding semiotics of the bourgeois drama and the allegorical drama, these two forms meeting clumsily in the multiple *tableaux* that depict embraces.[39]

Schiller's historical dramas neither solve the representational problems of the bourgeois tragedy nor shy away from the ideals of bourgeois *Häuslichkeit* [domesticity] that he parodies in his poem "Shakespeares Schatten" [Shakespeare's Shadow]. *Wilhelm Tell*, like *Die Jungfrau von Orleans*, is full of *tableaux* that are cued by the cessation of speech and an emotional pause: "*alle stehen gerührt*" [all stand emotionally moved]. The political narrative of regional Swiss independence condenses, in the end, into an ideal of bourgeois *Häuslichkeit*. Indeed, freedom is defined in the play in material terms: as the ability to live in one's own house, inherited from one's family. Villagers Gertrud and Melchtal both express this ideal at different points in the play: "Gertrud: Er ist dir neidisch, weil du glücklich wohnst. Ein freier Mann auf deinem eignen Erb." [Gertrud: He is jealous of you because you live happily. A free man on your own inheritance.][40] Melchtal refers with respect to strangers who "wie wir, frei sitzen auf Erbe" [like us sit free on their own inheritance].[41] And Walter Fürst expresses a similar link between subjecthood and the domestic idyll as he anxiously considers whether he should put a lock and bolt on the door in order to protect his domestic tranquility.[42]

Yet despite the characters' fixation with a very bourgeois notion of domestic harmony, none of the many *tableaux* in the play depict this space in a manner comparable to Diderot's ending *tableaux*. On the contrary, the concluding *tableau* in the final scene of *Wilhelm Tell* seems gratuitously to move Wilhelm and his beloved wife Hedwig outside of their idyllic domestic space to a spot in the valley where a group picture with multiple characters from the play can be choreographed:

Man sieht in der letzten Szene den ganzen Talgrund vor Tells *Wohnung, nebst den Anhöhen, welche ihn einschließen, mit Landleuten besetzt, welche sich zu einem Ganzen gruppieren. Andre kommen über einen hohen Steg, der über den Schächen führt, gezogen.* Walter Fürst *mit den beiden Knaben,* Melchtal *und* Stauffacher, *kommen vorwärts, andre drängen nach; wie* Tell *heraustritt, empfangen ihn alle mit lautem Frohlocken.*

Alle: Es lebe Tell! der Schütz und der Erretter!

Indem sich die vordersten um den Tell drängen und ihn umarmen, erscheinen noch Rudenz *und* Berta, *jener die Landleute, diese die* Hedwig *umarmend. Die Musik von Berge begleitet diese stumme Szene.*

[*One sees in the final scene the entire space of the valley in front of Tell's home in addition to the hills that enclose it, filled with country folk who are grouped in an organic whole. Others come over a high bridge that leads over the Schaechen.* Walter Fürst *with the two boys,* Melchtal *and* Stauffacher, *come forward, others crowd behind; as* Tell *comes out, all receive him with loud cheers.*

All: Long live Tell! The marksman and the savior!

As the ones in front crowd around Tell and embrace him, Rudenz *and* Berta *appear, and he embraces the country folk, she* Hedwig. *The music from the mountains accompanies this wordless scene.*[43]

Here Schiller has taken the Tell couple out of their domestic sphere and carefully choreographed a group painting that stretches the boundaries of the ideal of the natural *tableau*. Although we can imagine an image of village celebration here, we are unable to forget the frame and the fourth wall. The scene, although almost without dialogue, is accompanied by music that suggests it is being produced for representation and has not simply naturally appeared for the lucky, accidental spectator. The claustrophobia of the domestic interior is mirrored by the hills that circumscribe the group. The various characters, however, serve more as extras than integral family members. Schiller includes so many characters in his drama that it is difficult to distinguish between them, and the characters self-consciously try to form a grouping that would be appropriate for a painting. Yet once again, there are too many hugs, too many insignificant figures. Schiller's decision to move Wilhelm and Hedwig outside of their bourgeois idyll into this crowded, self-conscious *tableau* brings to the fore, yet again, the conundrum of the representation of the organic.[44]

COUP DE THÉÂTRE MEETS TABLEAU: GOETHE'S CLAVIGO
AND STELLA, OR CLAUSTROPHOBIC DOMESTICITY
AND THE LURE OF POLYGAMY

Two early plays by Goethe, *Clavigo* (1774) and *Stella* (1775), offer a different perspective on the question of the German *tableau* and the representation of bourgeois *Häuslichkeit*. In both plays we are confronted with protagonists (Clavigo and Ferdinand, respectively) who are torn between the world of bourgeois domesticity on the one hand and the life of importance lived by a libertine and member of the court on the other. In each case, the protagonist wavers between desiring the bourgeois family idyll (while fearing entrapment), and the freedom and pleasures of the court. Each play offers concluding *tableaux* that are unable to reconcile the two worlds and their corresponding semiotic modes, and these *tableaux* portray excess in the form of overlapping worlds. Goethe famously wrote two endings for *Stella*, each of which represents excess in its own way.

In his lectures on *Aesthetics*, Hegel points to the weak, vacillating characters of Fernando and Clavigo before turning to his critique of German drama as a whole.[45] We might, indeed, see the two figures, and the two plays, as representative of the split quality of German literature in the eighteenth century. *Clavigo* is a bourgeois tragedy of sorts, given its prominent theme of the seduction and ruin of a bourgeois virgin (or a figure embodying bourgeois values). Clavigo rises from obscurity within the Spanish court in Madrid as an author and editor of a popular weekly publication and as a lady's man. He seduces and then rejects the financially vulnerable Marie, a transplant from France living with her sister, Sophie. Clavigo is unable to decide whether to marry her or seek his fortunes at the court when Marie's brother Beaumarchais (the historical figure on whom the play was loosely based) arrives to avenge his sister. Clavigo's friend Carlos repeatedly articulates the choice facing Clavigo: "Entweder du heuratest Marien und findest dein Glück in einem stillen bürgerlichen Leben, in den ruhigen häuslichen Freuden; oder du führest auf der ehrenvollen Bahn deinen Lauf weiter nach dem nahen Ziele." [Either you marry Marie and find your happiness in a quiet bourgeois life, in peaceful domestic joys; or you lead yourself on the honorable path further toward your goal.][46] The vision of his future at the court is never clearly painted, for success at the court broadly signifies a wide-open future beyond one's wildest dreams. In contrast, the contours of bourgeois life are repeatedly laid out in claustrophobic terms. For example, Carlos points out that "sich häuslich niederlassen" [to settle down domestically] is, in essence, the same as "sich einschränken." [constraining onself.][47] Later he taunts Clavigo: "Und so genieße das Glück einer ruhigen Beschränkung." [Enjoy the happiness of a peaceful confinement.][48] Choosing the path of what Carlos perceives as bourgeois narrowness would mean living a life without surprises. Bourgeois life, for Carlos, signifies death, immobility, and entrapment within an ever-repeating *tableau*. In Diderot's drama aesthetics, bourgeois life is embodied by the barely moving *tableau*, whereas the *coup de théâtre* of court life offers the unexpected and exciting movements for which humans live.

Clavigo, like *Miß Sara Sampson*'s Mellefont before and *Stella*'s Ferdinand after him, is drawn to the bourgeois life while living in mortal fear of the walls of the bourgeois home that seem to slowly close in on him. Ultimately, the play offers no solution to the problem of the collision of Clavigo's two worlds. He wavers until finally choosing not to act, thereby allowing Carlos to solve the problem for him so that he can continue his life at the court, and he stumbles into the final *tableau* of the play, which offers a bizarre and grotesque collision between the bourgeois milieu and the performative/allegorical representational aesthetics of the court. In the course of fleeing Madrid, Clavigo happens upon a domestic scene with Marie's family. Marie has died of a broken heart, and Clavigo encounters the funeral procession that is emerging from Marie's home. He fights with and is mortally stabbed by Beaumarchais, to whom Clavigo says, "Ich danke dir, Bruder! Du vermählst uns. *Er sinkt auf den Sarg.*" [I thank you, brother! You marry us. He sinks onto the coffin.][49] Repulsed, Beaumarchais responds, "Weg von dieser Heiligen, Verdammter!" [Get away from this saint, damned one!],[50] speaking the language of allegory in accordance with the Christian semiotics of the funeral procession.

The dialogue that follows occurs while Clavigo lies draped over Marie's coffin, dying and bleeding. He begs for forgiveness from all the figures in the scene, including Marie's former suitor, calling them "Bruder—Freunde." [brother—friends.][51] At one point he gets up only to lie down on the coffin again: "Clavigo, *sich dem Sarge nähernd, auf den sie ihn niederlassen.* Marie! deine Hand! *Er entfaltet ihre Hände und faßt die rechte.*" [Clavigo, nearing the coffin, upon which they lay him. Marie! Your hand! He unfolds her hands and clasps the right one.][52] By now Carlos has arrived, and it is clear that Beaumarchais must run for his life in order to escape punishment for the murder of Clavigo. Still lying on the coffin, Clavigo cries:

Ich hab ihre Hand! Ihre kalte Totenhand! Du bist die Meinige—
Und noch diesen Bräutigamskuß. Ah!

SOPHIE: Er stirbt! Rette dich, Bruder!

BEAUMARCHAIS: *fällt Sophien um den Hals.*

SOPHIE: *umarmt ihn, indem sie zugleich eine Bewegung macht, ihn zu entfernen.*[53]

[I have her hand! Her cold dead hand! You are mine—and still this bridegroom's kiss. Ah!

SOPHIE: He's dying! Save yourself, brother!

BEAUMARCHAIS: *falls and clasps Sophie around the neck.*

SOPHIE: *embraces him while simultaneously making a movement to send him away.*]

The *tableau* that emerges in these few lines begs for interpretation. In a grotesque and theatrical gesture of bourgeois sentimentality, Clavigo's prostration on Marie's coffin creates a kind of marriage bed, thereby unwittingly parodying the intimacy associated with the bourgeois bedroom.[54] A few lines earlier, Clavigo had appealed to the "Geist meiner Geliebten" [ghost of my beloved],[55] mimicking Beaumarchais's allegorical naming of his sister as a "saint" and Clavigo as a "damned one."[56] At the same time as the exaggerated bourgeois marriage takes place in semi-allegorical form, Sophie performs the gestures of bourgeois sentimentality and danger. She embraces and then attempts to shoo her brother, combining the gesture of the immovable familial *tableau* with one associated with the *coup de théâtre* adventures of the court. The *tableau* contains a corpse, a dying man, a representative from the court, and the siblings Sophie and Beaumarchais, as well as servants and the coffin bearers who are mentioned in the stage directions. There is movement directed inward (Clavigo's joining of hands with Marie, Sophie's embrace of her brother) and movement directed outward (Carlos's arrival, Sophie's attempt to get Beaumarchais to leave). The *tableau* and *coup de théâtre* collide here as two irreconcilable worlds.

The excessive quality of emotions, semiotic codes, and characters in *Clavigo*'s closing *tableau* is mirrored both qualitatively and quantitatively in *Stella: Ein Schauspiel für Liebende* [Stella: A Play for Lovers]. Goethe famously wrote two endings for the latter in response to the moral outrage incited by the first version, which presents a *tableau* of the protagonist Fernando flanked by Cäcilia and Stella as they agree to a life of polygamy. Goethe rewrote the original ending and renamed the play *Stella: Ein Trauerspiel* [Stella: A Tragedy] (published in 1816). As in *Clavigo*, the weak Ferdinand is unable to choose between his wife, Cäcilia, who represents the feared *Häuslichkeit* from which Clavigo also retreated, and Stella, the noble for whom he has left Cäcilia. Cäcilia describes the life of bourgeois marriage in these terms: "Alle Stützen des menschlichen Herzens: Liebe, Zutrauen, Ehre, Stand, täglich wachsendes Vermögen, Aussicht über eine zahlreiche, wohlversorgte Nachkommenschaft." [All supports of the human heart: love, trust, honor, status, daily increasing wealth, a view to numerous descendants who are well provided for.][57] Her verbal catalogue of the rewards and traps of bourgeois marriage evokes slow movement, a lack of surprises, and a steadily increasing income reflecting a perfectly ethical notion of capitalism—in other words, a series of *tableaux* as opposed to *coups de théâtre*.

After escaping the scene of the bourgeois *Häuslichkeit* he shares with Cäcilia and their daughter Lucie, Ferdinand seduces the young noble Stella, of whom he also eventually tires. Far from blaming Ferdinand for his inability to choose, both women are perfectly aware that for a man like him, the *coup de théâtre* is preferable to the *tableau*. Cäcilia expresses her sympathy with Ferdinand in so many words:

> Ich seh ihn als einen Gefangenen an. . . . Ich nun gar konnte ihm zuletzt nichts sein als eine redliche Hausfrau, die zwar mit dem festesten Bestreben an ihm hing, ihm gefällig, für ihn sorgsam zu sein; die dem Wohl ihres Hauses, ihres Kindes, all ihre Tage widmete, und freilich sich mit so viel Kleinigkeiten abgeben mußte, daß ihr Herz und Kopf oft wüste ward, daß sie keine unterhaltende Gesellschafterin war, daß er mit der Lebhaftigkeit seines Geistes meinen Umgang notwendig schal finden mußte. Er ist nicht schuldig![58]

> [I see him as a prisoner. . . . In the end I couldn't be anything to him but an honest housewife, who was attached to him with the most intense ambition to please and care for him; one who dedicated all her days to the well-being of her household, her child and certainly had to concern herself with so many trivialities that her heart and head were often empty, so that she was not an entertaining companion; so that he must have found my company shallow, given the vibrancy of his spirit. He is not guilty!]

Cäcilia's discourse here mirrors the court intrigant Carlos's view of bourgeois *Häuslichkeit* in *Clavigo*: it is a space of entrapment, of boredom for the man, of predictability. The problem is not a man's lack of loyalty to his wife but instead the inability of the bourgeois domestic space to satisfy the demands of male desire.

The final *tableau* of the first version of the play might be said to present the ideal *Rührstück* ending. All three main characters are represented, and they engage in a series of gestures of moving closer to one another and, finally, embracing. Ferdinand's inability to choose between the two women—in effect, between bourgeois *Häuslichkeit* and the adventurous life of the libertine—is not actually solved in the final scene. Stella represents for Ferdinand a more aristocratic and only marginally less stifling domestic context than that offered by the much more bourgeois Cäcilia. The happy ending both doubles the potential for entrapment (two wives) and diffuses it; the solution of bringing the three main characters together as a polygamous unit both tightens the grip the women have on Ferdinand and loosens it, as their bond with one another is also strengthened through the agreement.

The solution to the problem of bourgeois monogamy comes in the form of the famous fable of the Graf von Gleichingen, a popular narrative of the time that was frequently adapted for the stage. The story as Cäcilia tells it in *Stella* initially mirrors Ferdinand's story: "Er war ein Biedermann; er liebte sein Weib, nahm Abschied von ihr, empfahl ihr sein Hauswesen, umarmte sie, und zog." [He was an honest man; he loved his wife, said goodbye to her, left his household matters to her, embraced her, and departed.][59] In the fable, he is taken prisoner and rescued by his captor's daughter, whom he finally brings home to his wife, where the three of them share "Eine Wohnung, Ein Bett, und Ein Grab." [One home, one bed, and one grave.][60] It is significant that Cäcilia comes up with the solution to the boredom produced by the bourgeois *tableau*. Could it be that Cäcilia, too, prefers a more dynamic life than the rigidly confined one dictated by bourgeois monogamy?[61] The final *tableau* offers a picture of mutual embrace, representing both a circumscribed bourgeois semiotics and excess:

Stella, *an ihrem* [Cäcilia's] *Hals*: O du!—
Fernando, *beide umarmend*: Mein! Mein!
Stella, *seine Hand fassend, an ihm hangend*: Ich bin dein!
Cäcilia, *seine Hand fassend, an seinem Hals*: Wir sind dein![62]

[Stella, *hanging on her* [Cäcilia's] *neck*: O you!
Fernando, *embracing both*: Mine! Mine!

Stella, *clasping his hand, hanging on him*: I am yours!
Cäcilia, *clasping his hand, hanging on his neck*: We are yours!]

We will never know whether Fernando eventually flees the scene of double love. The semiotics of the bourgeois family are here mimicked in the repeated embraces and in the language of possession that reflects early capitalism's importance for bourgeois discourses. And the triangulated love between Stella and Cäcilia potentially opens up additional space within the smothering embrace of *Häuslichkeit*. The revised ending from 1816, in which Stella and Fernando die, does not solve the problem of excess that threatens the naturalness of the *tableau*. We are still dealing with extra lovers. Cäcilia and her teenage daughter, Lucie, are forced to run between Ferdinand and Stella, each of whom is dying, in an attempt to demonstrate their love for both.

Both endings of Goethe's *Stella* point to the lure of additive love, of polygamy, as an antidote to the claustrophobia of monogamous *Häuslichkeit* that oppresses Clavigo and Ferdinand.[63] German cameralists such as Christian Thomasius and English philosophers such as David Hume wrote about polygamy as a possible solution to certain social problems (prostitution, unwed mothers), cognizant of its ubiquity in the Bible and in non-European cultures. Concerns about population (either too many people or not enough) prompted thinkers to consider polygamy's possible utility (whereas polyandry was generally rejected out of hand). German Enlightenment thinkers were, on the one hand, keen to preserve the social unit of monogamy, but on the other hand, almost all agreed that polygamy was in line with natural law.[64] As Hull shows, this belief was underscored by considerations about "natural" male sexual passions.[65] Yet the suturing of the couple to the modern nation-state model clearly necessitated the institutionalization of monogamy. As Hull writes, "Introducing polygamy would immediately have revolutionized the lives of all Germans, turned law, custom, inheritance, and economy (which was still tied to the couple-centered household) topsy-turvy in ways neither the introduction of capitalism nor republicanism would have done (or did, when they occurred)."[66] Hume's ultimate rejection of polygamy was based on the concern that polygamy would engender anarchy, since the patriarch would have trouble controlling his many subjects.[67] In contrast, Hegel argues in *Elements of the Philosophy of Right* that the polygamist is a despot and hence unfit for rule. In each case, the deciding factor is the analogical utility of the nuclear family/monogamous couple model for the modern nation-state. Competing pictures of these relationships or families would, it was feared, undermine the project of building a German nation, destroying the heuristic scaffolding of modernity.[68]

August von Kotzebue's *La Peyrouse* (1798) likewise flirts with the topic of polygamy, functioning as a loose adaptation of Goethe's *Stella*.[69] The play is set in the South Seas and is based on the biography of the French explorer La Peyrouse, who was lost at sea in the 1780s. Like *Stella*, Kotzebue's play is inspired by the well-known Graf von Gleichen story of polygamy, a story upon which Kotzebue also based his later play, *Der Graf von Gleichen: Ein Spiel für lebendige Marionetten* [The Count of Gleichen: A Play for Living Marionettes] (1808), in which he parodied Goethe's *Stella* even more explicitly. Kotzebue was the most popular playwright of his day, yet the critical reception of his works was generally negative.[70] Hegel and Schiller, as we saw, associated his plays with a stifling and trivial bourgeois *Häuslichkeit*. In *La Peyrouse*, the eponymous hero has been shipwrecked somewhere in the South Seas and lives the bourgeois family ideal together with his native wife Malvina and their son. The arrival of La Peyrouse's wife Adelaide on the otherwise uninhabited island creates a crisis for all involved, as both women are originally invested in the institution of monogamy. The solution to the problem mimics Goethe's original ending for *Stella*: the three will live together, along with one son per couple, on the island. The virtues and pleasures of bourgeois *Häuslichkeit* are therefore not reducible to monogamy, for the characters have chosen this option precisely for its ability to produce a domestic haven in light of what they perceive as the post-revolutionary dangers awaiting them in France. Indeed, the island provides the ideal parameters for bourgeois *Häuslichkeit*, as La Peyrouse articulates early in the play:

> Wohl dem Menschen, der alles was er liebe in einem kleinen Raum zusammendrängen kann! wohl dem Menschen, der zufrieden von seiner Handbreit Land hinausblickt auf die übrige Welt, die ihm so fremd geworden, als die Gestirne, die über seinem Haupte wandeln. Hier darf ich nur die Hand ausstrecken, um ein Wesen zu berühren, das mich liebt.

> [How lucky the person who can crowd everything together that he loves in a small space! How lucky the person who contentedly looks out from his small piece of land to the rest of the world that has become as foreign to him as the stars that wander over his head. Here I only have to stretch out my hand in order to touch a creature that loves me.][71]

The narrowness Auerbach attributes to the lives of the characters in Schiller's *Kabale und Liebe* is magnified tenfold in La Peyrouse's description of his milieu: it is a space in which he need only reach out his hand to touch the familiar; indeed, there is no need to ever move at all. Kotzebue has very cleverly shown that the ideal space of bourgeois *Häuslichkeit* is an island far away from Germany.

As with the case of *Stella*, in *La Peyrouse* the solution to the problem of monogamy is polygamy. Like Cäcilia before her, Adelaide is aware that she is the older of the two women and that La Peyrouse is chained to her through gratitude.[72] How is it that adding members to the family creates *fewer* stifling bonds and responsibilities? The solution is suggested by Adelaide's brother Clairville, who insists that bourgeois *Häuslichkeit* need not be predicated on monogamy: "Seltsam, das Himmelreich teilt man gern mit jedem guten Menschen, und mag ein Herz nicht teilen." [Strange, one is happy to share the Kingdom of Heaven with every good person, yet one doesn't want to share a heart.][73] The solution is for the two wives ("wir Schwestern") [we sisters][74] to live together in a hut, with La Peyrouse in another. During the day they will build a family. Like *Stella*, the play ends with multiple embraces, this time including not only the three principals but also the brother Clairville and the two offspring of La Peyrouse. Clairville has the last tongue-in-cheek word: "Das Paradies der Unschuld!" [The paradise of innocence!][75] Kotzebue wrote a second, tragic ending in 1806, although it was not published until 1818. In this ending, Malvina, like Stella, commits suicide.[76] The death of Malvina does not, however, solve the problem of excess, for Malvina's offspring, like Marwood's Arabella in *Miß Sara Sampson*, continue to haunt the monogamous bourgeois scene.

ARISTOCRATIC EXTRAS AND THE *TABLEAU*

Extra figures in dramatic *tableaux* come in the form of lovers and aristocratic secondary figures. The central plot of J.M.R. Lenz's *Die Soldaten* [*The Soldiers*] (1776) ends with a rare touching reunion between the fallen bourgeois daughter and her father. Yet this scene is followed by a final framing scene in which the "Colonel Count of Spannheim" and the "Countess La Roche," two well-meaning aristocrats, discuss solutions to the problem of the ruin of bourgeois daughters by soldiers indulging in their "natural" excessive passions.[77] Lenz composed two different versions of the final scene, but in each case the soldiers' sexual desires are not to be restrained; instead, young women are sacrificed either as prostitutes or well-trained (and tolerant) soldier brides. Polygamy, the potential solution to the common problem of excessive male desires, is the appropriate topic for these frame characters, themselves unnecessary additions to the development of the plot.[78] If the play's penultimate scene provides a rare and unusual bourgeois father-daughter reunion, the framing scene dutifully reinserts aristocratic bridge characters who can ennoble the bourgeois milieu.

Aristocratic bridge figures likewise appear in Kotzebue's highly popular *Menschenhaß und Reue* [Misanthropy and Regret] of 1790. In this *Rührstück* a separated family that learns to perform and then internalize bourgeois values is reunited, and the concluding *tableau* in which this reunion takes place is framed by two external noble figures, a countess and her brother, a major, who are in no way crucial for the plot. Eulalia, who lives alone as a simple bourgeois beautiful soul, is revealed to be the wife of a melancholic "Unbekannter" [stranger] who resides in her vicinity, although their proximity is unknown to either of them. Eulalia, having married the "Unbekannter"—in reality a baron—at a very young age, was seduced by a libertine, and her behavior led to her separation from her husband. The reconciliation between the two is orchestrated with the help of their two children, who are living nearby with a village woman. In the end, we have a *tableau* of familial intimacy (comprised of Eulalia, the baron, and their two children, Wilhelm and Amalia), but this *tableau* likewise includes the seemingly gratuitous presence of the countess and her brother. The German bourgeois dramatic *tableau* simply cannot easily stand on its own without the self-conscious frame created by the aristocratic characters. As the two separated lovers run into each other's arms and are reunited, it is the duchess and the major who help create the complete concluding *tableau*: "The Countess and the Major raise the children into the air as they cling to their parents and cry dear Father! dear Mother!"[79]

Likewise considered a trivial production, Otto Heinrich von Gemmingen-Hornberg's only play, *Der deutsche Hausvater oder die Familie* [The German Father of the Family or the Family] (1780), was also extremely popular in its time and explicitly takes on the task of offering a German *Father of the Family* to German-speaking audiences.[80] The work's ending *tableau* comes very close to emulating the heightened interiority, simplicity, and claustrophobia of Diderot's concluding *tableau*. As in Diderot's play, a financially successful family with tendential bourgeois values awaits the return of the father as the offspring enmesh themselves in troubles: the daughter fights with her husband, one son drowns in gambling debts, and the other has fallen in love with a poor bourgeois girl, the daughter of a painter. In the end, not only is Karl allowed to marry his bourgeois beloved, Lotte, but all other problems in the family are solved by the father. The play ends with what is *almost* a family *tableau* worthy of Diderot. With the problems solved, "The whole family collects around the father of the family, and without ado, the curtain falls."[81]

We therefore have a family *tableau* with a father, his three grown-up children, the husband of his daughter, and the betrothed of his son. Why, then, did Gemmingen-Hornberg feel he also had to include the family bene-factress, Countess Amaldi, in this scene? Why, as was the case with Lenz's *Die Soldaten* and Kotzebue's *Menschenhaß und Reue*, must the bourgeois family be framed by aristocratic extras? In *Der deutsche Hausvater*, Count-ess Amaldi leaves the scene shortly before the play's end but her presence is a reminder of the many "extras" we encounter in German dramatic *tableaux*. Yet the father's discourse deviates substantially from the sentimental father in Diderot's play, who almost suffocates his offspring in his embrace. Gemmingen-Hornberg's father is exhausted from solving all the problems in his family; he is so stiff and upright as to stand as an allegory of patrio-tism, referring repeatedly to Germanness and the German state. The play ends with him sending Karl and the petit bourgeois Sophie to his properties in the country (to prevent them from offending anyone with their transgres-sions of class and rank) and then reiterating his values:

> I will come, too, whenever my business allows it, but otherwise, as long as I have the strength, I will stay here in order to serve my state and my Prince. Also hear it, Heaven, for this day I dedicate the rest of my life to my family and my Fatherland. My reward?— that you all love me?—and then, when one day I am dead, that an honorable German will pass by my grave and say, he was worthy of being a German![82]

The ending *tableau* of the play presents a scene not of embrace but of collect-ing together. In translating *The Father of the Family* as "Hausvater," we are in a realm of household economics. Where Diderot's father pulls his off-spring closer and closer, the German father of the family stands in the center as his offspring draw close but not too close. What comes first for the German *Hausvater*? The state, his sovereign. His family? The inclusion of a question mark after "My reward?—that you all love me?" is curious. The true reward for the *Hausvater* is recognition not by the members of the family but by a German peer, one who can sanction the father as the family members never can.

The figure of the *Hausvater*, idealized by post-1945 historians of the family such as Otto Brunner, is relegated to the past, and Gemmingen-Hornberg's "Hausvater" seems to know this. In Goethe's 1814 "Festspiel" [festival play] *Des Epimenides Erwachen* [The Awakening of Epimenides], a deeply allegorical play about the ramifications of the Napoleonic Wars, Epimenides sleeps through much of the violence of the period, waking up to dreamlike images. One of these is a beloved, "well-known image" of the family hearth, a hybrid picture of the bourgeois family and the premodern "Haus" in which servants are included. The picture is indicated in the play through the otherwise unmotivated use of quotes that function as a framing device for the familial scene:

> Was seh' ich hier! Ein wohlbekanntes Bild!
> Im Marmorglanze, Glanz vergangner Tage.
> "Der Vater ruht auf seinem breiten Polster,
> Die Frau im Sessel, Kinder stehen umher
> Von jedem Alter; Knechte tragen zu,
> Das Pferd sogar es wiehert an der Pforte;
> Die Tafel ist besetzt, man schwelgt und ruht."[83]

> [What do I see here? A well-known image!
> In the marble sheen, the radiance of days past.
> "The Father rests on his wide pillow,
> The wife in a chair, the children stand around them
> Of every age; Servants mill about,
> Even the horse whinnies at the gate;
> The table is full, one feasts and rests."]

We have here the idealized *tableau* of the family that is so elusive in German bourgeois drama from the long eighteenth century. This is the imagined family *tableau* of the past, one that, as we have seen, is unrepresentable as a natural phenomenon (hence the quotes, even in Epimenides's imagination). There is no indulging ("schwelgen") or resting ("ruhen") in the bourgeois dramas leading up to Goethe's "Festspiel." Nor does the German dramatic *tableau* manage to picture this moment as Diderot had imagined it. Goethe's *Des Epimenides Erwachen* ends with a *tableau*, but it is one of allegorical pageantry, featuring figures such as "Unity," priests, and a chorus of warriors. The domestic *Häuslichkeit* is notably a picture of the imagined past, at odds with the energies of the present.

The cross-section of dramatic family *tableaux* examined in this chapter reveals that there is no clear naturalness, interiority, or privacy in the eighteenth-century German literary family. Indeed, the intact nuclear family is nowhere to be found. Instead, these *tableaux* feature "extras," figures often not central to the plot who represent a variety of social and cultural groups. Aristocratic characters frequently serve as framing figures, highlighting the formality of the representation and the presence of the frame/fourth wall. They are carriers of a semantic and semiotic system that precedes bourgeois literature and that imbues the *tableaux* with heightened significance. Alex Hernandez's argument that *tableaux* are not simply "passive" forms is important here.[84] In their ability to bring together seemingly conflicting systems of kinship, class, rank, and aesthetics they nudge us to see human relations as dynamic collisions and intersections. Like the filmic stationary camera long take, they invite a reflection on metonymic relations within the scene that might easily be erased through an exclusive focus on plot.

CHAPTER FOUR

Against Interiority

Letters and Portraits as Dramatic Props

THE EIGHTEENTH CENTURY IS often viewed as the era of the letter, a genre that formally mirrors a shift in the discourse on human relations. For Jürgen Habermas it is the newly emerging, intimate nuclear family sphere that fosters enthusiasm about the exchange of letters, because this is the sphere in which individuals communicate with one another in a manner that he calls "purely human."[1] Habermas views the relationship between the family and the production of "humanity" as a dialectical one. The unfolding of the newly conceptualized interior subject is realized in the process of letter writing: "In writing letters the individual unfolds his subjectivity."[2] This subject is one who experiences, through letters, intimacy with another "Mensch," a mode of relations that was new in the period.[3] As Thomas Beebee puts it, there is a shift from letters being seen in the Middle Ages as the "discourse of the absent" to their function as "the mirror"[4] or "imprint of the soul."[5]

Habermas explicitly connects the tropes that circulate in our contemporary discussions of the eighteenth-century letter: interiority, intimacy, subjectivity, authenticity, truth, and family. Repeatedly called forth and utilized, these metonyms harden, over time, into metaphor. For Habermas the intimate sphere is the space in which the nuclear family, and hence the interior subject, unfolds its individual self; the new obsession with the pure "Mensch" grows directly from the bourgeois nuclear family hearth. The increased interest in "humanity" is a direct product of the intimate relationships between "humans as simply humans within the protection of the family,"[6] and this family resides precisely in the intimate sphere in which humans can relate to one another in a purely human manner. The tautology is purposeful and telling. It reflects Habermas's modern dependence, and our own, upon the metonymic, and hence metaphorical, linkages between the nuclear family, the interior subject, and the nation-state.

Habermas cites the example of a letter written by Herder's bride, Caroline Flachsland, in order to highlight the shift from a discourse of sharing news that characterized the family letter in the seventeenth century to one of intimacy and openness in the following century. Flachsland explicitly writes to her beloved that she fears her letter might contain "nothing but a story," thereby reflecting the function of letters in the period as "containers for the 'pouring of the heart'" instead of "cold news."[7] This new mode of intimate communication was, however, predicated upon a sense of privacy and what Habermas calls a "public-oriented subjectivity."[8] Family members and friends wrote letters with the explicit knowledge that they would likely be read aloud to others in salons and other communal gatherings. Letters were even "bound together and made available to house guests."[9] In this sense, intimacy and privacy are delinked in eighteenth-century letter writing culture.[10] Goethe writes about the period in *Dichtung und Wahrheit* [Poetry and Truth] in precisely these terms:

> There was such a general openness amongst people that it was not
> possible to speak or write to someone else without observing that
> it was simultaneously passed on to others. One spied on his own
> heart and on that of others.[11]

The letter emerges in the eighteenth century as a marker of authenticity and truth, values that are of central concern to the bourgeois class in this period. The letter becomes a privileged genre at the same time as an aesthetics of mimesis emerges. It constitutes a "bridge genre," as Rachael Scarborough King argues, by embodying pre-eighteenth-century modes of mediality as well as new media that arise in the eighteenth century.[12] We might also call it a "bridge genre" due to its ability to stand both for a kind of immanent transcendence connoting the soul of the letter writer and for Enlightenment notions of reality and truth. A mode of representation inherently at odds with allegory's attempt to unambiguously connect signifier and signified (the letter represents words that represent something else), the eighteenth-century private letter, understood as a "mirror of the soul," reintroduces a premodern transcendence into an object otherwise seen as indexical and mimetic. What is more, the hand is central to the letter's simultaneous immanence and transcendence, serving as synecdoche for the individual who animates the letter with a soul.[13]

The authenticity of the letter is a product of its verisimilitude, "its ability to mimic and reflect reality" and function as a "document of reality."[14] The letter contains a "patent of authenticity" that lends it particular weight in a culture ever more concerned with observable and verifiable truth.[15] As C. F. Gellert asks in his 1751 letter primer, "Who is a more faithful betrayer than a letter?"[16] For Gellert, the letter equals the truth: it reveals, and therefore *betrays*, secrets. Beebee writes that "the letter thus acquired the power to mediate between conflicting claims of realism and propriety."[17] Realism has the capacity to transgress the bounds of propriety, as we learn in Diderot's "Conversations on *The Natural Son*." Dorval's ideal *tableau* pictures a weeping father lying across the dead body of his son. As the mother enters the scene she falls into the arms of her husband, provoking shock in the narrator with whom Dorval speaks and who objects to the improper representation of "a bed, a mother and father asleep, a crucifix, a corpse."[18] The proposed, very real *tableau* of grieving parents threatens to "betray" too much in a manner akin to the "authentic" letter, complicating the moral and pedagogical principles that seemingly underlie these new modes of representation and communication.

WRITING THE "GERMAN" LETTER

The literary letter that emerged in the eighteenth century traveled from England and France to Germany. Seminal examples include Richardson's epistolary novels *Pamela, or Virtue Rewarded* (1740) and *Clarissa* (1748) and, in France, Rousseau's *Julie, or the New Heloise* (1761). Norbert Elias shows that the letter and the book were vital to the German cultural sphere around 1750, but this sphere lacked a social and political center. Indeed, the "political fragmentation of Germany" in this period profoundly influenced German intellectuals: "In France the members of the intelligentsia were collected in one place, held together within a more or less unified and central 'good society'; in Germany, with its numerous, relatively small capitals, there was no central and unified 'good society.' Here the intelligentsia was dispersed over the entire country." Whereas in France, conversation was cultivated in the metropolis, the book stood as the central means of communication in Germany, reflecting a "unified written language, rather than a unified spoken one."[19] The German intelligentsia, "floating," as it were, without an economic, political, or social center, consistently looked to France and England for models, yet bourgeois realist aesthetics developed differently within these three cultural contexts.

Rachel King points out that the purely "private" letter emerges in England only in the middle of the nineteenth century after the democratizing postal reforms of 1840.[20] The cost of sending a letter was reduced to a penny nationwide, and new features such as "prepaid postage, envelopes, stamps, and letterboxes" were introduced so that a notion of privacy could be realized.[21] Prior to these postal reforms, letters straddled the public-private divide. As King demonstrates, letters were often written communally, and were thus often not products of individual writers. As a "bridge genre," the letter frequently combined elements of manuscript culture and print culture: for example, King explains that books were often printed with gaps that were then filled in by hand in manuscript style, so that new and old media forms overlapped.[22]

King problematizes what she rightly sees as Habermas's overemphasis on the private nature of the letter in the eighteenth century,[23] demonstrating that in eighteenth-century England the letter never lost its status as the bearer of news.[24] However, her study is firmly circumscribed within the context of eighteenth-century England, and the differences between the cultural spaces of England, France, and Germany in the period are not negligible. In the politically fractured German states there was no unified postal service, and people often avoided using regional postal services, instead relying on friends or relatives to deliver letters.[25]

Janet Altman notes that there were clear differences between the epistolary fiction of Germany, France, and England: in Germany, epistolary novels took on a diary form; in France, they were bound up with "conversational and rhetorical arts, and in England with an esthetic that valued realistic, immediate description of phenomena."[26] It is telling that the diary form is associated with the relatively isolated German context. Communication via writing occupies a unique position in the context of isolation. Albrecht Koschorke thematizes this privileging of distance over nearness, showing how writing served in eighteenth-century Germany to replace a model of communication in which bodies were perceived as less bounded and the individual was hence a more fluid entity. Communication shifted from an exchange of bodily fluids and organic material to a system in which exchange with others occurred in a noncorporeal manner. In this context, orality becomes obsolete, phantasms of immediacy and intimacy are created, and letters and the epistolary novel represent a particularly powerful collision of physical distance and emotional intimacy.[27] The letter, then, bridges the gap, standing in for intimacy while retaining this distance.

Christian Fürchtegott Gellert's paradigm-changing *Briefsteller* [letter primer] entitled *Gedanken von einem guten deutschen Briefe* [Thoughts on a Good German Letter], published in 1751,[28] reiterates the German letter's connection to the trope of isolation. This work provides a discussion of the rules of letter writing followed by examples of letters that readers could use to approximate the new letter writing style. Gellert's letters published in the primer, models for a new mode of epistolarity, reveal a discomfort with proximity to others (i.e., to family members with whom he had once lived in close proximity) and an indulgence in the melancholy produced by distance from loved ones.[29]

Primers (*Briefsteller*) like Gellert's included a variety of model letters (petitions, condolence letters, letters of education) that were useful for legal and private purposes. *Briefsteller* were particularly prevalent in the sixteenth and seventeenth centuries, although important exemplars were also published in the eighteenth century. These books were pedagogical, often resembling encyclopedias, featuring information about practically everything that was considered "worth knowing."[30] They generally included letters translated from French and Italian, modeled after the letters of Cicero and Plinius that frequently appeared in school primers. As Beebee points out, it was not until the eighteenth century that letter writing came to be considered an *art* in its own right. He highlights the image of the muses on the cover of Johann Neukirch's popular *Briefsteller* published in 1729. One of the three muses in this image holds an envelope that presumably contains a letter, and another muse holds a lyre. As Beebee argues, the image marks an unusual moment in which the letter is set on an equal footing with poetry, represented by the lyre, thereby demonstrating "the extraordinary cultural importance which the art of letter-writing had assumed by the early eighteenth century."[31]

The letter was not, however, qualitatively equal across Europe. Gellert is quick to write in his own *Briefsteller* that the Germans are sorely in need of foreign models to produce good letters in their own tongue. He emphasizes repeatedly that Germans lack taste and that the lack of good letters written in German shames the Germans in front of foreigners: "I don't know what foreigners, when they learn our language, should think of us, that we don't write any good letters." For national "Geschmack" [taste] can be most surely detected "from the mode of letter writing that people love in a certain period."[32] The plan of the *Briefsteller* was to publish a collection of good German letters written in the style of "a German Plinius . . . so that we have something of this kind to present to the foreigners and no longer have to suffer the accusation that we would rather write miserable French letters than beautiful German ones."[33] Gellert's impetus for publishing his *Briefsteller*, then, is not a desire to share his letters with interested readers and students but instead a feeling of shame vis-à-vis England and, in particular, France. In other words, the very lack of self-consciousness that he demands from the letter writer—the "natural" and "light" style "ohne Zwang" [without constraint]—is foreclosed via one of the project's explicitly stated purposes, which is to prove to other nations that Germans, too, have taste.

Gellert's work was hailed by his contemporaries, including Lessing, as a radical departure from the "cold" manuals that preceded it, and it is generally viewed as a turning point in the function of the letter as an "imprint of the soul." The "Kanzleistil" [bureaucratic style] characterized both professional and familial/private letters up until the eighteenth century. Letters were expected to follow a rigid model of discourse taught through primers throughout the early modern periods.[34] Gellert emphasizes again and again in his own *Briefsteller* that all letters, regardless of genre, should be "natural, beautiful, pleasant, lively."[35] His work offers no less than a damning critique of all the *Briefsteller* that preceded his own, including those by Talander, Manantes, Weise, and Junker, in which the formal and stylistically rigid "bureaucratic style" is preserved, a style Gellert calls "artificial."[36] Indeed, he suggests that we should retain only "the fewest" rules for letter writing.[37] Yet Gellert's few rules cannot easily be distilled. One should create light, natural letters, ones that do not bore the reader. In fact, Gellert concedes that many women write beautiful letters, in particular those women who are not "gelehrt" [overeducated],[38] thereby articulating the emerging ideals for femininity that prioritize "naturalness" over formal education.[39] Steinhausen formulates the letter aesthetics of the period as "a general striving for naturalness,"[40] a formulation that reveals the fissures in the labored construction of naturalness.

Gellert writes in his *Briefsteller* that letter writing should produce something *natural* and beautiful, although the representation of naturalness should, in keeping with the concerns of propriety, not be exaggerated: "When I write: I only do as when I speak, and there is no need to emphasize the natural to the point of the disgusting."[41] Gellert points out that "there is a mode of writing that is displeasing because it is . . . too natural. Like water it doesn't have a good taste."[42] Some artifice is necessary to create the experience of authenticity and to avoid the ugliness and vulgarity that lurks within realism.

The reception of Gellert's work by his contemporaries was universally positive, and the published reviews often highlight precisely the authenticity of the letters included in the volume. A review published on May 6, 1751, praises in particular the unselfconsciousness that adheres to letters not initially intended to be published: "His letters are full of nature, beautifully thought out, and delicately expressed. . . . One can immediately see that they were originally not written for the press and bookstores. They were simply dedicated to good friends (male and female); this is why they are not stiff."[43] In his review for the *Berlinische Privilegirte Zeitung* that appeared on May 8, 1751, Lessing likewise underscores the superiority of Gellert's letters to those published in earlier *Briefsteller*, calling them "durchgängig Meisterstücke" [through and through masterworks].[44] Here again, the naturalness of the letters is linked to their status as *real* documents originally written by Gellert without any intention of being published: "The conviction that the author wrote the letters to real people substantially increases the reader's interest in that which is written."[45] Letters signify authenticity, and the author of these letters—Gellert himself—is presented as a man with a pure heart precisely because he is presumably unaware ("ihm unbewußt") of the effect his personal letters will have on their readers.

Despite the new sentimental tone of Gellert's letters, only two out of the seventy-three letters included in the *Briefsteller* are written to family members: the twenty-third letter is addressed to "Liebe Mama" [dear Mama] and the forty-third is written to "Hochzuehrende Jungfer Schwester" [deeply honored Maiden Sister]. All the other letters are written to friends, both male and female; to fans who have written with requests; and to other acquaintances unrelated by blood to Gellert. In other words, the sentimental letter that Gellert officially introduces into German Enlightenment intellectual circles is not a product of, or geared toward, the family. The hierarchy of relations as expressed in the letters is underscored by Gellert in his assertion that good taste can be learned through the imitation of a few good model letters; this good taste will then flow "from friend to friend, from father to son, from the reasonable mother to daughter, and becomes the dominant taste."[46] It is telling that the first relationship listed is that of friendship, followed by father-son and mother-daughter relationships.

The discourses surrounding Gellert's "authentic" letters rehearse Diderot's discussions about the "fourth wall" and the *tableau* a few years later.

Just as Diderot's dramatic *tableau* was meant to represent the *real* domestic
scene as if there were no spectators and as if the actors were standing behind
a fourth wall that made them oblivious to the audience's presence, so too
should the letter embody a natural whole, "ein Ganzes," as Gellert writes,
in which all of the pieces are connected organically.[47] In this way, the new
letter prefigures the aesthetics of the fourth wall/*tableau* of the emerging
bourgeois drama. The letter is a product that reflects the natural and cohesive thoughts of its writer, who ideally composes it without any knowledge
of its future publication or wider dissemination, an odd conceit that parallels the fourth wall idea that actors should act *as if* they were not being
watched. Any letter is, after all, written to be read by at least one other
person.

Like a *tableau*, Gellert's ideal letter is a framed whole in which the frame
should be invisible. Also like the dramatic *tableau*, Gellert's model letters
quite frequently convey almost no content. Just as Diderot's ideal drama represents a series of moments of stillness resulting, in the end, in the suspension of plot, Gellert's letters often constitute expressions of feelings devoid
of narrative or action. The *Briefsteller* includes seventy-three letters, many
of them written to friends. In these texts, the author (presumably Gellert)
expresses his love for the friend, his sorrow at the distance between them,
an homage to friendship itself, a complaint about a lack of correspondence
from the other, or a plea for the friend to visit. Very rarely are stories or news
included in these letters. In the twenty-fifth letter written to "my lazy friend,"
Gellert complains about his friend's failure to write and then includes a fictional letter he himself has written in his friend's name, requesting that the
latter correct it as needed and send it back.[48] Here we see the monologic
potential of the letter and its ability to circle around a lack of action.

The sixty-fourth letter, written to "den Herrn von S**," is a case in
point; the letter to this friend includes Gellert's expressions of love, his refusal
to send his friend his own comedies (which he has perhaps not yet finished),
and his advice that Herr von S** should not allow his son to become an
author. In short, not only does the letter express no action except writing
itself; it twice thematizes the suspension or curtailing of action: "I don't know
what to write you except that I don't have anything to write you. For I have
written you for the last ten years that I love you and respect you highly. I
can't send you the comedies. . . . Yes, my dear S——, if you notice at any time
that a son of yours wants to become an author: have his right hand made
lame."[49] This letter is astonishingly devoid of action. The single action it
thematizes, writing itself, is present only in the mention of comedies that

Gellert hasn't completed and the recommendation that it be curtailed should Herr S**'s son show an interest in it. In this sense, the letter signifies a temporal slowing, a pause.

The temporality and framing of many of Gellert's letters mirror the aesthetics of the *tableau*. In one letter written to Herr Baron Gr** during Gellert's stay at the country estate of Frau von K, he writes in an ekphrastic style about servants eating that conjures a *tableau* worthy of Diderot. Gellert highlights the fourth wall framing of the meal as he watches the feasting unobserved: "At twelve o'clock the servants bell is rung, and I am never happier than when I see, without being noticed, a large table full of healthy and hungry maids and servants eating."[50] Gellert's description of the meal sets the parameters for a *tableau* with "natural" subjects in the vein of an emerging aesthetics of realism:

> Everyone eats and speaks at the same time. The men sit in one row, and the village beauties sit in the other one. A loaf of bread as wide as the table is consumed within a half an hour. You can imagine that amongst these two sexes there are sensual ones and that whenever one servant wants to look into his bowl, he temporarily forgets and looks his beloved in her black eyes.[51]

The lovers gaze at one another without shyness or coquetry, unaware that they are being watched. The naturalness of the scene overwhelms the presence of the frame that is pictured here as a large loaf of bread and is literally consumed by the subjects pictured.[52]

The self-conscious *tableau* of Gellert's ideal letter links it formally to the emerging bourgeois drama. It is well known that the epistolary novel developed in tandem with the letter in eighteenth-century German intellectual life,[53] but the striking formal connections between the letter as *tableau* and the bourgeois drama invite further investigation. As I have shown in my analyses of German dramatic *tableaux*, the nuclear bourgeois family is not positioned at the center of these dramas. Similarly, the literary letter, long connected to the nuclear family interior, offers, as we saw with Gellert's *Briefsteller*, a *tableau* of constructed "naturalness" that pictures numerous figures but rarely the bourgeois nuclear family.

LETTERS AS PROPS: *COUP DE THÉÂTRE*

A look at the letter's function in eighteenth-century German bourgeois dramas reveals that it does not cue the interiority/interior subject/nuclear family metonymic chain; instead, the letter is almost exclusively linked to court intrigue and to a semiotic crisis provoked by collisions between allegorical and mimetic representational systems. Family members are not intimately connected via letters; rather, letters function as *props*, as material agents and catalysts of tragic results. The literary letter in German bourgeois dramas of the period does not stand as a signifier for interiority; its content is frequently empty, and its form is utilized to highlight a crisis of representation.

In his theoretical writings on the bourgeois drama, Diderot—a great fan of Richardson[54]—links the letter not to the *tableau*, the representation of domestic naturalness, but to the *coup de théâtre*. In delineating the difference between the *tableau* and the *coup de théâtre* Dorval gives an example from *The Natural Son*: "The second act of the play opens with a *tableau* and ends with a *coup de théâtre*."[55] The *coup de théâtre* is then defined as "an unforeseen incident that takes place in the action and abruptly changes the situation of the characters."[56] It is striking that Diderot's sole example of a *coup de théâtre*, precisely the mode of theatricality he seeks to avoid in his plays, revolves around a letter, the presumed signifier for interiority. Dorval refers here to the scene in which the Dorval of the play has hastily written a letter to his beloved Rosalie, who is betrothed to his friend Clairville and hence off-limits. Dorval is interrupted in his writing by a servant, and he leaves the unfinished letter on the table. Clairville's sister Constance, who is in love with Dorval, enters, finds the letter, and reads it aloud, believing it was written for her and that Dorval has proclaimed his love for her. The Dorval of the "Conversations" dislikes this scene, calling it not natural but contrived.[57] The content of the letter is, we might say, "true," but it could not be completed and is misinterpreted. Gellert reminds his readers again and again in the *Briefsteller* that the letter is distinguished from speech precisely by the fact that we take more time writing letters.[58] In this scene the letter functions, as Dorval complains, not to communicate the feelings of the heart but simply to move the plot forward.

As Peter Szondi has argued, the *coup de théâtre* adheres to the logic of *Zufall* (accident and coincidence), a mode of relationality associated with the court, intrigue, and unpredictability. In contrast, middle-class values were understood to produce the conditions to avoid coincidences, since everyone in the bourgeois nuclear family is reasonable and hence behaves in a predictable manner. This notion of the incompatibility of the *coup de théâtre* with the bourgeois world also extends to an early notion of capitalism in which all players act in the interest of reason.[59] The eighteenth-century letter, presumably recoded as the marker of bourgeois interiority, is, ironically, the ideal prop for "unnatural" and anti-realist plot twists. Additional instances of the use of the letter in German bourgeois dramas (Lessing's *Miß Sara Sampson*, Schiller's *Kabale und Liebe*, Goethe's *Egmont* [1789], and Kotzebue's *Menschenhaß und Reue*) follow this seemingly contradictory model: letters in these and other bourgeois dramas of the period do not connote a natural interiority. They likewise neither present a window/*tableau* onto a domestic scene of familial intimacy nor connect family members. Letters function instead as metonyms, material objects that flatten interiority and are acted on by figures in the plays in a manner that resembles empty allegory.

THE DRAMATIC LETTER AS PROP

Lessing and his contemporaries frequently turned to Aristotle's *Poetics* in order to ground their judgments of eighteenth-century drama. The interest in mimesis is profoundly informed by interpretations of Aristotle, and, as Andrew Sofer has pointed out, Aristotle was completely uninterested in the materiality of the stage:

> The Spectacle has, indeed, an emotional attraction of its own, but, of all the parts, it is the least artistic, and connected least with the arts of poetry. For the power of Tragedy, we may be sure, is felt even apart from representation and actors. Besides, the production of spectacular effects depends more on the art of the stage machinist than on that of the poet.[60]

Props, and even actors, are superfluous to the play's essence in Aristotle's formulation. But we know that props and the bodies of actors can serve as symbols, icons, metonyms, and even allegorical figures. They are important signifiers in the eighteenth century, a period of semiotic transition.

The fetishization of bourgeois interiority leads us in the direction of Diderot, toward a theater whose objects are "transparent," just like the individuals represented.[61] But the objects in German bourgeois drama are frequently not "transparent." In particular, the letter, signifier on the one hand of interiority and on the other of the arbitrary via the use of language, appears again and again as material, highlighting the semiotic shifts underway. As Sofer shows, props can be "volatile".[62] They become important when they no longer signify what they used to in earlier dramas;[63] this is when they "draw the spectator's attention in their own right."[64] Hence, props speak to a semiotic crisis in a particular period.[65] The eighteenth-century dramatic letter is a case in point. The letter emerges as a nontransparent prop in dramas at the very moment that it is coming to signify the new interior subject. In its refusal to be linked, even metonymically, to the family or interiority, it *resists*, we might say, the forward-looking pull of mimetic aesthetics.

Erika Fischer-Lichte lays out the various uses of props in different dramatic periods. In baroque, Romantic, and symbolist theater, props have symbolic meanings; in realist and naturalist theater, props point to the subject and to interactive processes between subjects; and in Goethe's Weimar theater, props are given a subordinate role.[66] In this schema, eighteenth-century German bourgeois theater stands somewhere between baroque and realist theater. Taking cues from Fischer-Lichte, Sofer, and Elaine Freedgood, I interpret props in this period as initially serving a metonymic function and then a metaphorical or symbolic one. Props can refer to situations metonymically: "For example, suitcases piled up at the door point to an impending departure."[67] Freedgood focuses on objects rather than plots in the nineteenth-century British novel.[68] This enables her to alight on a metonymic journey via the objects in the novels, viewing them in relation to other figures and objects surrounding them, and to thereby reflect on the shifted picture of the novel that emerges.

If we take our cue from Freedgood and look not at what the letter symbolizes but at what it *does* and to whom it is linked in eighteenth-century German bourgeois drama, then we are struck by its resistance to narratives of domestic interiority; the letter frequently gestures in this direction but cannot and will not reach its destination. Serving as a "bridge genre," it is the material representative of both "authentic" handwriting and the arbitrary sign.

Appearing fifteen years after Richardson's epistolary novel *Pamela*, Lessing's *Miß Sara Sampson* nods to the centrality of the letter genre in the period while likewise presenting the letter as intermedial prop. Drama normally resists the letter precisely because of the slowing of action that letter writing and reading demands.[69] If the ideal modern letter post-1750 is, as I have suggested, a *tableau* in written form (ekphrasis)—a suspension of action and reflection on interiority—then this notion of the letter is particularly at odds with the tenets of tragedy. The letter in drama must function, then, as a prop, indicating metonymically the interiority that it wants to represent. But any scene in which characters read letters aloud confronts the spectators with an intermediality that pushes the semiotics of the theater to its limits. *Miß Sara Sampson* reveals the impossible expectations put upon the genre of the letter, showing how it does not forge intimate familial relations or cue interiority. The letter does not function in Lessing's play as a *coup de théâtre*, but neither is it able to mirror the *tableau* of the domestic family scene. Rather than representing naturalness and thereby erasing its own frame, as the *tableau* tries to do, the letter in Lessing's drama constantly calls attention to its own constructedness and its inability to successfully forge intimate ties.

The central correspondence with which I am concerned is between the sentimental father, Sir William, and his daughter, Sara. William and Sara are residing at the same inn, but in the first scene in Act 3 William chooses to contact his daughter initially via letter. His servant Waitwell is instructed to take the letter to her while William awaits an answer: "Sir William: Es ist der Brief eines zärtlichen Vaters, der sich über nichts, als über ihre Abwesenheit beklaget. Sag ihr, daß ich dich damit vorweggeschickt, und daß ich nur noch ihre Antwort erwarten wolle, ehe ich selbst käme, sie wieder in meine Arme zu schließen." [Sir William: It is the letter of a tender father who is complaining about nothing but her absence. Tell her that I sent you ahead for this reason and that I only want to wait for her answer before I come and wrap her again in my arms.][70] The letter is important, in particular, as the document of a sentimental father. Even as its content, according to William, is a complaint about his distance and absence from his daughter, it is likewise sent in order to extend the period of separation between the two. Rather than seeking out his daughter immediately, William is content to delay the reunion and await an answer, itself in the form of a letter.

William delays his reunion with Sara because he wants Waitwell to observe her while she reads the letter. The letter, as a signifier of authenticity and intimacy, will presumably create, by association, a situation in which Sara will be unable to dissemble: "Gieb auf alle ihre Mienen acht, wenn sie meinen Brief lesen wird. In der kurzen Entfernung von der Tugend, kann sie die Verstellung noch nicht gelernt haben, zu deren Larven nur das eingewurzelte Laster seine Zuflucht nimmt. Du wirst ihre ganze Seele in ihrem Gesichte lesen." [Watch her expressions carefully as she reads my letter. In her short absence from virtue, she cannot have learned to dissemble, in whose larvae only a deeply rooted vice takes refuge. You will read her whole soul in her face.][71] The letter, as we know from Gellert, is the perfect "Verräther" [traitor]. It reveals the truth of both the writer and the reader, creating a kind of X-ray machine in which those initiated into the bourgeois domestic world (despite the nobility of William's family) reveal their true selves via letter writing and reading.

The scene in which Waitwell brings the letter to Sara, Act 3, scene 3, is the longest in the entire play. The discussion between them focuses entirely on the letter. Sara is loath to read it, but not because she is afraid to discover that her father no longer loves her; on the contrary, she fears William's indulgence of her, his embrace of the role of the sentimental father that puts demands on everyone within the (mediated) familial sphere. Sara strenuously resists accepting the letter from Waitwell precisely because Waitwell tells her it is filled with "Liebe und Vergebung" [love and forgiveness], the qualities of the sentimental father: "So behalte nur deinen grausamen Brief!" [Keep your cruel letter!][72] Sara rejects the modern letter of interiority and intimacy that brings with it the messy emotions of guilt for the receiver.

The scene drags on for pages and depicts Sara's stubborn resistance to reading the letter and engaging with a mediated discourse of sentimentality: "Wenn sein Brief alles enthielte, was ein aufgebrachter Vater, in solchem Falle Heftiges und Hartes vorbringen kann, so würde ich ihn zwar mit Schaudern lesen, aber ich würde ihn doch lesen können." [If his letter were to contain everything impetuous and strict that an enraged father can summon in such a case, then I would read it with a shudder, but I would be able to read it.][73] Her comment is characterized by the subjunctive mode: Sara *would* read the letter if it were to simply present the position of the premodern father figure. As this is not the case, she asks Waitwell to take the letter back to its author. After an extensive back-and-forth, Waitwell is only able to get Sara to read the letter by telling her the lie that it contains the full force of the tyrannical father's anger. Although in the end she is moved by her father's love, throughout the course of the entire play Sara is unable to finish the response to the letter that her father desires.

The next scene, Act 3, scene 4, depicts Sara in the *tableau* of the solitary letter writer, feather in hand: "*Sie setzt sich zum Schreiben nieder.*" [*She sits down to write.*][74] The letter codes the scene as connoting intimacy and interiority. But the authentic letter that reflects the true heart of the loving, wayward daughter simply cannot be written. The scene offers a fascinating picture of the bumpy transition to the letter of "authenticity":

> Wenn man mir es vor Jahr und Tag gesagt hätte, daß ich auf einen solchen Brief würde antworten müssen! Und unter solchen Umständen!—Ja, die Feder hab ich in der Hand.—Weiß ich aber auch schon, was ich schreiben soll? Was ich denke; was ich empfinde.—Und was denkt man denn, wenn sich in einem Augenblicke tausend Gedanken durchkreuzen? Und was empfin-

det man denn, wenn das Herz, vor lauter Empfinden, in einer tiefen Betäubung liegt?—Ich muß doch schreiben—Ich führe ja die Feder nicht das erste Mal. Nachdem sie mir schon so manche kleine Dienste der Höflichkeit und Freundschaft abstatten helfen: sollte mir ihre Hülfe wohl bei dem wichtigsten Dienste entsehen?—*Sie denkt ein wenig nach, und schreibt darauf einige Zeilen.* Das soll der Anfang sein? Ein sehr frostiger Anfang. Und werde ich denn bei seiner Liebe anfangen wollen? Ich muß bei meinem Verbrechen anfangen. *Sie streicht aus und schreibt anders.* Daß ich mich ja nicht zu obenhin davon ausdrücke!—Das Schämen kann überall an seiner rechten Stelle sein, nur bei dem Bekenntnisse unserer Fehler nicht. Ich darf mich nicht fürchten, in Übertreibungen zu geraten, wenn ich auch schon die gräßlichsten Züge anwende.—Ach! warum muß ich nun gestört werden?

[If one had told me in the past that I would have to answer such a letter! And under such conditions!—Yes, I have the feather in my hand.—But do I know yet what I should write? What I think; what I feel.—And what does one think when in one moment a thousand thoughts crisscross one another? And what does one feel when the heart, full of feeling, is deeply numb?—But I must write—I am, of course, not using the feather for the first time. After it helped me pay many a small service of courtesy and friendship: Should it not help me with this most important service?—*She reflects a little and then writes some lines.* That is supposed to be the beginning? A very frigid start. And will I want to start with his love? I have to begin with my crime. *Sie crosses the words out and writes something else.* I shouldn't express myself too fleetingly about this!—Shame is appropriate everywhere except when we confess our mistakes. I can't be afraid of getting entangled in exaggerations even when I already use the most horrible terms.—Oh! Why do I have to be disturbed now?][75]

The scene provides an "authentic" picture of the impossible task of writing the letter that purports to be an "imprint of the soul." Sara is self-conscious throughout, unable to simply write her heart's impressions on the page. Adept at letter writing, she is nevertheless aware that the intimate, sentimental letter demands a mode of communication that is ultimately impossible—such a letter should convey unmediated feelings in a mediated form. Sara's frustration ends with her pronouncement that exaggeration would actually be appropriate in the letter she is writing. In allowing herself to include "exaggerations," she has, in fact, resorted to an earlier mode of letter writing, one that deviates significantly from Gellert's dictates for "authentic" letter writing.[76]

Sara is interrupted while trying to write this letter, and she is depicted trying and failing to finish it in two subsequent scenes. In Act 3, scene 5, she tries again to continue the letter: "*Sie will sich niedersetzen zu schreiben.*" [She wants to sit down to write.][77] And again in Act 5, scene 7, after being poisoned by Marwood, Sara promises a letter to Waitwell, a letter that is *not quite* finished: "Sie ist fertig, bis auf einige Zeilen." [It is ready, except for a few lines.][78] Indeed, the letter cannot and will not be completed, and although the daughter and father reside at the same inn, the father's insistence that communication between them must take the form of the authentic letter almost ensures that they will never see each other. This anxiety is expressed by the poisoned and dying Sara: "Wenn du mit dem unvollendeten Briefe der unglücklichen Sara an den unglücklichern Vater abreisen müßtest, Waitwell?" [What if you had to leave with the unfinished letter written by the unhappy Sara to the even unhappier father, Waitwell?][79]

The drama of the authentic letter that cannot be composed dominates much of Lessing's play. In the end, the reunion between father and daughter occurs, as the daughter dies, without letters, since Sara never completes hers. Functioning in the play as a suspender of action, the letter arguably contributes to Sara's demise. Had the father immediately gone in person to his daughter, scolded or forgiven her, and taken the young lovers away with him, Sara might have escaped Marwood's murderous revenge. Not only is the sentimental bourgeois family absent from the final *tableau* of the play; the genre associated with this new social grouping is likewise revealed to create more confusion than clarity. Only the father is able to write a letter in the new style; Sara cannot do it.

Everyone in the play is aware that the new letter should connote authenticity, intimacy, and "Rührung." Even Mellefont, in Act 4, scene 1, expresses his plans to write to the father, once he learns that Sir William has forgiven the lovers: "Ich will sogleich schreiben, und Sir William, hoffe ich, soll mit den Beteurungen meiner Reue, mit den Ausdrückungen meines gerührten Herzens, und mit den Angelobungen des zärtlichsten Gehorsams zufrieden sein." [I want to write immediately, and Sir William will, I hope, be content with the asseverations of my regret and the expressions of my moved heart, and with my oath of the most tender obedience.][80] This letter is, of course, never written. But the aristocratic Mellefont, hovering halfway between court intrigue and bourgeois transparency, is perfectly aware that this letter demands not only promises of future obedience but also the "expressions of a moved heart."

Letters take on a variety of functions in German bourgeois drama, but they generally do not serve as the signifier of the heart. On the contrary, they appear as props cueing the topos of interiority while nevertheless representing exaggerations or superficiality in lieu of depth and interiority. Schiller's *Kabale und Liebe* contains an important letter, written by the musician's daughter Luise at the prince's command via his secretary. The prince is determined to break up the liaison between his son Ferdinand and the bourgeois girl Luise, and Luise is tricked into believing she must write a love letter to the silly Hofmarschall von Kalb in order to save her imprisoned parents from what she believes will be their death ordered by the prince. Again, the letter is written by the bourgeois daughter, the figure embodying virtue, transparency, and authenticity. Yet the letter is a lie. Hence, we are confronted with the seeming impossibility of a letter written by the hand of a bourgeois daughter containing a lie. Ferdinand is struck by the authenticity embedded in the handwriting: "Es ist ihre Hand." [It is her hand].[81] The hand touches the letter, which should therefore be coded with the true emotions of the writer. Yet Luise's letter belies the truth, and her reunion with her distrustful father occurs at the moment when she rips the letter in two.[82] Communication between father and daughter is only possible in this instance via the destruction of a letter. As Luise confesses to Ferdinand in the final scenes of the play, "Meine Hand schrieb, was mein Herz verdammte—dein Vater hat ihn diktiert." [My hand wrote what my heart condemned—your father dictated it.][83] The body of the virtuous daughter is no longer coded as transparent; her hand and her heart are at odds, and the letter contains the lie this confrontation produces. Does the letter serve as a *coup de théâtre* here? It seems instead to function, as in *Miß Sara Sampson*, to complicate assumptions about the truth of the hand and the heart and the belief in the letter as the window onto this truth.

Kotzebue's *Rührstück Menschenhaß und Reue* [Misanthropy and Regret] highlights the letter's continued association with court intrigue, transnational commerce, and a "bureaucratic" style despite the play's focus on a reunion between members of the nuclear (if not quite bourgeois) family. Bittermann, the count's administrator, speaks continually of letters; he purports to receive them daily from members of courts all over Europe, and the letter functions here not to connote bourgeois interiority but instead as a mask. The letter is likewise not a German signifier but a transnational one, thereby complicating the function of patriotism in the *Rührstücke* of the time. Bittermann takes on the role of the updated harlequin or *Hanswurst*, and the letter functions simply as a signifier of false identity:

> Bittermann: And furthermore I had an important letter in my bag; it almost became wet and unreadable; a letter from France from a *chevalier*—what is his name again? *He pulls the letter out, puts it back in.* You see, you might have thought that it wasn't true. Oh, it contains interesting things.[84]

Letters are repeatedly mentioned by Bittermann as material proof of his important transnational connections. In contrast, letters are never exchanged between estranged husband and wife or between family members.

In this sense, the letter in Kotzebue's *Rührstück* takes on the ironic significance it holds in Goethe's *Faust II* (1830–1831), where it is compared to paper money. Printed paper money, by necessity, introduces yet another layer of mediation into the genre of the letter, insofar as the "truth" of the piece of paper is based on its representative function. There is no hand that gives the paper its authenticity, and no heart that empties its contents into it. In fact, Mephistopheles compares the meaning of paper money to a love letter:

> Ein Blättchen ist im Busen leicht zu tragen,
> Mit Liebesbrieflein paart's beqeum sich hier.
> [A small bit of paper is easy to carry in the breast,
> It couples comfortably here with love letters.][85]

This is the fate of the love letter by the time Goethe writes the second part of *Faust*. What could very well be seen as a parody of the fetishized letter in *Menschenhaß und Reue* is called out in *Faust II* in a particularly harsh manner. The prop of the letter is linked here, as in the earlier plays, to its materiality and ability to stimulate or stifle action, but Goethe's blatant comparison, through the voice of Mephistopheles, between the letter and money deconstructs any sentimentality that the letter might connote within a modern discursive realm.

THE PORTRAIT AND THE INVENTION OF INTERIORITY
The letter is not the only prop that frequently appears in German bourgeois dramas: jewelry boxes, roses, mirrors, and rings abound and carry their

significance through and across a variety of plays. The portrait, however, is linked, like the letter, to the complex shift to a modern aesthetics of mimesis and valuation of interiority, and it appears as a prop in multiple plays of the period. Like the letter, it is introduced as an intermedial form that calls particular attention to itself within the drama genre. And in tandem with the letter, the portrait points to both mimesis and interiority, representing a multi-coded aesthetic form within the Enlightenment.

The portrait, like the modern letter, is metonymically linked to the family.[86] Portraits have historically not been associated primarily with the individual; even in the case of portraits of individual subjects, they tend to connote kinship and social status. Catherine M. Soussloff argues that the portrait is always dialectical, reflecting the communication between sitter, artist, and viewer, who desire "social connection through visible means."[87] Considering Roman portrait masks called *imagines*, Soussloff shows that these images were "signifiers of the family's prominence and kinship."[88] Laura R. Bass highlights the genealogical function of portraits in early modern Spain, showing that royal portraits project "dynastic continuity." "Visual genealogies" were created via the use of common portrait conventions in order to legitimize and naturalize "the royal sitter's sovereignty on the basis of his or her likeness to predecessors."[89] In Sebastián Herrera Barnuevo's *Charles II Surrounded by Images of His Ancestors* (1670) the child king stands dressed magnificently, surrounded by portraits of his ancestors and relatives. This painting connects the young king metonymically to his kin, underscoring the portrait's social, familial, and class function far beyond its representation of an individual.[90]

Soussloff argues convincingly that the portrait connotes both exteriority and interiority, which she also calls indexicality and spirituality. One might also think of these two functions of the portrait as mimetic and allegorical (or iconic). The "functional dialectic of portraiture" is experienced, according to Soussloff, as resemblance and interiority.[91] The Enlightenment shift in art is informed by secularism, as the immanent sacredness of religious art ceases to be a central concern. Henceforth, "images could represent the quotidian and the real," but a "lingering cultural belief in the immanence of the subject's presence remained."[92]

Like the letter, the portrait transcends its indexical qualities, such that it hovers somewhere between resemblance and icon. Aristotle highlights the indexical/mimetic qualities of portraiture when he compares the portrait painter to the dramatist, but he nevertheless stipulates that the portrait should exceed the limitations of the real person so that something more ideal is represented: "Since Tragedy is an imitation of persons who are above the common level, the example of good portrait-painters should be followed. They, while reproducing the distinctive form of the original, make a likeness which is true to life and yet more beautiful."[93] Hence, even for the architect of mimetic drama, the portrait stands as a hybrid genre between the real and the ideal, between the indexical and the transcendent.

The connection between portraiture and interiority—or inner spirit—is at the core of Hegel's lectures on painting given in the 1820s and published as the *Aesthetics*. At the point corresponding to painting in Hegel's teleological schema, the dialectic between external and internal starts to give way to a privileging of interiority and, for Hegel, the human face. Painting should therefore not be overly concerned with appearance, or with trivialities and coincidences. In contrast, he privileges "a genuinely historical portrayal which does not accept what is purely external and reveals only that in which the inner spirit is vividly unfolded."[94] Hegel nods to Aristotle's notion of mimetic portraiture while highlighting the task of the painter to exceed a mere representation of the exterior in favor of a picture of the soul:

> In this way too the painter must set before us by means of his art the spiritual sense and character of his subject. If this is done with perfect success, then we can say that such a portrait hits the mark better as it were, is more like the individual than the actual individual himself.[95]

We see here the tension between mimesis and transcendence that dynamizes the portrait. Hegel is, of course, far less interested in the quotidian side of the dialectic than in the inner spirit that will transform history.

Hegel's ideal portrait is Correggio's *Mary Magdalene* (1528), a painting that, unlike a family portrait, depicts Mary Magdalene alone in a natural setting with a book, looking squarely in the direction of the viewer. The painting contains multiple markers of Magdalene's eroticism, which are not of interest to Hegel here:

> So her profound but reserved withdrawal into herself is but a return to herself and this is no momentary situation but her whole nature. In the whole presentation, in the figure, facial traits, dress, pose, surroundings, etc., the artist has therefore left no trace of reflection on one of the circumstances which could hint back to sin and

guilt; she is unconscious of those times, absorbed only in her present situation, and this faith, this sensitiveness, this absorption
seems to be her entire and real character.[96]

Magdalene's absorption represents, for Hegel, the ideal "accord between
inner and outer, between specific character and its situation."[97] Her splendid isolation and her engagement with the props within the painting—the
book as well as a lamp or vessel, objects that, for Hegel, do not hint of her
former sins (although, again, the erotic pose of the figure is hard to miss)—
characterize the inward turn of her absorption. Hegel takes Magdalene out
of her social-historical context, ignoring what are likely signifiers of precisely that context (the book, the vessel, Mary's erotic gesture and immod-
est attire), and privileges a moment in which absorption, a turn inward that
ultimately mimics transcendence, provides an experience in which the frame
itself can fall away. Here we have again the desire inherent in Diderot's *tableau* and in Gellert's ideal letter for a representation so real that it both produces a fourth wall between artwork and spectator and dissolves the frame
that circumscribes the figures.

A tension between mimesis and interiority, between the real and the
transcendent, characterizes the (post-)Enlightenment portrait and letter as
well as the *tableau*. It is telling that one of the two family letters included in
Gellert's *Briefsteller*, one between the author and his mother, is concerned
with the ownership of a portrait. The impetus for the letter is precisely to
explain that he has given to his beloved "girl" a miniature portrait of himself
that his mother would like to have. In the letter the mother's voice is inter-
jected/imagined three times by the son/author, and each time the mother's
voice is remonstrative, which suggests that the letter writer has internalized—
like an eighteenth-century Norman Bates—a kind of maternal superego
that he represents in the letter.[98] The fight over the portrait, which is the mis-
sive's sole and central purpose, is a fight for the possession and soul of the
son. Gellert suggests he might be able to borrow the portrait briefly from
his beloved "and see if I can have it copied" for his mother.[99] At the end of
his letter Gellert dangles the possibility of sitting for a second portrait, but
it is not the *copy* of the portrait the mother wants but the *original copy*, so to
speak. The portrait stands in as a genealogical product; the portrait is both
mimetic and transcendent, and the mother cannot overcome its lack by
possessing any other object, not even, presumably, the son himself. The
portrait represents the power associated with biological kinship, with

resemblance and transcendental immanence, the heart and soul of the subject depicted. Just as the letter is both hand and heart, indexical and transcendent, so too the portrait embodies both the aesthetics of mimesis and of
iconicity.

THE DRAMATIC PORTRAIT AS PROP

Like letters, portraits often appear as props in German bourgeois drama.
Portraits were central to early modern Spanish drama, and Pedro Calderón
de la Barca was celebrated by the German Enlightenment and Romantic dramatists.[100] The jilted Rosaura in Calderón's *Life Is a Dream* (1635) spends a
significant portion of the play trying to retrieve her portrait, which is linked
not just to her exterior qualities but also to her soul. The portrait in early
modern drama holds allegorical significance, but a lingering semiotics of
transcendence accompanies the portrait into the modern age. In this section
I will examine the role of the portrait in Lessing's *Emilia Galotti*, along with
Goethe's comedy/tragedy *Stella* and Gemmingen-Hornberg's popular *Rührstück, Der deutsche Hausvater oder die Familie*. And let us not forget that in
Mozart's *The Magic Flute* (1791), with a libretto by Schikaneder, Tamino first
falls for Pamina in the form of a portrait!

The first act of Lessing's *Emilia Galotti* famously concerns two portraits
and a number of letters. In the opening scene, Hettore Gonzaga, Prince of
Guastalla, is at his desk dealing with letters containing various requests. He
picks up one of the letters because the name it bears, "Emilia," reminds him
of his fascination with Emilia Galotti. He then signs the request in accordance with the semiotics of metonymy—the letter's writer, Emilia Brunes-
chi, shares a signifier with Emilia Galotti, and this link trumps any content
within the letter. A letter from the Countess Orsina arrives, and the prince
picks it up but immediately discards it. Its message has been received simply via the sender's name, a material link to the letter writer. Once again,
the content is perceived to be irrelevant: *"Bitter, indem er den Brief in die Hand
nimmt:* So gut, als gelesen! *und ihn wieder wegwirft." [Bitter, as he takes
the letter in his hand:* As good as read! *and throws it away again.*][101] Because
her letter is never read, Orsina arrives at Dosalo Palace at the beginning of
Act 4 with the assumption that the prince has received her message and is
awaiting her. Act 4, scene 3, is concerned primarily with the semiotic
betrayal of that assumption. Orsina assumes that the letter has been valued
not for its materiality but for its "interiority"—which contains not just her
"hand" but her heart, according to a new mode of semiotics. Orsina even-

tually learns the truth from Marinelli after repeatedly prodding him: "Orsina *heftig:* Nicht gelesen?—*Minder heftig:* Nicht gelesen?—*Wehmütig, und eine Träne aus dem Auge wischend:* Nicht einmal gelesen?" [Orsina, *vehemently:* Not read?—*Less vehemently:* Not read?—*Wistfully, and wiping a tear from her eye:* Not even read?][102] Lessing shows us here a court society that is shifting, taking on the values of the bourgeoisie. Orsina depends on a semiotics of interiority, according to which the letter reveals the truth of love, but the prince applies his newly developed bourgeois aesthetic to the portrait and thus neglects the letter entirely.

Although the first act of the play contains numerous pieces of paper (*"Briefschaften und Papiere"* [correspondence and papers], as the stage directions indicate),[103] it is the portrait that primarily carries the weight of a bourgeois aesthetics of interiority. The artist Conti brings two paintings to the prince, a commissioned one of Orsina and one of Emilia Galotti, a portrait he claims he painted of his own accord as a study in female beauty.[104] Orsina is a countess, a prominent member of the local aristocracy, whereas Emilia Galotti is a member of a lower order of aristocrats whose father explicitly espouses bourgeois virtues. The prince finds the painting of Orsina to be— like the ideal of mimesis proposed by Aristotle—a recognizable but superior version of its original, the woman he no longer loves. Orsina is coded here, like Marwood in *Miß Sara Sampson*, as an allegorical figure of female fury, as the prince refers to the real Orsina's "Medusa eyes."[105] By contrast, the portrait of Emilia inspires the painter to call her an "angel."[106] The allegorical roles of Emilia and Orsina are thereby set in accordance with those presented in *Miß Sara Sampson*: angel/Virgin Mary vs. fury/Medusa.[107]

This new portrait of the bourgeois feminine ideal, that of Emilia Galotti, demands a dialectical encounter that resembles Hegel's notion of absorption. The stage directions point continually to the prince's difficulty in looking away from the painting: "Der Prinz *indem er sich zu fassen sucht, aber ohne ein Auge von dem Bilde zu verwenden*" [The Prince, *trying to calm himself, but without turning an eye away from the painting*]; "*Noch immer die Augen auf das Bild geheftet*" [*Still with his eyes glued to the painting*]; "*Die Augen wieder auf das Bild gerichtet.*" [*His eyes turned again to the painting*].[108] Indeed, his fantasy in Act 1, scene 5, is to spend the entire morning alone with the painting ("Was für einen Morgen könnt ich haben!" [What a morning I could have!]).[109] Like Gellert's mother and betrothed in his letter to his mother, the prince connects his ownership of the portrait with ownership of the "Meisterstück der Natur" [masterpiece of nature] that is Emilia herself.[110]

Orsina's portrait will hang in the gallery, but the prince has decided that Emilia's portrait will stay with him ("gern bei der Hand" [with pleasure at hand],[111] away from the social/rank context of the exhibition hall.

Even though the portrait is seemingly delinked from a genealogical context, it immediately prompts the prince to think of Emilia's father, Odoardo. Let us not forget that the original painting for which Emilia sat belongs to her father: "Die Schilderei selbst, wovor sie gesessen, hat ihr abwesender Vater bekommen. Aber diese Kopie—" [Her absent father received the painting itself for which she sat. But this copy—].[112] The referential jump from the picture to Emilia's father is immediate. When Conti shows the painting to the prince, he asks him: "Wie, mein Prinz? Sie kennen diesen Engel?" [What, my Prince? You know this angel?][113] After staring intently at the painting, the prince responds:

> So halb!—um sie eben wiederzukennen.—Es ist einige Wochen her, als ich sie mit ihrer Mutter in einer Vegghia traf.—Nachher ist sie mir nur an heiligen Stätten wieder vorgekommen—wo das Angaffen sich weniger ziemet.—Auch kenn ich ihren Vater. Er ist mein Freund nicht. Er war es, der sich meinen Ansprüchen auf Sabionetta am meisten widersetzte.—Ein alter Degen; stolz und rauh; sonst bieder und gut!—
>
> CONTI: Der Vater! Aber hier haben wir seine Tochter.—
> DER PRINZ: Bei Gott! wie aus dem Spiegel gestohlen!
>
> [Sort of!—enough to recognize her now.—It has been a few weeks since I encountered her with her mother in a vegghia.—After that I only came across her in religious locales—where staring is less appropriate.—I know her father, too. He is not my friend. He was the one who resisted my claims on Sabionetta the most.—An old dagger; proud and tough; otherwise honest and good!—
>
> CONTI: The father! But here we have his daughter.—
> PRINCE: My God! as if stolen from the mirror!][114]

When asked if he knows Emilia Galotti, the prince links this knowledge first to the mother and then to the father, lingering on a description of the latter, whom he admires, until Conti redirects him to the daughter.[115] The exclamation "as if stolen from the mirror!" highlights the centrality of a mimetic aesthetics (the painting resembles the subject so closely that it looks like her mirror image) while reminding us that the prince has introduced another level of mediation into the picture via both the mirror and the father. And it is not clear whether the painting of the daughter is stolen from the mirror in front of her or whether the mirror might instead reflect the father. In the latter case, the daughter's resemblance to her father would be at stake, and Lessing leaves this question open. In any case, the genealogical nature of the portrait and its connection to the family are reasserted in *Emilia Galotti*, despite the prince's attempts to cordon the painting off from any social contexts.[116]

A crisis of materiality inheres in the portrait, as it does in the letter.[117] As multi-coded props, the letter and the portrait in German bourgeois dramas are connected to a hand (that of the letter writer or painter) as well as all of the objects and figures around them. Perhaps this is why the question of possession becomes so central, particularly in the case of the portrait, where there is no salutation indicating ownership. The painting of Emilia Galotti is fetishized by both Conti and the prince, with Emilia's represented body parts serving as synecdoches for the "angel" to which they are connected: "Conti: Dieser Kopf, dieses Antlitz, diese Stirn, diese Augen, diese Nase, dieser Mund, dieses Kinn, dieser Hals, diese Brust, dieser Wuchs, dieser ganze Bau, sind, von der Zeit an, mein einziges Studium der weiblichen Schönheit." [Conti: This head, this face, this forehead, these eyes, this nose, this mouth, this chin, this neck, this breast, this figure, this whole build are from now on my only study of female beauty.][118] We see that mimesis and the fetish are linked in interesting ways. The object must, indeed, be recognizable and actually replaceable, be itself a replacement, in order to serve as a fetish—an object, as Freud defined it, that is both a reminder of and a solution to the problem of castration, of anxiety about lack. "Prinz: Am liebsten kaufte ich dich, Zauberin, von dir selbst!—Dieses Auge von Liebreiz und Bescheidenheit! Dieser Mund! und wenn er sich zum Reden öffnet! wenn er lächelt! Dieser Mund!" [Prince: Most of all I would love to buy you, magician, from yourself!—This graceful and demure eye! This mouth! And when it opens to speak! When it smiles! This mouth!][119] The prince will ideally purchase Emilia, or particular parts of her, from the object herself. The angel has morphed into a prostitute as the aesthetics of mimesis and allegory collide.

The colliding representational systems embodied in the modern portrait are on display again in Goethe's *Stella*, where the portrait serves as a prop of recognition that cues Cäcilia to the fact that Stella's beloved is

Cäcilia's husband. When the two women meet, Stella begins to gush about her beloved Fernando, despite the pain his abandonment has caused her, pointing to his portrait as a more powerful signifier for that which cannot be represented in words: "Stella: Ihr sollt sein Porträt sehn!—sein Porträt—O, mich dünkt immer, die Gestalt des Menschen ist der beste Text zu allem, was sich über ihn empfinden und sagen läßt." [Stella: You should see his portrait!—his portrait—oh, I always think that the outline of the person is the best text representing everything that can be felt and said about him.][120] Here, the portrait functions as idealized resemblance. Lucie, the daughter of Cäcilia and Fernando, recognizes Fernando immediately as the man from the inn (she does not remember her father). Cäcilia recognizes her husband in the painting, and she immediately draws the link between portrait and family vis-à-vis her daughter: "Der Gemahl—Das Bild—Der Erwartete—Geliebte!—Das ist mein Gemahl!—Es ist dein Vater!" [The husband—the picture—the awaited one—beloved!—that is my husband! It is your father!][121]

Yet the mimetic function of the portrait is complicated in the next scene, Act 3, scene 1, when Fernando arrives and is reunited with Stella. The stage directions interestingly invite Stella to interact with a painting of Venus hanging on the wall, introducing thereby a less mimetic mode of representation into the play:

> Stella: *ʒu den Wänden.* Er ist wieder da! Seht ihr ihn? Er ist wieder da! *Vor das Gemälde einer Venus tretend.* Siehst du ihn, Göttin? Er ist wieder da! Wie oft bin ich Törin auf und ab gelaufen, hier, und habe geweint, geklagt vor dir. Er ist wieder da! Ich traue meinen Sinnen nicht. Göttin! ich habe dich so oft gesehen, und er war nicht da—Nun bist du da, und er ist da!

> [Stella, *to the walls:* He is back! Do you see him? He is back! *Moving in front of a painting of Venus.* Do you see him, goddess? He is back! How often have I, fool, run back and forth here and cried, lamented to you. He is back! I don't trust my senses. Goddess! I have seen you so often, and he was not here—Now you are here, and he is here!][122]

The painting of Venus overlaps here with the sitter for the portrait; the allegorical figure of love meets the real-life lover who is represented mimetically in the portrait. Stella expresses precisely the collision between the two representational forms in her amazement that the Venus and Fernando could coincide in the same time and place.

By the end of the play, when everyone is aware of Fernando's multiple liaisons, Stella turns again to the portrait of Fernando, this time both fetishizing it and threatening to destroy it and reduce it to pure material. In Act 5, scene l, Stella is in her room in the moonlight: "*Sie hat Fernandos Porträt und ist im Begriff, es von dem Blendrahmen loszumachen.*" [She has Fernando's portrait and is just about to take it out of the frame.][123] Releasing the portrait of Fernando from its frame would represent a complete fetishization of the painting, as Stella plans to carry it around with her when she flees the others. Just as Cäcilia proposes to Fernando that letters will be her only comfort in her plan to renounce him so that he can live with Stella, so too does Stella plan on clinging to the prop that holds the tension between resemblance and material transcendence. Her cries of terror in this scene are framed by her engagement with the portrait as icon and material canvas:

Stella: O mir ist schwindelig!—Leb wohl!—Lebt wohl? Nimmer wiedersehen?—Es ist ein dumpfer Totenblick in dem Gefühl! Nicht wiedersehen? Fort! Stella! *Sie ergreift das Porträt.* Und dich sollt ich zurücklassen? *Sie nimmt ein Messer und fängt an, die Nägel loszubrechen.* O daß ich ohne Gedanken wäre! daß ich im dumpfen Schlaf, daß ich in hinreißenden Tränen mein Leben hingäbe!—Das ist und wird sein:—du bist elend!—*Das Gemälde nach dem Monde wendend.* Ha, Fernando! da du zu mir tratst und mein Herz dir entgegensprang, fühltest du nicht das Vertrauen auf deine Treue, deine Güte?—.

[Stella: Oh, I am dizzy!—Adieu!—Adieu? To never see again?—A hollow gaze of death is in this feeling! To never see again? Away! Stella! *She grabs the portrait.* And I should leave you behind? *She takes a knife and begins to break the nails free.* Oh, if only I were free of thoughts! That I could give up my life in a dull sleep, in ravishing tears!—It is so and will be so:—You are miserable!—*Turning the painting toward the moon.* Ha, Fernando! When you walked up to me and my heart sprang toward you, didn't you feel the trust in your loyalty, your goodness?—.][124]

Having been de-framed, so to speak, the portrait becomes both more and less than the subject that it represents.

Stella's gothic ceremony in removing the portrait from its frame ultimately reduces it to fetish material. Shifting wildly from reproaches to expressions of love, she threatens the portrait with destruction, only to protect it in the end:

> Stella: Wo bist du, Stella?—*Das Porträt anschauend.* So groß! so schmeichelnd!—Der Blick war's, der mich ins Verderben riß!—Ich hasse dich! Weg! wende dich weg!—So dämmernd! so lieb!—Nein! Nein!—Verderber!—Mich?—Mich?—Du? Mich?—*Sie zuckt mit dem Messer nach dem Gemälde.* Fernando!—*Sie wendet sich ab, das Messer fällt, sie stürzt mit einem Ausbruch von Tränen vor den Stuhl nieder.* Liebster! Liebster!—Vergebens! Vergebens!

> Stella: [Where are you, Stella?—*Looking at the portrait.* So grand! So flattering!—It was this gaze that tore me into ruin!—I hate you! Away! Turn away!—So dimly lit! So dear!—No! No!—Destroyer!—Me?—Me?—You? Me?—*She twitches with the knife in the direction of the painting.* Fernando!—*She turns away, the knife falls, she falls down in front of the chair with an outburst of tears.* Dearest! Dearest!—In vain! In vain!][125]

Stella's ontological crisis ("Mich?—Du? Mich?") coincides with her engagement with the portrait, not with Fernando himself. Having taken the portrait out of its frame, she has, we might say, broken the fourth wall so that the illusion of the portrait's transcendence is no longer possible. In the end, a servant appears as she is trying to flee, and she tells him to take the painting, which he rolls up like a rug or any other object:[126] "Stella: Das Gemälde! *Bedienter nimmt das Messer auf und schneidet das Gemälde von dem Rahmen und rollt's.*" [Stella: The painting! Servant picks up the knife and cuts the portrait out of the frame and rolls it up.][127] Stella is now in full possession of the portrait, but it has been reduced to a rolled canvas in a telling reminder of the crucial role of the frame for the retention of the portrait's transcendent immanence.[128]

Interestingly, Gemmingen-Hornberg includes a painting representing Goethe's character Stella in *Der deutsche Hausvater oder die Familie* (1780), his German version of Diderot's *Father of the Family*. It is difficult to understand the scene in which this painting is featured except as a reflection on the questions of framing, interiority, and materiality that come to the fore in Goethe's play. Gemmingen-Hornberg's painter is the father of Lottchen, the beloved of Karl, the count's son who has impregnated her (unbeknownst to the father) and has come to break off his relations with Lottchen in the interest of pleasing his own father. Act 4, scene 4, is concerned with the painter's work; he exclusively creates images of unmarried mothers, referring sometimes explicitly, sometimes implicitly to German literary works published a few years before *Der deutsche Hausvater*, namely *Die Leiden des jungen Werthers* (1774), *Stella* (1776), and Heinrich Leopold Wagner's *Die Kindermörderin* [The Child Murderess] (1776). In the scene, the painter shows Karl his paintings and drawings, and Lottchen suffers quietly in the background until she collapses, ending the scene. Here, literary mimesis meets mimesis in painting and drawing, and both point metonymically to the pregnant Lottchen who sits in the same room. First, the painter shows Karl his painting, taken from a scene in *Stella*:

> It is from our felicitous Goethe's *Stella*. You know how Madame Sommer tells of her walks at her child's grave.[129] Here you can see the vale of tears that fall onto the child's grave, here the urn of the little grave; lit by the moon's twilight; notice how the night stars shine down onto the sad spot. And there the poor, lovesick, abandoned Stella, standing at the grave of her child; it is the moment in which, after friendly and hopeful dreams, it becomes clear to her that she is alone, in which she stretches out her arms in vain, and in the desire of full love seems to want to pull the moon down towards her.[130]

The painter's description of the scene is so detailed as to highlight his intense desire to represent mimetically how he imagines the scene would look. We have here something that sounds like stage directions. Whereas in *Emilia Galotti* and *Stella* the paintings invite an intensive dialogue with the viewer, this painter's work is in need of the arbitrary signs of words.

The first scene of ekphrasis ends with the painter showing Karl additional drawings that will serve as studies for a painting representing a child murderess. Without knowing about his own daughter's pregnancy, the painter nevertheless expresses his rejection of the laws that condemn unmarried mothers who kill their offspring, stating that "our laws are responsible for this."[131] His commentary demonstrates that the painter's art is political and no longer linked explicitly to allegory or transcendence. His detailed explanations about the preliminary drawings for the painting of the child murderess gesture beyond the medial boundaries of painting:

PAINTER: Look here, Count, at the sketches I made; here is the unhappy girl as she strangles her only child. Do you notice there at the top of the line a branch, the frenzy of the mother, do you feel it, Count?

KARL: Yes, unspeakable.

PAINTER: And now this second drawing. There she lies, the mother, the complete image of unhappiness, the dead child, whom she seems to not want to let go, pressed against her breast. Here is the guard who wants to lead her to the court, and there the poor, old father, utterly confused, who his dear, his only. . . . *At this point Lottchen faints.*[132]

Here, even more than in the *Stella* painting, the visual scene that the painter describes in such detail constitutes what could only be characterized as a *tableau*. The *tableau* includes the mother, her dead child, and the mother's own father. As in Lessing's interpretation of the *Laocoön*, the father's pain is both at the composition's center and potentially so difficult to represent that it would break the fourth wall, leading to an excess of suffering on the part of the spectators due to intense compassion. When Lottchen collapses behind the two men, it is a sign of this excess.

The mimesis and doubling in this scene produce not a collision between allegorical and mimetic aesthetic modes but instead an excess of the real. The paintings of the literary scenes are described in words, and they likewise figure the real lives of the lovers in the room. Ekphrasis, for Murray Krieger, is precisely the moment when literature "takes on the 'still' elements of the plastic form which we normally attribute to the spatial arts."[133] This kind of troubling of the specificity of media aesthetics is underscored by a feeling of ambivalence.[134] Why did Gemmingen-Hornberg include this scene of ekphrasis in his only play? Does it contribute to the overall dramatic plot? We can answer this question in the negative, since Karl continues with his plan to renounce Lottchen. There is, in fact, something sadistic about the scene. On the one hand, the father expresses his deep compassion for poor young women who become impregnated and have no choice but to become child murderers due to draconian laws. On the other hand, his excruciating descriptions of the paintings cause undue suffering for both Karl and Lottchen. Do these descriptions inspire a sense of compassion in the spectator? Perhaps. But more important, they bring the complex modern aesthetics of the *tableau* and the portrait to a head in such a way as to upend the hierarchical relationship between the natural (pictorial) and the arbitrary (language) sign.

❧❦❧

CHAPTER FIVE

Material Kinship

The Economy of Props in
G. E. Lessing's *Nathan der Weise*

PROPS PLAY A surprisingly central role in Lessing's *Nathan der Weise* (1779), a play that is often called an "Ideendrama" [drama of ideas] for its polemical take on religious tolerance.[1] Lessing's drama contains numerous stage directions that cue extras (often playing enslaved people) to bring piles of goods and money onto the stage; props and property become one, constituting material manifestations of the increasing wealth accruing to key figures in the play. In the opening stage directions to her 2008 play *Abraumhalde* [Rubble Heap], which relies heavily on *Nathan der Weise* as an intertext, Elfriede Jelinek highlights a logic of excessive addition that is reflected in staging and prop choices for the performance: "*Es soll eine Vermehrung und/oder allgemeine Vergrößerung von allem stattfinden.*" [*An increase and/or general enlargement of everything should occur.*][2] These stage directions capture the essential dramatic economy of Lessing's play: more begets more, as in a protocapitalist fantasy, and this logic defines not only the function of wealth and money in the play but also that of kin structures. Just as props in the form of sacks of money and costly goods crowd the stage in *Nathan der Weise*, kin groupings in Lessing's drama likewise form and expand in ways that exceed and break open any "walled-off" notion of the family that is sutured to the ideal of nation in the period.

Goethe, who produced the first successful stagings of the play at Weimar in 1801,[3] underscored the role of Lessing's play in imagining a German nation, writing: "Möge das darin ausgesprochene göttliche Duldungs—und Schonungsgefühl der Nation heilig und wert bleiben!" [May the feeling of divine tolerance and protection expressed therein remain sacred and valuable to the nation!][4] The play's protagonist, the Jewish merchant Nathan, is often viewed as the ideal father of a utopian German nation. The drama was famously banned during the Third Reich for its positive representation of a Jewish merchant as the ethical leader of the state, and it was the first play performed in Berlin after the defeat of the Nazis.[5] That a unified German nation was only a distant ideal at the time of the work's publication and yet would be realized 100 years later reminds us that *Nathan der Weise* is a dream of sorts that imagines a complex fusion of kinship and economic systems linking the past to the future.

A focus on the function of props and property in the play highlights the power of objects within a drama valued for its presentation of ideas. *Nathan der Weise* is best known as a play that advocates tolerance for religious and cultural difference. Set in Jerusalem during the Third Crusade (1189–1192), it depicts a moment of reconciliation between members of each of the major monotheistic religions, Judaism, Christianity, and Islam. The work's generic categorization as an "Ideendrama" corresponds to its early critical reception, which considered the play to be "cold" and didactic.[6] Nathan is a teacher who frequently lectures his daughter Recha, her Christian nanny, and a young Templar (who saves Recha from a fire and falls in love with her) about the moral value of reason. Ideas, then, rather than material—arbitrary, and not natural, signs—are often seen as driving the play. But *Nathan der Weise* cannot easily be categorized generically, because it borrows elements from the bourgeois tragedy and comedy as well as from early modern morality plays, and its hybridity open ups more possibilities than it forecloses.[7] Critics who have emphasized the importance of objects in the play often point to the ring in the seminal ring parable, as well as the coin that serves as a metaphor for Nathan's reflections on truth. It is customary to analyze these objects by following the trajectory laid out in Lessing's *Laocoön*, which moves from natural to arbitrary signs, from material to ideal. As Stefani Engelstein reminds us, Lessing's *Die Erziehung des Menschengeschlechts* [The Education of the Human Race] (1780) traces the path of education and Enlightenment from the materialism of the Jewish book to a universal and ideal Christianity.[8] Helmut Schneider interprets the ring in the ring parable as a "Dingsymbol" [symbolic thing] that symbolizes the shift from the particular (the past) to a universal future.[9] But a focus on the play's many props representing the accrual of wealth should give pause to assumptions about the transcendence of materiality within Lessing's drama. The play is about expansion, in both economic and kin terms, but expansion and addition need not imply transcendence. We can instead interpret *Nathan der Weise*, via the onstage accumulation of props, property, and kin, as a material vision of precapitalist surplus in which the usually repressed signifiers of the exploitation that produced this wealth are surprisingly manifest for all to see (i.e. figures of enslaved people crossing the stage).

The play's ending *tableau*, to which I have referred in earlier chapters, is staged as a group hug featuring the principal players surrounded by the precious goods piling up around them. In the end, all of these main characters (with the exception of the wise and rich Jew, Nathan) are determined to be biologically related, and we learn that Nathan adopted his daughter Recha. It is left to dramaturgs and directors to decide whether Nathan is included in the group hug. For example, the Berliner Ensemble production of the play in 2013–2014 chose to leave Nathan out of the final *tableau* embrace, a decision that highlights the porous nature of the play's kin groupings.[10] Many of Lessing's contemporaries were dissatisfied with the ending *tableau*.[11] Indeed, despite the tragic elements in Nathan's past (his wife and seven sons were killed in what was likely a pogrom), the play is generally understood to approximate a comedy. Yet the lack of any wedding leads to what Peter Demetz calls a "sterile tableau" in the final scene.[12] Indeed, an early prose draft of the play indicates that Lessing had initially modeled the narrative not only after Boccaccio's *Decameron* (tale 1, 3) but also Denis Diderot's *The Natural Son*.[13] In his play, Diderot resolves the crisis of potential incest between siblings through an elegant double marriage at the end in which one of the siblings marries the sister of the other. In an early draft of *Nathan der Weise* Lessing opened the possibility for a double wedding between Sittah and the Templar and Saladin and Recha. However, the crisscrossing biological connections of the final version excluded this more traditional option for a happy ending. Lessing ultimately chose to emphasize the expansive nature of a multicultural community rather than containing the individuals within neat dyads.

Surplus is the dominant topos in the final act of the play. Indeed, material surplus in the form of goods and bodies is a central motif throughout *Nathan der Weise*, inviting us to consider anew both the play's final "Menschheitsfamilie" [family of humanity] *tableau* as well as its economy of things and human relations.[14] Willi Goetschel writes that "for Lessing, everything is connected to everything else."[15] If we begin by remarking on the motif of tolerance, for example, we might easily end up discussing the role of family, religion, or even economics in Lessing's works. Already at the beginning of the play we are invited to consider the connections between the good (*Güte*) and goods (*Güter*), as Nathan the wise, wealthy, and good merchant returns home from his travels bringing riches and gifts for everyone in the household. In the first scene, Daja, the nursemaid of Nathan's adoptive daughter Recha, receives beautiful cloth in abundance: "Was in Babylon für einen schönen Stoff ich dir gekauft. So reich, und mit Geschmack so reich! Ich bring für Recha selbst kaum einen schönern mit." [What lovely cloth I bought you in Babylon. So rich, and so rich in taste! I've hardly brought more lovely cloth for Recha herself.][16] Daja perceives the gift as a bribe (which she, of course, accepts, and thus stays silent about the true circumstances of Recha's birth), thereby immediately inviting us to link goodness with generosity, generosity with self-interest, and self-interest with family.

But what happens if we linger a little longer with the fine goods and "Beutel" [sacks] of money that arrive with Nathan in the opening scene and that continue to be piled onto the stage at key moments in the play? How might such a reading offer new insights into the play's material and erotic economies? Nathan himself teaches us that God's rewards are material and earthly, thereby investing the material with a transcendental weight and the transcendental with a material imperative: "Denn Gott lohnt Gutes, hier Getan, auch hier noch." [For God rewards here the good deeds done here.][17] If we follow Nathan's teachings in parallel with the onstage accumulation of goods throughout the play, then we must consider the weight and value of the material itself. Indeed, a focus on props and property in Lessing's drama offers unexpected insights into the relationships formed between humans, as well as those between humans and things.

In Lessing's *Nathan der Weise* material and affective surplus are intricately linked. It is precisely a delay in the arrival of goods and luxuries to Saladin's court that motivates communication between the Muslim ruler and Nathan, leading also to the latter's telling of the famous parable of the ring. The tale itself connects material value (the ring, a gift from the father) with an additive mode of love; it speaks not of an either/or model for familial alliances but instead a both/and one. For generations, a special ring is handed down from father to son, until one day a father of three sons impossibly promises the ring to all of them. He subsequently has indistinguishable copies of the ring made in order to indicate his nonexclusive love for them: each is equally loved, not one is left out. Similarly, as the family (both biological and adoptive) grows exponentially in the course of the drama, so do the piles of luxury goods and wealth that begin to appear in Saladin's palace as well as in Nathan's house. Economic wealth coincides with an expansive, seemingly limitless mode of love. And once again, it is not the nuclear family that is of central concern here but the extended and extending family with its logic of surplus. The final *tableau* of the play offers us a kin grouping that consists of thwarted erotic attachments between siblings (as with the Templar and Recha, whose love introduced the incest taboo); unexpected blood connections (between Recha and the Templar, and between Saladin and Sittah); and adoptive and elective affinities (Nathan as the ideal father and yet one who has no biological relation to the characters on the stage).

MONEY AND MATERIALITY

The complex relationship between material (via props/property and money) and ideas (religious tolerance) in Lessing's play is represented discursively via a number of famous dialogues concerning money. The European Enlightenment is often seen as a period that marked a fundamental shift in the perception of signs: to follow the trajectory of Lessing's *Laocoön*, signs become arbitrary and symbolic, while material becomes commodified and metaphorical. Nathan himself seems to thematize this shift in an oft-cited passage from act 3, scene 6, where, during the moment of delay at Saladin's court, he considers how he will respond to the Sultan's question about which of the three monotheistic religions is the superior one:

> —Ich bin auf Geld gefaßt; und er will—Wahrheit.
> Und will sie so—so bar, so blank—als ob
> Die Wahrheit Münze wäre!—Ja, wenn noch
> Uralte Münze, die gewogen ward!—
> Das ginge noch! Allein so neue Münze,
> Die nur der Stempel macht, die man aufs Brett
> Nur zählen darf, das ist sie doch nun nicht!
> Wie Geld in Sack, so striche man in Kopf
> Auch Wahrheit ein? Wer ist denn hier Jude?
> Ich oder er?

> [—I am prepared for money, and he wants—truth!
> And he wants it so bare, so blank, as though
> The truth were a coin! Now if it were an ancient coin that is
>   weighed!—
> That would still work! But such new coins,
> That only a stamp can make, that you can just count on a board,
> That's not what the truth is!
> Like money in a bag, you would pocket truth
> In your head? Who's the Jew here?
> I or he?][18]

It is precisely the arbitrary, nonliteral nature of stamped coins that disturbs Nathan. Richard Gray argues that two modes of truth are reflected in the two modes of money Nathan is comparing: the older coin, whose weight corresponded to its intrinsic value, can be linked with an "ancient" truth, one that is "already known or believed"; the new coin (or bill), with its value indicated arbitrarily by a stamp, stands "as a mere placeholder of absent value" and as a "speculative form of knowledge that employs arbitrary signs to generate new 'truths.'"[19] Indeed, we are here reminded of Nietzsche's reference to Lessing in "On Truth and Lies in an Extramoral Sense": "Truths are illusions which we have forgotten are illusions; they are metaphors that have become worn out and have been drained of sensuous force, coins which have lost their embossing and are now considered as metal and no longer as coins."[20]

Nathan's monologue highlights the problem of metaphor. Minted coins say nothing about the context, about the contingencies of meaning involved in a particular exchange, or about their own materiality and the materials to which they relate. In the first scene of act 2, the Sultan Saladin makes a similar complaint about smooth chess pieces that do not reflect the roles they represent: "Wer giebt uns denn die glatten Steine Beständig? Die an nichts erinnern, nichts Bezeichnen?" [Who keeps giving us these smooth stones, which don't remind us of anything, don't signify anything?][21] In both instances, Nathan and Saladin not only offer a critique of a modern system of signs; they likewise invite us once again to consider the materiality of the object, to read less metaphorically and more literally, to look at the thing as a thing. Indeed, money and goods are not simply metaphors for wealth in the play. Although "Geld" [money] is mentioned numerous times in the play (thirty-five times, to be precise), wealth is represented as material through the stream of goods and *Beutel* of money arriving on the stage. If we attend, in this sense, to the surface of the play, we can learn something about the ways in which material goods interact with and influence human relationships.

Mark Lehrer warns against exaggerating the modernness of Lessing's "treatment of money."[22] Does Lessing really offer here, as Hinrich Seeba has argued, a critique of the commercialization of human relations?[23] Such an interpretation is informed by a modern notion of capitalism that, in the context of my materialist reading of the play, may constitute an anachronism. The consistent return to questions of money and materiality within Lessing's drama points to a less critical view of wealth than modern readers might assume would be the case. The relationship between arbitrary and natural signs is not clearly worked out in the play, but wealth and riches are unambiguously seen as holding great value.

In his essay "Geld" (1844), Marx points to the power of money to travel between the material and the imagined. Money, according to Marx, both separates and binds.[24] In its ability to turn the imagination into reality, it is "die *wahrhaft schöpferische Kraft*" [the truly creative force].[25] Money creates the material from the idea:

> Whenever I desire food or need the postal van because I am not strong enough to go all the way on foot, then money supplies me with the food and the postal van, that is, it transforms my wishes from the essence of an idea, it translates my wishes from their thought, imagined, desired being into their *sensible, real* being, from the idea into life, from imagined being into real being.[26]

This is the sense in which money works within *Nathan der Weise*—as an idea that creates objects (viewed as props on the stage) that comprise the building blocks of the newly created kin structure. Whereas Marx is notably suspicious of the seemingly magical powers of money to conjure objects of the imagination, the manner in which objects as props and property circulate and function within Lessing's play points to money's ability to foster material relations.

The constant delivery and display of money and goods on the stage of Lessing's play is informed by the one-to-one semiotics of allegory. Allegorical drama is, as Jane Brown points out, based on concrete signifiers—personifications that make ideas material.[27] Figures such as "Strength," "Death," and "Goods" personify the insubstantial and the abstract in the morality plays that were popular in the late medieval and early modern period; they can be seen as an initial step toward the secularization and democratization of drama, moving away from Corpus Christi performances and processionals, staged for the court, to public performances in towns. This mode of representation made identity and meaning visible and material. The shift away from the valuation of allegorical representation in the seventeenth and eighteenth centuries was, as I have argued earlier, surely informed by the interest in the emerging interior subject. "Visibility became equated with superficiality," and allegory came to seem "outmoded."[28]

THE SEMIOTICS OF ALLEGORY

Lessing's *Nathan der Weise* invites an allegorical mode of reading. The most prominent example of allegory in the play is the material representation of money and goods, which is reminiscent of the character named "Goods" in the morality play *Everyman* that was produced extensively beginning in the

late fifteenth century (first in Holland and then in England and beyond).[29]
Goods expresses his identity in terms of piles of goods, admitting, in a precapitalist self-critique, that these items cannot accompany Everyman to the
reckoning to which God has called him:

> Goods: I lie here in corners, trussed and piled so high,
> And in chests I am locked so fast,
> Also sacked in bags, thou mayst see with thine eye,
> I cannot stir: in packs low I lie.[30]

It is notable that Goods is both hidden ("in corners"; "in chests I am locked
so fast") and visible for all to see ("trussed and piled so high"; "thou mayst
see with thine eye"). Serving as an allegorical figure within the play, Goods
nevertheless takes on the role of the prop: property accumulating under our
nose but without calling attention to itself.

Goods in Lessing's *Nathan der Weise* play a similar role: they are piled
just as high as the Goods in *Everyman* and are likewise often overlooked
despite their constitutive role in the creation of relationships within the play.
Aside from the human characters, money and goods are the central players
in Lessing's drama. The play begins with the arrival of goods, and an additive logic likewise structures the rest of the play. In the opening act, Nathan
arrives with the luxury goods that he has brought back from his travels
thanks to collecting on debts ("Schulden einkassieren"),[31] and throughout
the play, goods and money consistently arrive at Nathan's home and at Saladin's palace. By the drama's end there are too many goods and too much
cash, with the characters remarking frequently on the excessive surplus.

After Nathan's recounting of the ring parable in act 3, the following
two acts feature stage directions indicating the arrival of goods.[32] Act 4,
scene 3, begins with a stage direction stipulating that enslaved people should
bring goods and sacks of money to the stage: "*Szene: Ein Zimmer im Palaste
des Saladin, in welches von Sklaven eine Menge Beutel getragen, und auf dem
Boden nebeneinandergestellt werden.*" [*A room in Saladin's palace into which
slaves carry a large quantity of bags and set them side by side on the floor.*][33] The
characters likewise express their amazement at the seemingly endless sup-
ply of material goods:

> Saladin: Nun wahrlich! Das hat noch kein Ende.—Ist
> Des Dings noch viel zurück?
> Ein Sklave: Wohl noch die Hälfte.

[Saladin: Now truly! This has no end. Is
There much more of the stuff left behind?
A slave: Still about half of it.][34]

Scene 6 of the same act opens with a view of a hallway in Nathan's house, in which goods are piled up: *"Ein Teil der Waren und Kostbarkeiten liegt ausgekrampt, deren ebendaselbst gedacht wird."* [A portion of the wares and valuable objects have been unpacked, and these are the subject of conversation.][35] As in scene 3, figures in the drama take notice of and interpret the meaning of these goods: "Daja: 'Oh, alles herrlich! Alles auserlesen! Oh, alles—wie nur Ihr es geben könnt.'" [Oh, everything's splendid! Everything's exquisite! Everything, as only you can give it.][36] In response, Nathan explains that the goods are for Daja herself, and that even more will be arriving for Recha. Three scenes later, scene 1 of act 5 begins similarly, with the stage direction, *"Szene: Das Zimmer in Saladins Palast, in welches die Beutel mit Geld getragen worden, die noch zu sehen"* [Scene: The room in Saladin's palace into which the money bags, which are still visible, have been carried], followed by additional commentary from one of the characters: "Saladin *im Hereintreten:* Da steht das Geld nun noch!" [Saladin, stepping in: The money is still sitting there!][37] We cannot fail to see the arrival of riches when we are cued both by the stage directions ("money bags, which are still visible") and by Saladin's commentary. And Nathan's gifts to Saladin are subsequently followed by news of the arrival of a caravan of goods from Egypt that Saladin himself had been awaiting.

The last scene of the play is likewise structured around the arrival of goods, and in the midst of the extended kin narrative that is unfolding in Saladin's palace, the Sultan's first words to the arriving Nathan refer to money:

Saladin: Ah, meine guten lieben Freunde!—Dich,
Dich, Nathan, muß ich nur vor allen Dingen
Bedeuten, daß du nun, sobald du willst,
Dein Geld kannst wiederholen lassen!
[. . .] Die Karawan ist da! Ich bin so reich
Nun wieder, als ich lange nicht gewesen.—

[Saladin: Ah, my good, dear friends!—You,
You, Nathan, I must tell you first of all
That you can retrieve your money as soon as you like!

[. . .] The caravan is here! I'm richer now again
Than I've been in a long time.—][38]

By the end of the play, money and goods flow with a material vibrancy that is apparent to all of the figures. When Saladin tells Nathan that he can "Dein Geld . . . wiederholen lassen," he is suggesting not only that Nathan can be repaid for the money he gave to Saladin but that the money itself will reproduce: "Wiederholen" also signals repetition and growth, a process of surplus production that is as much a part of the play as the religious and familial narratives.

The sacks of money and goods arriving throughout Lessing's drama connote material wealth as well as the divine and the immaterial. Sittah and Saladin discuss the origin of Nathan's money before they meet with him in Act 2, and Sittah suggests Nathan has a special and magical connection to Solomon and David and can therefore access God's infinitude via the riches held within their graves: "Aus ihnen bringt er dann von Zeit zu Zeit, die unermeßlichen Reichtümer an Den Tag, die keinen mindern Quell verrieten." [From them he brings from time to time such immeasurable treasures to light as no other source could produce.][39] The "unermeßliche Reichtümer" emerge from a secret source and represent a direct link to God.

Marx uses similarly allegorical language in his discussion of money: money is material and God at the same time. He quotes Shakespeare in this context: "Thou *visible* God!"[40] Money, Marx shows, can both create and destroy human connections. Deploying a discourse connoting both economics and family, he suggests that money can destroy the natural family and also create new ones: money is "die Verbrüderung der Unmöglichkeiten— die *göttliche* Kraft" [the joining of impossibilities as brothers—the *divine* power].[41] Money is imagined here by Marx as binding and separating, as producing kin, in a manner similar to a transcendental power.

The allegorical signification attributed by Sittah to Nathan's "riches" is complicated when she reminds her brother Saladin that it is in fact the merchant who holds the keys to God's temple:

Sittah: Auch
Ist seines Reichtums Quelle weit ergiebiger,
Weit unerschöpflicher, als so ein Grab
Voll Mammon.

Saladin: Denn er handelt, wie ich höre.
[Sittah: Also

His source of riches is far more abundant,
Far more inexhaustible than such a tomb filled with Mammon.
Saladin: Because he trades, as I've heard.][42]

The verb *handeln* means not only to trade but also to act. Trading is precisely one step from God in this line of thought because it is the realization of productive action. Jane Brown links the figure of the merchant in allegorical drama to Christ, citing Calderón's *The Merchant's Ship* (1674) as a prime example of this allegory. In Calderón's play, the merchant represents a new cosmopolitan class, and he brings back golden grain from the New World that will, as Brown notes, be made into the Host.[43] Similarly, Nathan is linked to Good and God through his magical access to a bottomless well of riches that can be used to create good in the world. Yet the allegorical elements of the play also require a metonymic mode of interpretation, as Nathan is made ethically good not only by his allegorical linkage to goods but by his possession of and proximity to them.

UNLIMITED GROWTH: WEALTH, KINSHIP, AND METONYMY

The exponential growth of riches in the play reflects a utopian, protocapitalist logic. As Lehrer writes, "When money steps onto the stage, it does so exclusively as the positive life- and love-saving hero."[44] Nathan is, of course, a "Kaufmann" [merchant] embodying the values of the free-market economy espoused by Adam Smith in *The Wealth of Nations* (1776), who famously argued that an "invisible hand" regulates the economy in a manner that should create a win-win situation for all involved. Eighteenth-century thinkers did not consider self-interest and charity to be at odds.[45] Rather, they generally viewed the free market as a mode of communication between equals, a back-and-forth in which self-interest and sympathy could complement one another. The merchant was a "Bürger par excellence."[46] As Max Weber observed, after the Reformation, *Beruf* [profession] came to serve as a marker for future salvation.[47] Willi Goetschel points to the productive nature of *Handel* [trade] in the context of Lessing's play; indeed, Goetschel sees the role of the merchant as that of the mediator, one who produces relations.[48] As Daniel Fulda argues, the "maxims of trade" of the eighteenth-century tradesman can be likened to general "rules of life" of the time.[49] And as Jörg Schönert points out, the exchange of goods and money in the eighteenth century was imagined as a pragmatic manifestation of the ideals of equality in liberalism, a reciprocal mode of valuation.[50] *Wirtschaftsbürgerlich* [economically bourgeois] meant *bildungsbürgerlich* [intellectually bourgeois], an idealized mode of win-win exchange.[51]

Saladin hesitates initially to speak the word *Geld*. When Sittah asks, "Was klemmt? Was fehlt?" [What's wrong? What's missing?], Saladin responds, "Was sonst, als was ich kaum zu nennen würd'ge? Was, wenn ich's habe, mir so überflüssig, Und hab ich's nicht, so unentbehrlich scheint . . . —Das leidige, verwünschte Geld!" [What else but what I hardly think worth naming? The thing that, when I have it, seems so superfluous. And when I don't have it, it seems so indispensable . . . —The exasperating, accursed money!][52] But once the word comes out of his mouth, Saladin repeats it again and again, like a mantra: "Und soll das alles, ah, wozu? Wozu?—Um Geld zu fischen! Geld!—Um Geld, Geld einem Juden abzubangen? Geld!" [And I should do all of this, ah, what for? What for?—To fish for money! Money!—To scare up money, money from a Jew? Money!][53] The word, once spoken, multiplies exponentially. If in Lessing's play *Handel* is the practice of collection and accumulation of money and goods that mirrors social ethics, then money need not be hidden. As allegory, it is visible throughout *Nathan der Weise*, and as prop/property it creates relations metonymically.

Elaine Freedgood highlights the contingent character of metonymy, describing it as "the figure of arrested development, 'thick description,' the readable, the readerly." She notes (in a formulation that recalls reactions to the final *tableau* in *Nathan der Weise*) that metonymy "embarrasses interpretation because of its apparent contingency, its seeming inability to provide a unitary or singular meaning, or a kind of critical 'truth' (or the appearance thereof). It is the nightmarish opposite of the interpretive dead end: an interpretive open end of dizzying potential."[54] Whereas metaphor has been traditionally seen as indicating a "necessary link" between sign and signified, metonymy is contingent, open, and subject to proximities.[55]

Freedgood observes that metonymy and allegory are frequently at odds with one another. Indeed, Angus Fletcher submits that allegory requires a *kosmos*, a world to which it refers.[56] But Lessing's drama, poised at a transitional moment in Enlightenment semiotics, joins together these two modes of signification. His play represents a cosmos through its allegorical representation of Nathan's money and goods as well as of the Jewish Nathan as Christ figure and merchant. But the world of the play is also a radically contingent one: Nathan's paternal identity is based on an arbitrary relationship through adoption, and the other relationships and identities in the drama are likewise contingent and fragmented.

What are the contingencies suggested by the scenes in which goods and money arrive in *Nathan der Weise?* If we read these scenes both allegorically, as making the insubstantial visible, and metonymically, in terms of proximity and relation, we see fascinating connections between money and familial ties. The arrival of Nathan's gifts at Saladin's palace in Act 4 ("Das Ding hat kein Ende!" [The thing has no end!]) is followed immediately by the revelation that the Templar is the nephew of Saladin and Sittah, the son of their long-lost brother. In response to this revelation, Saladin exclaims, "Zuviel Gewinn für einen Tag! Zuviel!" [Too much profit for one day! Too much!][57] The material of the arriving goods is literally embedded in this sentence. The excess inherent in the surplus goods is metonymically linked to the familial excess in the form of an extra nephew and the return, via memory, of a lost brother. Similarly, the arriving caravans filled with goods invest the rapidly extending family with a material value that rebuts the abstract non-truth of the minted coin.

The relationships between characters in the play are conceived in terms of a debt that does not cheapen them but imbues them with greater substance. Therefore, while Nathan was busy collecting debts before the opening of the play, the Templar was receiving the gift of life from Saladin, a gift that allowed him to save Recha's life from a fire and thereby created a relationship of debt between him and Nathan. The materiality and value of the body itself is experienced viscerally via the discourses of debt and gifts:

TEMPELHERR: Das Leben, das ich leb, ist sein [Saladin's] Geschenk.
NATHAN: Durch das es mir ein doppelt, dreifach Leben schenkte.
Dies hat alles zwischen uns verändert; hat mit eins ein Seil mir umgeworfen, das mich seinem Dienst auf ewig fesselt.

[TEMPLAR: The life I live is his [Saladin's] gift.
NATHAN: From which he has doubly, triply given me life. This has changed everything between us; it has in one fell swoop thrown a rope around me that will forever bind me in his service.][58]

The relationship of debt between individuals, established thanks to the gift of the body and of life, is represented here as something that creates an intimate linkage to the other and thereby nurtures an ethics of sociality.

In this sense, the discourse of ownership surrounding Recha takes on a unique ethical tone, complicating a straightforward reading of the daughter as an objectified possession of the father. In the first scene, as Nathan arrives home to be met by news of the fire, he becomes frantically concerned about Recha's safety, engaging in a discourse of ownership that reflects not the distance often associated with the relationship to possessions but instead an intimacy, a relationship of love:

> NATHAN: O Recha! Meine Recha!
> DAJA: Eure? Eure Recha?
> NATHAN: Wenn ich mich wieder je entwöhnen müßte, dies Kind
>   mein Kind zu nennen!
> DAJA: Nennt Ihr alles, was Ihr besitzt, mit ebensoviel Rechte das
>   Eure?
> NATHAN: Nichts mit größerm! Alles, was ich sonst besitze, hat
>   Natur und Glück mir zugeteilt. Dies Eigentum allein dank
>   ich der Tugend.

> [NATHAN: Oh Recha! My Recha!
> DAJA: Yours? Your Recha?
> NATHAN: If I ever had to get used to not calling this child my
>   child!
> DAJA: Do you call everything you possess *yours* with equal
>   justification?
> NATHAN: Nothing with greater justification! Everything else I pos-
>   sess, Nature and Fortune have given me. For this possession
>   alone I have Virtue to thank.][59]

All of Nathan's possessions are perceived by him as a gift from God, and an appreciation of the materiality of his adoptive daughter only heightens the love he feels for her. Here, possessions are simultaneously intimate extensions of the self and gifts to be cherished and shared. Nathan emphasizes that he received Recha as a reward for his virtue, making her a particularly valuable possession.

The repetitive exclamations of ownership between Nathan and Recha at the end of the play imbue the notion of possession of another body with a particular weight, since it is not blood but love of the possession that creates intimacy between the two:

> NATHAN: "Was fehlt dir?—bist doch meine Tochter noch?
> RECHA: Mein Vater! . . .

NATHAN: Wir verstehen uns. Genug!—Sei heiter! Sei gefaßt!
Wenn sonst dein Herz nur dein noch ist! Wenn deinem Herzen
sonst nur kein Verlust nicht droht!—Dein Vater ist Dir
unverloren!

[NATHAN: What's the matter? Aren't you still my daughter?
RECHA: My father! . . .
NATHAN: We understand each other. Enough!—Be happy! Be
calm! As long as your heart is still yours! As long as no other
loss does not threaten your heart!—You haven't lost your
father!][60]

Recha's heart belongs to Nathan as long as it also belongs to her. The
double negative ("As long as no other loss does not threaten your heart!")
complicates a reading of the love between father and daughter as exclusive,
particularly because Saladin quickly steps in as a second father to Recha.
One heart can belong simultaneously to the self, to one's adoptive father,
and to another adoptive father—who is also one's uncle—and in each case
not be threatened by "Verlust" [loss]. There is no theory of compensation
at work in this affective logic; although Nathan lost his original family, gain
is not imagined here as necessitating a future loss.

In contrast to the notion that biological relations are meant to cement
the bourgeois family as the ideal model for a German state, Nathan and
Recha negotiate their relationship in terms of consent. Their relationship is
reminiscent of Hobbes's early Enlightenment discussion of the parent-child
relationship in *De Cive* (1642), in which he writes that "the right of dominion by generation . . . is not so derived from the generation, as if therefore
the parent had dominion over his child because he begat him, but from the
child's consent, either express or by other, sufficient arguments declared."[61]
As Silke-Maria Weineck writes, "What is generated here, then, is not a child
but a particular relationship *to* the child."[62] Dominion is not determined by
biological reproduction, for as Hobbes points out, both a mother and father
are necessary for reproduction and there can only be one ruler. The dialogue
between Nathan and Recha in which he asks for her consent to be in his
dominion reveals that the most intimate relationship in the play is one of consent and not of natural ties.

A similarly arbitrary picture of generation and succession is painted in
the ring parable recounted by Nathan in Act 3, in which an opal ring serves
as the material signifier of God's favor:

"Vor grauen Jahren lebt' ein Mann im Osten, der einen Ring von unschätzbarem Wert aus lieber Hand besaß. Der Stein war ein Opal, der hundert schöne Farben spielte, Und hatte die geheime Kraft, vor Gott und Menschen angenehm zu machen, wer in dieser Zuversicht ihn trug."

[Many years ago in the east there lived a man who owned a ring of inestimable worth, which someone dear to him had given him. The stone was an opal that sparkled with a hundred beautiful colors and had the mysterious power of making whoever wore it agreeable to God and human beings, as long as the wearer believed in its power.][63]

The origin of the ring is unknowable, but it was given with love ("aus lieber Hand") and gains its value (which cannot be quantified) from this love. An opal is an opaque jewel, a material that diffracts light, and is therefore oddly unsuited to be the symbol of absolute truth. And the materiality of this jewel leaks into the narrative, as the ring is passed from father to favorite son, from generation to generation. Again, eventually one of the fathers is unable to choose between his three sons and therefore orders that two identical rings be made, telling all three sons that they possess the true familial ring. Here, Nathan/Lessing teaches us to read metonymically. The ring as metaphor (the signifier of God's favor) gives way to the ring as metonymy, an object associated with the love of the father not as a "necessary link" but instead via the familial history that associates the gift of an opal ring with love and favor. Nathan advocates here for religious tolerance, and this tolerance is predicated upon the diffusion of power, on a deconstruction of what Nathan calls the "Tyrannei des einen Rings" [tyranny of the one ring].[64] The message of tolerance is heightened and increased quantitatively through the multiplication of the rings: all three of them are imbued with the value of the "liebe Hand" [dear hand] that bequeaths them to the sons. Lessing's drama teaches us that materiality is about the relationship to the thing, not the thing itself. In this sense, each ring is a gift from the father and represents a debt to him. And yet excess (the gift) and lack (debt) do not cancel each other out. Both indicate a direct and meaningful relationship, and both enhance the value of the ring, an object that is constructed by a craftsman in a manner similar to the father's creation of his ideal family.

The motto by Gellius at the beginning of *Nathan der Weise* points to the plurality of gods: "Introite, nam et heic Dii sunt!" [Enter, for here, too, are gods!][65] The play is usually interpreted as a representation of the reconciliation of the three monotheistic religions (Christianity, Islam, and Judaism) via familial ties, but the multiplicity of gods to which the motto refers throws a wrench in such an interpretation. Who, then, are these many gods in the play? Whereas the ring parable ostensibly centers on the number three, the play actually presents us with fours: four fathers, four religions, and four rings. In the parable, the judge tells the three sons who are fighting over their inheritance, "Der echte Ring vermutlich ging verloren. Den Verlust zu Bergen, zu ersetzen, ließ der Vater die drei für einen machen." [The real ring must have been lost. To hide the loss, to replace it, the father had three made for one.][66] If the original ring is lost, then there are actually four rings, or perhaps a multitude of rings, as rings are easily lost. The three fathers of the play—Nathan, Saladin, and the Christian Patriarch—are joined by at least one additional father, who is generally left out of the equation: Saladin's father. In fact, we learn that Saladin is actually only in charge of the smaller treasure that is in Jerusalem and that the larger treasure is kept with Saladin and Sittah's father in Lebanon (Al-Hafi: "denn des größern waltet sein Vater noch—" [for his father still manages the larger one—]).[67] The money Saladin is waiting for is being sent by the father, and in this sense the great leader of Jerusalem is both son and father figure. And it is Nathan's friend Al-Hafi, the elusive dervish and erstwhile beggar who serves for a short period as Saladin's treasurer, who tells Nathan about the financial power of Saladin's father; Al-Hafi's religious identity is neither Christian, Jewish, nor Muslim, thereby reminding us that the four rings and four fathers are also joined by four religions. Scholars have argued about Al-Hafi's religious identity, connecting him variously to Hinduism, Zoroastrianism (a religion both monotheistic and pantheistic), Buddhism, and Sufism (a mystical current within Islam).[68] Al-Hafi longs throughout the first half of the drama to escape the stress of financial dealings and return to the Ganges. He bids farewell to Nathan in the last scene of Act 2, having decided to depart from Jerusalem forever, and he invites Nathan to go with him. Hence, the origin of the ring (the "Orient") is marked as the place of return and thereby further opens up the presumed constellation of threes to a more polyvalent reading.

THE ECONOMIES OF KINSHIP

The focus on material wealth in the play tells us a great deal about the true foundation of kinship in the work. Family is not based on "blood" in *Nathan der Weise*. In the prehistory of the ring parable, each father gives the ring to one son "ohne Ansicht der Geburt" [without reference to birth]. This formulation refutes the inheritance law that states that the oldest son should receive the greatest inheritance, but it also suggests that circumstances of birth are irrelevant to the father's choice of favored son. The latter interpretation opens up the possibility that the father might choose as his favorite a bastard son, a nephew, a daughter, or an adoptive son over a biological one. Saladin states this in the final act: "Das Blut, das Blut allein macht lange noch den Vater nicht!" [Truly blood, blood alone does not the father make!][69] We might instead conclude that it is capital and material goods that make the father and, indeed, the family. The history of the family is a history of wealth, property, and economic alliances, of debts and gifts, and Lessing's drama revives this history metonymically. Hence, Nathan's suitability for fatherhood is not based on blood bonds, precisely because blood was never the true foundation of the family. In this sense, Lessing's play complicates the relationship between the eighteenth-century family and capital imagined by the Frankfurt School theorists. Whereas Habermas argues that the family is propped up by capital, the domestic sphere nevertheless serves as a refuge from the vicissitudes of capital. In contrast, in *Nathan der Weise*, public, private, and intimate spheres are flattened in light of a parallel semiotics of material wealth (props/property) and kin groupings.

A logic of addition, rather than balance, underlies the economic and libidinal economies in the play. Indeed, the economy of "both/and" in *Nathan* invites a rethinking of both familial and economic models. A utopian notion of early capitalism is at play. Kierkegaard's renunciative Protestantism (*Either/Or*),[70] taken up by Weber, does not define the moral universe of these works; instead, we must look to an additive notion of self and community that complicates a modern paradigm of compensation and equilibrium. In *Nathan der Weise*, profit yields profit while producing very little deficit.

SURPLUS AND THE VISIBILITY OF EXPLOITATION

If surplus is the name of the game in Lessing's play, then we are in a very different world from the one to which Marx refers in his *Kapital*. In his discussion of commodity fetishism, Marx is critical of the equivalence that economist Samuel Bailey makes between "riches" as "the attribute of men" and use value.[71] Marx, in contrast, sees "riches" as a surplus produced through the capitalist extension of the duration of labor. There is no wealth without exploitation, a point Wendy Sutherland makes via an analysis of props in *Die Mätresse* [The Mistress] (1780), a play by Lessing's brother Karl Gotthelf Lessing. The drama tells the story of Otto von Kronfeld, who has returned to Prussia after a long stay in America during which he married a Black woman. The woman died in childbirth, along with the child, mirroring Gotthold Ephraim Lessing's tragic loss of his own wife Eva and his son in childbirth. Sutherland focuses on the racial semiotics in *Die Mätresse* as they play out in a *tableau* at the dining table while stage props in the form of tea, coffee, chocolate, and tobacco are brought to the family by servants. As Sutherland writes, "The invisibility of colonialism and slavery 'at home' in Europe is therefore made visible through the stage properties of the global trade, and like that which is hidden but in full view, they are visible but not seen."[72]

In *Nathan der Weise* the early structures of colonialism are likewise made visible via the enslaved servants who carry riches across the stage. In this sense, Lessing's play brings to the surface the normally repressed source of riches enjoyed by the characters. We can contrast the representation of colonial exploitation in Lessing's play to that of its source drama, Diderot's *The Natural Son*, which not only represses the colonial source of the family's wealth but also embeds this repression within the "walled-off" family circle within the domestic home. When Clairville is in need of money in *The Natural Son*, he decides to go into business: "There are many ways to gain wealth quickly; but business is almost the only way where the gains are in proportion to the effort and the risks you take."[73] When the father Lysimond returns from his business travels after having been captured by British sailors, he brings with him great wealth from his colonial enterprises: "I leave you a great fortune. Enjoy it in the same way I earned it. My wealth never affected my integrity. You can now own it without remorse."[74] Lysimond claims (without any prompting from skeptics) that the wealth produced in a capitalist society through global trade represents the honest efforts of the businessman. Exploitation and alienation are terms anathema to capitalism in *The Natural Son*, but Lysimond's anxious reassurances reveal a repressed nervousness about ill-begotten wealth.

The importance of wealth is repeatedly made clear in Diderot's play, although its source is repressed. The virtuous Dorval insists, "a family demands wealth."[75] Indeed, Diderot's plays as well as German bourgeois dramas reflect this truth again and again. Virtue and wealth must not merely coexist but should mutually enrich one another. Caroline Weber shows how the colonial source of the family's wealth constitutes a fully repressed motif in *The Natural Son*. Whereas the threat of incest—the traditional "secret" within the bourgeois family—is clearly revealed and resolved within the play, this secret serves as a foil for the dirtier secret of colonialism that taints

Dorval's and the family's wealth.[76] It is clear that colonial exploitation likewise lies at the heart of the goods delivered to Saladin in *Nathan der Weise*, as these are carried onto the stage by actors playing enslaved people. But what about Nathan's wealth? Andrea Schatz argues that Lessing's play "turns the colonial fantasy of a 'single family' against itself." She notes that no single family in the story is reunified, contrary to the case in *The Natural Son*. Instead, the final *tableau* in Lessing's drama reveals "the impossibility and undesirability of perfect integration."[77] Indeed, while Lessing's play does not resolve the colonial issues that confront us when reading it and other plays from the period, it nevertheless points to a more humanist, relational model for economic encounters than we see in Diderot's plays.

A case in point is the topic of inheritance that connects biology and wealth. When the Commander in Diderot's *Father of the Family* offers to bequeath his wealth to Cäcilia, his niece by marriage, she resists, making the argument that blood relatives have a natural right to the money: the "inheritance should rightfully go to those for whom it was destined by the laws of nature and society."[78] Some decades before the publication of Hegel's *Elements of the Philosophy of Right*, Cäcilia has internalized the belief that natural law and social law must unite in questions of inheritance. As Hegel argues, inheritance must always go to the biological relations, for otherwise arbitrariness will rule the question of inheritance.[79] It is the family that stands as a harbinger against the arbitrary, just as the *tableau* temporarily fends off the threat of the fragmentary. In *Nathan der Weise* we are confronted, in contrast, with a final *tableau* predicated on adoption and assumption.

Szondi highlights the economic prosperity that adheres to the *tableau*. Where the *coup de théâtre* is associated with theatricality and chance, the *tableau* is imagined as rational and predictable. Along these lines, the capitalist model appropriate to the *tableau* is precisely an early one in which the bourgeois nuclear family represents a humanist capitalism reflecting good intentions on all sides.[80] In the world of early bourgeois tragedies, capitalism is still perceived as ethical and "direkt als gottgewollt" [directly ordained by God]. There is no issue with the rational accrual of wealth, only with the irrational use of possessions.[81]

LESSING'S POLYVALENT *SCHLUβTABLEAU*

The benevolent notion of protocapitalism on display in *Nathan der Weise* does not rest on the biological family the way it does in Diderot's *The Natural Son*. The celebration of surplus traverses material and human bonds but not genetic ones. In response to Recha's fear that she will lose Nathan if fatherhood is defined simply by blood, Saladin responds expansively:

"Sobald der Väter zwei
Sich um dich streiten:—Laß sie beide; nimm
Den dritten!—Nimm dann mich zu deinem Vater!"

[As soon as two fathers
Start to fight over you:—leave both of them;
Take the third!—Then take me as your father!][82]

The surplus of goods arriving at Saladin's palace from Nathan's house and from Egypt shapes the family structure within the play. Meaning is not derived vertically and hierarchically; rather, it is given weight through expansion and contagion. The increased number of fathers does not lessen the value of the first father but instead creates an excess of value, along the lines of the surplus money arriving at the palace.

By the end of the play, relations between the figures resist strict hierarchies and even transcend generational boundaries. Sittah tells Recha: "Nenn mich Sitta, deine Freundin—deine Schwester. Nenn mich dein Mütterchen!" [Call me Sittah, your friend—your sister. Call me Little Mother!][83] Not only is a traditionally patriarchal nuclear family nowhere in sight; figures such as Sittah are able to take on at times contradictory familial roles. More money signifies more value, and more value creates a better kin grouping. The economic and kin model here is open-ended and not contained, inviting, perhaps surprisingly, a democratic ethics in which figures can play multiple roles and where patriarchal power is diffused. Even Assad, the brother of Saladin and Sittah, played numerous roles in his life, Muslim and Christian, to the point of taking the name of his German wife (von Filneck) in one of his incarnations.

The ethics of horizontal expansion and multiplication are seemingly at odds with an Enlightenment notion of virtue, but Lessing's utopian *Nathan* has as much to tell us about the practice of virtue as those works that locate resignation and renunciation as the keys to virtue. The only character who briefly experiences the pang of resignation is the Templar upon learning that Recha can never be his wife because she is his sister. Yet he is soon convinced that the logic of material excess applies to him as well as to the others: "Ihr gebt mir mehr, als Ihr mir nehmt! Unendlich mehr!" [You've given me more than you've taken from me! Infinitely more!][84] The value of the newly created extended kin group exceeds that of the monogamous bond the Templar had hoped to form with Recha. The material is the thing, and more is better. Loss, like debt, is also conceived in terms of gain. In the final *tableau*, in which the figures hug one another repeatedly, the stage directions stress the excess displayed in their intimacy: *"Unter stummer Wiederholung allseitiger Umarmungen fällt der Vorhang."* [*The curtain falls while all present onstage repeatedly embrace in silence*.][85] The hugging is intensified here both quantitatively ("Wiederholung") and in terms of quality ("allseitiger"), and the excessive emotions are conveyed through a lack of words.

The final *tableau* of the play collects the major figures in a performance that combines traditionally allegorical and modern (mimetic and bourgeois) modes of representation. In its slow movements, the *tableau* is, once again, reminiscent of the allegorical roots of bourgeois theater—the pageantry, mumming, and spectacle that were subordinated, at least in theory, to the focus on the individual actor in the eighteenth century.[86] Yet the pageantry in this scene is rendered chaotic by the material crowding induced by the incessant appearance of goods on the stage. In turn, this material surplus is mirrored in the characters' frequent and excessive verbal repetitions of kin markers. The word "Bruder" [brother] is repeated sixteen times in the final act, joined by repeated exclamations of the words "Schwester" [sister] and "Vater" [father]. Although the characters have names, the signifiers indicating their relational roles are given more weight than their individual names. The revelation that the Templar is Recha's brother is spoken in declamations; "Bruder" is repeated in the same manner as "Geld" was earlier in the play, like a mantra:

> TEMPELHERR: Nicht mehr! Ich bitt
> Euch!—Aber Rechas Bruder? Rechas Bruder . . .
> NATHAN: Seid Ihr!
> TEMPELHERR: Ich? Ich ihr Bruder?
> RECHA: Er mein Bruder?
> SITTAH: Geschwister!
> SALADIN: Sie Geschwister!
> RECHA *will auf ihn ʒu*: Ah! Mein Bruder!
> TEMPELHERR *tritt ʒurück*: Ihr Bruder!

> [TEMPLAR: Enough! I beg you!
> What about Recha's brother? Recha's brother . . .
> NATHAN: You're her brother!

TEMPLAR: I? I'm her brother?
RECHA: He's my brother?
SITTAH: Siblings!
SALADIN: They're siblings!
RECHA, *wanting to approach him*: Oh! My brother!
TEMPLAR, *stepping back*: Her brother!][87]

The scene is a remarkable performance of the production of family based on a meeting of two semiotic systems—one based on belief and one on arbitrary signifiers.[88] In fact, there is no hard proof that Recha and the Templar are siblings; the assumption is based on Saladin's insistence that the Templar physically resembles his brother Assad, whom he hasn't seen in twenty years and whose handwriting he believes he recognizes in the family book.

It is thus surprising when, in a seeming nod to a bourgeois aesthetics of interiority, we are presented with a final *tableau* (Act 5, scene 6) that takes place in Sittah's harem, where Sittah and Recha are communicating about the latter's new identity crisis. The harem is a "forbidden and sacred space" that excludes unrelated men or outsiders.[89] In terms of dramatic space, the harem serves in the eighteenth-century European imaginary as the interior of the interior. Whereas earlier scenes in Lessing's play had taken place within the transitional spaces of a hallway or sitting room in Nathan's house or in Saladin's palace, the portrayal of the harem is the equivalent of taking the spectator into the very core of the intimate sphere. In his analysis of bourgeois architecture, Habermas sees the interior space of the home as the refuge for the bourgeois nuclear family. Since the harem serves as the exoticized mirror image of this bourgeois interior space, it is therefore all the more surprising when, in scene 7, Saladin barges in to talk to both women, and Nathan and the Templar join them in the final scene of the play (scene 8). What can be seen as a performative pageant of political symbolism takes place in a sphere that connotes both bourgeois intimacy and the kind of exotic polymorphic sexuality that the eighteenth-century European imagination associated with the harem.[90] This scene thus presents a bizarre juxtaposition of interiority (the exoticized harem/bourgeois domestic sphere) with courtly pomp and political and economic exchange (formal relations and negotiation between men). It displays that which is normally hidden for all to see. It should not be surprising, then, that the incest taboo, in the form of love between the siblings, rears its head in this scene. The notion of an interior subject that contains a hidden secret (one that is therefore true and connected to sex) collides here with an older model of representation that foregrounds visuality and materiality.

In the end, the incest taboo does not delimit but instead opens up possibilities. The specter of polygamy that adheres to the harem provides the expansive affective structure for the play, although no one marries and consummation is foreclosed. Reproduction is replaced by what Helmut Schneider calls a "future-oriented education"—it gives way to production as surplus.[91] The utopian community created at the end of the play is seemingly capable at any moment of spontaneously spawning new members. In this sense, Nathan is often viewed as the adoptive father of a utopian "nation." In light of my materialist reading of the play, this nation can be seen as embodying cosmopolitanism in its most basic form—as *Handel* [trade] that knows no lack. Zedler's *Large Complete Universal-Lexicon* of 1737 includes the following entry on *Handel*: "Kauffmannschaft oder Kauff-Handel: Ihrer Beschaffenheit nach ist sie [die Kauffmannschaft] die unerschöpfliche Quelle des Reichthums eines Staates" [Merchant class or purchase trade: in its constitution, the merchant class is the inexhaustible source of the wealth of a state].[92] This entry uncannily echoes the source of the "unermesslichen Reichtum" [immeasurable riches] to which Nathan has access. In *Antigone's Claim*, Judith Butler reminds us that kinship both produces and is predicated on the state.[93] In Lessing's play, it is not the nuclear bourgeois family with its limiting vertical structure of power that stands as a microcosm of the successful nation; instead, the extended kin grouping, as presented in the horizontal relations of consent and elective affinity in the final *tableau*, provides the affective material for a seemingly inexhaustible source of riches.[94]

Another way of thinking about the play would be to say that money makes the queer family possible. As Butler points out, if kinship produces the state, which in turn produces kinship, then there is no "natural" or organic reason why this state should be modeled on a biological nuclear family. In Nathan's ideal polis a queer family produces and is produced by the utopian state. However, this family would not be possible had Nathan been a poor man. In such a case, Saladin and Sittah would not have summoned him, and the web of connections would not have been discovered or, as it were, created. To the extent that the play utilizes an older, allegorical mode of representation, the slippage that allegory always inevitably produces is likewise productive in a queer sense. As Alice Kuzniar puts it, "allegorical narratives tell the truth about the failure to read" and hence offer a queer mode of semiotics: "Through its privileging of visibility allegory pretends to open, direct statement, while actually it calls attention to the breach between sign and referent."[95] Kuzniar writes that allegory is "extravagant, an expenditure of surplus value; it is always *in excess.*"[96] Along these lines, the excessive crowding within the space of the harem at the end of Lessing's play offers up a queer image that belies "reproductive futurism."[97]

And what future does the play offer us? A future that is not based on the past? Nathan has moved beyond the trauma of losing his original family and created a complex new constellation of kin members. Recha expresses her distaste for the past when she describes to Sittah the moment when Daja revealed her Christian origins to her at the site of a ruined Christian temple. She sees

> Mit Graus die wankenden Ruinen durch.
> Nun steht sie wieder; und ich sehe mich
> An den versunknen Stufen eines morschen
> Altars mit ihr. Wie ward mir?

> [With dread through tattering ruins.
> Now she stands again; and I find myself
> On the sunken steps of a molding
> Altar with her. How did I feel?][98]

Recha does not experience the ruins as the Romantics would, as a fragment of a more perfect past. Instead, this stolidly Enlightened girl chooses a productive future over a moldy past.[99]

Indeed, Lessing's *Erziehung des Menschengeschlechts* [Education of the Human Race], written the year after *Nathan der Weise* (in 1780), reflects a similar notion of futurity that neither idealizes the past nor fixates on biological generation and inheritance. In this treatise, Lessing famously tells the story of the Enlightenment of mankind. God first chooses the Jews as his pupils, and they, in turn, are the teachers of the Christians, leading to a world in which humankind comes perilously close to doing away with God altogether. In the same work Lessing writes of the impatience on the part of humans who want to develop at a speed that far outpaces the temporality of a human life:

> 90: Der Schwärmer tut oft sehr richtige Blicke in die Zukunft, aber er kann diese Zukunft nur nicht erwarten. Er wünscht diese Zukunft beschleuniget; und wünscht, daß sie durch ihn beschleuniget werde. Wozu sich die Natur Jahrtausende Zeit nimmt, soll

in dem Augenblicke seines Daseins reifen. Denn was hat er davon, wenn das, was er für das Bessere erkennt, nicht noch bei seinen Lebzeiten das Bessere wird? Kömmt er wieder? Glaubt er wiederzukommen?

[90: The enthusiast often casts true glances into the future, but for this future he cannot wait. He wishes this future accelerated, and accelerated through him. That for which nature takes thousands of years is to mature in the moment of his existence. For what is it to him if what he recognizes as that which is better does not become the better in his lifetime? Does he come back? Does he believe he will come back?][100]

Nature, Lessing writes, is too slow to provide development at the speed humans desire. Indeed, the desired experience of time would be so accelerated as to bypass biological hindrances.

But Lessing does not rule out the idea of nonlinear experience for humans; indeed, his notion of generation is decidedly queer by the end of *Die Erziehung des Menschengeschlechts*. The desire for an accelerated life of learning in which one would overtake one's own history points to the possibility of reincarnation, a possibility that Lessing celebrates in the last few paragraphs of the essay:

93: Eben die Bahn, auf welcher das Geschlecht zu seiner Vollkommenheit galangt, muß jeder einzelne Mensch (der früher, der später) erst durchlaufen haben.—"In einem und eben demselben Leben durchlaufen haben? Kann er in eben demselben Leben ein sinnlicher Jude und ein geistiger Christ gewesen sein? Kann er in eben demselben Leben beide überholet haben?"
94: Das wohl nun nicht!—Aber warum könnte jeder einzelne Mensch auch nicht mehr als einmal auf dieser Welt vorhanden gewesen sein?

[93: The very same path by which the race reaches its perfection, every individual human (one sooner, another later) must have traveled before.—"Have traveled in one and the same life? Can he have been, in one and the self-same life, a sensual Jew and a spiritual Christian? Can he in the self-same life have overtaken both?"][101]

94: Surely not that!—But why could not every individual human
have existed more than once in this world?]¹⁰²

What is reincarnation? It is a return that is not a repetition. Reincarnation
makes reproduction unnecessary. Perhaps the mature Lessing, having himself been a father for less than a day, wanted his readers/spectators to imagine a future quite different from the one prescribed by the path of biological
reproduction and perceived necessity. "Es ist nicht wahr," he writes, "daß
die kürzeste Linie immer die gerade ist." [It is not true that the shortest line
is always the straight one.]¹⁰³

An additional alternative future is escape, and the play also offers us this
possibility. After Al-Hafi leaves Jerusalem, he never again appears on the
stage, but he is sorely missed. Throughout the second half of the play Saladin continually asks, "Wo bleibt Al-Hafi?" [Where is Al-Hafi?]. Has he
gone, or has he returned and is staying (*bleiben*)? In any case, Al-Hafi represents a remainder in the play that cannot easily be accounted for, and when
he invites Nathan to join him at the Ganges, Nathan is clearly keenly
tempted:¹⁰⁴

> Al-Hafi: Kommt! Kommt!
> Nathan: Ich dächte zwar, das blieb uns ja
> Noch immer übrig. Doch, Al-Hafi, will
> Ich's überlegen. Warte . . .
>
> [Al-Hafi: Come! Come!
> Nathan: I would think we could always still do that.
> But, Al-Hafi, I'll think it over. Wait . . .]¹⁰⁵

In accord with the fathers in Lessing's other dramas, Nathan imagines
escape from the scene of responsibility.¹⁰⁶ The play presents us with two
possible futures for the German state: one a form of reincarnation without
reproduction and the other a state without a patriarch. In some stagings of
the play, Nathan stands to the side during the group hug of the drama's
final *tableau*, as if he were going to sneak out a side door. The possibilities
for a future nation/family model offered by the play are, in this sense,
multiple.

❦

CHAPTER SIX

The *Tableau* of Relations

Novels in Stillness and Motion

IN HIS *Salon* of 1765, Denis Diderot praises his favorite artist, Jean-Baptiste Greuze, for his ability to paint *tableaux* that he likens to the building blocks of novels: "Here we have your painter and mine; the first who has set out to give art some morals, and to organize events into series that could easily be turned into novels."[1] Greuze's paintings, according to Diderot, not only model the *tableaux* that structure the idealized domestic scenes of Diderot's new bourgeois drama, they likewise correspond in form to the novel. We are confronted here with a porousness of genre and media that, yet again, complicates the polemical position Lessing takes on media-specific semiotics in the *Laocoön*. Indeed, it is especially in the second half of the eighteenth century, when the domestic drama and the modern novel are just beginning to emerge as dominant genres in Europe, that intermedial cross-pollination and genre borrowing are rampant. Diderot reminds us that the *tableau* holds a central place not only in the bourgeois drama but also in the new literary form of the novel.

Meant to offer a freeze-frame of domesticity (*Häuslichkeit*), of life behind the fourth wall, the *tableau* is predicated on the sense of sight; it offers a visual composition, a grouping of individuals linked to one another. For Diderot, of course, this grouping constitutes a nuclear family, but we have seen how expansive the social groupings in bourgeois German dramatic *tableaux* are. How is it, then, that the *tableau* becomes a formal feature of the emerging modern German novel? How does the freeze-frame composition function within a genre that utilizes only what Lessing would call "arbitrary signs" and is meant to be read?

C. F. Gellert, the first German sentimental novelist, writes that a successful narrative is predicated on its presentation of visual *tableaux*. In his *Briefsteller* he maintains that the letter, the experimental locus for the modern novel,[2] should tell a story in such a manner that creates pictures, or what he calls "*die kleinen Gemälde*" [small paintings] "which one constructs while telling the story of the conditions or people, especially when one sometimes allows them to speak themselves, thereby making us familiar with their character."[3] Gellert likewise highlights the importance of sight for successful storytelling, proposing that letters should be narrated in such a way "that one doesn't only understand the thing, but that one believes one has *seen* it oneself and is a *witness* to it; that is called lively storytelling."[4] Epistolary narrative not only calls for an outside reader; the "small painting" it mentally creates positions that reader as a "witness." I have shown in earlier chapters how the *tableau* is predicated on an "invisible observer" who is "cited" through the symmetry of the "tableau-like static compositions."[5] Of importance here is the way in which the visual scene is organized "around an internal frame"[6] that mirrors Diderot's fourth wall.

The *tableau*, as we see, is not only a flexible form producing representations of groupings of kinship and community in eighteenth-century German bourgeois drama; it is likewise an important intermedial trope cueing sociality in the German novel of the period.[7] Manuel Frey argues that the *tableau* and the *tableau vivant* appear in popular literature around 1800 precisely because social structures could be modeled via these descriptions of groupings.[8] In this sense, we can think about literary *tableaux* as a form of what Anna Kornbluh calls "social modeling."[9] Kornbluh points to Marx and Engels's materialist method articulated in *Die deutsche Ideologie* [The German Ideology] (1846) as a way of thinking about social collectives: "Thus the first fact of the case to be established is the physical organization of these individuals and their consequent relation to the rest of nature."[10] Organization is key—in other words, the ways in which individuals form groups create imaginative realities. German literary *tableaux* picture these groupings during a period in which an imaginative sociality was needed for the creation of a national future, and we see again and again that the forms this sociality takes are far more expansive than the nuclear *tableau* associated with bourgeois domesticity.

Via the lens of the *tableau* and social constellations represented therein, the eighteenth-century German drama and novel genres are not as easily distinguished as one might imagine. When Goethe began working on

Wilhelm Meisters Theatralische Sendung, he wrote to Merck on August 5, 1778, that he was ready to present ("vorzutragen") "das ganze Theaterwesen in einem Roman" [the entire essence of theater in a novel].[11] Goethe is referring explicitly to Wilhelm's passion for and experiences with the theater, but the statement also tells us something about the generic conventions of the novel itself. The "essence of theater" to which he refers might well point to the ways in which his novel project represents heterogeneous communities and a "theatrical" aesthetics of exteriority instead of the interiority and intimacy we have learned to expect from the novel form. Schiller famously called the "Tower Society" plot within *Wilhelm Meisters Lehrjahre* a "theatrical game"[12] that compromised the organicism of the novel, and likewise criticized both Goethe's purpose ("Zweck") and literary techniques ("Mittel") as "theatrical."[13] The fact that Schiller never himself wrote a novel and yet called the writer of novels a "Halbbruder des Dichters" [half brother of the poet] may well have influenced his rigid understanding of genre distinction; in any case, he highlights here the vast disparity between genre theory and practice in the period.[14]

This chapter traces the paths the *tableaux* of social groupings take within exemplary eighteenth-century German novels, from the birth of the sentimental novel to the epistolary novel and *Bildungsroman*. At some point, the *tableau* becomes less static and begins to move, a phenomenon that underscores the connection between the social *tableau*, notions of modernity, and the aesthetic surface-depth dichotomy. In Goethe's *Wahlverwandtschaften* (1809), which is the focus of my analysis in chapter 7, the *tableau vivant* becomes a key marker for sociality. The current chapter follows the heterogeneous social groupings depicted in *tableaux*-like descriptions in novels that span the "trivial/Kunstroman" [trivial/quality novel] divide, beginning with C. F. Gellert's *Das Leben der schwedischen Gräfin von G****[The Life of the Swedish Countess of G***] (1747–1748), a work that serves both as the first German sentimental novel and the first German "Familienroman" [family novel].[15] Sophie von La Roche's epistolary novel *Die Geschichte des Fräuleins von Sternheim* [The History of Lady Sophie Sternheim] (1771), Goethe's *Die Leiden des jungen Werthers* [The Sorrows of Young Werther] (1774, revised in 1787), and *Wilhelm Meisters Lehrjahre* (1795–1796) and Dorothea Schlegel's *Florentin* (1801), a literary response to *Wilhelm Meister*, constitute a string of intertextually and intermedially intertwined novels whose *tableaux* of social groupings and nonnuclear kin structures open a web of intimate connections that point us away from the nuclear family and toward more complex social constellations. *Wilhelm Meisters Lehrjahre* famously ends as Wilhelm and many of the other main characters in the novel collect at the estate of the ubiquitous avuncular figure of the "Oheim" [uncle], thereby configuring a community that includes figures representing diverse nationalities, classes, and biological families. *Das Leben der schwedischen Gräfin von G****, *Die Geschichte des Fräuleins von Sternheim*, *Die Leiden des jungen Werthers*, and *Florentin* likewise depict heterogeneous social groupings, and each novel ends with a *tableau* of community that belies the centrality of the nuclear family.

RETHINKING INTERIORITY: THE ENGLISH, FRENCH, AND GERMAN NOVEL

The sentimental novel tradition emerged out of England and France and arrived in Germany, like the drama, by the second half of the eighteenth century. Samuel Richardson's epistolary novels about heroines sexually pursued by rakes, *Pamela, or Virtue Rewarded* (1740) and *Clarissa, Or the History of A Young Lady* (1748), were monumentally influential for German novelists of the period, and the German "Familienroman" emerged in response to Richardson's novels.[16] *Pamela* concludes with a "happy ending" marriage, while *Clarissa* ends with the heroine's death from emotional suffering after she has been deceived and raped by Robert Lovelace.[17] *Clarissa* was translated into German the year after it appeared in English, and it was a rousing success.[18] Thomas Beebee writes that professors and students at Göttingen University were "gripped with *Clarissa* fever. In their enthusiasm, medicine and literature met each other on an equal footing," as Haller discussed possible narratives for a sequel with his anatomy students.[19] And this popularity and influence continued in the German states for decades: fully one-third of novels written between 1774 and 1781 were Clarissa clones.[20]

Scholars of English literature locate the rise of the modern novel firmly in England, with Richardson, Daniel Defoe, and Henry Fielding. Indeed, almost all major works by these authors were published prior to Gellert's *Das Leben der schwedischen Gräfin von G**** and Rousseau's *Julie, ou la nouvelle Héloïse* [Julie, or the New Héloïse] (1761). Watt argues convincingly that the rise of the English novel is a product of an established English middle class in the early part of the eighteenth century, as well as a middle-class reading public.[21] The focus of the eighteenth-century English novel is the individual, reflecting the new values of secularization, innovation, and breaking with tradition.[22] The rise of the individual "weakened communal and traditional relationships" and fostered a focus on a "private and egocentric mental life."[23] McKeon writes that "the emerging novel internalizes the emergence of the middle class and the concerns that it exists to mediate."[24]

English novels of the period reflect a new aesthetic realism.[25] Characters are given proper names to reflect their individuality, in contrast to the figures representing social types in earlier novels.[26] Watt underscores the "clumsy" manner in which both Defoe and Richardson wrote and for which they were criticized by their contemporaries, but this writing style was necessary so that these novelists could break with established "canons of prose style," and was the "price they had to pay for achieving the immediacy and closeness of the text to what is being described."[27] These novels work through "exhaustive presentation rather than by elegant concentration"[28] and thereby contribute to the "formlessness" of the genre vis-à-vis other literary forms such as the epic or lyric.[29]

The aesthetics of realism are often sutured to the letter in novels of the period.[30] The epistolary form of Richardson's novels offers the letter as the signifier of the subtle shifts in emotions felt by the heroines Pamela and Clarissa. Jane K. Brown highlights the "increased sense of interiority" generated by these characters' constant writing of letters that document a seemingly uncensored stream of feelings and thoughts: "Because their being is contained entirely in writing, they seem to possess a new form of psychological depth."[31] In Rousseau's extraordinarily influential *Julie, ou la nouvelle Héloïse*, the narrative of the forbidden love between Julie and her tutor St. Preux represents a milestone in literary interiority via letters that trace nothing more than the nuanced movement of feelings on the part of the letter writers. In particular, the first part of the novel has virtually no descriptions of locales, consisting almost exclusively of letters presenting the outpourings of feelings on the part of Julie and St. Preux.

As Brown puts it, subjectivity was generally characterized in terms of interiority and consciousness in the eighteenth century. The latter emerges from Descartes's *cogito, ergo sum*, and the former is produced in large part through literary language in the novels of writers such as Richardson, Lawrence Sterne, and Rousseau. The isolation of characters creates the conditions for letter writing, a form of writing that can contain the entire being of the characters in these situations. In Sterne's *The Life and Opinions of Tristram Shandy* (1760), narrative voice is so radically delinked from action (it even precedes the hero's birth) that "identity is so interiorized as to be almost inaccessible."[32]

Interiority is seen in the period, almost anti-intuitively, as an indicator of truth. Within this epistemological system, that which is hidden is *more true* than that which lies on the surface.[33] Michel Foucault connects this knowledge system not only to the emergence of depth psychology but also to modern concepts of "sexuality" that are predicated upon the hypothesis that "sexuality" is always repressed and, hence, a cipher for the subject's truth.[34] In modern thought there is *one* self and *one* truth, and that truth is sexual, binary, hidden, and *at home* in the nuclear family.

Theories of the German novel have historically reiterated the metonymic chain of signifiers—subjective interiority/organicism/bourgeois family/domestic interior—that we associate with the English and French novels of the period, but we potentially overlook the unique qualities of the German novel when we focus on the English novel as generic exemplar. Friedrich von Blanckenburg's *Versuch über den Roman* [Theory of the Novel] of 1774 is frequently cited as the first German theoretical work to take the novel seriously as an art form.[35] Blanckenburg traces the shift from the connected series of events of the epic and the baroque adventure novel to the organic development of the main character in the modern novel. The focus here is no longer external actions but inner experience: "If the poet does not have the ability to shed light on the *interiority* of the character and teach himself to know him as well: then he actually has—no 'subject'."[36] Blanckenburg essentially tells Watt's story of the novel almost 200 years earlier. In line with secular shifts in the eighteenth century, the novel is about the essence of the individual human being: "And so it seems the *Being* of the character, his *inner condition* is the main thing."[37] The perspectival shift moves from God's bird's-eye view to a low-angle one focused on the minutiae of the individual soul: "And isn't this *Interiority* the most important thing in our entire being?"[38] Similarly, Blanckenburg's understanding of the principle of *Bildung* relies on Herder's organic notion of *Bildung* focused on *internal action* as the individual unfolds their personality like a plant.[39]

The rhetoric of interiority that characterizes eighteenth-century theories of the German novel since Blanckenburg is frequently tied to the prosaic, the bourgeois, and even the domestic (*häuslich*). Six years after Blanckenburg published *Versuch über den Roman*, the novelist Johann Carl Wezel coined the term "bürgerliche Epopöe" [bourgeois epic] to describe the novel genre.[40] Hegel takes up this terminology in his discussion of the novel form in the *Ästhetik*, defining the novel as a "modern bourgeois epic."[41] Just as Hegel critiques the narrowness of bourgeois drama by playwrights such as Iffland and Kotzebue, he faults the novel genre for its narrowness in milieu, what he sees as the focus on the private, the bourgeois, and the domestic: "Epic poetry has fled from great national events into the restrictedness of private domestic situations in the countryside of a small town."[42] For Hegel, the novel is a form of trivial degeneration: interiority is folded into bourgeois domesticity and narrowness. Here we encounter the same kind of critique that was made about the bourgeois "Rührstück," yet it is astounding to see it as a response to a novel such as *Wilhelm Meisters Lehrjahre*, that focuses on a bourgeois domestic sphere only in portions of book 1, and that otherwise presents us with a picaresque journey in which the hero encounters the world of the theater, the German aristocracy, and numerous other milieus and characters.

Blanckenburg and Hegel displace, in a nutshell, a theory of the interiority of the English novel onto the eighteenth-century German literary world, and this model is taken up in the whirlwind of theories of the modern novel despite numerous aesthetic clues that tell a different story. Yet theory and practice often diverge, and these points of divergence provide us with important insights into both the ideological interests of a period and the alternative narratives being told. The modern depth-based epistemology of the literary (private) subject that characterizes eighteenth-century English and French novels does not figure nearly as prominently in the eighteenth-century German bourgeois novel. Just as Goethe's novels can be seen as "theatrical," German *Familienromane* and *Bildungsromane* beginning with Gellert's *Das Leben der schwedischen Gräfin von G**** likewise exhibit an *exterior* quality, a style more suited to the representations of *tableaux* and landscapes than to interior bourgeois spaces and the inner workings of the modern mind.

German authors and scholars around 1750 were frequently dismayed by what they perceived as the inferior German novel, just as Gellert bemoaned the lack of good models for German letter writing. Thomas Beebee writes that the German translator of *Clarissa*, Johann David Michaelis, lacked "confidence in the German language of the time," based on the fractured nature of the German states, the lack of schooling for common people, and the lack of a precise, shared language.[43] These kinds of self-conscious views about German language and letters vis-à-vis their French and English counterparts not only plagued authors and critics in the eighteenth century but are often expressed by modern literary scholars.[44] Such critical views are likely motivated by an aesthetic hierarchy that privileges realism and bourgeois interiority over nonrealist aesthetic modes.

Gellert's *Das Leben der schwedischen Gräfin von G**** is often read as a wooden mimicry of Richardson,[45] and this critique was already articulated in 1875 by Erich Schmidt.[46] Whereas Richardson is able to create a complete and round character in conjunction with a simple plot, Schmidt argues,

Gellert neglects psychological depth and instead relies on excessive narrative turns reminiscent of the adventure novel.[47] Schmidt's denigration of Gellert's novel reiterates the self-critique of eighteenth-century Germans that is informed by reverence for the English interior novel. Gellert's novel features an intricate plot consisting of adventures in Siberia, multiple seductions, incest, and returns from the dead, with only occasional insights into the emotional world of the countess. However, it is precisely these stories that create an ever-expanding community around the countess who tells and listens to them.

Gellert's aesthetic combines didacticism with a weak interiority. Gellert himself looked self-consciously to Richardson when writing his novel. In a poem dedicated to his literary hero, Gellert praises Richardson's ability to combine "Natur, Geschmack, Religion" [Nature, Taste, Religion] in his works.[48] Indeed, didacticism and interiority are potentially at odds, and Germans at the time were particularly keen on didactic interpretations.[49] Beebee stresses that Michaelis's translation of *Clarissa* was intent on highlighting and preserving the "didactic elements of the original," whereas the French translation invited readers to sympathize with the rake Lovelace.[50] Although *Das Leben der schwedischen Gräfin von G**** includes a number of letters, they serve as didactic tools and carriers of the plot and not as windows onto individual souls. Letters in the novel are frequently read aloud to the countess's community, and they also often arrive by post after the letter writer has already arrived. In this sense, the letters stand in for the eyewitness narrative of the returning character and do not map the minute contours of the character's emotional life. To the extent that they teach the reader and the community that is constructed within the novel, they model friendship and sociality and are constitutive of this community.

Like *Das Leben der schwedischen Gräfin von G****, Sophie von La Roche's *Die Geschichte des Fräuleins von Sternheim*—the first German novel known to have been written by a woman[51]—is modeled after the novels of Richardson,[52] but like Gellert's novel, it remains highly descriptive in its multiple plotlines and its depictions of exteriors and the milieus in which Sophie resides.[53] Like Richardson's Clarissa, Sophie Sternheim's compassion for the poor exemplifies her status as an ideal, virtuous woman. In his preface to the novel, C.M. Wieland nods explicitly to Richardson and Fielding as literary models that far exceed the abilities of German authors of the time.[54] Yet despite Wieland's insistence on the "internal and singular examples of beauty"[55] represented in the novel, *Sternheim* reads much more like a description of events and actions than a narrrative of psychological interiority.

Rousseau's *Julie*, a model for literary interiority, is an intertext both for La Roche's *Sternheim* and Goethe's *Werther*, although this interiority tends to be exteriorized in the German novels. A famous review (generally assumed to have been written by Goethe) asserts that La Roche's novel is not a book but a "Menschenseele" [human soul.][56] Sophie Sternheim is constructed, like Julie, as an ideal of "natural" femininity. In contrast to the performative beauty of Parisian women, St. Preux calls Julie a "unique masterpiece of nature!"[57] Sophie's admirers, including the seducer and rapist Lord Derby, use these words to describe her in the rape scene, calling her "the imprint of the first masterpiece of nature."[58] But as we shall see, this scene is presented as a static *tableau* and not as a window onto Sophie's soul. Goethe's Lotte in *Die Leiden des jungen Werthers* is likewise depicted as a transparent product of nature, and this novel's plot is closely based on that of *Julie*, with an outsider falling passionately for a woman he cannot possess and whose family expects her to marry another man. Jane K. Brown has argued convincingly that while Rousseau was pivotal for the development of Goethe's novels, Goethe's *Werther* represents "an emphatic 'no'" to the sentimentalism of *Julie*.[59]

Instead of indulging a radically subjective language in the manner of Rousseau, German novelists of the period retain what we can call a more theatrical relationship to their characters.[60] Even Goethe's *Werther*, an epistolary novel oozing with Werther's feelings, includes concrete descriptions of Werther's surroundings, something that is largely missing from Rousseau's *Julie*. Brown gives the example of Lotte cutting bread for her siblings as a significant gesture "of entirely visual effects."[61] This reading contrasts with Niklas Luhmann's terminology for the semiotics of this scene in *Werther* as "Schwarzbrot-Semantik" [black bread semantics],[62] in which "domestic life, the garden, etc." are privileged.[63] Luhmann thereby traces the theoretical path laid for him by Blanckenburg and Hegel, who interpret literature as a dialectical product of ideological shifts and, in the process, look past formal aesthetic elements that represent deviation from the larger theory.

The readiness to overread realism into literary works from this period is a case in point. Lukács's distinction between description and narration is a useful way to think about the eighteenth-century German novel's resistance to a realist aesthetic. Lukács approaches this distinction from a Marxist perspective, advocating for a mode of realism that reflects social change. Comparing the horse race in Émile Zola's *Nana* with the one in Leo Tolstoy's *Anna Karenina*, he argues that the race in *Nana* is a superficial description, whereas the race in Tolstoy's novel, resulting as it does in Vronsky's fall and a dramatic turn in Anna's life, draws the reader into the narrative in a significant way: "The race is not a 'picture' [Bild] but rather a row of highly dramatic scenes, a turning point in the entire plot."[64] Lukács's "picture" is a *tableau*, one that interpellates the reader into the position of the observer: "The race is described by Zola from the perspective of the spectator, by Tolstoy from the perspective of the participant."[65] Description, like the *tableau*, slows time— contemporizes the moment—whereas narration engages with significant moments from the past: "Description makes everything present. One narrates what is past."[66] Description is likened to the *tableau* and to still life ("Stillleben"),[67] connoting death, whereas narrative is vital.

Lukács codes his recipe for realism in the language of interiority and a surface/depth topography that mirrors the shifting aesthetic values in the modern period. The realist novel should dialectically reflect the interiority of its characters and, thereby, the relations among humans. Social praxis is experienced ("miterleben") by the reader through narration that is informed by a larger ideology. Description, in contrast, invites observation and lacks ideology, producing a temporality and form that is not organic but instead episodic.[68] For Lucáks, description resides temporally in the Now and makes one event qualitatively indistinguishable from another. What was deep ("tief") becomes flat ("Verflachung"):

> Obviously there is here [with Zola] no correct and *deep* reflec-
> tion of objective reality but rather a flattening and distortion of its
> principles. . . . The real knowledge of the driving forces of social
> development, the impartial, true, *deep* and comprehensive poetic
> reflection of their effectiveness in human life must appear in the
> form of *movement*, a *movement* which exposes the legitimate unity
> of the normal and the exceptional.[69]

An exteriorizing, descriptive mode of narrative, exemplified in the aes-thetics of the *tableau*, flattens reality into surface, resisting a true and deep reflection of social realities. Aesthetic value is sutured to depth, whereas a flat, surface representation indicates distortion. Interestingly, movement becomes sutured in Lukács's analysis to an aesthetics of depth, a concept to which I return later in this chapter.

In Lukács's discussion of prose forms we have, once again, an under-standing of realism that devalues nonmimetic aesthetics and that does not map cleanly onto eighteenth-century German literary aesthetics. Although deeply indebted to the English and French realist novels that paved the way for the bourgeois German novel, German language authors often rely on aesthetic strategies of description and *tableaux*. Letters are frequently not mere windows onto the soul but adventure stories or narrative devices. And very importantly, *tableaux* and exteriorized descriptions appear again and again in early German bourgeois novels. In the transposition of the modern bourgeois novel into the German states, the metonymically linked tropes of interiority and the family become refracted in a distorted mirror: truth as a moral value appears on the surface, and the figures in the frame multiply, creating heterogeneous and porous "still lives." Instead of implementing the devalorizing terms of Lukács's vocabulary to interpret these *tableaux*, we should see them as imaginative alternative pictures that have the potential to expand our understanding of sociality.

VERWANDTSCHAFT/BEKANNTSCHAFT
[RELATION/ACQUAINTANCE]

The descriptive and episodic "Bilder" [pictures] that we encounter in the eighteenth-century German novel are celebrated by Dorothea Schlegel[70] in her dedication and preface draft to the unfinished second part of *Florentin*, her homage of sorts to Goethe's *Wilhelm Meisters Lehrjahre*.[71] She writes here that the generic category of the novel makes claims to excite a "zarte innige Sympathie" [tender, inner sympathy] in the reader, but that *Florentin* will disappoint in this regard. Instead, Schlegel hopes her readers will "sich einige Augenblicke an den bunten Bildern dieser fremden Welt ergötzen" [delight for a few moments in the colorful pictures of this foreign world]. The reader will not be confronted with a mirror but with a "Bildergalerie wo die verschiedenen Porträte und Figuren uns bald mit teurn bald mit verhaßten jetzt mit wehmütigen und jetzt mit lächerlichen Erinnerungen umgeben" [picture gallery where the different potraits and figures surround us with sometimes dear, sometimes hateful, and at times melancholy and at times laughable memories].[72] Rather than representing the dialectical "depth" of human struggle and social practice that Lukács prescribes, Schlegel offers "colorful pictures" through which one would wander, taking in images as entertaining episodes.[73] The picture and the portrait do not serve as signifiers of the modern interior subject;[74] they do not offer a mirror image with which the reader can identify. Instead, Schlegel describes her novel as a literary space in which the reader is not alone with a few well-rounded modern characters but becomes a part of a larger social constellation. This is not the realm of the isolated, modern interior subject but instead of a heterogeneous collection of *tableaux* containing diverse figures who evoke multifarious affective responses.[75]

The portrait and the "Ahnengallerie" [ancestral gallery] are thematized within *Florentin* in a manner that mirrors the surface aesthetics described by Schlegel in her preface and which corresponds to the fetish nature of the portrait in eighteenth-century German dramas. Painterly representations of novel characters often tend in the direction of allegory. Early in *Florentin*, the novel's eponymous hero encounters the central family when he rescues its father, a count, from the attacks of a wild boar. Florentin immediately imagines the count and his servant as types represented in an ancestral gallery:

> Der feierliche, umständliche, höfliche Alte! Der empfindsame exaltierte Knabe! Repräsentanten ihrer Zeit und ihres Standes, . . . wenn ich ihre Porträte zu einer Ahnengallerie zu machen hätte, so malte ich den ersten, wie er mit großer Devotion ein von Pfeilen durchbohrtes Herz darbringt, und den andern in erhabenen und rührenden Betrachtungen vertieft über ein Büschel Vergißmeinnicht. Es ist das Lächerlichste von der Welt, außer ich selbst, der ich mich verleiten lasse, ihnen zu folgen, und mich in Prozessions aufzuführen. . . . Was will ich dort?

> [The solemn, ceremonious, courteous old gentleman! The sensitive, exalted boy! Representatives of their age and class, . . . if I had to paint their portraits for an ancestral gallery, I would paint the first one as he presented in great devotion a heart pierced with arrows, and the other deep in sublime and moving meditations over a bouquet of forget-me-nots. It is the most ridiculous thing in the world, except for me, who is allowing himself to be led into following them so they can stage me in a procession. . . . What do I want there?][76]

Florentin's imagined portraits are ludicrous parodies of allegorical pictures in which gender and class are queered: in Florentin's mind the count and his servant take on the roles of Cupid and a melancholy woman. Florentin imagines his trip to the count's home not as a journey that might lead to *Bildung* but somewhat ironically as a procession, a premodern performance of roles.

The picture of the count's family that Florentin experiences cannot be called modern, but the larger family constellation strikes him nevertheless as ideal. When Florentin encounters the count's entire family, they gather in a manner that resembles an organic, barely moving *tableau*, a heterogeneous collection of individuals that strikes Florentin as utopian:

Auch mußte das offne, zutrauliche, arglose Benehmen der Eltern, Kinder, Geschwister, Hausgenossen, Domestiken gegeneinander wohl jeden Zwang und jedes Mißtrauen verscheuchen. Nicht leicht konnte man *eine Familie* finden, in der so wie in dieser jedes Verhältnis zugleich so rein und so belebt zu sein schien, indem jeder einzelne zugleich seinem eigenen Werte treu blieb.

[The open, trusting, guileless conduct of the parents, children, siblings, houseguests, and domestics toward one another chased away all coercion and distrust. One could not easily find a family like this one in which each relationship seemed to be both pure and animated and in which each individual remained true to one's own worth.][77]

In its structure, this ideal family is not a modern one; the class relations remain firmly in place. "Familie" refers here not to the nuclear grouping of the parents and their daughter but to the larger community of servants and visitors, everyone who is living at this point in the castle. It is a feudal family with a modern sense of communication, one in which every individual is heard and listens.[78]

Florentin's ideal family/community is made up of characters who are related biologically and others who are not, forming "colorful pictures" for a variety of moods. In the preface draft Schlegel lays out this network model of relations, one in which *Bekanntschaften* are just as important as *Verwandtschaften*:

Doch, blicken wir auf unser vergangenes Leben zurück, so finden wir nicht selten, daß Begebenheiten oder Bekanntschaften, die wir anfänglich als fremd, oder zufällig anzusehen geneigt waren und denen wir weder Folge noch Wichtigkeit zugestanden: daß gerade diese, nicht allein von entschiedenstem Einfluß auf unser Leben waren, sondern sogar in so innigem Zusammenhange mit demselben gestanden, daß wir nun nicht mehr einsehen, was ohne jene aus diesem geworden wäre.

[But if we look back at our past life, we frequently find that events or acquaintances that we initially tended to view as strange or coincidental and to which we neither conceded consequence nor importance: that precisely these not only had the most decisive

influence on our life but even stood in an intimate connection to it,
and that we no longer understand what would have become of our
life without these events or acquaintances.]⁷⁹

Here Schlegel expresses a central tendency in the eighteenth-century German novel and drama: communities represented therein do not settle on the
nuclear family grouping but instead trace a variety of social connections
between diverse characters that, as in the picaresque and baroque adventure novel, retrace the slippage between the concepts of *Bekanntschaft* and
Verwandtschaft. Isn't this precisely the picture of social relations that a novel
like *Wilhelm Meisters Lehrjahre* paints for us?

EXCURSUS ON *VERWANDTSCHAFT/ BEKANNTSCHAFT* IN GOETHE

The concepts "verwandt" and "Verwandtschaft" appear in many of Goethe's
literary and theoretical texts and shed light on eighteenth-century concepts
of relationality and kinship. A look at the various connotations of these concepts in Goethe's works points to a notion of relationality that is rather more
metonymic/associative than oppositional; one, indeed, that is not dialectical.

In Paul Fischer's *Goethe-Wortschatz* [Goethe-Vocabulary], being related
("verwandt") to something/someone means "zu ihm in nähere Beziehung
treten" [to enter into a closer relation to him].⁸⁰ We have here both the
approach of the Other and the concept of proximity. Indeed, the term "nah"
[near] appears frequently in connection to "verwandt" and "Verwandtschaft."
In *Faust II*, Act 2 (the "Classical Walpurgis Night" scene), Mephistopheles
experiences proximity vis-à-vis "Verwandte" as a threat and a nuisance:

Empuse *zu Mephistopheles:* Begrüßt von Mühmichen Empuse,
Der Trauten mit dem Eselsfuße!
Du hast nur einen Pferdefuß,
Und doch, Herr Vetter, schönsten Gruß!
Mephistopheles: Hier dacht' ich lauter Unbekannte
Und finde leider Nahverwandte;
Es ist ein altes Buch zu blättern:
Vom Harz bis Hellas immer Vettern!

[Empuse *to Mephistopheles:* Greetings from Aunty Empuse,
Your cousin with the ass's foot!
You only have a horse's foot,

And yet, Mr. Cousin, my warmest greeting!
Mephistopheles: I thought there would only be strangers
And unfortunately I find close relatives;
It is an old, familiar book;
From Harz to Hellas, always cousins!]⁸¹

The slippage between acquaintances and those to whom one is closely related is ubiquitous and frequent. How are Empuse and Mephistopheles "ver-wandt"? One has a donkey's foot, the other a horse's foot, yet they are "cousins." Indeed, Mephistopheles bemoans the encroaching proximity of "cousins" everywhere. "Vetter" and "Muhme," or "Tante" [aunt] for that matter, are kinship titles that indicate either loose or nonbiological connections. Mephistopheles is put off by the nearness of Empuse, her assumption of similarity and intimacy. She is neither completely the same nor entirely different, but she is, at any rate, too close.

When, in *Faust I*, Mephistopheles first appears in Faust's study as a poodle, Faust is likewise disturbed by his nearness/proximity:

Solch einen störenden Gesellen
Mag ich nicht in der Nähe leiden.

[I don't want to suffer such a bothersome companion
In my proximity.]⁸²

Like Mephistopheles vis-à-vis Empuse, Faust expresses his anxiety at the excessive closeness of another. The relationship between Faust and Mephistopheles is characterized in this scene as one of extreme proximity to the point where the boundaries of the self are threatened ("Doch willst du mit mir vereint, Deine Schritte durchs Leben nehmen . . ." [If you want to take your steps through life with me . . .]).⁸³ Mephistopheles articulates his own role vis-à-vis Faust as that of a servant:

So will ich mich gern bequemen,
Dein zu sein, auf der Stelle.
Ich bin dein Geselle,
Und mach' ich dir's recht,
Bin ich dein Diener, bin dein Knecht!
Faust: Sprich die Bedingung deutlich aus;
Ein solcher Diener bringt Gefahr ins Haus [. . .]

Mephistopheles: Ich will mich hier zu deinem Dienst verbinden,
Auf deinen Wink nicht rasten und nicht ruhn;
Wenn wir uns drüben wiederfinden,
So sollst du mir das Gleiche tun.

[I will gladly adapt myself
To be yours, here and now.
I am your companion,
And if I please you,
I am your servant, your slave!
Faust: Speak clearly the conditions;
Such a servant brings danger into the house [. . .]
Mephistopheles: I will bind myself to your service here.]
Be at your beck and call without respite;
And when we meet beyond,
Then you shall do the same for me.[84]

The "servant" is precisely a figure whose relation to the self is neither the same nor opposite; the servant lives in close proximity, in intimate nearness, to their master. Yet the relationship between Mephistopheles and Faust is not that of Hegel's master and slave. As Mephistopheles articulates it, the two will remain in close proximity into perpetuity, even as power roles morph. Fischer points out that Goethe uses the term "verwandt" for a wide variety of employees, "Kanzleiverwandter, Kassenverwandter, Bibliotheksverwandter, Kunstverwandter, Ratsverwandter" [chancellory relation, finance relation, library relation, art relation, council relation], and utilizes the term "Stallverwandten" [stable relation] for "Stallknecht" [stable servant] in the *Wanderjahre*.[85] If Mephistopheles and Faust mutually function as each other's "servants," we have circled around to a notion of "verwandt" that is, again, not about identity or difference but about proximity, a proximity that is frequently threatening.

This notion of relationality ("verwandt") appears again in the essay "The Experiment as Mediator between Object and Subject." Goethe writes here that one phenomenon can only be understood in its relation to another, and yet the more similarity that exists between them, the more attention must be paid to difference: "Two phenomena can be related ('verwandt') to one another but then again not as near ('nah') as we believe."[86] How close is too close? Where is the line between similar and same? These are questions that haunt the period.

The notion of *Verwandtschaft* is central to *Die Wahlverwandtschaften*, a subject at the center of chapter 7. The Hauptmann famously articulates the notion of "Wahlverwandtschaften" in book 1, chapter 4. As Norbert Puszkar points out, the chemical process of "elective affinities" presents an impasse between the concepts "oppositional" ("entgegengesetzt") and "related" ("verwandt").[87] We are not dealing with a clear dialectic but instead with a kind of relationality that eschews both oppositionality and sameness. One of the many cases in point is the description of Ottilie's relation to the baby Otto, to whom she is not related by blood, as *"so viel als eine Mutter, oder vielmehr eine andere Art von Mutter"* [*as much as a mother, or even more another kind of mother*].[88] In being both "as much as" (quantitatively similar) and "a different kind" of mother (different but still of the same species), Ottilie embodies relationships both to Otto and to motherhood that elide the same-other dichotomy.

As Eve Sedgwick points out, male and female are not true opposites: "Under no matter what cultural construction, women and men are more like each other than chalk is like cheese, than ratiocination is like raisins, than up is like down, or than 1 is like 0."[89] Sedgwick's metonymic mode of thinking surely represents a different worldview than Goethe's, but Goethe nevertheless invites us, again and again, to consider notions of relationality metonymically, in terms that elide both dichotomous and dialectical thought structures.

Mephistopheles himself, the figure who is always too close for comfort, deserves to be at the center of these deliberations. The relationship of part to whole that he embodies is more metonymic (or synecdochic) than dichotomous:

MEPHISTOPHELES: Ein Teil von jener Kraft,
Die stets das Böse will und stets das Gute schafft.
FAUST: Du nennst dich einen Teil, und stehst doch ganz vor mir?

[MEPHISTOPHELES: A part of that force
Which always wills evil and always produces good.
FAUST: You call yourself a part, and yet you stand complete in front
     of me?][90]

Here, the part-whole/Mephistopheles is important not as a harmonious principle but instead for his relationality vis-à-vis others that stimulates affective and moral responses in them.

KINSHIP AND THE *TABLEAU*

In each of the five novels at the center of this chapter we see a metonymic notion of *Verwandtschaft*, as illustrated by the *Florentin* and Goethe examples, one that is not limited to blood relations but that creates fluid lines between relationality, affinity, acquaintance, and proximity, as well as frequently traversing class distinctions. What is more, these social constellations are often pictured intermedially as *tableaux*, as still lives, and, eventually, as moving pictures.

Das Leben der schwedischen Gräfin von G***

In Gellert's *Das Leben der schwedischen Gräfin von G****, proximate relations are just as important as those of marriage or blood. *Verwandtschaft* includes friendship and erotic ties, and the distinction between these relationship categories is porous.[91] We see this model for community formation throughout the novel, as romantic connections are fostered between individual characters and lovers or friends. The novel tells the narrative of the countess as she marries the count and then believes he has died in the course of a military expedition, only to experience his return from Siberia (seemingly from the dead) after she has married his best friend, the bourgeois Herr R***. The count's return leads not to a crisis but to an expansion of the community. When the count learns that his wife has married his best friend, his response is one not of jealousy but joy: "'Also . . . ist mein liebster Freund Ihr Gemahl? Dieses macht mein Unglück noch erträglich.'" [Then . . . my best friend is your husband? This makes my unhappiness bearable.][92]

There is an additive logic at work in the relationships within Gellert's novel, as *Bekanntschaften* become *Verwandtschaften* and a polyamorous group is formed via, in part, the activity of reading aloud one another's letters. These letters depict the adventures of the various characters and help construct an intimate community within the novel.[93] The countess's friendship with Herr R*** through her husband becomes a marriage bond, and this bond transforms again into an eroticized friendship. Caroline, the count's (bourgeois) former beloved, likewise remains one of the permanent "Hausgenossen" [house companions], and the count continues to flirt with her after his return.[94] An additional love triangle is created between Caroline's daughter Mariane (who was raised by Caroline's brother), Mariane's beloved, her brother Carlson (a fact unknown to the lovers during their courtship), and Carlson's friend Dormund.[95]

The Mariane-Carlson incest narrative is caused by Mariane's separation from her family. The narrative, told from the perspective of the countess, provides a complex view of the slippages between blood relations and erotic ones. On the one hand, the countess writes of the familiarity that is produced between blood relations and which discourages erotic love; but, on the other hand, she articulates the ultimate "naturalness" of the bonds between siblings:

> Sie hatten einander in ihrem Leben nicht gesehen, und also kam ihnen die Vertraulichkeit nicht zu Hülfe, die sonst die Liebe unter Blutsverwandten auszulöschen pflegt. Ihre Natur selbst tat den Ausspruch zu ihrem Besten. Wie konnten sie etwas in sich fühlen, das ihre Liebe verdammte, da sie den Zug der Blutsfreundschaft nie gefühlt hatten.

> [They had never before seen each other in their lives, so that familiarity, which otherwise takes care to extinguish love between blood relatives, did not come to their aid. Their nature used their claim to its advantage. How could they feel something inside themselves that damned their love, since they had never felt the affinity of blood before.][96]

The tension between familiarity and erotic love and between blood relatives and friendship is already softened by the countess's interchangeable use of "Blutsverwandte" [blood relations] and "Blutsfreundschaft" [affinity of blood]. *Verwandtschaft* and *Bekanntschaft* inform one another in ways that could easily produce the incest crisis that befalls Mariane and Carlson, although this love affair, seen from the perspective of the loose boundaries between these terms, places incest on a spectrum rather than outside of a closed circle of acceptable relations.[97] Interestingly, when Carlson dies, Mariane quickly shifts her devotion to his friend Dormund, reiterating the logic of affective substitution within the novel as a whole.[98]

The additive logic that inheres to this community is, as we have seen in the case of German dramas, both affective and economic: an increase of chosen people within the group corresponds to more wealth for the entire community. The (bourgeois) marriage between the countess and Herr R*** leads to the production of a child and a corresponding increase in riches: "Unsere kleinen Kapitale hatten sich binnen sechs Jahren in der Handlung fast um noch einmal soviel vermehrt, und wir hätten beide sehr gemächlich davon leben können." [Our small capital almost doubled within six years of business, and we both could have lived very comfortably from it.][99] Money creates not only comfort but moral character; the more money one has, the more charity one can engage in: "Wir hatten mehr, als wir begehrten, und also genug, andern wohlzutun." [We had more than we desired and enough to help others.][100] As the community grows with the addition of Caroline, the capital increases: "Unsere Kapitalia brachten mehr ein, als wir verlangten, und weit mehr, als wir brauchten." [Our capital brought in more surplus than we demanded of it, and much more than we needed.][101] The growth of wealth corresponds to the wealth of the extended kinship group; with the exception of the tale of Mariane and Carlson, addition in the novel is always a happy event, even when characters lose their specific place vis-à-vis a loved one. The bourgeois values enjoyed by the countess and Herr R*** spill over into the larger mixed group of aristocrats and bourgeois characters.

The *tableau* of embracing kin, so important in *Nathan der Weise*, serves as a central gesture of inclusion and expansion within Gellert's novel, connoting almost limitless possibilities for addition. When the countess admits to the recently returned count that she has born a child with Herr R***, the count insists on kisses and hugs all around: "'Und Ihr, mein Lieber R*** . . . schlagt Eure Augen immer wieder auf, und seht zu Eurer Strafe Eure vorige Gemahlin in meinen Armen.' Er küßte ihn, und ich mußte es auch tun." ["And you, my dear R*** . . . open your eyes again and see as a punishment your former wife in my arms." He kissed him, and I had to do the same.][102] The group immediately turns to Caroline, inviting her into their circle. By the end of the novel, the countess/count/Herr R***/Caroline quartet has become a sextet, as Steely, the count's beloved English friend from his Siberia days, joins the group with his own beloved, Amalia. The count and Steeley embrace in a scene that the countess describes as a theater of emotions: "Der Graf zitterte, daß er kaum von dem Sessel aufstehen konnte, und wir sahen ihren Umarmungen mit einem freudigen Schauer lange zu." [The count trembled so that he could hardly stand up from the chair, and we watched their embraces with a joyful shiver for a long time.][103] The countess immediately runs to Steeley, who is speechless: "'Ach, Madame,' fing er an, 'ich—ich—ja, ja, Sie sind es—,' und das war sein ganzes Kompliment." ["Oh, Madam," he began, "I—I—yes, yes, you are it—," and that was his entire greeting.][104]

Within this *tableau* it is the physical that creates meaning; words, Steeley makes clear, cannot adequately articulate the significance of the moment. In "Conversations on *The Natural Son*," Diderot advocates for the privileging of gesture over speech. For Diderot, it is precisely when words fail that we are particularly moved in the theater: "What is it that affects us in the spectacle of a man fired by some great passion? Is it his words? Sometimes. But what is always moving are cries, inarticulate words, moments when speech breaks down, when a few monosyllables escape at intervals, a strange murmuring from the throat or from between the teeth."[105] It is not only the lack of words but the performance of speech breaking down that imparts the intensity of the passion experienced by the character. Gellert utilizes precisely this kind of active speechlessness in the novel (Steeley's "I—I— yes, yes, you are it—") in order to cue the intense emotional experience that is pictured by the physical gestures of embrace.

Luhmann points to the "discovery of incommunicability" in the period, an inability to express clearly that signifies intimacy;[106] indeed, it is precisely the lack of speech that provides the code for intimacy. Gellert highlights gestures of physical intimacy in the scene, as the countess embraces Steeley and the count joins them in a group hug that eventually includes Herr R*** and Caroline:

> Der Graf kam auf uns zu, und wir umarmten uns alle drei zugleich. Oh, was ist das Vergnügen der Freundschaft für eine Wollust, und wie wallen empfindliche Herzen einander in so glücklichen Augen-blicken entgegen! Man sieht einander schweigend an, und die Seele ist doch nie beredter als bei einem solchen Stillschweigen. Sie sagt in einem Blicke, in einem Kusse ganze Reihen von Empfin-dungen und Gedanken auf einmal, ohne sie zu verwirren. Caro-line und der Herr R*** teilten ihre Freude mit der unsrigen, und wir *traten alle viere um Steeleyn und waren alle ein Freund.*

> [The Count approached us, and all three of us embraced at the same time. Oh, what revelry the joy of friendship is, and how sensitive hearts flutter toward each other in such happy moments! One looks silently at one another, and yet the soul is never more eloquent than during such silence. It speaks in one gaze, in one kiss a whole series of feelings and thoughts at once, without confusing them. Caro-line and Herr R*** shared their joy with ours, and all four of us sur-rounded Steely and were all one friend.][107]

One friend is created through the embrace of the five erotically and emo-tionally connected figures. The kinship demarcations within the novel become loose: "friend" is the overarching term that blends the distinction between "Verwandtschaft" and "Bekanntschaft."

Die Geschichte des Fräuleins von Sternheim

In Sophie von La Roche's *Die Geschichte des Fräuleins von Sternheim, Verwandtschaft* is explicitly defined as a relationship of the heart, one that is frequently delinked from blood relations. Sophie Sternheim's mother dies giving birth to her, and her father dies early in the novel. Sophie has a number of remaining relatives, but her speech and behavior deny this fact. After the death of both her parents, Sophie kneels before their graves with her friend Emilia: "'Ich habe keine Verwandten mehr, als diese Gebeine,' sagte sie." ["I no longer have any relatives, except for these remains," she said.][108] Although Sophie has an aunt, she explicitly rejects the possibility that the term *Verwandtin* could express their relationship: "Die Gräfin Löbau ist nicht meine Verwandtin; ihre Seele ist mir fremde, ganz fremde, ich liebe sie nur, weil sie die Schwester meines Oheims war." [The Countess Löbau ist not my relative; her soul is strange to me, very strange. I only love her because she was the sister of my uncle.][109] Blood does not make kin; what is more, love is a product of duty. In contrast, Sophie is drawn to a charitable canoness with whom she desires to remain and whom she calls "mütterlich" [motherly].[110] Her desire to remain with this maternal figure prompts Sophie to write in a letter to Emilia that blood relations are only important if they help one gain access to desired people: "Nur um dieser Dame willen habe ich mir zum erstenmal alte Ahnen gewünscht, damit ich Ansprüche auf einen Platz in ihrem Stifte machen, und alle Tage meines Lebens mit ihr hingbringen könnte." [Only because of this lady have I wished for the first time for ancestors so that I could lay claim to a spot in her foundation and spend all the days of my life with her.][111]

By the end of *Die Geschichte des Fräuleins von Sternheim* Sophie has created a community of lovers and friends that defies the *Verwandtschaft/Bekanntschaft* dichotomy and that resembles the community formed within *Das Leben der schwedischen Gräfin von G****. Having been abducted by Derby (her Lovelace) after being lured into a sham marriage, she travels to the idealized space of England. Abduction and rescue are followed by a utopian ending in which she lives in harmony with two brothers who share a passion for her, along with two children.[112] The novel ends with a letter written by the elder brother Lord Rich to a friend, in which he describes his initial melancholic resignation to his brother Seymour's marriage to Sophie and his subsequent joy when she names her second son after him:

> Der kleine Rich hat die Züge seiner Mutter; diese Ähnlichkeit
> schließt ein großes Glück für mich in sich; wenn ich das Leben
> behalte, soll dieser Knabe keinen andern Hofmeister, keinen andern

Begleiter auf seinen Reisen haben als mich.—Alle Ausgaben für ihn sind meine; seine Leute sind doppelt belohnt; ich schlafe neben seinem Zimmer; ja ich baue ein Haus am Ende des Gartens, in das ich mit ihm ziehen werde, wenn er volle zwei Jahre alt sein wird.

[Little Rich has the features of his mother; this similarly entails great happiness for me; if I live long enough, this boy shall have no other tutor, no other companion on his travels than me.—All payments for him are mine; his servants are doubly rewarded; I sleep next to his room; yes, I am building a house at the end of the garden into which I will move with him once he is two years old.][113]

Sophie has lured Rich into her world permanently by giving him a son, the biological offspring of his brother. With the plan that Rich and the boy will move into a house on the estate when the boy turns two, the community becomes polyamorous, as multiple fathers share their children and one wife.

The community created by the end of La Roche's novel is articulated by Rich using the pronoun "our"; proximity creates kin groupings and property alike. There is no distinction between "they" and "I," as is illustrated in the following examples: "*Unsere* Abende und *unsere* Mahlzeiten sind reizend" [*Our* evenings and *our* meals are delightful];[114] "Fröhlich treten wir in die Reihen der Landtänze *unserer* Pächter, deren Freude wir durch *unsern* Anteil verdoppeln" [We joyfully step into the rows of the country dances of *our* tenants, whose joy we double with *our* participation].[115] Quotidian experiences are shared, as are the tenants and property. Perhaps most telling is that Lord Rich writes twice in this section about "unser Haus" [our house]: "Sie können hoffen, *in unserem Hause* wechselweise jede Schattierung von Talenten und Tugenden zu finden" [You can hope to find alternately *in our house* every kind of talent and virtue];[116] "Das einfache, obgleich edle Aussehen *unserer Kleidung und unsers Hauses* läßt auch die ärmste Familie unserer Nachbarschaft mit Zuversicht und Freude zu uns kommen" [The simple yet noble appearance of *our clothing and our house* enables even the poorest family to come to us with confidence and joy].[117] Shared material and experiences culminate in the shared "Haus," with all of its connotations in 1771.

Die Leiden des jungen Werthers

Verwandtschaft in Goethe's *Die Leiden des jungen Werthers* connotes, as in La Roche's novel, emotional rather than biological kinship.[118] *Vetter* functions in the work as a queer kinship term, anticipating Mephistopheles's

appropriation of this slippery identity, one that connotes intimacy based on
Bekanntschaft instead of blood relation. When Werther first meets Lotte in
the famous scene in which she feeds her younger siblings bread, she calls
Werther "Vetter" when speaking to her little brother. Werther is elated:

> "Vetter?" sagte ich, indem ich ihr die Hand reichte, "glauben Sie,
> daß ich des Glücks wert sei, mit Ihnen verwandt zu sein?"—O,"
> sagte sie mit einem leichtfertigen Lächeln, "unsere Vetterschaft ist
> sehr weitläufig, und es wäre mir leid, wenn Sie der schlimmste
> drunter sein sollten."

> ["Cousin?" I said, while giving her my hand, "Do you believe that
> I am deserving of the happiness of being related to you?"—"Oh,"
> she said with a giddy smile, "our cousins are extensive, and it would
> be too bad if you were the worst amongst them."][119]

While we might think about Lotte's statement that her "cousins are extensive" as a comment on extended biological relatives, her use of "Vetter" for
Werther cues the slippage between biology and affinity. We are reminded
of Mephistopheles's complaint in *Faust II* about what he sees as an
oppressive network of "Vetter": "From Harz to Hellas always cousins!" For
Mephistopheles, elective affinities morph into a claustrophobic world of
interweaving relationships.

Nuclear family relationships likewise slip and slide within *Werther*: Lotte
is a sister and a mother to her siblings. Werther spends as much time as possible with Lotte, her siblings/children, and her father, desiring to be an integral member of the family: "Ein Glied der liebenswürdigen Familie zu
sein, von dem Alten geliebt zu werden wie ein Sohn, von den Kleinen wie
ein Vater, und von Lotten!" [To be a member of this lovable family, to be
loved by the old father like a son, by the little ones like a father, and by
Lotte!][120] The constellation resembles in many ways the one constructed at
the end of *Die Geschichte des Fräuleins von Sternheim*, with Werther in the
role of Lord Rich.[121] But whereas Sternheim's affective precursor to Werther,
the melancholic Seymour, is rewarded with marriage to Sophie, the reasonable Rich models the way forward for a mature Werther; Rich resigns
himself to his fate and is then rewarded with an adoptive son.[122]

The blurring of familial relationship categories within *Werther* takes
place despite the relatively small cast of characters, in contrast to the multiple figures and contexts represented in Gellert's and La Roche's novels.

In his final letter to Lotte, Werther utilizes three signifiers for his relationship with Lotte, son, friend, and lover: "dein Sohn, dein Freund, dein Geliebter."[123] The sentiment is formulated in a manner that ambiguously suggests that these relational categories apply in his connection both to nature and to Lotte. Werther takes on each and every role named here (son, friend, lover) vis-à-vis Lotte, and he also calls into question the narrowness of relationship categories in general. Why, Werther's letter suggests, should relationships be fixed in the manner usually prescribed by modern familial structures when humans take on multiple roles within social contexts?[124] This question appears again and again in Goethe's later novels.

Wilhelm Meisters Lehrjahre

Goethe's *Wilhelm Meisters Lehrjahre* offers numerous scenes that invite the reader to pause and consider the heterogeneous social constellations the novel portrays and perhaps prescribes. The novel begins not in Wilhelm's bourgeois home but at the theater, where Wilhelm's beloved, Mariane, is performing. Although often considered to be the quintessential *Bildungsroman*, Goethe's novel deviates from the organic path that typically structures the form.[125] *Wilhelm Meisters Lehrjahre* maps out Wilhelm's picaresque journey away from his bourgeois family and through various stations with a theater troupe, aristocrats, a secret Tower Society, and, finally, a grouping at the estate of an uncle figure consisting of a variety of characters from diverse points in his journeys.[126] As I have argued elsewhere, the plot is episodic, and the novel's movement is not structured by the nuclear family.[127] Wilhelm creates communities in tandem with various characters throughout the novel, and a bourgeois nuclear family model is never reintroduced into the plot as a source of stability.

Throughout the novel a variety of family-like groupings are created, but none is based clearly on biological relations, and all are temporary.[128] One of these family-like groupings includes the "wunderbare Familie" [miraculous family] consisting of the harpist, Mignon, Felix, and Wilhelm: "Der Alte und Mignon nahmen den Wiederkehrenden freundlich auf, und alle drei verbanden sich nunmehr, ihrem Freunde und Beschützer aufmerksam zu dienen und ihm etwas angenehmes zu erzeigen." [The old man and Mignon warmly welcomed the returning one, and all three were united henceforth to attentively serve their friend and protector in as pleasing a manner as possible.][129] Felix is a child whom Wilhelm later believes is his biological son, and the harpist and Mignon are two Italian performers who have unofficially joined the theater troupe with which Wilhelm is temporarily engaged. The harpist and Mignon (the latter an offspring of the harpist's incestuous liaison with his sister) are literally "foreign" (Italian) and unable to form traditional nuclear families due to the incest bonds between them. Temporality is important here: Wilhelm sees this group as his family "seit einiger Zeit" [for some time now]. This family has a short history, as he is perceived as returning to it. Wilhelm is then named not as a father but as a friend and protector of the misfit group.

The *Verwandtschaft/Bekanntschaft* divide in *Wilhelm Meisters Lerhjahre* is queered in more ways than one. Mignon, a frequent member of various kinship groupings in Wilhelm's travels, is an adolescent, that liminal point between childhood and adulthood. She is likewise described as a "zwitter-haftes Geschöpf" [hermaphroditic creature],[130] one who consistently falls between numerous categories—child/adult, male/female, foreign/familiar, and, in the end, vibrant/ghostlike. As a hermaphroditic figure, Mignon's relationships are of necessity queer, since she does not occupy a firm position within established societal roles.[131] The figure of Philine, a whimsical and flirtatious member of the theater troupe, is likewise queer in many ways, her name connoting a snail.[132] Philine's notion of family relations and reproduction is exemplified in her resistance to pregnancy, a state she perceives as ugly: "'Es wäre doch immer hübscher,' rief Philine, 'wenn man die Kinder von den Bäumen schüttelte.'" ["It would really be much lovelier," Philine exclaimed, "if one could shake children from the trees."][133] Philine's fanciful notion of reproduction invites an understanding of childbirth delinked from generation; every apple is different, and some even fall far from the tree. We might also think of the figure of the "beautiful soul" in this context. Natalie's aunt, the "beautiful soul," remains a queer figure, as aunts are wont to do,[134] in the end choosing the life of a hermit over marriage. In particular, she writes about her connections with those considered "fremd" [strange]: "Meine Bekanntschaften wurden erst recht weitläufig, nicht nur mit Einheimischen, deren Gesinnungen mit den meinigen übereinstimmten, sondern auch mit Fremden." [My acquaintances then became really extensive, not only with locals, whose sensibilities were in accord with mine, but also with strangers.][135] The use of the word "extensive" here is reminiscent of Lotte's fluid use of the term in *Werther* to describe her own relations.

Perhaps the most important line in the novel that reveals the slippage between *Verwandtschaft* and *Bekanntschaft*—and that further reminds us of the central role of affinity in human relations[136]—is the jokester Friedrich's comment about paternity: "Die Vaterschaft beruht nur überhaupt auf der Überzeugung; ich bin überzeugt, und also bin ich Vater." [Paternity actually only rests on conviction; I am convinced, therefore I am a father.][137] Friedrich is referring here to his own ignorance about the paternity of Philine's child, but his formulation is also grammatically tentative, as he uses the modifying terms "nur" [only] and "überhaupt" [at all] to soften the force of "Überzeugung" [conviction]. The utterance reminds the reader that there is no proof of Wilhelm's paternity of Felix. The Tower Society pronounces that Wilhelm is the father, and Wilhelm believes it, but we have learned in the course of the novel that no pronouncements are fixed or eternally true.[138] Hence, Friedrich's utterance points not only to the uncertainty attached to fatherhood in an era prior to genetic testing but also to the willed nature of the father-child relationship. In this sense, paternity is just one of many relationships along the *Verwandtschaft/Bekanntschaft* spectrum, a spectrum that reveals a consistent slippage between roles. The father role is particularly vexed, and *Wilhelm Meisters Lehrjahre* contains numerous cases in which paternity is either unknown (Felix, Philine's child) or kept secret (Mignon). The novel's sequel, *Wilhelm Meisters Wanderjahre* (1821), begins as Wilhelm and Felix encounter a series of biblical Joseph figures depicted in the form of paintings in a chapel and embodied by a similar character named Joseph.[139] It is striking that at the outset of the novel, Wilhelm and his son, whose paternity is never clearly established, are drawn to Joseph as the iconic adoptive father figure.[140]

Fatherhood is shown to be just one of many roles that a character may take on vis-à-vis another character. At the end of the novel, when Felix has survived what was feared to be a poisoning, Wilhelm claims that Felix is not only a (likely) son but also a mother and brother figure: "Du warst mir zum Ersatz deiner geliebten Mutter gegeben, du solltest mir die zweite Mutter ersetzen . . . komm, mein Sohn! komm, mein Bruder." [You were given to me as a replacement for your beloved mother, you should replace my second mother . . . come, my son! come, my brother.][141] Kinship relations, those of blood and those of choice, are interchangeable, such that a son figure can likewise serve as a mother and brother figure.

Heterogeneous communities are formed throughout Wilhelm's travels. The theater troupe consists of a variety of figures; some with aristocratic histories, some with bourgeois backgrounds like Wilhelm, others from artist families, and still others from cultural spaces outside of the German-speaking world. At times, Wilhelm is ecstatic about what he imagines to be a utopic community formed with the members of the troupe. In book 4 he tells them that the theater could provide a model for an ideal nation with a democratic structure; Wilhelm is chosen as the troupe's director, a senate is created, and women are able to hold seats in it and vote. The actor Laertes reminds everyone that that they represent a "wanderndes Reich, . . . wir werden wenigstens keine Grenzstreitigkeiten haben." [traveling empire, . . . at least we won't have any border skirmishes.][142] The ideal community imagined by Wilhelm is therefore modeled neither on the nuclear family nor on a modern state model, insofar as fixed borders are crucial to both. The community nonetheless frequently lapses into fighting, undermining Wilhelm's utopian hopes.

The secretive Tower Society is yet another community model represented in Goethe's novel, and the beloved figure of Lothario, the brother of Natalie (who rescued Wilhelm and whom he eventually marries), is the initial lure for Wilhelm to join the community. Lothario and Natalie's family is aristocratic, but their genealogy is fuzzy. After Wilhelm's encounter with Natalie, he searches through maps and genealogical books in order to find out more information about her family: "Man suchte nach dem Orte, den die edle Familie während des Kriegs zu ihrem Sitz erwählt hatte, man suchte Nachrichten von ihr selbst auf; allein der Ort war in keiner Geographie, auf keiner Karte zu finden, und die genealogischen Handbücher sagten nichts von einer solchen Familie." [One searched for the location that the noble family had chosen as its seat during the war, one searched for news of the family itself; but the location was not in any geography book or on any map, and the genealogical handbooks said nothing about such a family.][143] Hence, Natalie's family must be understood as a collection of unique individuals and not as a group of similar characters related by a bloodline. The Tower Society is just as much of a puzzle and includes figures such as the mercurial Jarno and the Abbé. Indeed, this society is radically homosocial yet opaque, differing substantially from both the nuclear family model and the heterogeneous theater community. Interestingly, the narrator uses the term "Familie" (albeit in the subjunctive mood) when Wilhelm undergoes initiation rituals choreographed by Jarno and the Abbé, two figures who are not part of any traditional family: "Von diesem Augenblick an ward unser Freund im Hause, als gehöre er zur Familie, behandelt." [From this moment on our friend was treated within the house as if he belonged to the family.][144]

The final chapters of the novel, which take place at the Oheim's [uncle's] estate, include a collection of characters from Natalie and Lothario's family, members of the Tower Society, Mignon, Felix, and numerous visitors, and yet Wilhelm expresses the feeling that he is in the midst of a "Familienkreis" [family circle].[145] Indeed, yet another kind of *Verwandtschaft* is explored in these final chapters, as Wilhelm discovers the paintings that had belonged to Wilhelm's grandfather in the Oheim's estate, producing kinship via art works: "Diesen unsern alten Familienschatz, diese Lebensfreude meines Großvaters, finde ich hier zwischen so vielen andern würdigen Kunstwerken aufgestellt, und mich, den die Natur zum Liebling dieses guten alten Mannes gemacht hatte, mich Unwürdigen, finde ich auch hier, o Gott! in welchen Verbindungen, in welcher Gesellschaft!" [Here I find this, our old family treasure, my grandfather's life's joy, displayed amongst so many other valuable artworks, and I find here, too, my unworthy self, whom nature made into the darling of this good old man. Oh, God! Amongst such connections, in such a society!][146] The Oheim's grand estate stands as a *Haus* in the premodern sense, one that connects diverse characters, inviting the reader to think anew about genealogy and the notion of *Erbteil* [inheritance] in the broadest sense.[147] The final chapter at the Oheim's castle (book 8, chapter 10) resembles the scenes of plays in which all the characters are assembled in a final *tableau*. Goethe seems to poke fun at this convention, as the house becomes so crowded that people start to avoid one another:

> Nun waren nach und nach so viele Menschen angekommen, daß man sie im Schloß und in den Seitengebäuden kaum alle unterbringen konnte, um so mehr, als man nicht gleich anfangs auf den Empfang so vieler Gäste die Einrichtung gemacht hatte. Man frühstückte, man speiste zusammen und hätte sich gern beredt, man lebe in einer vergnüglichen Übereinstimmung, wenn schon in der Stille die Gemüter sich gewissermaßen auseinander sehnten.

> [And now so many people had arrived, one after the other, that one could barely house them in the castle and in the auxiliary buildings, especially since one hadn't prepared for a reception of so many guests right from the beginning. One ate breakfast and other meals together and would have liked to convince oneself that one lived in a pleasurable state of accord, even if in quiet moments the characters in some measure desired some separation.][148]

The heterogeneous grouping of characters almost breaks the idealized community open, much as Wilhelm's fantasies of a utopian theater troupe world were similarly frustrated.

The failure of utopia, however, does not lead to the establishment of more streamlined kinship structures.[149] Instead, the excess of the final scenes is mirrored in the happy ending solution of a double marriage: Lothario will marry Therese, and Wilhelm will marry Lothario's sister Natalie. Wilhelm gives up his plan to marry Therese, and the pairs are quickly shuffled to create a larger grouping of characters linked via a mixture of blood and elective relations: "Sie [Therese] schwur, daß dieses doppelte Paar an einem Tage zum Altare gehen sollte." [She (Therese) swore that this double couple should go to the altar on the same day.][150] Goethe's novel, said to be the quintessential *Bildungsroman*, here resembles a *Possenspiel*, a premodern comedy in which characters join together in the final *tableau*. Excess is the quality characterizing the collection of characters in the castle and the erotic and kinship connections that continue to remain opaque, and Wilhelm never forms a neat nuclear family structure with Natalie and Felix. Indeed, this family never materializes in Goethe's subsequent novel about Wilhelm, *Wilhelm Meisters Wanderjahre*. The *Wanderjahre* depicts Wilhelm's travels, sometimes in the company of Felix and sometimes with a vast collection of characters, but Natalie is always located at a distance.[151] As Goethe's work exemplifies, the nuclear family is simply not a kinship form that resonates in German novels of the period.

Florentin

Schlegel's *Florentin* similarly represents multiple slippages between *Bekanntschaft* and *Verwandtschaft*, and these queer kin relations are likewise depicted via paintings that empty the portrait of its presumed modern interiority. Scholars have famously been unsuccessful in attempting to sketch out the various genealogies and blood ties within the novel.[152] We never find out who Florentin's mother is, though clues point in multiple directions.[153] It is as if Schlegel has laid a trap for her readers in order to teach us, once and for all, to abandon the hierarchy of *Verwandtschaft* over *Bekanntschaft*. The central figure of Clementina is the matron "aunt" of Juliane, a friend of Juliane's mother who cared for Juliane in her childhood. Clementine eventually takes on a role that merges Goethe's avuncular figures the Beautiful Soul and the Oheim from *Wilhelm Meisters Lehrjahre*. Clementine is the virginal aunt figure whose castle provides the context for a gathering of characters near the end of the novel and where, in a manner mirroring Mignon's funeral in *Wilhelm Meister* that I discuss later in the chapter, a grand musical performance takes place that transfigures the hero Florentin. Florentin first encounters this virginal aunt figure in the form of a painting of Saint Anne and the Virgin Mary in which Juliane stands for Mary and Clementine for Mary's mother Anne. Florentin is so moved by this painting that he wonders if it could be a portrait:

Und diese Anna, gewiß eine Heilige! Diese Hoheit, dieser milde Ernst in den verklärten Augen! Mit welcher Liebe sich ihr Haupt zu dem Liebling hinneigt, sich ihre Tugend lehrenden Lippen öffnen! Ruhe und Würde in der ganzen Gestalt, und wie erhaben diese Hand, die gegen den Himmel zeigt! Ist auch diese Anna ein Porträt?

[And this Anna, certainly a saint! This majestic dignity, this mild gravity in the transfigured eyes! With what love does her head look down to her darling, do her lips that teach virtue open! Peace and dignity in the entire figure, and how sublime this hand, that points toward heaven! Points! Is this Anna also a portrait?][154]

The description of the painting highlights its gestural, *tableau*-like nature. Indeed, the painting seems to be a *tableau vivant* that has been reified as a work of art.

However, Florentin learns that "Aunt" (Clementine) did not sit for this picture but rather, as a young woman, for a painting of Saint Cecilia that was later copied for the composition Florentin is now looking at

sowohl dieses Bild, das sie dem Grafen auf sein Bitten malen zu lassen erlaubte, um ein Denkmal der Zeit zu stiften, in der sie Julianens Lehrerin war, als das, welches unter den andern Familiengemälden in der Galerie hängt, und auch das Miniaturbild, das Juliane an ihrer Brust trägt, sind Kopien nach dieser Cäcilia.

[this picture, that she allowed to be painted at the count's wish as a memorial to the time during which she was Juliane's teacher, as well as the one that hangs amongst the other family portraits in the gallery, and also the miniature that Juliane wears on her breast, are all copies of this Cäcilia painting.][155]

Here, again, we are confronted by copies, and a copy that has been reimagined in a new religious context. The original portrait was made at a time when none of the characters in the novel knew Clementine. The multiple roles (Saint Anne and Saint Cecilia) she takes on in the original painting and the copy complicate the temporality of the portrait, a work of art that captures the subject in a particular moment of time. In the case of the Clementine portraits/paintings, the face of the young Clementine clashes with the matron's clothing worn by Saint Anne. Instead of functioning as a modern portrait, the various iterations of young Clementine's likeness render her ghostly, like a floating ideal. Hovering between portraiture and religious iconography, these renderings of Clementine approximate allegorical *tableaux*. And like Sophie Sternheim, Juliane wears a copy as a talisman in a gesture that both undercuts the aura of the original painting and codes it as a mnemonic prop.

The reflected engagement with paintings and *tableaux* in *Florentin* suggests that by 1800 the frozen image of the social grouping is beginning to loosen. There are many moments in the novel in which paintings are mentioned in order to cue the other characters or readers to imagine the *tableau* and reconstruct the *tableau vivant* for themselves. This cueing occurs not only when Florentin experiences the picture of the count's extended family and guests as utopic and when he is fascinated by the paintings of Juliane and Clementine. The wedding party for Juliane and her betrothed Eduard is likewise imagined by Florentin, himself a painter, as a *tableau vivant* of a Teniers painting: "'Mir ist,' sagte Florentin, 'als sähe ich eine Szene von Teniers lebendig werden!'" ["It seems to me," said Florentin, "as if I were seeing a scene from a Teniers painting come alive!"][156]

THE LITERARY *TABLEAU* AND MOVEMENT

What does it mean that the *tableau* begins to move in the German novel? The delicate tension between stasis and movement is particularly apparent in *Die Leiden des jungen Werthers* and *Wilhelm Meisters Lehrjahre*. As we have seen, for Lukács, movement is sutured to the depth he associates with a socially relevant mode of realism. As he writes, "The impartial, true, *deep* and comprehensive poetic reflection of . . . human life must appear in the form of *movement*."[157] In *The Theory of the Novel* (1916), Lukács connects movement in the novel to a concept of modernity (in contrast to the stasis of the epic), and this is one way of thinking about the tendency in Goethe's first two novels for *tableaux* to represent both stillness and movement. But it would be too simple to smoothly ally the *tableaux* of social groupings within these novels to Goethe's interest in vitalism and *Bildung*. The development and change at the center of works like "Die Metamorphose der Pflanzen" [The Metamorphosis of Plants] (1798) does not map cleanly onto the representation of social groupings in the novels. Whereas *Bildung* is organic, movement as "Bewegung" indicates dynamism without development. In this sense, the episodic structure of *Wilhelm Meisters Lehrjahre* reveals an affinity with a form of movement that deviates from the telos of *Bildung* and does not map onto the development of an interior subject.

Lukács distinguishes the hero of the premodern epic from the hero of the modern novel: the former has no interiority, while the latter does. The epic hero is not an "individual" in the modern sense.[158] The epic hero resides at the center of the adventures he experiences, "the internally most immobile point of the rhythmic movement of the world." In contrast, the novel is "the form of adventure of the intrinsic value of the individual"[159] and represents "a Becoming,"[160] an encounter between a fragile hero and the "fragility of the world."[161] As a "Becoming," the novel, along with its hero, is constantly in motion within a destabilized post-sacral world. Yet despite his praise for *Wilhelm Meisters Lehrjahre*, Lukács expresses frustration with the "epic character"[162] of the Tower Society narrative strand of the novel, complaining "that it destroys in a dissonating manner the unity of tone: it becomes about producing secrets without any hidden depth of meaning, and it becomes a strongly emphasized plot motif without true importance, a playful ornament without decorative grace."[163] For Lukács, the Tower Society thread within Goethe's novel destroys the organic unity of the work, gesturing toward depth via secrets while remaining flat and "inorganic."[164]

Deleuze's reflections on film are helpful here, as he distinguishes between the premodern "privileged instant" and the "any-instant-whatever" of our modern times. Central here is the category of movement: How does one movement transition to the one that follows? "Privileged instances" reflect the older notion of movement as "the regulated transition from one form to another, that is, an order of *poses* or privileged instants, as in a dance." "Any-instant-whatevers" are modern and Cartesian, not Euclidian: moments that are equal in time and importance.[165] In this sense, the movement between "any-instant-whatevers" is constant, making it difficult for modern spectators to register the transition. Modern movement, in this sense, is an uninterrupted whir instead of a careful shift from one pose to another.

Novel *Tableaux*

Die Geschichte des Fräuleins von Sternheim incorporates a number of *tableau* scenes that picture nonbiological groupings and themes. *Tableaux* in the novel represent scenes of suffering and recall biblical iconography theatrically performed. Often, figures seek God's grace with eyes or hands stretching up to heaven, a gesture we encounter multiple times via Ottilie in Goethe's *Wahlverwandtschaften*.

A key concept for understanding eighteenth-century German literary *tableaux* is the term *Anblick* [sight, view]. The entry on *Anblick* in the *Goethe-Dictionary* indicates that it connotes both an objective and a subjective gaze as well as the conscious presentation of the self to others: "das Angeblickte, das sich dem Blick Darbietende" [that which is viewed, that which offers itself to the gaze.][166] *Anblick* indicates not only "the visually perceived presence of a person" but also always points to the "presence of the observer."[167] Along these lines, there is a complex relationship between the looker and the one being looked at that belies a naive naturalness on the part of either individual within the *Anblick* scene.

There is a static character to *anblicken* that adheres to the *tableau*, even when that which is being observed is moving. *Tableaux* in the novels discussed here are cued by the reference to a witness (Diderot's "invisible observer"), one who, as Elsaesser points out, is "cited" through "tableau-like static compositions."[168] Gazing, of course, functions differently in a novel than in a film or play, but novel *tableaux* are cued via looking, either from the first-person perspective of the passive observer or when the narrative voice makes clear that the characters in the *tableau* are being observed. This cue is crucial to the creation of an invisible frame that creates an aesthetic of exteriority and flatness; emotions are legible via gesture and not through access to the interior subjectivity of the characters in the *tableau*. What is more, both *Anblick* and *tableau* point to the outlines of a frame within which time slows. Indeed, the *tableau demands* a slowing of time and movement in order for the observer to take it in.

La Roche's *Die Geschichte des Fräulein von Sternheim* contains numerous *tableau* scenes that are marked by the term *Anblick*. The scenes highlight the slippery relationships between genres and media in the period (drama and novel, painting, theater and writing) and frame characters in a manner that depicts them allegorically, as figures in religious paintings. A case in point is the silent scene of mourning depicted from the perspective of Sophie's passive suitor Lord Seymour, and this *tableau* is cued by the term *Anblick*. Seeing and watching are doubly at play, since the *tableau* is observed not by Seymour, who describes it in a letter to Doktor B., but by Derby, who relays it to Seymour. Despite the assumption of Sophie's transparent goodness, the scene is called an "Aufführung" [a show], suggesting that performance is at play. In the *tableau* Sophie comforts Rosina after the death of the latter's father:

> Und wie er in ihr Zimmer gegangen sie abzuholen, habe er ihre
> Kammerjungfer vor ihr knien gesehen; das Fräulein selbst halb

angezogen, ihre schönen Haare auf Brust und Nacken zerstreut, ihre Arme um das knieende Mädchen geschlungen, deren Kopf sie an sich gedrückt, während sie ihr mit beweglicher Stimme von dem Wert des Todes der Gerechten und der Belohnung der Tugend gesprochen. Tränen wären aus ihren Augen gerollt, die sie endlich gen Himmel gehoben. . . . Dieser *Anblick* hätte ihn staunen gemacht.

[And as he went into her room in order to get her, he saw her chambermaid kneeling before her; the maiden herself half-dressed, her beautiful hair scattered over her breast and neck, her arms wrapped around the kneeling girl, whose head she pressed against her as she spoke to her with an animated voice about the value of the death of the righteous and the reward of virtue. Tears, he said, rolled out of her eyes that she finally raised to heaven. . . . This sight, he said, amazed him.][169]

Gesture is key here. Though words are presumably spoken, their content is not important. Gestures of kneeling, resting one's head upon another, and turning one's hands or eyes to heaven are common "stage directions" in these *tableaux*. In fact, we have two *tableaux* combined in this image: Sophie shifts from holding Rosina with her head presumably facing downward to finally ("endlich") turning her eyes toward heaven. We encounter here the slow movement from one *tableau* to another related one. The turn toward heaven is repeated again and again in the novel, for instance when Sophie learns that people at the court believe she has become the count's mistress: "Das Fräulein antwortet mit nichts als einem Strom von Tränen, die aus ihren gen Himmel gerichteten Augen flossen, und ihre gerungenen Hände benetzen." [The maiden answers with nothing but a stream of tears that flowed from her eyes turned to heaven and that moistened her clasped hands.][170] The ekphrastic description of gesture and mood in the Rosina/Sophie *tableau* is detailed enough that a corresponding painting could easily be produced.

The rape scene in La Roche's novel includes a number of *tableaux* observed by the abducter and rapist Derby as well as by Rosina; each *tableau* highlights the static, religious, and painterly quality of the scene. After bringing Sophie to an inn under the guise of marrying her, Derby insists that Sophie prepare to share her bed with him:

Ich ging mich umzukleiden, kam bald wieder, und sah durch eine
Türe sie auf der Bank sitzen, ihre beiden Arme um den Vorhang
des Fensters geschlungen, alle Muskeln angestrengt, ihre Augen in
die Höhe gehoben, ihre schöne Brust von starkem tiefen Atemho-
len langsam bewegt; kurz, das Bild der stummen Verzweiflung!
Sage, was für Eindrücke mußte das auf mich machen?

[I went to change my clothes, came back soon, and, through the
door, saw her sitting on a bench, both of her arms wrapped around
the window curtain, her muscles strained, her eyes raised to the sky,
her lovely breast slowly moved by strong and deep breaths, the picture of mute confusion! Tell me, what kinds of impressions must
this have made on me?][171]

The scene is cued by Derby's passive observer position. Sophie's gestures
replace speech, as her eyes are again turned to the heavens. What is particularly notable here is Derby's reflection on his own reception of this
scene ("what kind of impressions must this have made on me?"). In this
sense, the *tableau* is a moment in the novel in which characters stop, watch,
and reflect, as if contemplating a static artwork. But, as we see, movement
cannot be fully avoided, as Derby notes the slow breaths that move her
chest.

The *tableaux* highlight the tenuousness of stasis. In a *tableau* scene following the rape, Rosalia describes this tension:[172] "Sie ißt nichts; sie ist den
ganzen Tag auf den Knieen vor einem Stuhl, da hat sie ihren Kopf liegen;
unbeweglich, außer, daß sie manchmal ihre Arme gen Himmel streckt, und
mit einer sterbenden Stimme ruft; '*Ach Gott, ach mein Gott!*'" [She eats nothing; she remains on her knees before a chair the entire day, that's where she
lays her head; motionless, except that she sometimes stretches her arms
toward heaven and calls with a dying voice, "Oh God, oh my God!"][173]
Sophie's words do not express the content of her suffering: they mimic Jesus's
lament on the cross and connote Christian suffering in general. Though
Rosalia codes the scene as "motionless," she nevertheless describes the
repeated gestures of kneeling, of laying one's head down and then stretching the arms to heaven. These singular iconic movements complicate the stasis of the scene, rendering it something like a GIF, in which movement is
contained and repeated, as if in a loop. These *tableaux* create intimate connections through proximity, desire, or empathy.

In one passage in the novel the *tableau* becomes a *tableau vivant*: a familiar painting (like those static biblical artworks that inform the gestures in the *tableaux*) begins to move—to become modern, we might say. The collection of figures represented in the painting does not change, but the two-dimensional world becomes uncannily three-dimensional in Sophie's description of her first experience of the world of the court:

> Aber denken Sie sich eine Person voll Aufmerksamkeit und Empfindung, die schon lange mit einem großen Gemälde von reicher und weitläufiger Komposition bekannt ist! Oft hat sie es betrachtet, und über den Plan, die Verhältnisse der Gegenstände, und die Mischung der Farben nachgedacht, alles ist ihr bekannt; aber auf einmal kommt durch eine fremde Kraft das stillruhende Gemälde mit allem, was es enthält, in Bewegung; natürlicherweise erstaunt diese Person, und ihre Empfindungen werden auf mancherlei Art gerührt. Diese erstaunte Person bin ich; die Gegenstände und Farben machen es nicht; die Bewegung, die fremde Bewegung ist's die ich sonderbar finde.

> [Consider an attentive and sensitive person who has long been familiar with a large painting of a rich and spacious composition! She often observed it and reflected upon the relationships between the objects and the mix of colors, it is all familiar to her; but suddenly a strange force makes the quietly resting painting move; of course, this person is astonished, and her sensibilities are moved in various ways. I am this astonished person; the objects and colors aren't causing it; the movement, the strange movement is the thing I find peculiar.][174]

Already familiar with images of the court, Sophie's entrance into its lived world is described as a *tableau vivant*, as Sophie becomes aware of materiality, of precisely the vitality and strangeness of movement. The fleshing out of the court as figures begin to move and objects take on a three-dimensional complexity shifts the perspective from a premodern to a Renaissance one. Suddenly, Sophie's own perspective becomes the focal point of the painting as things and figures move around her. We have presumably shifted from a flat representation of allegorical figures to a more modern and complex world in which subjective perspective is key to comprehending the world. The *tableau vivant* of the court is potentially unstable—movement always threatens order. But how is it that the temporary rounding out of Sophie's experience occurs not within her bourgeois home but at the court, which she despises, the place where individuals are not interior subjects in the modern sense but instead take on prescribed roles? The conflation of a more modern sense of experience with the old/aristocratic world provides us with yet another instance of the German novel of the period destabilizing a neat bourgeois domestic/interior, subject/*Bildung* paradigm.

The inclusion of what we might call a *tableau vivant* amongst the many static scenes within *Die Geschichte des Fräuleins von Sternheim* points to the emergence of a self-consciousness vis-à-vis self-presentation. The onset of movement in the static picture of society creates not only a feeling of vitality but also fear of instability as the perspective shifts to viewers whose own positions are no longer clearly fixed. In Goethe's novels, as well, we see the *tableau* of social constellations shifting from a static to a more dynamic moving picture. Both *Die Leiden des jungen Werthers* and *Wilhelm Meisters Lehrjahre* depict *tableaux* cued by the description of gestures and marked by the presence of an observer who frames the extended moment, yet these *tableaux* frequently do not remain static; instead, the figures represented in them often begin to stir just as the picture is becoming fully formed.

Tableaux in *Die Leiden des jungen Werthers* retain a tension between stasis and movement in which relationships are framed and then dissolve. They are often cued by the term *Anblick* or by the clearly delineated presence of an observer within the narrative frame. When Werther first discovers the rural and idyllic village of Wahlheim,[175] he describes in detail the exact gestures of two children sitting on the ground, a scene in which one child holds the smaller one in a motherly embrace that quiets the child and creates the *tableau*:

Es war alles im Felde; nur ein Knabe von ungefähr vier Jahren saß an der Erde und hielt ein anderes, etwa halbjähriges, vor ihm zwischen seinen Füßen sitzendes Kind mit beiden Armen wider seine Brust, so daß er ihm zu einer Art von Sessel diente und ungeachtet der Munterkeit, womit er aus seinen schwarzen Augen herumschaute, ganz ruhig saß. Mich vergnügte der Anblick.

[Everyone was in the field; only a boy of about four years sat on the ground and held another child, about half a year old, sitting between his feet in front of him, with both arms against his chest so that he created for him a kind of chair and, notwithstanding the playfulness with which he looked around out of his black eyes, sat very calmly. The sight gave me pleasure.][176]

The gestures of the children are described in such detail that Wilhelm is able to draw the scene. The children remain still ("very calmly"), although this stillness is produced through the tight grip of the child playing the role of mother. One has a sense that the scene will burst into motion at any moment.

Scenes with Lotte include ekphrastic descriptions of gesture that dissolve in motion. The most famous of these *tableaux* is the "reizendste[s] Schauspiel" [most charming play] Werther experiences when he first meets Lotte, who is playing the dual roles of sister and mother to her siblings:[177]

In dem Vorsaale wimmelten sechs Kinder von eilf zu zwey Jahren um ein Mädchen von schöner Gestalt, mittlere Größe, die ein simples weißes Kleid, mit blaßroten Schleifen an Arm und Brust, anhatte. Sie hielt ein schwarzes Brod und schnitt ihren Kleinen rings herum jedem sein Stück nach Proportion ihres Alters und Appetits ab, gab's jedem mit solcher Freundlichkeit, und jedes rief so ungekünstelt sein "Danke!", indem es mit den kleinen Händchen lange in die Höhe gereicht hatte, ehe es noch abgeschnitten war, und nun mit seinem Abendbrote vergnügt entweder wegsprang, oder nach seinem stillern Charakter gelassen davonging nach dem Hoftore zu, um die Fremden und die Kutsche zu sehen, darin ihre Lotte wegfahren sollte.

[In the entrance hall six children from eleven to two years old swarmed around a girl with a lovely figure and of medium build, who had on a simple white dress with pale red ribbons on the arms and chest. She held a loaf of black bread and cut for each of the little ones circled around her a piece according to their age and appetite and gave it to each with such friendliness, and each cried so unaffectedly their "thank you!," for each child had reached with their little hands into the air for a long time before the bread was cut, and now pleased with their bread each child either sprang away or with a quieter character nonchalantly walked to the gate in order to see the strangers and the carriage within which Lotte was supposed to drive away.][178]

The scene is set up as a dramatic *tableau* or painting with detailed descriptions of color and gesture. Indeed, by highlighting the transparent and natural ("unaffected") behavior of the characters in the scene, Werther as narrator creates a *tableau* to Diderot's taste, one in which the fourth wall is firmly in place. By the end of the description the characters, members of a fragmented family community, are beginning to run away, some quickly and others more calmly, as the idyllic scene is disrupted at the margins through the introduction of movement into the controlled stasis.

Other *tableaux* in *Werther* likewise paint an initially static picture and then show the process of its dissolution. After Werther kisses Lotte, the narrative describes a *tableau* in which Werther lies on the floor with outstretched arms, interpellating Lotte into the role of the heavens, recalling the *tableaux* in La Roche's novel. The narrator/editor of the novel indicates that Werther holds this frozen *tableau* position for over half an hour. Yet the description, and Werther himself, is interrupted by a noise that cues his movement: "Werther streckte ihr die Arme nach, getraute sich nicht, sie zu halten. Er lag an der Erde, den Kopf auf dem Kanapee, und in dieser Stellung blieb er über eine halbe Stunde, bis ihn ein Geräusch zu sich selbst rief." [Werther stretched his arms out to her but didn't dare hold her. He lay on the ground, his head on the sofa, and remained in this position for over half an hour, until a noise brought him back to himself.][179]

The final scene of the novel, likewise told from the ironic perspective of the novel's editor,[180] presents a *tableau* of Werther's disfigured body after the suicide attempt. In this representation of the hero as mangled flesh we have the culmination of the epistolary novel,[181] told through two levels of narrative perspective, that of the editor and that of the doctor, as the former details the latter's observation of the body:

Als der Medikus zu dem Unglücklichen kam, fand er ihn an der Erde ohne Rettung, der Puls schlug, die Glieder waren alle gelähmt. Über dem rechten Auge hatte er sich durch den Kopf geschossen, das Gehirn war herausgetrieben. Man ließ ihm zum Überfluß eine Ader am Arme, das Blut lief, er holte noch immer Atem.

Aus dem Blut auf der Lehne des Sessels konnte man schließen, er habe sitzend vor dem Schreibtische die Tat vollbracht, dann ist er heruntergesunken, hat sich konvulsivisch um den Stuhl herumgewälzt. Er lag gegen das Fenster entkräftet auf dem Rücken, war in völliger Kleidung, gestiefelt, im blauen Frack mit gelber Weste.

[As the doctor came to the unfortunate one, he found him on the ground beyond saving; his pulse beat, his limbs were all paralyzed. He had shot himself above the right eye, through the head, the brain was expelled. Needlessly, a vein was opened in his arm, blood was running; he was still breathing.

The blood on the back of the chair allowed for the conclusion that he committed the act while sitting in front of the desk; then he sank down and writhed convulsively around the chair. He lay enfeebled on his back against the window, fully clothed and in boots, in the blue coat with the yellow vest.][182]

The well-known scene reads like a forensics protocol, preceded by stage directions that detail the preparations for the *tableau*.[183] Ekphrastic language is used here to describe in great detail the most profane of scenes, a suicide *tableau*. The "objective" nature of the view being presented is underscored not only by the doctor's viewpoint but also by the use of the subjunctive to emphasize the distant perspective from which the imagined scene is being described. And in this scene, as in the others, the freeze-frame nature of the *tableau* is complicated by *movement*: Werther's blood is still flowing, and he is still breathing.

This *tableau* of the body is followed by a more traditional death scene *tableau*. Here it is not a family that surrounds Werther but instead the sons of the bailiff, who kneel at his feet:

> Seine ältesten Söhne kamen bald nach ihm zu Fuße, sie fielen neben dem Bett nieder im Ausdrucke des unbändigsten Schmerzens, küßten ihm die Hände und den Mund, und der älteste, den er immer am meisten geliebt, hing an seinen Lippen, bis er verschieden war und man den Knaben mit Gewalt wegriß.

> [His oldest sons arrived soon after him; they fell down next to the bed with expressions of irrepressible pain, kissed his hands and mouth, and the oldest one, whom he had always loved the most, hung on Werther's lips until he passed and one pulled away the boy by force.][184]

The oldest boy kisses Werther like a lover, taking on the role of wife or child. The gestures of mourning are rendered in great detail by the editor in this *tableau*, yet the description ends with the violent ripping away of the older boy from the scene, the dissolution of the *tableau* through movement. The kinship structure in the *tableau* is anything but familial: Werther, the doctor, Albert, the bailiff, and his two sons constitute a homosocial hodgepodge that notably excludes Lotte.

Within *Wilhelm Meisters Lehrjahre* the queer figure of Mignon, always foreign, always in between, stands at the center of *tableaux* that depict an intense dialectic of stillness and movement.[185] Mignon is a daughter and potential lover figure to Wilhelm and a sister and mother figure to Felix, as well as an androgynous saint by the end of the novel when her funeral service is performed as a spectacle at the Oheim's castle. The *tableaux* with Mignon invariably include few or no words spoken by characters and combine an intense energy and movement with a sudden or forced stillness. An early encounter between Wilhelm and Mignon pictures this tension between stasis and movement: "Es ging die Treppe weder auf noch ab, sondern sprang; es stieg auf den Geländern der Gänge weg, und eh' man sich's versah, saß es oben auf dem Schranke und *blieb eine Weile ruhig*." [It neither climbed nor descended the stairs but rather jumped; it climbed onto the banister of the hallway and, before one could apprehend the moment, it sat on top of the closet and *remained calm for a while*.][186] Bodily gestures are described here, but Mignon moves too quickly for the ekphrasis to be complete. She climbs onto the banister of the stairwell and perches on top of the closet faster than Wilhelm can perceive her movement. The convention of cueing the *tableau* ("before one could apprehend the moment") is still used here, but the movement is simply too quick and abrupt. Yet the scene also includes a moment of stillness ("remained calm for a while"). The movement between postures is both premodern in the sense that Deleuze describes, as a movement that shifts from one posture to the next, and modern, as certain movements are not perceivable in the whir of activity, and it is difficult to ascertain which one is most important.

Three additional *tableaux* featuring Mignon and Wilhelm depict the tension between stillness and movement. In these scenes, Wilhelm frequently introduces stillness by force, as he attempts to hold Mignon tighter, and his action in this regard correlates with the fixed role he has chosen as the girl's adoptive father. The tension of movement that he seeks to tame reflects the blurring of boundaries between kinship roles as he and Mignon hover on the edge of an erotic relationship. Book 2 ends as Wilhelm tells Mignon he is leaving her in order to continue his travels, followed by a *tableau* in which Mignon kneels in front of Wilhelm and puts her head on his knee:

Sie sah ihm in die Augen, die von verhaltenen Tränen blinkten, und kniete mit Heftigkeit vor ihm nieder. Er behielt ihre Hände, sie legte ihr Haupt auf seine Kniee und war ganz still. Er spielte mit ihren Haaren und war freundlich. Sie blieb lange ruhig. Endlich fühlte er an ihr eine Art Zucken, das ganz sachte anfing und sich, durch alle Glieder wachsend, verbreitete.

[She looked him in his eyes, which shimmered with restrained tears, and kneeled down with fervor in front of him. He held her hands, she laid her head onto his knees and was completely still. He played with her hair and was friendly. She remained calm for a long time. Finally he felt in her a kind of tremor that began very gently and then spread out through all of her limbs.][187]

The *tableau* resembles Magdalene kneeling before Christ and is cued by descriptors of time ("She remained calm for a long time."). Yet the moment is fleeting and is followed immediately by seemingly involuntary movements in Mignon's body. She lets out a scream: "Der mit krampfigen Bewegungen des Körpers begleitet war. Sie fuhr auf und fiel auch zugleich wie an allen Gelenken gebrochen vor ihm nieder. Es war ein *gräßlicher Anblick!*" [That was accompanied by cramped movements of the body. She stood up and simultaneously fell in front of him as if all of her limbs were broken. It was a horrible sight!][188] The *Anblick* of cramped movement and a broken, fragmented body is "horrible" in its resistance to any clear frame. Is Mignon remembering a past trauma? Having a sexual experience?[189]

Wilhelm's response to Mignon's seemingly formless movement is to call her "Mein Kind!" [My child!][190] and hold her ever tighter as she cries: "Ihre starren Glieder wurden gelinde, es ergoß sich ihr Innerstes, und in der Verwirrung des Augenblickes fürchtete Wilhelm, sie werde in seinen Armen zerschmelzen, und er nichts von ihr übrigbehalten. Er hielt sie nur fester und fester." [Her rigid limbs became limp, her inner self poured out of her, and in the confusion of the moment Wilhelm feared she would melt in his arms and nothing would be left of her. He only held her tighter and tighter.][191] In response to the perception that Mignon is dissolving in his arms, Wilhelm forcefully tries to hold her still. Details of gesture common to the novel *tableau* are combined with subjective description ("and in the confusion of the moment Wilhelm feared she would melt in his arms"). *Anblick* as objectively perceived vision and *Anblick* as something subjectively experienced and performed for another meld in this scene.

The word "fester" [tighter] is used throughout the novel to express the forceful action of trying to press Mignon into a role in order to ward off the dissolution of the contours of the frame. Later in the same chapter, once Mignon has somewhat calmed down, the narrator again uses the formulation "fester" to describe Wilhelm, "der, sein Kind immer fester in Armen behaltend, des reinsten, unbeschreiblichsten Glückes genoß." [who, holding his child ever tighter in his arms, enjoyed the purest, most indescribable happiness.][192] In a similar *tableau* in book 4, chapter 2, Mignon places her head on Wilhelm's breast in a rare moment of stillness: "Mignon hatte sich ihm unter diesen Worten genähert, schlang ihre zarten Arme um ihn und blieb mit dem Köpfchen an seine Brust gelehnt stehen." [Mignon had approached him as he spoke, wrapped her tender arms around him, and remained standing with her head leaning on his chest.][193] Yet the *tableau* is intensified by Mignon's movement not away from Wilhelm but actively *closer* to him: "Mignon drückte sich immer fester an ihn." [Mignon pressed herself ever more tightly to him.][194] The narrator again uses the words "immer fester" to picture the intensive force of Mignon's attempts to be still. The *tableau* can, ironically, only be held through motion and not rest.

The tension between motion and stillness, the *tableau* and the loss of its frame, is beautifully rendered in the description of Mignon as moving in a restless stillness, and Mignon's state is framed by the narrator as eliciting discomfort in Wilhelm ("Wir müssen, da wir gegenwärtig von ihr sprechen, auch der Verlegenheit gedenken, in die sie seit einiger Zeit unseren Freund öfters versetzte." [We must, since we are currently speaking of her, also consider the embarrassment into which she often put our friend recently.]):[195]

Die zuckende Lebhaftigkeit schien sich in ihrem Betragen täglich zu vermehren, und ihr ganzes Wesen *bewegte sich in einer rastlosen Stille*. Sie konnte nicht sein, ohne einen Bindfaden in den Händen zu drehen, ein Tuch zu kneten, Papier oder Hölzchen zu kauen. Jedes ihrer Spiele schien nur eine innere heftige Erschütterung abzuleiten.

[The quivering liveliness in her demeanor seemed to increase daily, and her whole essence *moved in a restless calm*. She couldn't be without turning a string in her hands, kneading a towel, or chewing paper or wood. Each of her games seemed only to deflect an intense inner shock.][196]

Mignon's restless stillness points to the tension between new and old time as well as new and old modes of identity, a tension that creates a contagious anxiety within the world of Goethe's novel.

Mignon's death follows immediately after Natalie agrees to marry Wilhelm and one of her roles (as Wilhelm's lover) is extinguished. Her memorial service is held using large wax torches[197] so that even though her body is enshrined "in der angenehmsten Stellung" [in the most pleasing position],[198] it does not appear as completely still. The torches are reminiscent of those Goethe describes in Italy that illuminate the Laocoön statue group, giving one the impression that it is moving:

> Um die Intention des Laokoons recht zu fassen, stelle man sich in gehöriger Entfernung, mit geschlossnen Augen davor, man öffne sie und schließe sie sogleich wieder, so wird man den ganzen Marmor in Bewegung sehen, man wird fürchten, indem man die Augen wieder öffnet, die ganze Gruppe verändert zu finden. . . . Dieselbe Wirkung entsteht, wenn man die Gruppe Nachts bei der Fackel sieht.

> [In order to experience this intention in the *Laocoön* group, face the sculpture from a proper distance with eyes closed. If you open and then immediately close your eyes, you will see the whole marble in motion, and you will fear that when you open your eyes again, you will find the entire group changed. . . . The same effect arises whenever one views the group at night by torchlight.][199]

The description here of the tension between stasis and movement and the fleeting nature of individual movements reiterates the Mignon *tableaux* sketched above. Mignon's death is likewise depicted as a *tableau* of movement and stasis, ending, in contrast to the representation of Werther's death, with no movement: "Mignon fuhr auf einmal mit der linken Hand nach dem Herzen, und indem sie den rechten Arm heftig ausstreckte, fiel sie mit einem Schrei zu Nataliens Füßen für tot nieder . . . keine Bewegung des Herzens noch des Pulses war zu spüren." [Mignon suddenly brought her left hand to her heart, and while fiercely stretching out the right arm, she fell down dead with a scream at Natalie's feet . . . no movement of either her heart or her pulse was detected.][200] The *tableau* of falling or kneeling before another is followed by "no movement." Yet the movement begins again during her funeral service when the large wax torches reanimate seemingly dead objects and bodies.

The dialectic of movement and stasis that I have traced through *tableaux* of the figure of Mignon mirrors the form of the novel, as Wilhelm travels from one community to another, settling in one place and then moving to the next station, in a manner recalling the picaresque hero. Perhaps this not-quite-modern novel structure is the reason why the one scene in the novel that resembles a more traditional family *tableau* points to an empty future. In the final chapter, in the midst of the gathering at the Oheim's castle of seemingly every character and imaginable guest, Natalie, Wilhelm, and Felix appear in a family *tableau*, following Felix's feared consumption of poison:[201]

> Wilhelm saß vor ihr auf einem Schemel; er hatte die Füße des Knaben auf seinem Schoße, Kopf und Brust lagen auf dem ihrigen, so teilten sie die angenehme Last und die schmerzlichen Sorgen und *verharrten*, bis der Tag anbrach, in der unbequemen und traurigen Lage; Natalie hatte Wilhelmen ihre Hand gegeben, sie sprachen kein Wort, sahen auf das Kind und sahen einander an.

> [Wilhelm sat in front of her on a stool; he had the feet of the boy in his lap, the head and chest lay on hers. This is how they shared the pleasant burden and the painful worries and *persisted* in this uncomfortable and sad state until the day broke; Natalie had given Wilhelm her hand; they didn't say a word; they looked at the child and at one another.][202]

The self-conscious *tableau* of the adoptive nuclear family is not a comfortable one to perform. Although it wants to point to a nuclear family future, this future will, we know, never come to pass. Wilhelm plans to marry Natalie in a double wedding and to depart on his travels soon thereafter. We know that Natalie never joins Wilhelm in *Wilhelm Meisters Wanderjahre*, that no biological offspring is produced by the pairing, and that Wilhelm travels restlessly, encountering communities of all kinds along the way and never stopping to rest in the stillness he had tried to impose upon Mignon.

MOVING PICTURES: MOVEMENT WITHOUT *BILDUNG*

Movement and *Bildung* are not synonymous. Lukács's suturing of movement to the modern novel hero and the modern world does not mean that literary movement is always a sign of organic growth. Novalis was one of the few harsh critics of *Wilhelm Meisters Lehrjahre* among the Romantics, calling it a "poeticized machinery" as well as "prosaic."[203] "Prosaic" connotes here something like Luhmann's "bready semantics," in which "bürgerlich" and "häuslich," terms Novalis likewise uses as qualifiers for Goethe's novel, are metonyms. In calling Goethe's novel a "poeticized machinery," Novalis undercuts any organic force within it, likening its movements to repetition and not development. In this sense, Novalis anticipates Lukács's later critique of the epic quality of the Tower Society narrative thread that he sees as flattening the novel's characters and their world.

Schiller's response to the novel was mixed, as expressed in the published correspondence between him and Goethe during Goethe's production of the novel, and his criticism prefigures Lukács's concern with the excessive plotting of which the Tower Society story line is indicative.[204] Schiller complains that the novel is not sufficiently organic because there is too much going on: "die erstaunliche und unerhörte Mannigfaltigkeit" [the astonishing and egregious plurality].[205] Like Lukács, Schiller frets that the novel is too similar to an epic in form, since "er Maschinen hat, die in gewissem Sinne die Götter oder das regierende Schicksal darin vorstellen." [it has machines within it that in a certain sense represent the gods or the ruling fate].[206] In particular the Tower Society is seen as a kind of premodern deus ex machina/"machinery" that interrupts the novel's organic development.

> Bei dem allen aber hätte ich doch gewünscht, daß Sie das Bedeutende dieser Maschinerie, die notwendige Beziehung derselben auf das innere Wesen, dem Leser ein wenig näher gelegt hätten. . . . Viele Leser, fürchte ich, werden in jenem geheimen Einfluß bloß ein theatralisches Spiel und einen Kunstgriff zu finden glauben, um die Verwicklung zu vermehren, Überraschungen zu erregen u. dgl.

> [With all of this I would have wished that you had made more clear to the reader the meaning of this machinery, its necessary connection to the inner essence. . . . Many readers, I fear, will see in that secretive influence simply a theatrical game that increases the entanglements, arouses surprises, etc.][207]

For Schiller, there is no "necessary" connection between all of the parts in Goethe's novel, no clear relationship between the exterior and the interior. He compares this flatness both to the premodern epic form and, as we saw earlier, to the theater as spectacle.

Harping on the weakness of the Tower Society plot, Schiller is concerned with the retention of a notion of a whole, fretting that in Goethe's

novel "die Einbildungskraft zu frei mit dem Ganzen zu spielen scheint . . .
—Mir deucht, daß Sie hier die freie Grazie der Bewegung etwas weiter getrieben haben, als sich mit dem poetischen Ernste verträgt." [the imagination seems to play too freely with the whole . . . —It seems to me that you
have pushed the free grace of movement further than poetic seriousness can
bear.][208] "Bewegung" [movement] and "Ganzes" [a whole] are at odds here.
Too much movement disrupts the organic whole. This tension is present in
Goethe's novel not only in the multiple plots and literary forms it includes
(a diary, songs, ekphrasis, etc.) but also in the constant threat of movement
embodied in the *tableaux* featuring Mignon. Schiller's reception of Goethe's
novel reveals his desire to tame and streamline it, to introduce a formal classicism that is utterly absent from the novel, something that Goethe refuses
to do. On October 23, 1796, Schiller writes to Goethe that his sister-in-law
read the novel and was deeply moved, and he takes this opportunity to
emphasize his privileging of a calm, sublated beauty above all else: "Immer
ist es doch das Pathetische, was die Seele zuerst in Anspruch nimmt; erst
späterhin reinigt sich das Gefühl zum Genuß des ruhigen Schönen." [It is
always the pathetic that initially engages the soul; only later does the feeling purify itself into the pleasure of the tranquil Beautiful.][209]

Schiller's concern about the excess of movement without resolution
might reflect an anxiety vis-à-vis a notion of movement without *Bildung*. The painting of "Der kranke Königssohn" [The Sick Prince] that is
mentioned three times in the novel provides a window onto the melding of
movement with flatness/lack of interiority within the novel. The painting
is mentioned in book 1, when Wilhelm meets the Abbé who has procured
Wilhelm's grandfather's art collection; in book 7, when the Abbé asks
Wilhelm, in the context of a Tower Society ritual, where the painting
might reside; and once again in book 8, when Wilhelm sees the painting in
the Oheim's castle. Schiller famously notes in his correspondence with
Goethe that the painting collection of Wilhelm's grandfather is "ordentlich
eine mitspielende Person und rückt selbst an das Lebendige" [actually a
proper character that practically comes alive].[210] More importantly, Schiller
argues that Wilhelm's fascination with this painting is too repetitive, suggesting that Wilhelm has not developed at all over the course of the novel:

> Er ist mir noch zu sehr der alte Wilhelm, der im Hause des Groß-
> vaters am liebsten bei dem kranken Königssohn verweilte, und den
> der Fremde, im ersten Buch, auf einem so unrechten Weg findet.
> Auch noch jetzt bleibt er fast ausschließend bei dem bloßen Stoff

fig. 6.1. Antonio Bellucci, *Antiochus and Stratonice*, circa 1700, oil on canvas, Kassel, Germany. Image courtesy of Museumslandschaft Hessen Kassel, Gemäldegalerie Alte Meister.

der Kunstwerke stehen und poetisiert mir zu sehr damit. Wäre hier nicht der Ort gewesen, den Anfang einer glücklicheren Krise bei ihm zu zeigen, ihn zwar nicht als Kenner, denn das ist unmöglich, aber doch als einen mehr objektiven Betrachter darzustellen, so daß ein Freund wie unser Meyer Hoffnung von ihm fassen könnte?

[He is for me still too much the old Wilhelm who liked best to linger by the sick prince in the house of the grandfather. Even now he remains almost exclusively with the bare material of the artworks and poeticizes too much about them for my taste. Would this not have been the place to show the beginning of a more fortunate crisis in him, to represent him not as an expert, for that is impossible, but as a more objective observer so that a friend like our Meyer could have some hope about him?][211]

In essence, Schiller complains that the novel is not a *Bildungsroman*: What has Wilhelm learned in the space of eight books? He is still "too much the old Wilhelm," fascinated by what the art conoisseurs in the novel consider to be a mediocre painting. Wilhelm is fixated on the story of the prince and the materiality of the painting when he should want to learn more about the form of art or utilize this moment to experience a crisis that would lead to the kind of sublation worthy of a *Bildungsroman*.

With the recurring motif of the painting of "Der kranke Königssohn," we are confronted again with the motif of movement without development. Not a *tableau vivant* but a painting that moves, Wilhelm's favorite painting both signifies the static nature of Wilhelm as hero and tracks the picaresque movement within the novel's plot. We first learn of the painting when Wilhelm meets the Abbé seemingly by chance at a guesthouse in book 1. In the dialogue we learn that the painting represents the story of a young prince who is ill due to the passion he feels for his father's wife.[212] The source of this scene is likely a painting by Antonio Bellucci (ca. 1700), which Goethe purportedly saw in Kassel, depicting Antiochos I Soter, the son of Seleukos I Nikator, who has fallen ill due to his love for his young stepmother Stratonike I. In the Rococo painting a doctor and Seleukos are present at what looks like the deathbed of young Antiochos. The father gestures to Stratonike, who is approaching Antiochos, to indicate that he is ready to give up his bride in order to save his son's life.[213] We see the sick son of the king looking at his father weakly but hopefully as Stratonike approaches with a gentle smile.

Throughout *Wilhelm Meisters Lehrjahre* Wilhelm is fixated on the content of the painting, the tormented kinship structure of the family, and not its artistic merit. Indeed, the Abbé points to the painting's mediocrity:

> "Es war eben nicht das beste Gemälde, nicht gut zusammengesetzt, von keiner sonderlichen Farbe und die Ausführung durchaus manieriert."

> "Das verstand ich nicht und versteh' es noch nicht; der Gegenstand ist es, der mich an einem Gemälde reizt, nicht die Kunst."

> ["It was actually not the best painting, not well composed, with no particular color and the presentation thoroughly mannered."

"I didn't understand that and still don't: it is the subject that appeals
to me in the painting, not the art."][214]

Wilhelm's obsession with the impossible and potentially destructive family
story depicted in the painting, despite the painting's lack of greatness, connects his lack of development within the novel to kinship constellations that
expand far beyond the confines of the nuclear family.

The Abbé mentions the painting of the sick prince again at Lothario's
castle in the context of the gothic Tower Society rituals Wilhelm undergoes.
He asks where Wilhelm's grandfather's art collection might be located now:
"'Erinnern Sie sich des Gemäldes nicht mehr, das Ihnen so reizend war? Wo
mag der kranke Königssohn jetzt schmachten?' . . . 'Vielleicht,' fuhr dieser
fort, können wir jetzt über Schicksal und Charakter eher einig werden.'"
["Do you no longer remember the painting that was so appealing to you?
Where can the sick prince be languishing now?" . . . "Maybe," this one continued, "we can more readily be unified in our views on fate and character."][215] What is the purpose of mentioning the painting in this scene? It has
been moved, and the Abbé hints in his final sentence that its movement might
correspond to the development of character. We are invited here to consider
that Wilhelm may have moved far enough along in the process of *Bildung*
as to be able to distinguish good from bad art and to focus not only on the
story depicted but also on artistic merit.

The suggestion that the painting might give us a window onto Wilhelm's
development is born out in book 8 of the novel, but not in the way that either
the Abbé's point about character or the genre of the *Bildungsroman* would lead
us to expect. The painting signifies instead the utter lack of development on
the part of Wilhelm. He is not able to let go of his fascination with the scene of
pseudo-incest represented in the painting, but he also never quite warms to an
idealized "bourgeois" marriage and family life with Natalie. Wilhelm sees
the painting again at the Oheim's castle amongst his grandfather's other art
works: "Mit Verlangen eilte er dem Bilde vom kranken Königssohn entgegen,
und noch immer fand er es reizend und rührend." [Full of longing, he hurried
up to the picture of the sick prince, and he still found it delightful and moving.][216] "Noch" [still] is key. Often when we encounter loved objects from our
youth, we are disappointed: the dishes we savored with our childish palates
are not nearly as delicious now; the objects we cherished seem smaller and less
shiny. But this is not the case with Wilhelm's fascination with the painting; he
finds it just as moving and exciting as ever.

Indeed, Wilhelm is still fixated on the painting at the end of the novel after Felix is found to be free of poison and the house is filled with a heterogeneous grouping of guests. Wilhelm has fallen ill, and the narrator makes it clear that he is psychologically overwrought.[217] In this moment, Wilhelm rips open the doors leading to the entrance hall where the painting hangs (it is not important enough to hang in the "Hall of the Past") and screams hysterically to the entire gathering about the passion and empathy represented in the painting:

"Wie hieß der König?" rief er aus und hielt einen Augenblick inne. "Wenn Ihr mir nicht einhelfen wollt," fuhr er fort, "so werde ich mir selbst zu helfen wissen." Er riß die Türflügel auf und wies nach dem großen Bilde im Vorsaal. "Wie heißt der Ziegenbart mit der Krone dort, der sich am Fuße des Bettes um seinen kranken Sohn abhärmt? Wie heißt die Schöne, die hereintritt und in ihren sittsamen Schelmenaugen Gift und Gegengift zugleich führt? Wie heißt der Pfuscher vom Arzt, dem erst in diesem Augenblicke ein Licht aufgeht, der das erste Mal in seinem Leben Gelegenheit findet, ein vernünftiges Rezept zu verordnen, eine Arznei zu reichen, die aus dem Grunde kuriert, und die ebenso wohlschmeckend als heilsam ist?"

In diesem Tone fuhr er fort zu schwadronieren. Die Gesellschaft nahm sich so gut als möglich zusammen und verbarg ihre Verlegenheit hinter einem gezwungenen Lächeln.

["What was the name of the king?" he cried out and paused for a moment. "If you don't want to help me," he continued, "I will know how to help myself." He ripped open the wings of the doors and pointed toward the large painting in the entrance hall. "What is the name of the goatee with the crown, who is perched careworn at the foot of his sick son's bed? What is the name of the beauty, who steps in and whose imp eyes contain both poison and its antidote? What is the name of the bumbler of a doctor, in whom only in this moment a light dawns, who finds for the first time in his life the opportunity to write a reasonable prescription, to offer a medicine that therefore cures and that is just as delicious as it is curative?"

In this tone he continued to rant. The group pulled itself together as well as possible and hid their embarrassment behind a forced smile.][218]

Wilhelm's melodramatic reveal of the painting creates not only embarrassment in the community at the castle but surely also confusion in the reader. Only Wilhelm finds this painting important, and it speaks just as viscerally to him at the endpoint of his *Lehrjahre* as it had when he was a child. The reader might ask: Who do the king and the stepmother represent in Wilhelm's life, if he takes the role of the sick prince? But there is no clear correlation between the painting and Wilhelm's own biography.[219] His rant has been produced by his illness, and if the scene reveals anything, it underscores yet again the delinking of movement from development within the novel. The culmination of *Wilhelm Meisters Lehrjahre* is not the emergence of an interior subject primed to begin his role as father of the family; instead, the vague displacement of roles and feelings onto the painting of the sick prince mirrors the expansive grouping that collects at the end of the novel and includes figures such as the Abbé, Lothario, and Friedrich, whose relational roles are constructed via proximity and affinity. The novel promises a double (not single) wedding that is to take place in a future to which the reader is never privy, and our closing *tableau* includes a vast cast of characters reminiscent of the final curtain call in a play.

A focus on *tableaux* and social constellations in eighteenth-century German novels offers a picture of malleable groupings of interconnected characters. What the German novel of this period presents to us mirrors the social imaginings represented in German dramas of the time, ones that cannot be aligned with the ideology of the nuclear family. The liberal use of the *tableau* of heterogeneous relations lends a flatness to these works that highlights the experimental, transitory quality of imaginative social formations. If we delink movement from *Bildung*, as, in particular, Goethe's *Wilhelm Meisters Lehrjahre* invites us to do, we are prompted to think expansively, to reject the trappings of teleology and hence be less invested in a particular narrative direction. In this way, the energies of literatures of the period remain vibrant and urgently relevant for readers today.

CHAPTER SEVEN

Kinship and Aesthetic Depth

The *Tableau Vivant* in Goethe's
Wahlverwandtschaften [Elective Affinities]

IN HIS *Aesthetics*, Hegel famously reveals a conflicted reaction to Goethe's
novel *Die Wahlverwandtschaften* [Elective Affinities] (1809), one that mirrors
in many ways the conundrum the novel has represented for readers since its
publication.[1] Despite being a great fan of Goethe's, Hegel expresses ambivalence about the novel in his critique of a mode of aesthetics (exemplified
for Hegel by the writings of Jean Paul) that uses "a baroque combination of
things, which have no real connection with one another":[2]

> A similar collection of individual traits which do not arise from the
> subject-matter we find over again even in Goethe's *Wahlver-
> wandtschaften*: the parks, the *tableaux vivants*, and the swinging of
> the pendulum, the feel of metals, the headaches, the whole picture,
> derived from chemistry, of chemical affinities are of this kind. In a
> novel, set in a specific prosaic time, it is true that this sort of thing
> is more permissible, especially when, as in Goethe's case, it is used
> so skillfully and gracefully, and, besides, a work of art cannot
> entirely free itself from the culture of its time; but it is one thing to
> mirror this culture itself, and another to search outside and col-
> lect materials together independent of the proper subject of
> representation.[3]

Is Hegel comparing *Die Wahlverwandtschaften* here to the writings of Jean
Paul and others who bring together "the most heterogeneous material"[4] in
a manner resembling what the postmoderns would call pastiche? Or is
Goethe absolved of the crime of a lack of organicism because of the skill

and grace of his genius? Hegel's conundrum about Goethe's novel is unresolved in this passage, and the point is not picked up again in the *Aesthetics*.

Hegel's concern about a seeming lack of organicism in Goethe's novel singles out the work's *tableaux vivants*, the odd scenes in which Goethe's characters perform well-known paintings for a salon audience. Goethe famously included two long descriptions of *tableau vivant* performances in chapters 5 and 6 of the second part of *Die Wahlverwandtschaften*: one series of three performances of famous paintings starring the superficial and aristocratic Luciane, and two nativity scene performances featuring Ottilie, the shy ward of Luciane's mother Charlotte.[5] Indeed, these scenes do present a puzzle for the reader, introducing not only a seemingly random activity but also a heterogeneous and potentially slipshod form of art that combines painting, theater, and sculpture. As Gertrude Brude-Firnau has pointed out, scholars have long sought to explain why Hegel is wrong in his view that certain parts of *Die Wahlverwandtschaften* detract from the novel's organicism, and her own essay argues forcefully for a meaningful connection between the *tableau vivant* scenes in the novel and Goethe's feelings about the Napoleonic invasion of Weimar in 1806.[6] But what if we follow Hegel's line of thought about Goethe's unexpected use of the intermedial form of the *tableau vivant*? Indeed, Hegel's observation about the novel is productive, providing a window not only onto the function of the *tableaux vivants* within Goethe's novel but also onto the ways in which heterogeneous aesthetic forms offer crucial insights into social forms.

Hegel makes one other mention of *tableaux vivants* in the *Aesthetics* in the context of his discussion of portrait painting, where he reveals a similar concern for the mismatching of exterior and interior that mirrors his distaste for the "heterogeneous" mixing of diverse elements in modern novels. In his discussion of portrait painting, Hegel emphasizes that "the purely natural side of imperfect existence, little hairs, pores, little scars, warts," should not be the subject of a portrait; instead, the artist should reproduce "the subject in his universal character and enduring personality":

> It is one thing for the artist simply to imitate the face of the sitter, its surface and external form, confronting him in repose, and quite another to be able to portray the true features which express the inmost soul of the subject. For it is throughout necessary for the Ideal that the outer form should explicitly correspond with the soul. So, for example, in our own time what has become the fashion, namely what are called *tableaux vivants*, imitate famous

masterpieces deliberately and agreeably, and the accessories, costume, etc., they reproduce accurately; but often enough we see ordinary faces substituted for the spiritual expression of the subjects and this produces an inappropriate effect.[7]

The inappropriate effect to which Hegel refers is brought about by the conflict between the internal (the beautiful soul) and the external (ordinary faces) produced in the haphazard process of copying that is part and parcel of the *tableau vivant* performance. The "expression of the inmost soul of the subject" can surely not be reproduced in the "heterogeneous" process of collecting and bringing together that characterizes the *tableau vivant*. For Hegel, external appearance can reveal the soul in a work like Rafael's Madonna, in which the spiritual expression has not been rendered inaccessible by the "purely natural side of imperfect existence" made visible in a flawed, living human face.

I propose that we understand the *tableau vivant* in Goethe's novel along the lines put forth by Hegel: as a coming together, or *collision*, of heterogeneous elements that brings the "purely natural" and the material to the fore. Goethe's use of the *tableau vivant* in *Die Wahlverwandtschaften* renders the novel a mixture of historical realism (the fashion of the time) and artifice/theatricality.[8] The *tableau vivant* makes manifest the line between the external (the natural body) and the internal (the soul); it stages both the natural and the theatrical simultaneously, skirting the dichotomy between surface and depth. The *tableau vivant* itself and its role in Goethe's novel likewise represent the joining of two seemingly incompatible representational modes: allegory and mimesis. As we have seen, allegorical aesthetic elements abound in artworks deemed mimetic/realist, works that presumably represent a modern notion of the self as interior subject and a corresponding modern epistemology of truth as depth.[9]

The appearance of the *tableau vivant* in the classical novel brings to the fore this collision between old and new representational and epistemological regimes. August Langen and Manfred Frey both draw the link between the *tableau vivant* and traditional, premodern art forms such as pantomime and passion plays, connecting the *tableau vivant*—along the lines suggested by Brown with regard to allegory—to older, "outmoded"[10] types of representation.[11] Indeed, allegorically staged *tableaux vivants* were often performed in seventeenth-century theaters during scene intervals.[12] Hence, instead of joining oppositional aesthetic modes synthetically, the *tableau vivant* in *Die Wahlverwandtschaften* presents a series of collisions: between various old and new art forms; between the novel form and the *tableau vivant*;[13] between diverse understandings of character and subject; and between old and new social and kinship forms. The coming together of the classical novel and the *tableau vivant* in Goethe's work likewise offers a window onto the intimate relationship between sociopolitical and aesthetic forms. Performed in the drawing room for and with diverse social groups, the *tableau vivant* combines allegory and mimesis; it joins the extended kin community of the premodern aristocratic social system with the modern nuclear family social form. The *tableaux vivants* in *Die Wahlverwandtschaften* are embedded in a genre (the modern novel) normally understood as the aesthetic complement to bourgeois interiority. In this sense, these scenes are a "baroque" reminder of the coexistence of aesthetic and social forms normally understood to be situated along a developmental trajectory (ancient to modern).[14]

KINSHIP AS AESTHETIC FORM

The *tableau vivant* scenes in Goethe's novel stage the nonsynthetic meeting of aesthetic and social forms. Rather than reading literature as being unambiguously shaped by ideology, Caroline Levine reminds us to look at what happens when different forms "meet."[15] This is a particularly productive way to attend to the work that literature does, work that cannot be subsumed under monolithic hegemonic social narratives. In the case of Goethe's novel, we might ask: What happens when the aesthetic form of the *tableau vivant* collides with that of the modern novel? What does this collision tell us about the parallel collision between allegorical and mimetic representational regimes? As an art form concerned with choreographed groupings of figures ("Gruppierungen" [groupings]), the *tableau vivant* likewise stages a collision between premodern kinship and nuclear family constellations.

The kinship structures that inhere in *tableau vivant* performances likewise reflect shifting social constructions and relational ties across classes, as Frey has argued.[16] *Tableaux vivants* became a popular pastime in the early part of the nineteenth century and were initially performed primarily by aristocratic dilettantes, but members of the educated middle class quickly began to appropriate the form as their fortunes improved. As Birgit Jooss points out, the "frozen moment" of the *tableau vivant* pictures beautifully the aspirational nature of the bourgeois engagement with the form that attempts to model itself after the extravagance represented in painting.[17] Frey similarly describes the complex mixing of social groups that occurs in the frozen moment of the *tableau vivant*.[18] The *tableaux vivants* described in Goethe's novel feature collections of performers from a variety of contexts (the bourgeois architect; village children; Charlotte's aristocratic daughter;

and so on) who join together to represent particular roles in a manner that is both contingent and transparent. The *tableaux vivants* collect not only members of diverse ranks but also nonbiological kin (for example, a soldier, a fallen general, and charitable women in the performance of Luciano Borzone's "Belisarius" painting).

As Walter Benjamin observes, Goethe's *Wahlverwandtschaften* "like to represent groups," reminding us of Goethe's fondness for statuary groupings over individual statues.[19] In his reflections on the *tableau vivant*, Karl August Böttinger likewise emphasizes that these "lebende Bilder" [*tableaux vivants*] consist of living figures arranging themselves into groups in order to create temporary frozen images.[20] We do not normally think of the novel as a genre focused on the construction of social groups, but Goethe's use of the *tableau vivant* in *Die Wahlverwandtschaften* reminds us yet again of his particular interest in social networks. Through the repeated staging of groups, *Die Wahlverwandtschaften* not only presents a collision between diverse aesthetic forms (the novel and the *tableau vivant*); the social constellations within the novel also prompt us to reconsider assumptions about the smooth shift at the end of the eighteenth century from the premodern, precapitalist extended family household (*Haus*) to the modern bourgeois nuclear family.

The formal distinctions between kinship (old) and family (new) are mirrored in the focus on materiality and interiority in eighteenth-century discussions about neoclassical and modern art. In his *Laocoön*, Lessing associates the fine arts such as painting and sculpture with materiality in contrast to the "Einbildungskraft" [imagination][21] that is sparked by reading the immaterial and hence higher aesthetic form of poetry. Indeed, when Lessing links poetry to mimesis and painting to allegory, he makes clear his preference for the dyad poetry/mimesis:

> Die Götter und geistigen Wesen, wie sie der Künstler vorstellet, sind nicht völlig eben dieselben, welche der Dichter braucht. Bei dem Künstler sind die personifierte Abstrakta, die beständig die nämliche Charakterisierung behalten müssen, wenn sie erkenntlich sein sollen. Bei dem Dichter hingegen sind sie wirkliche handelnde Wesen, die über ihren allgemeinen Charakter noch andere Eigenschaften und Affekten haben, welche nach Gelegenheit der Umstände vor jenen vorstechen können.[22]

> [The gods and other spiritual beings represented by the artist are not precisely the same as those introduced by the poet. To the

artist they are personified abstractions which must always be characterized in the same way, or we fail to recognize them. In poetry, on the contrary, they are real beings, acting and working, and possessing, besides their general character, qualities and passions which may upon occasion take precedence.][23]

Allegory (personified abstraction), for Lessing, is sutured to the art of painting in order for painting to be legible, whereas poetry can liberate itself from allegory in the practice of mimesis of action.

A discussion about material vs. imaginative/intellectual art forms continues into the nineteenth century, with a preference often given for that which is "light" and imaginative over the "heavy" and material. As Catriona MacLeod reminds us, the distinction between the "pittoresk" [picturesque] and the "plastisch" [plastic] was important for the early Romantics; A. W. Schlegel associated the latter term with the past and with a "material resistance to the imagination."[24] Hegel continues this line of preference for the imaginative/spiritual/intellectual over the material when he writes that sculpture's "corporeal externality presented in terms of heavy matter" resembles the sensuous beauty of nature and therefore forecloses an engagement with the spirit.[25] Hence, whereas sculpture and the material correspond to the past, painting and, even more so, poetry correspond to the modern, the imaginative, the less "plastic"[26] that characterizes "inner life."[27]

The preference for the imaginative over the "plastic" that emerges over the long eighteenth century is also mirrored in Hegel's critique of allegory: "Far below historical subjects in intellegibility are the so-called allegorical presentations which once had a considerable vogue and, apart from the fact that they must usually lack inner life and individuality of figure, they become vague, uninteresting, and cold."[28] Allegory, a mode of signification that flattens the dichotomy between interior and exterior, is left behind in Hegel's Romantic and highest stage of aesthetics.[29]

In contrast to the cold materiality of allegory, painting's content is, for Hegel, "the spiritual inner life."[30] Painting of the Romantic period corresponds, for him, to the shift away from the classical form of art that offers a conceptually adequate representation of the ideal of Beauty but that is lacking in spirit. In the shift to the final and "new" stage of art, the Romantic form, the spirit knows

that its truth does not consist in its immersion in corporeality; on the contrary, it only becomes sure of its truth by withdrawing from the external into its own intimacy with itself and positing external reality as an existence inadequate to itself. . . . The truth content of romantic art is absolute inwardness.[31]

It is the "realm of the external" that corresponds to "an unsatisfying existence."[32] Externality maps here onto corporeality and a cold, hard materiality.[33] And if we return to the correlates between aesthetic and social forms, we arrive with Hegel at the point of the ideal "holy family" (nuclear) that stands for invisible truth in the form of the soul and that is meant to replace the outdated and heavy premodern kinship grouping.

KINSHIP AND MATERIALITY

Goethe's *Die Wahlverwandtschaften* is ostensibly a novel about marriage,[34] but it is famously unorthodox in its treatment of the affective and elective affinities of eros and kinship.[35] The power of eros to complicate traditional social structures stands at the center of the novel.[36] Susan Gustafson has recently expanded this line of analysis by highlighting the centrality of "same-sex, nonexclusive, and adoptive affinities" in the novel.[37] The kinship structures represented are therefore both traditional (a civil marriage between Charlotte and Eduard) and unorthodox (Eduard's uncontrollable passion for Ottilie, Charlotte's love for the Captain, her maternal fondness for Ottilie, the pseudomarriage between Charlotte and Ottilie as they care for the child Otto, and so on). The chemical theory of "Wahlverwandtschaften" is the presumed model for understanding affective and elective kinship relations.[38] In this theory, chemicals "choose" to combine with another element and can just as easily cathect to a third one if it enters the scene. A unites with B; but if C and D appear, then new constellations of affinities are formed: A unites with D, and B unites with C. But the formula breaks down quickly. Even if we focus exclusively on the four characters in the novel living on the estate (Charlotte, Eduard, the Captain, and Charlotte's ward Ottilie), the theory produces multiple groupings: A and B (Eduard and Charlotte); A and D (Eduard and Ottilie); B and C (Charlotte and the Captain); B and D (Charlotte and Ottilie, the midpoint that presents a temporary moment of stillness); and B, C, D, etc. Affinities are structural rather than qualitative and do not produce social harmony. For example, when the child Otto dies, the Captain suggests that Ottilie's erotic love for Eduard can serve as a replacement for the loss of Eduard's child.

In terms of familial models, the theory of "Wahlverwandschaften" is explicitly *not* about relations defined by blood ("blutsverwandt" [blood

relation], as Charlotte points out [303]).[39] The trope of grafting that opens
the novel (Eduard is grafting shoots onto young trees) provides another
way of thinking about the encounter of diverse forms, in this case of the
natural and the unnatural. In their merging, the two plant types do not
produce an organic third but retain their character—as the graft joint continues to make visible. Eduard is particularly disinterested in "natural"
family structures. For example, he believes that individual children are
unimportant, because the rich can always adopt additional children. He
also claims that inheritance is potentially bad for a child's character, a prop-
osition that undercuts Hegel's notion of an ideal state based on the married
couple and a system of biological inheritance that resists arbitrary decisions
about inheritance:[40]

> Es ist bloß ein Dünkel der Eltern, versetzte Eduard, wenn sie sich
> einbilden, daß ihr Dasein für die Kinder so nötig sei. Alles was lebt
> findet Nahrung und Beihülfe, und wenn der Sohn, nach dem frühen
> Tode des Vaters, keine so bequeme, so begünstigte Jugend hat, so
> gewinnt er vielleicht eben deswegen an schnellerer Bildung für die
> Welt, durch zeitiges Anerkennen, daß er sich in andere schicken
> muß, was wir denn doch früher oder später alle lernen müssen. Und
> hievon ist ja die Rede gar nicht: wir sind reich genug, um mehrere
> Kinder zu versorgen, und es ist keineswegs Pflicht noch Wohltat,
> auf ein Haupt so viele Güter zu häufen. (*Wahlverwandtschaften*,
> FA I, 8, 484–485)

> ["Parents just delude themselves to think their presence so neces-
> sary for their children," answered Eduard. "All living things find
> support and nourishment; and if a son, having lost his father early,
> does not have such a comfortable, well-favored youth, he may, for
> that very reason, gain an education for the world all the faster
> through the early recognition that he must consider others. It's not
> even a question of that: we have enough money to take care of sev-
> eral children, and it is by no means a duty or a benefit to heap so
> many advantages on a single head."][41]

Quite radically, Eduard even hands over his paternal rights to his wife's lover
(the Captain). Here Eduard refers to the complex affinities that produced the
group child, "Otto," who has multiple fathers and mothers but is nonetheless sorely neglected.[42]

The unorthodox and shifting affinities that produce the social category of kinship in *Die Wahlverwandtschaften* are reflected in its aesthetic form. Paul Stöcklein calls *Die Wahlverwandschaften* a "swelling novella," evoking an image of crowding.[43] Yet another metaphor for the novel, one that Goethe uses twice in *Die Wahlverwandtschaften*, is the "Sauerteig" [sourdough], which suggests an excess of growing materiality. The narrator describes the family as a body that cannot be contained, as something that ferments ("gärt"):

> Überhaupt nimmt die gewöhnliche Lebensweise einer Familie, die aus den gegebenen Personen und aus notwendigen Umständen entspringt, auch wohl eine außerordentliche Neigung, eine werdende Leidenschaft, in sich wie ein Gefäß auf, und es kann eine ziemliche Zeit vergehen, ehe dieses neue Ingrediens eine merkliche Gärung verursacht und schäumend über den Rand schwillt. (321)

> [Indeed, it is generally true that the life of a family, consisting of a certain set of persons and an unavoidable set of circumstances, contains within itself, like a wine-vat, any extraordinary affection or growing passion, and some time can elapse before this new ingredient sets up a noticeable fermentation and over-flows the top.][44]

The family is depicted here in stark contrast to the walled-off nuclear unit: like an active sourdough starter, it grows uncontainably and oozes over the given boundaries. When Mittler later uses the sourdough metaphor to connote the characters of the earl and his mistress, the baroness, we are invited to read kinship once again as an ever-shifting and uncontrollable form: "und nehmt euch in acht; sie bringen nichts als Unheil! Ihr Wesen ist wie ein Sauerteig, der seine Anstekkung fortpflanzt" (338) [and be careful; they bring nothing but harm! Their essence is like a sourdough that reproduces its own contagion]. The earl and the baroness in no way represent a traditional family, but their ability to reproduce and grow in "contagious" ways likens their natures to the "Familie" in the previously quoted passage. Family and kinship are not qualitatively different in the novel. Goethe's "swelling novella" resembles the organic unpredictability of a sourdough starter, contained and uncontainable and with no discernible interior or exterior, reflecting both the constellations and emotions that make up kin groupings and the excessive materiality that adheres to them. Indeed, Friedrich Jacobi understood the novel along these lines: "Dieses Goethesche Werk ist durch

und durch materialistisch oder, wie Schelling sich ausdrückt, rein physiolo-
gisch" [This Goethean work is materialistic through and through or, as
Schelling puts it, purely physiological].[45]

As critics have pointed out, *Die Wahlverwandtschaften* is itself a collision of diverse genres, having begun as a novella that was to have been
included in *Wilhelm Meisters Lehrjahre* and containing within it the novella
Die wunderlichen Nachbarskinder [The Fantastical Neighbor Children] (a child
within the child, we might say).[46] Walter Benjamin bases much of his analysis of the novel on this generic tension. The modern novel takes many
forms, but it is generally seen as coinciding with and helping to construct
the modern interior subject, as I discussed in the previous chapter. Interiority, uniqueness, and development are central to the modern novel, as are the
bourgeois (and Protestant) values of productivity and marriage (reproduction). Benjamin's categorization of *Die Wahlverwandtschaften* as a "Grenz-
form" [liminal form] between the novel and the novella precisely hinges on
this understanding of the novel as sutured to interiority: "Denn wenn der
Roman wie ein Maelstrom den Leser unwiderstehlich in sein Inneres zieht,
drängt die Novelle auf den Abstand hin." [For if the novel pulls the reader
irresistibly into its interior, the novella presses the reader into distance.][47]

If the novel is presumed to be sutured to the modern interior subject
and, by extension, to the bourgeois family form, then the *tableau vivant* hear-
kens back to the realm of materiality and to the notion of the individual
defined by clothing and assigned roles. What happens, then, when the novel
form and the *tableau vivant* meet? Indeed, the *tableau vivant* is itself a hybrid
form, as Goethe pointed out in a letter to Johann Heinrich Meyer written in
1813, calling it a "Zwitterwesen zwischen der Mahlerei und dem Theater"
[hybrid creature between painting and the theater].[48] In his tongue-in-cheek
remark, Goethe neglects to include sculpture in the mix. Do we have here
a collision or an encounter? In *Die Wahlverwandtschaften* the novel form
meets the *tableau vivant* form, itself a collision of painting, theater, and, without a doubt, sculpture. It is the materiality of the living bodies, their inability
to remain completely static and likewise to transcend their own materiality,
that makes the *tableau vivant* fascinating. In it, the ideal elements of theater
and painting are confronted again and again with an excess of materiality.
In Goethe's novel the salon audience marveling at the performances based
on paintings by Borzone, Poussin, and ter Borch is titillated yet also repelled
by the extreme corporeality that comes to the fore in the collision of the three
aesthetic forms. The encounter between corporeality and ideal art produces
anxiety: "nur daß die Gegenwart des Wirklichen statt des Scheins eine Art

von ängstlicher Empfindung hervorbrachte" (428) [only that the presence of the real in place of appearance produced a kind of anxious sensation]. We can say here that intermediality renders the material apprehensible again.[49]

The *tableau vivant* also represents an encounter between the imagined and the real, and its ontological status is always that of the copy, the double.[50] As such, it is a deeply uncanny art form. As the character Ottokar states in Johanna Schopenhauer's 1819 novel *Gabriele, tableaux vivants* "bleiben doch nur die Kopie einer Kopie der Natur, und zwar eine unvollkommne" [remain only a copy of a copy of nature and, to be sure, an incomplete one].[51] The *tableaux*'s actors (usually amateur) painstakingly attempt to recreate the scene and affect of a painting familiar to all. Hence, a substantial part of the pleasure experienced by the performers, the set designers, and the audience is that of recognition, of knowing the reference. Yet this "aha" moment is quickly followed by the anxiety provoked by the double, as is reflected in the anxious response to the "presence of the real in place of appearance" in Goethe's fictional community. Indeed, the author of a review of *tableaux vivants* in Munich in 1815 refers to the anxiety that the dialectic between stillness and motion produces: "Die ruhige Beschauung wird noch immer durch die bange Sorge, es möchte sich eine oder die andere Figur im Gemälde bewegen, gestört, und diese Furcht wird durch die sichtbare Anstrengung der Figuren, sich ruhig zu halten, immer wieder angeregt." [The calm observation is always disturbed by the nagging fear that one or another figure in the painting might move, and this fear is ever again stimulated by the visible attempt of the figures to hold themselves still.][52]

The anxiety that accompanies the *tableau vivant* performance is generated not only by the collision between materiality and the ideal but by the fear that movement will ruin the performance at any moment. Martin Meisel draws a productive distinction between the dramatic *tableau* and the *tableau vivant* that is predicated on the meeting of stillness and movement. Whereas the introduction of a *tableau* into a drama stops the movement, *tableaux vivants* attempt (often unsuccessfully) to introduce stillness into the movement of life.[53] Perhaps this is why repetition is key to the *tableau vivant*—an art form that ultimately cannot succeed, due to the vitality of the performers. Not only does repetition increase the spectators' pleasure,[54] but repeated *tableau vivant* performances can also be understood as a form of repetition compulsion: the attempt to master that which cannot be mastered; the movement that inheres to all life forms.[55]

Repetition and doubling remind us of the ontological instability of the notion of the original, and the presence of physical bodies resembling statues brings to the fore the blurred distinction between life and death exemplified in statue narratives such as the Pygmalion myth, which was highly popular during Goethe's time. Freud made clear that the uncanny is a product of the blurring of boundaries between life and death. The life and death dichotomy likewise maps onto a movement-stillness binary that, as I discussed in the previous chapter, posits movement as modern. Birgit Jooss suggests that the discomfort generated during a *tableau vivant* performance is similar to the experience of viewing wax figures. But in the *tableau vivant*, in contrast to the lifelike copy produced in a wax figure, stillness and movement collide, and this collision of opposing concepts cannot be resolved within the performance.[56] The stillness of a painting or sculpture cannot quite be realized by the performers, who are hindered by their vitality; yet they do not have the freedom of the theater actor who, as Lessing writes, is at liberty to represent ugliness because the dramatic moment is fleeting. *Tableau vivant* performers, constrained by their living materiality, always fall just short of what Martin Meisel calls "realization" of the painting that is being performed. This "realization," for Meisel, carries "the sense of materialization, even reification."[57] Hence, a successful *tableau vivant* performance would be one in which the art form of painting becomes material, thereby making the form akin to sculpture. We might therefore say that the form must always become "heavy." Is this a degradation of the form of painting? Of theater? Or are we instead reminded in these performances of the centrality of materiality even within aesthetic and social forms that aim toward the imaginative and ideal?

THE "OPEN SECRET" OF THE *TABLEAU VIVANT*

The first three *tableau vivant* performances in Goethe's novel (part 2, chapter 5) star Luciane and are based on etchings of three paintings that were well known to Goethe and his peers, although they likely did not see the originals of any of them:[58] Luciano Borzone's *Belisarius Begging for Alms* (ca. 1620), Nicolas Poussin's *Esther before Ahasuerus* (1655), and Gerard ter Borch's *The Gallant Conversation* (1654–1655).

Critics have pointed out possible historical, as well as symbolic and allegorical, reasons for Goethe's choices, but of particular interest here is the Johann Georg Wille engraving, entitled *Die väterliche Ermahnung* [The Paternal Admonition] (1765), based on the ter Borch painting. Whereas scholars have generally agreed that ter Borch's original painting depicts some kind of erotic transaction, such as that of a prostitute being sold to a client, Wille's title suggests a bourgeois family whose daughter is being scolded by

fig. 7.1. Luciano Borzone, *Belisarius Begging for Alms*, 1620s, oil on canvas, Chatsworth, England. Image courtesy of the Devonshire Collection, Chatsworth. Reproduced by permission of Chatsworth Settlement Trustees.

fig. 7.2. Nicolas Poussin, *Esther before Ahasuerus*, 1655, oil on canvas, Hermitage, St. Petersburg, Russia. Photo Credit: Scala/Art Resource, NY.

fig. 7.3. Gerard ter Borch (II), *Gallant Conversation*, circa 1654, oil on canvas, Amsterdam, Netherlands. Image courtesy Rijksmuseum, Amsterdam.

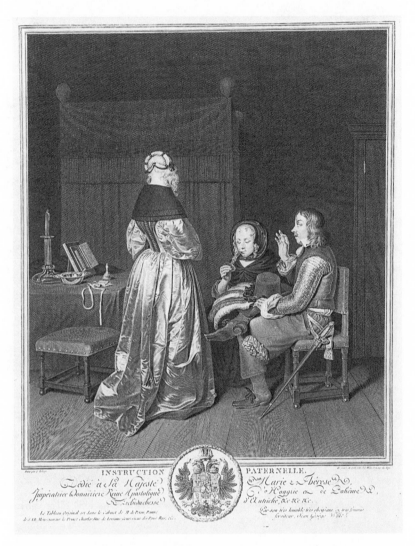

fig. 7.4. Johann Georg Wille, *Paternal Admonition*, 1765, engraving, after the younger Borch, Cologne, Germany. Photo: © Rheinisches Bildarchiv, rba_180813.

her father.[59] As mentioned in chapter 3, art historians have argued about the exact context of the scene in the painting, but some have claimed the man is holding a coin in his hand, and the scruffy dog and the makeup on the table evoke erotic exchange.[60] Likewise, there is general agreement that the male figure (perhaps a soldier) and the young woman are not separated in age by many years and are therefore unlikely to be father and daughter.[61] Hence, it is likely that neither ter Borch's original (*The Gallant Conversation*) nor Wille's etching (*The Paternal Admonition*) represents a nuclear family scene, despite the coding implicit in Wille's title. Indeed, these two artworks—as well as the Borzone and Poussin paintings and their accompanying etchings—are not concerned with interior subjects in possession of secrets but instead with individuals who take on multiple roles. And the three *tableau vivant* performances of these compositions in part 2, chapter 5, of Goethe's novel depict "niederländische Wirtshaus—und Jahrmarktsszenen" (429) [Dutch inn— and carnival scenes]; that is, groupings that likewise highlight figures playing particular roles within larger, heterogeneous constellations.

The *Gruppierungen* in the three paintings in question present figures with complex affective relationships to one another. In each case, the attachments are intimate but not biological. (The two "stars" of the corresponding *tableaux vivants* in the novel are likewise marked by this complexity of attachment: Charlotte's daughter Luciane, with whom Charlotte has a rather cool relationship; and Charlotte's goddaughter Ottilie, whose kinship status vis-à-vis Charlotte is intimate but likely not biological.) In the case of the ter Borch painting, we are initially led to believe (via the interpretation in Wille's etching) that we are dealing with a nuclear family depiction, but contemporary interpretation of the composition's double entendres complicates such an understanding. Borzone's painting of Belisarius, which depicts a fallen, noble man—the Roman general Belisarius who was blinded by Emperor Justinium—likewise eschews a focus on blood relations. The painting shows the begging Belisarius receiving alms from three women while a sympathetic soldier stands to the side, presumably one who has remained loyal to the former general despite his fall from grace. Belisarius was a popular subject for representation in etchings and *tableaux vivants* in Goethe's time, and he served as a projection screen for empathy in a manner akin to the figure of Laocoön, although Belisarius is depicted here as a noble father figure who has lost his social standing.[62] The father figure of Belisarius has earned the love of the "son" figure, the soldier who watches him. The figures in the painting are loosely connected, creating a kinship grouping bound by emotions rather than blood.

The famous *tableaux vivants* in part 2, chapter 5, are preceded in chapter 4 by a performance by Luciane of an "attitude"[63] of Artemisia II of Caria, and followed by discussions of marriage. Hence, the framing of the *tableau vivant* performances within the narrative links these events to kinship and subjectivity in interesting ways.[64] The performance of "attitudes" was popularized by performers such as Lady Hamilton and Henriette Hendel-Schütz, the former of whom Goethe witnessed in Naples in 1787.[65] Attitudes were presented by a single (female) performer who would mimic the gestures and emotions of a particular mythical or historical figure in a frozen image akin to the grouping of the *tableau vivant*. In the novel, we learn that the Artemisia performance is a standard one of Luciane's. Artemisia's premodern, incestuous marriage with her brother Mausolus does not represent a model for the modern couples in *Die Wahlverwandtschaften*. Indeed, the architect who draws Luciane's "attitude" is reluctant to depict the famous urn containing Mausolus's ashes that Artemisia drinks, and the narrator's description of the scene not only reminds us of the taboo kinship structure of the Artemisia-Mausolus marriage (sister and brother) but also of the awkwardness of the performance as everyone waits for the architect to finish his drawing. In this sense, it is precisely the problem of bodies in time and space that distorts the aesthetic experience:

> Die Vorstellung zog sich daher in die Länge, der Klavierspieler, der sonst Geduld genug hatte, wußte nicht mehr in welchen Ton er ausweichen sollte. Er dankte Gott als er die Urne auf der Pyramide stehn sah und fiel unwillkürlich, als die Königin ihren Dank ausdrücken wollte, in ein lustiges Thema; wodurch die Vorstellung zwar ihren Charakter verlor, die Gesellschaft jedoch völlig aufgeheitert wurde. (416)

> [The performance dragged on; the pianist, usually patient enough, was at a loss to know what key to modulate to next. He was so relieved when he saw the urn on the pyramid that he moved unconsciously into a happy theme. Although the performance lost its character, the party was thoroughly cheered.][66]

As Goethe's narrative marks the movement of time, the problem of synchronization—of the "realization" of the attitude performance—becomes evident to the reader. The longer it takes to produce the ideal attitude or *tableau vivant* moment, the more the ever-looming threat of failure becomes manifest.

The Artemisia scene that precedes the following chapter's *tableau vivant* performances also metonymically highlights the uneven temporalities that inhere in nontraditional kinship units. Again, the *tableaux vivants* in part 2, chapter 5, are followed, immediately and abruptly, by issues around marriage raised in a description of the departure of the lovers (the earl and the baroness): "Der Graf und die Baronesse reisten ab und versprachen in den ersten glücklichen Wochen ihrer nahen Verbindung wiederzukehren, und Charlotte hoffte nunmehr, nach zwei mühsam überstandenen Monaten, die übrige Gesellschaft gleichfalls los zu werden." (429) [The count and the baroness departed, promising to return in the first happy weeks of their approaching marriage, and Charlotte now hoped, after two difficult months, that she could get rid of the other guests too.] The narrative thus invites the reader to think metonymically: What is the connection between the *tableaux vivants* and the anti-bourgeois love represented in the dyads Artemisia and Mausolus and the earl and the baroness? The nonnuclear and premodern groupings presented in the *tableaux vivants* jut up against the tropes of incest and divorce (the earl is planning a divorce in order to marry his lover, the baroness), and these scenes are represented temporally as excessive slowness and excessive speed. The uncomfortable waiting that accompanies the delayed Artemisia performance presents a temporality that is too slow, whereas a spectator of the ter Borch/Wille *tableau vivant* experiences so much excitement that he expresses his desire for a closer view. Charlotte, for her part, is painfully aware of the two long months that represent the real time of the three chapters during which Luciane, her only blood relative represented in the novel, visits the villa.

In the painting that serves as the model of the second *tableau vivant* performance in part 2, chapter 5, "Esther before Ahasuerus," the married couple that is portrayed is anything but modern. Poussin depicts the moment when Esther confesses her Jewish identity to her husband, the Persian king Ahasuerus, in order to save the Jews from extinction. In sharp contrast to the modern ideal of marriage as the meeting of two souls, Ahasuerus is ignorant of Esther's Jewish identity until this moment of her revelation. They are in fact strangers to one another, although connected by ambivalent feelings. In the composition they are surrounded by seven other figures, three of Esther's attendants and three counselors to Ahasuerus, as well as an additional figure who is gingerly entering the room between two columns in the background. The latter figure points to the self-reflexive nature of the painting, but Goethe's description of the scene gives no indication that his novelistic characters include this figure in their *tableau vivant*.[67] What we do know is that Luciane plays Esther, and that she chooses the most attractive man of the party to perform the Ahasuerus role; and the couple is surrounded by additional figures from Luciane's entourage.

The revelation of the secret that is at the heart of Poussin's painting provides another avenue of access to the encounter between materiality and interiority that characterizes the *tableau vivant*. Eve Sedgwick connects the story of Esther's "coming out" to Ahasuerus about her Jewish identity with the "open secret" that characterizes queer epistemologies. In *The Epistemology of the Closet*, Sedgwick reiterates Foucault's thesis that sexuality and the modern "secret" are always intertwined. For the queer, the closet is never fully open nor fully closed; queer sexuality (which in modern parlance means "queer identity") resides in the space of the "open secret."[68] Hence, we might say that the "open secret" is the structuring metaphor of modern sexuality, always the product of every confession, coaxed out as the "truth" again and again.[69] The comparison between the modern closet and Esther's confession is productive: in Poussin's painting Esther swoons at Ahasuerus's wrath; she is both condemned and saved by him. Her act of confession is both personal and political and stands as a picture of the tensions between multiple narratives, media, and meaning worlds embedded in Goethe's novel. While completing the novel, Goethe himself called *Die Wahlverwandtschaften* an "open secret" in a letter he wrote to Karl Friedrich Zelter on June 1, 1809: "Ich habe viel hineingelegt, manches hinein versteckt. Möge auch Ihnen dies offenbare Geheimnis zur Freude gereichen." [I put a lot inside and hid some things. May this open secret provide you, too, with joy.][70] Esther's secret, already known to the spectators in Eduard and Charlotte's villa, points to the epistemological structure of modernity and of Goethe's novel: The public knows the "truth" of Esther's story without the need for any words during the *tableau vivant* performance of the Poussin painting. Yet the moment must be enacted again and again; we must see Esther vulnerable and swooning, revealing yet again her "innermost" truth, a truth constructed as a secret that is known to all and resides on the surface.

Walter Benjamin likewise points to the metaphor of the veil and the false dialectic of revelation and truth in Goethe's novel, citing Goethe's remarks about the "open secret" and reminding us that Goethe destroyed all early drafts of the novel, creating a kind of mythic book.[71] Benjamin picks up the notion of the "secret" again in his discussion of Ottilie, the veil, and beauty.

Ottilie, for Benjamin, is the representation of beauty as "Schein" [appearance], as the semblance of purity. While not explicitly drawing the link between the *tableau vivant* and the "open secret," Benjamin mentions Ottilie's *tableau vivant* performance as the Virgin Mary (in part 2, chapter 6, of the novel) in his discussion of her beauty and the ambiguity that is tied to any representation of virginity:

> For the "living" picture, which portrays the grace and, transcending all ethical rigor, the purity of the Mother of God, is precisely the artificial one.
>   This is also confirmed in virginity. Above all, the ambiguity of its intactness is evident. For that which is considered the sign of inner purity is precisely what desire most welcomes. But even the innocence of unknowingness is ambiguous. For on its basis affection passes willy-nilly over into desire, which is felt as sinful.[72]

Virginity, the crux of Ottilie's performance in the *tableau vivant*, is always already ambiguous, revealing the open secret, the lure at the heart of the veil. It is fascinating to see Benjamin's discussion of beauty and sexuality develop along the lines put forth by Sedgwick decades later, as a question about depth epistemology and false revelation: "Like revelation, all beauty holds in itself the orders of the history of philosophy. For beauty makes visible not the idea but rather the latter's secret."[73] Benjamin's observation brings us around again to the notion that modern epistemology is based on the structure of the secret; and as Goethe already knew when he wrote *Die Wahlverwandtschaften*, the secret is an open one. And it is precisely the *tableau vivant* performances within the novel that bring to light the ways in which *Die Wahlverwandtschaften* refuses to prioritize an aesthetics and ontology of depth over surface.

GOETHE AND THE *TABLEAU VIVANT*

Goethe's *Wahlverwandtschaften* is generally credited with helping to popularize the *tableau vivant* as a salon activity among the landed gentry and middle classes of the early nineteenth century, but *tableaux vivants* were well known in Berlin and Vienna before the publication of Goethe's novel.[74] *Tableaux vivants* were popular not only at social gatherings but also at important political events, such as the Vienna Congress of 1814, reminding us that the art form intercedes in both social and political contexts.[75] The term *tableau vivant* can be traced back to the late eighteenth century.[76] The form is related to the dramatic "tableau" and harks back to the medieval and early modern pageant. Art historians suggest that the *tableau vivant* was occasionally featured between acts of plays in eighteenth-century France, but it only became widely known in European middle-class circles in the nineteenth century.

As discussed in chapter 2 of this book, the first documented public *tableau vivant* performance took place in Paris in 1761 during the staging of the *Comédie Italienne* play *Les Noces d'Arlequin*. The *tableau vivant* of *The Village Betrothal* included twelve actors, more than were needed for the performance of the play itself and thereby producing a "crowding" tendency that is characteristic of *tableaux vivants*, one that is further compounded by a perceived contraction of space generated both by the slowing of time as well as by framing devices used in these representations. Indeed, the *tableau vivant* is frequently at odds with the frame, which is key to the successful performance. *Tableaux vivants* were supposed to resemble the form of a contained painting in a salon setting, and for that reason were never performed outdoors. Jooss writes about a performance of the "Singspiel" [musical drama] *Adrian von Ostade* in Vienna in 1807 for which a golden frame was used to circumscribe the *tableau vivant* introduced during the play.[77] Another device employed—either to heighten the sense of enframement or to render the living picture more two-dimensional, like a painting—was a curtain, often made of gauze, through which the spectators could look and that, like a veil, signified concealment and revelation.[78] But this technique surely had the effect of blurring the boundaries of the figures and the represented image. Indeed, translating the dimensions of a painting to the three-dimensionality of a stage was rarely smooth, and figures in the background or on the sides were often left out of the *tableau vivant* in order to approximate the semblance of a contained picture.[79] Sometimes the figures were squished together on the stage in a manner that resembled a distorted aspect ratio.

Documents from the period show that *tableaux vivants* based on well-known paintings by Poussin, Rafael, Teniers, and others were interspersed with individual *tableau vivant* representations of allegorical figures.[80] For example, the *tableaux vivants* arranged by Goethe and Johann Heinrich Meyer at the Weimar court on February 2, 1817, included works by Rafael and Poussin as well as personifications of "Poetry," "Temperance," and "Intelligence."[81] Indeed, the allegorical quality of the *tableau vivant* is retained throughout the nineteenth century. Edmund Wallner's book *Eintausend Sujets zu Lebenden Bildern* [One Thousand Subjects for *Tableaux*

Vivants] (1876) is a do-it-yourself manual for *tableau vivant* performances among members of the middle class, including guidelines for staging and production and recommended allegorical motifs such as "Death," "Sleep," "Diligence," or "Freedom," accompanied by detailed information about props and secondary figures.[82] Despite the outmoded nature of allegory by Wallner's time, it is telling that the surface semiotics of allegory retains a central place in the *tableau vivant* well into the nineteenth century.

The *tableau vivant* exhibition practices of Goethe's time reflect the tension in *Die Wahlverwandtschaften* between surface/material and depth/interiority. Various *tableaux vivants* were usually performed simultaneously in a large room. The excessive materiality suggested by just one *tableau vivant* performance would then be heightened by spectators' access to multiple enactments in the same room. A "Hauptstück" [main piece] would take center stage and be based on historical, allegorical, or mythical paintings featuring numerous figures and elaborate costumes. A "Seitenstück" [secondary piece] would include fewer performers; for example, a self-portrait.[83] As Julie von Egloffstein wrote to her mother in 1817 after participating in the Weimar *tableaux vivants*, the main *tableau* consisted of six to eight performers "that had to be pressed closely together," whereas the secondary "paintings" presented on either side featured just one or two performers.[84] In the scenario Julie describes, the *tableau* framed as the central, interior installation is characterized by its excessive materiality and baroque surface aesthetics (generated by numerous characters portraying various social classes in elaborate costumes), whereas the secondary *tableaux vivants*—framing the "Hauptstück" as exterior to it—are defined by a more intimate and modern aesthetic (featuring domestic encounters between lovers or family members). This scenario points to a reversal of internal and external, interior and frame, that undermines the privileging of interiority.

Goethe's own stance toward the *tableau vivant* is clearly conflicted. He was famously critical of the mixing of aesthetic media, deeming the *tableau vivant* a "Zwitterwesen" [hybrid form].[85] In 1798 Goethe explicitly condemns aesthetic hybridity in the introduction to his *Propyläen*, a journal for criticism in the fine arts:

> Eines der vorzüglichsten Kennzeichen des Verfalles der Kunst ist die Vermischung der verschiedenen Arten derselben.

> Die Künste selbst, so wie ihre Arten, sind unter einander verwandt, sie haben eine gewisse Neigung, sich zu vereinigen, ja sich

in einander zu verlieren; aber eben darin besteht die Pflicht, das
Verdienst, die Würde des echten Künstlers, daß er das Kunstfach,
in welchem er arbeitet, von andern abzusondern, jede Kunst und
Kunstart auf sich selbst zu stellen, und sie aufs möglichste zu iso-
lieren wisse.[86]

[One of the prime markers of the decay of art is the melding of different types of art.

The arts themselves, as well as their types, are related to one
another. They have a certain tendency to unite with one another,
even to lose themselves in one another; but it is in this wherein the
duty, the merit, the dignity of the real artist consists—that he
knows how to differentiate the art form in which he works from
others, to refer each form of art to itself and to isolate it as much as
possible.]

Here, Goethe follows the central point of Lessing's *Laocoön*—that a distinct
semiotics should correlate with each individual aesthetic form. But Goethe's
language reveals an anxiety about mixing that is less apparent in Lessing's
work. Just as the characters in *Die Wahlverwandtschaften* understand the concept "verwandt" as a mixing and union of two discrete individuals ("Diejenigen Naturen, die sich beim Zusammentreffen einander schnell ergreifen
und wechselseitig bestimmen, nennen wir verwandt" [Those kinds of substances that rapidly combine and interact when brought together are what
we call "related"],[87] so too does Goethe express here the attraction ("Nei-
gung") between kindred art forms that leads to a loss of media and genre
boundaries. We recall Goethe's use of the metaphor of the sourdough as a
substance that unites with elements outside itself and becomes threatening
in its shapelessness.

    Despite his expressed distaste for the *tableau vivant* in his theoretical
writings, Goethe produced a variety of *tableaux vivants* for the Weimar stage,
including an 1813 performance of Jean-Louis David's Belisarius painting, in
which Goethe played the Roman soldier.[88] And "Frau von Goethe" Christiane Vulpius played Maria Magdalena in a performance of Rafael's "The
Ecstasy of St. Cecilia" (1516–1517) at the Weimar court toward the end of
December 1818.[89] Goethe also wrote exuberantly about the stunning *tableau vivant* staged at the conclusion of a performance of his play *Proserpina*[90]
directed by him in 1815.[91] In the *Journal für Literatur, Luxus und Mode*, he

describes in detail the final *tableau* in *Proserpina*, in which the ill-fated heroine must return to the side of her captor/husband, surrounded by the figures of the underworld. The *tableau vivant* was choreographed with accompanying music, elaborate costumes, and a painting behind the performers. In the same essay Goethe famously discusses the genre of the *tableau vivant* in more positive terms, locating as its origin (incorrectly) nativity scenes performed in Naples.[92] For the *Proserpina* performance, Goethe emphasizes, his own concluding *tableau* was created not to mimic an existing painting but as a *Gesamtkunstwerk* image stemming from his imagination: "Indem nämlich Proserpina in der wiederholten Huldigung der Parzen ihr unwiderrufliches Schicksal erkennt, und, die Annäherung ihres Gemahls ahnend, wo man das Schattenreich erblickt, erstarrt zum Gemälde, und auch sie die Königin zugleich erstarrend als Teil des Bildes." [As namely Proserpina recognizes in the repeated obeisance of the Parcae her irrevocable fate and, sensing the approach of her husband where one sees the realm of shadows, frozen into a painting, and also she the queen simultaneously freezes as part of the *tableau*.][93] Here again we have the intended freeze-frame of the *tableau*, yet the frozenness of this image is complicated not only by the use of living actors but also by the progressive tense of the adverb "ahnend" [sensing] that suggests Proserpina's mood is shifting within the scene.[94]

We know from the "Rules for Actors" that Goethe was fascinated with groups and the ways in which humans group themselves. Rather than seeking to garner interest by representing modern interior subjects, actors should think of themselves as props: "Das Theater ist als ein figurloses Tableau anzusehen, worin der Schauspieler die Staffage macht" [The theater is to be considered a figureless tableau, in which the actor is the decoration].[95] Seen as a prop, the actor is part of the whole, signifying not as metaphor, as an indication of a deeper meaning hidden within, but instead as metonym, as only meaningful in a relational sense. Indeed, Goethe writes that the actor should always remain conscious of their role as a prop, even offstage:

Da man auf der Bühne nicht nur alles wahr, sondern auch schön dargestellt haben will, da das Auge des Zuschauers auch durch anmutige Gruppierungen und Attitüden gereizt sein will, so soll der Schauspieler auch außer der Bühne trachten, selbe zu erhalten; er soll sich immer einen Platz von Zuschauern vor sich denken.

[Since one wants to have everything represented on the stage not only as true but also as beautiful, since the eye of the spectator also wants to be delighted by graceful groupings and attitudes, the actor should therefore strive even away from the stage to retain these characteristics; he should always imagine a space filled with spectators in front of him.][96]

In stark contrast to the "naturalness" that Diderot associates with the dramatic *tableau*, Goethe emphasizes theatricality as a relational mode. Actors, and one can infer, individuals, should constantly be cognizant of their place vis-à-vis "spectators" and one another.

Goethe's reflections on acting and the *tableau vivant* offer a clue to the curious mixture of surface and depth semiotics, of allegory and realism, within *Die Wahlverwandtschaften*. If we think about the order in which the *tableaux vivants* are presented in the novel, the performers choose to first represent historical works (Borzone's "Belisarius" and Poussin's "Esther before Ahasuerus") before introducing a work from an entirely different school, that of Dutch genre painting.[97] Prior to Denis Diderot's revolutionary reflections on painting, eighteenth-century art criticism favored historical painting over the Dutch style, viewing Dutch genre painting as inferior due to its choice of subjects, which were often still lives and ordinary humans in domestic spaces.[98] Historical painters paint for the soul, it was thought, whereas the Dutch painters, with their technical skill, paint for the eye. Peter Demetz argues that the revival of Dutch genre painting in the late eighteenth and early nineteenth centuries can be likened to the rise of the realist novel: although appreciated today as a window onto particular sociological truths and even as artworks beautiful in form (*l'art pour art*) if not in content, the conflicted reception of Dutch genre painting in Goethe's day mirrors the anxiety on the part of authors of the realist novel who fretted that their subjects were not worthy of them (i.e., Flaubert and his *Madame Bovary*).[99]

Consequently, Goethe's choice to present first the two historical paintings followed by the Dutch genre painting—itself potentially more "ordinary" than its etched manifestation as *Die väterliche Ermahnung* suggests—is quite interesting. Goethe rehearses the eighteenth-century argument about the value of historical painting versus Dutch genre painting and yet refuses to take sides. In none of the *tableaux vivants* is the realm of the material transcended or the depths of interiority highlighted, regardless of the style or school of the composition represented. It is clear that Goethe knew about Wille's modern interpretation of ter Borch's painting. The narrator calls the etching "die sogenannte väterliche Ermahnung" (428) [the so-called Paternal Admonition] and then uses the verb "scheint" [seems] three times when describing it: "ein edler ritterlicher Vater [sitzt] und *scheint* seiner vor ihm stehenden Tochter ins Gewissen zu reden" [an honorable knightly father sits and *seems* to admonish his daughter]; "ihr ganzes Wesen *scheint* anzudeuten, daß sie sich zusammennimmt" [her whole bearing *seems* to suggest that she is pulling herself together]; "und was die Mutter betrifft, so *scheint* diese eine kleine Verlegenheit zu verbergen, indem sie in ein Glas Wein blickt, das sie eben auszuschlürfen im Begriff ist" (428–429, italics mine) [and with regard to the mother, she *seems* to hide a slight embarrassment by looking into a glass of wine that she is about to slurp up.]

Goethe's insistent use of the verb "scheinen" [to seem] in the passage describing the *tableau vivant* performance of the Dutch master ter Borch's painting and Wille's etching suggests a circuitous dialogue with Hegel's aesthetics of interiority, which describes representation as the dialectic between "Schein" and "Innerlichkeit" [interiority].[100] According to Hegel, painting contracts the three dimensions into two, reducing the material to a level surface and producing interiority through the process of interiorization of the third dimension. Hence, unlike sculpture, painting is dependent upon the spectator for the production of its meaning, its subjectivity.[101] The *tableau vivant* would therefore be a "Zwitterwesen" [hybrid form] that gestures toward static two-dimensionality while always exceeding the contraction Hegel describes, thanks to the *tableau vivant*'s excessive three-dimensionality and the here-and-nowness of its physical bodies in the present—their status as living statues, so to speak. Is Goethe's use of the verb "scheinen" in the novel ironic? In his description of the ter Borch *tableau vivant*, the relationship between "Schein" and "Innerlichkeit" is flattened: the former is not something that reveals the depth of the latter[102] or that mirrors the interiority of the artist or actors (there is no clear artist here). Instead, "Schein" functions to underscore the theatrical nature of the performance and to undermine the dichotomy between surface and depth.[103]

OTTILIE AND THE AESTHETIC OF THE SURFACE

A common way of understanding the function of the *tableaux vivants* in *Die Wahlverwandtschaften* is to juxtapose the characters Ottilie and Luciane. Ottilie is viewed as representing an "antitheatrical" transparent interiority, and Luciane is seen as the representative of a vulgar materiality.[104] Of course, if there is a contest between them, Ottilie wins by losing the race. Luciane is ostensibly a narcissistic and superficial creature of society, whereas Ottilie is understood by the narrator to be shy, introverted, self-negating, and deep. The faster Luciane runs, the more alluring is Ottilie's stillness. But although the characters of the two young women are clearly different, their respective *tableau vivant* performances signify in uncannily similar ways.

Goethe's stated repugnance toward hybrid aesthetics could suggest that the *tableau vivant* scenes in the novel present a critique of the social world he describes—for its superficial dilettantism embodied most distastefully in the figure of Luciane. But there are reasons to question if Goethe shares this one-sided opinion of the *tableau vivant* and, by extension, whether he wholeheartedly dismisses Luciane as its representative. For one, the two women's *tableau vivant* performances are not qualitatively different despite their diverse themes. And for another, the novel never fully abandons the semiotics of these performances and their focus on gesture and materiality.

The dialectic of surface and depth that seemingly characterizes the two young women (Luciane as surface and Ottilie as depth) is deconstructed in multiple ways in the novel. For one, Ottilie's notable silence is accompanied by a highly theatrical gestural mode that recalls Luciane's Artemisia "attitude" performance. Ottilie's gestures are described in detail and are legible as allegory, as a denaturalized ritual that can be performed at diverse moments to signify a particular emotion.[105] One powerful example of Ottilie's use of coded gesture is her repeated use of the same body language to indicate negation. In the first instance, Ottilie's teacher describes her behavior as follows:

> Sie drückt die flachen Hände, die sie in die Höhe hebt, zusammen und führt sie gegen die Brust, indem sie sich nur wenig vorwärts neigt und den dringend Fordernden mit einem solchen Blick ansieht, daß er gerne von allem absteht, was er verlangen oder wünschen möchte. (310)[106]

> [She presses the palms of her hands together and holds them up, then brings them toward her breast, bending forward a little and looking at the person making the request with such an expression that one gladly gives up all that one might wish to demand.][107]

Later in the novel, the narrator utilizes this same description almost word for word when Eduard tries to convince Ottilie to run away with him:

> Dann drückte sie die flachen, in die Höhe gehobenen Hände zusammen, führte sie gegen die Brust, indem sie sich nur wenig vorwärts neigte, und sah den dringend Fordernden mit einem solchen

Blick an, daß er von allem abzustehen genötigt war, was er verlangen oder wünschen möchte. (511)

[Then she pressed her hands together and raised them to her breast, bending forward a little and looking at her urgent supplicant with such a gaze that he was forced to give up all his desires and demands.][108]

This choreographed gesture of feminine resistance functions as a transparent signifier that can be deployed in any situation. In these instances, we might be tempted to view Ottilie's gaze ("Blick") as a signifier of her interior self. But this gaze is produced within the context of her ritualized gestures, and is described, like those gestures, with such precision (by the teacher and the narrator) that the gaze becomes just one of the many essential elements within Ottilie's larger performance of emphatic gesture.

In "Notes on Gesture," Giorgio Agamben links what he calls modern society's "loss of gesture" to the moment when the bourgeoisie "succumbs to interiority." Agamben writes that the moderns lost their "sense of naturalness" in the course of the nineteenth century: "In this phase the bourgeoisie, which just a few decades earlier was still firmly in possession of its symbols, succumbs to interiority and gives itself up to psychology."[109] We normally ally "naturalness" with interiority, but Agamben argues convincingly that the premodern language of the transparent gesture is more "natural" than the self-fashioning necessary to create the interior subject model. Along these lines, Ottilie's mute physical performances belie an interiority that we would assume affixes to this character. What is more, these gestural scenes extend the semiotics of the *tableau vivant* beyond the *tableau* performances themselves and throughout the novel.[110]

Another indicator of the contagion—and "swelling," we might say—of the surface/material aesthetics of the *tableau vivant* in the novel are Ottilie's diary entries. The narrator invites the reader to see these writings as exclusive access points into her interior (hidden, and hence true) self. The first diary entry is introduced in the last line of the first part of the novel as a "Blick . . . in ihr Inneres" (393) [view into her inner life]. But how disappointed we are when her diary entries are subsequently described not as a privileged view of her interiority but as

häufiger auf das Leben bezügliche und vom Leben abgezogene Maximen und Sentenzen. Weil aber die meisten derselben wohl

nicht durch ihre eigene Reflexion entstanden sein können, so ist es
wahrscheinlich, daß man ihr irgend einen Heft mitgeteilt, aus dem
sie sich, was ihr gemütlich war, aufgeschrieben. (418)

[maxims and sayings referring to life and drawn from life . . .
Considering that most of them are presumably not her own
thoughts, it is probable that she was given some book from which
she copied out what suited her purpose.][111]

Ottilie's diary likewise includes passages she copies from letters written by
others: "Einen guten Gedanken den wir gelesen, etwas Auffallendes das wir
gehört, tragen wir wohl in unser Tagebuch. Nähmen wir uns aber zugleich
die Mühe, aus den Briefen unserer Freunde eigentümliche Bemerkungen,
originelle Ansichten, flüchtige geistreiche Worte auszuzeichnen, so würden
wir sehr reich werden" (462) [When we read an interesting thought or hear
a striking idea, we usually note it in our diary. But if we also took the trouble to write down original remarks, unusual opinions, brilliant flights of
genius from our friends' letters, we would be greatly enriched].[112] Here the
diary, the key to the secret of the modern interior self, provides not a window unto the soul but plagiarized anecdotal detritus.

The *tableau vivant* performances likewise frustrate the desires of the
reader and the spectators to gain access to a hitherto inaccessible interiority. In Luciane's performance of the Wille etching, the daughter or prostitute figure is seen only from the back. To assuage our frustration, the narrator
assures us that

diese lebendige Nachbildung weit über jenes Originalbildnis hinaus-
reiche und ein allgemeines Entzücken erregte. Man konnte mit dem
Wiederverlangen nicht endigen, und der ganz natürliche Wunsch,
einem so schönen Wesen, das man genugsam von der Rückseite
gesehen, auch ins Angesicht zu schauen, nahm dergestalt überhand,
daß ein lustiger ungeduldiger Vogel die Worte, die man manchmal
an das Ende einer Seite zu schreiben pflegt: *tournez s'il vous plait*, laut
ausrief und eine allgemeine Beistimmung erregte. (429)

[this *tableau vivant*, to everyone's delight, far surpassed the original. There was no end of curtain calls, and the very natural desire
to see the front of such a beautiful creature, visible only from the
back, became so strong that one impatient clown called out, using

the words you sometimes put at the end of a page, "Tournez s'il vous plait"—and everyone clapped assent.][113]

The scene beautifully illustrates the meeting of the *tableau vivant* and the novel: the desire for repetition, to remain in the moment, collides with the desire to see what comes next by turning the page.[114] Erotic, material desire meets imaginative desire;[115] painting meets sculpture meets theater meets novel.[116]

The *tableau vivant* performance can be likened to the suspension of strip-tease. As Peter McIsaac shows, the *tableau vivant* simultaneously represents the revelation of female desire and its containment.[117] And it is not only Luciane who stars in this hybrid/hermaphroditic art form. In part 2, chapter 6, the architect convinces Ottilie to play the role of the Madonna with her baby in two nativity scenes, surrounded by shepherds and angels. In this scenario, Ottilie performs a copy without an original painting as its explicit referent. The two *tableaux vivants* are likely modeled after Correggio's *Holy Night (Adoration of the Shepherds)* (1522–1530) or the *Adoration of the Shepherds* by Gerrit van Honthorst (1620), although these are simply images the spectators have in their minds.[118] But, here again, if readers had assumed that Ottilie's *tableau vivant* nativity scene performances would differ radically from those of her feminine opposite, Luciane, they are disappointed when they are presented with a similar seductive play marked by concealment and revelation of feminine eros:

> Glücklicherweise war das Kind in der anmutigsten Stellung einge-
> schlafen, so daß nichts die Betrachtung störte, wenn der Blick auf
> der *scheinbaren* Mutter verweilte, die mit unendlicher Anmut einen
> Schleier aufgehoben hatte, um den verborgenen Schatz zu offen-
> baren. In diesem Augenblick schien das Bild festgehalten und
> erstarrt zu sein. Physisch geblendet, geistig überrascht, schien das
> umgebende Volk sich eben bewegt zu haben, um die getroffnen
> Augen wegzuwenden, neugierig erfreut wieder hinzublinzen und
> mehr Verwunderung und Lust, als Bewunderung und Verehrung
> anzuzeigen; obgleich diese auch nicht vergessen und einigen ältern
> Figuren der Ausdruck derselben übertragen war. (439, italics
> mine)

> [Fortunately the baby had fallen asleep in the most charming pose,
> and nothing disturbed the contemplation when the gaze lingered

on the *ostensible* mother, who had raised a veil with infinite grace to reveal the hidden treasure underneath. At this moment the image seemed caught and transfixed. Physically blinded, mentally surprised, the surrounding villagers seemed to have just turned their dazzled eyes away and, in their curiosity and delight, to be taking another look, more in amazement and desire than in admiration and veneration, although these expressions had not been forgotten, but were reserved for several older figures.]

There are a number of fascinating moments in this description. First, despite Ottilie's presumed radical difference from Luciane, the scene nevertheless eroticizes her in a manner similar to Luciane's performance of concealment and revelation. If we had assumed that the "verborgener Schatz" [hidden treasure] was the Christ Child, the text instead gestures toward that which is hidden in Ottilie: her sexuality. There is a slippage in this scene between the reactions of performers within the *tableau vivant*: "das umgebende Volk" [the surrounding villagers] surely refers not only to the actors observing the nativity scene as performers but also to the audience enjoying the spectacle itself. In this sense, the implicit frame around the scene is broken both by the vitality of the performers' bodies and by the blending of the boundary between performer and spectator. The performer-spectators and salon spectators look on the Virgin Mary together, turning quickly away and then back with "Verwunderung und Lust" [amazement and desire] to the enticing scene with Ottilie at the center, mirroring the eroticized reaction to Luciane's performance. The dialectic between "naturalness" and "Verstellung" [deception] is, once again, brought to the fore in the *tableau vivant* form.

THE TIME AND PLACE OF KINSHIP

The temporal slowing that is described in Ottilie's Virgin Mary *tableau vivant* scene ("In diesem Augenblick schien das Bild festgehalten und erstarrt zu sein" [At this moment, the image seemed caught and transfixed]) brings us back to a reflection on the collision of two aesthetic forms: the novel and the *tableau vivant*. Readers of the novel, ever eager to "turn the page" and learn what will happen next, are forced to slow down; progress is hindered and time momentarily stands still. The privileging of the pause in the novel at this point also signals a break in assumptions about the teleological narrative of the novel form itself, as the insistent materiality of the *tableau vivant* has forced readers to reflect on this form and on their own desires. The frozen moment that is not perfectly frozen (since we are working with real bodies) recalls the revealing and concealing work of the fetish. Has Goethe described here Benjamin's "Dialektik im Stillstand"—a dialectical image?[119] Ottilie's performances are characterized by the narrator as "Die Wirklich-keit als Bild" (439) [reality as *tableau*]. As in the dialectical image, the *tableaux vivants* in the novel contain within them the histories of the paintings and their various interpretations in sedimented form.[120] As Manfred Frey points out, the social function of the *tableau vivant* might be either conservative or progressive—either halting history for a brief moment or revealing its inability to stand still.[121] What is more, the progression necessitated by the ideology of the nuclear family (production/reproduction) is likewise interrupted. In the scene of Ottilie's Virgin Mary performance, no one is interested in the mother-baby bond.

Another way of thinking about the "Zwitterwesen" of the *tableau vivant* is as a queer figure, the "hermaphrodite," and here again we might think of queerness along aesthetic and social lines. The notion of queer (if we think of the German *quer*) is a relation that is neither oppositional nor purely aligned but is instead—as the word suggests—askance or askew. Queer theory offers a particularly compelling critique of the ideology of interiority, revealing not only its links to constructions of "naturalness" and normativity but also its central place in binary constructions of sex and gender predicated upon the presumption that sex and desire are "internal" and "true."[122] Queer aesthetics hence revels in the excess materiality of *Schein* that reveals the constructedness of *Sein*'s presumed naturalness. The *tableau vivant* itself is a project of "realization," making material and simultaneously copying, we might say, the painting that it models. The copy, however, must of necessity fall short of its goal of unity with what is copied—the painting—as copies always do; it is both not quite the same and not entirely different. In this sense, we are reminded of the failure inherent in drag performance.[123] Luciane faithfully tries to imitate the daughter in Wille's "Paternal Admonishment," an impossible task, not only because she is a living body but because the daughter portrayed in the painting is likely not the innocent she appears to be. Just as drag performances must fail in reproducing "naturalness," so, too, all of the *tableau vivant* performances in *Die Wahlverwandtschaften* fail—either because of their inability to approximate the ideal, or conversely (as in the case of Ottilie as the Virgin Mary), due to the nature of corporeality itself, which is always subject to a visceral excess of materiality and eros.

The collision between the *tableau vivant* and the novel form in Goethe's *Wahlverwandtschaften* offers a window onto various social forms that attach to materiality and surface on the one hand, and invisibility/interiority and depth on the other. Toward the end of the novel the architect who performed the role of the soldier in the *tableau* rendition of Borzone's Belisarius painting visits the chapel to see Ottilie's enshrined corpse,[124] where he repeats the very same gesture of awe and respect he portrayed in the performance: "Schon einmal hat er so vor Belisar gestanden. Unwillkürlich geriet er jetzt in die gleiche Stellung" (525) [Already once he had stood in this way in front of Belisarius. Involuntarily he now took the same pose]. In sociopolitical terms, this seemingly spontaneous *tableau vivant* connotes war (the soldier) and religion (Saint Ottilie) as well as bourgeois productivity (the architect). In terms of kinship, we have yet another scenario of shifting social roles with no nuclear family in sight. Indeed, the architect's deep reverence in the scene is automatic: his body involuntarily, even mechanically, assumes the position of the gesture from the Borzone painting, thereby undercutting our assumptions about the spontaneous emotions a character in a novel would experience in such a moment and likening the scene to an allegorical tableau in which meaning is fixed and immediately visible and legible. The marriage bond and reproductive future involving Ottilie and the architect that was presented as a possible plotline earlier in the novel is here rendered utterly irrelevant in the logic of the *tableau*. Itself a copy of the earlier imitative performance of the Borzone painting, the final *tableau* with the architect and Ottilie lays out the semantics of the collision of the *tableau vivant* and the novel: meaning is temporarily frozen, a linear reproductive narrative is interrupted, and the future is unknown.

The *tableau vivant* semiotics outlined in this chapter can be traced throughout Goethe's novel; prominent examples include the five *tableau vivant* performance descriptions (three starring Luciane and two starring Ottilie); the *tableau* scenes in which Ottilie enacts her gesture of prayer; Luciane's solo performance of Artemisia; the Belisarius *tableau* in the church; and Ottilie's displayed corpse at the end of the novel.[125] These scenes present temporal, material, and social dissonances, reminding us that aesthetic form does not simply reflect social shifts; instead, it complicates ideological smoothness. In this way, the multiple formal collisions generated by the inclusion of the *tableaux vivants* in *Die Wahlverwandtschaften* invite us to reconsider the presumed teleology of both the interior subject and the nuclear family and to read the novel as a profoundly heterogeneous meditation on kinship and sociality.

Concluding Reflections

THIS BOOK OFFERS an alternative to the well-worn story of the rise of the nuclear family in eighteenth-century German literature in the wake of modern economic and political shifts. In tracing this alternative path, I am concerned not only with the ways in which the cementation of the social narrative of "the family" limits how we imagine self and community; I am also keenly interested in *how we read*. *The Aesthetics of Kinship* is a thought experiment in reading: What do we see if, while reading literature, we shift our focus away from plot and toward intermedial representations of social groupings? Is it possible to read retroactively (indeed, all attempts to read literature of the past are retroactive)[1] in a manner that resists the profoundly usable narrative of Oedipus, a narrative that rigidifies the metonymic chain of interior subject/family/nation? Temporarily turning away from the admitted delights of plot is one way; another is to try to read literature as in communication with, but not reflective of, ideology. To do this, aesthetic form is key. What forms traverse literary works, and how might we read them in communication with one another *before* connecting them to ideology? I have traced here literary uses of the *tableau*, the *tableau vivant*, and literary props such as the letter and the portrait, and, as we saw, a picture has emerged from this work of reading that cannot easily be framed as a nuclear family portrait. We are confronted instead with a porous but not completely open notion of kinship that, while by no means utopian, opens up enticing alternatives to the nuclear family model for social and political community.

We read, overread, and underread culture as we do literature. *The Aesthetics of Kinship* was completed in the midst of a global pandemic. The world has changed in as yet incomprehensible ways, but not, it seems, with regard to our attachment to the concept of "family," understood as nuclear family, and its power as a heuristic tool for conceptualizing our world. The term "family" remains a phantasmagoric building block of German and, indeed, Western cultures, despite the fact that it doesn't map onto our lived realities at all. It is astounding to see the intense emotional cathexis to the concept despite its failure in almost every example to which we look: individual families, families represented in literature and art, families depicted in popular culture, metaphorical families, and even the Christian biblical family. In contemporary German discourse, the terms *Haushalt* [household], *Hausstand* [household], *Familie* [family], *Kernfamilie* [nuclear family], and *Kleinfamilie* [small family] tend to be interchangeable.[2] The newer term *Haushaltsange-hörige* [household members] moves far beyond the narrowest circle of the traditional nuclear family. In fact, this term could refer to anyone, human or nonhuman, but it is rarely used. LGBTQ+ groups have asked for the use of *Haushalt* instead of *Familie*, since many queer folks no longer have ties with their families of origin.[3] But the formulation slippage we consistently see between more inclusive terms like *Haushalt* and *Hausstand* and the more restrictive *Familie* subtly undermine attempts to create consistency and equality. The intermittent yet persistent use of the terms *Familie*, *Kleinfamilie*, and *Kernfamilie* on the part of both official representatives of the German state and ordinary Germans re-sutures this modern, neoliberal democracy to *Heimat* and all of its ideological baggage. *Familie* contains within it an unmatched power to help us form what we believe is a cohesive picture of subject and world, even if this picture does not match what we actually see in this world.

The thought experiment of this book is, then, to put the heuristic "family" aside for a while as we read. We can always return to it; we know it isn't going anywhere soon. And we might, while we are at it, delink notions of self from the story of the subject emerging from this family, the one whose interiority has developed within the domestic sphere, as the story goes, an interiority that tells the truth of this round and deep autonomous subject. What kinds of formations of community appear to us? How would we describe them? I have focused on the presumed beginnings of discourses of the modern family, the eighteenth century, in an attempt to see what kinds of social constellations emerge, and the kin pictures that stand out in imaginative literature of the period are, as I have argued, as heterogeneous and porous as the contemporary *Haushalte* that we consistently and unsuccessfully attempt to squeeze into the *Familie* frame.

The social constellations that I have highlighted in dramas and novels of the long eighteenth century are neither ideal nor truly utopian; power relations continue to inhere, and aristocratic characters are fetishized. But these literary experiments in imagining and forming social groups are nevertheless, as I have tried to show, more open and malleable than we have historically believed them to be. Indeed, a focus on these literary kin constellations should prompt us to reconsider a presumed Western heritage of the nuclear family and instead to trace alternative kin lines that have the potential to liberate our social imaginary in the present. A critical eye toward the dominant model of the interior subject will likewise aid in this endeavor, as interiority cannot be thought outside the nuclear family, the privileged site of internalization and development of this subject. Indeed, the dyad interior subject/family, understood as the *Kernfamilie*, necessitates the kind of teleological thinking that overvalues the autonomous subject and limits possibilities for more ethical social configurations. What is more, the privileging of depth over surface teaches us to value linear development and goals over actions and the present. If imagination precedes action, which I believe it does, then the retroactive reimagining I am proposing of an eighteenth-century aesthetics of kinship can help us to see and, perhaps, to act in a manner that expands the family frame.

ACKNOWLEDGMENTS

I am deeply indebted to many people and organizations who supported this project along its circuitous path. I have been privileged to receive funding at various points in the research and writing process. I thank the University of Illinois at Chicago College of Liberal Arts and Sciences for supporting my research on the Enlightenment novel through a summer grant. A UIC Institute for the Humanities fellowship gave me time to focus exclusively on this book during the 2017–2018 academic year. I am truly grateful to Mark Canuel and Linda Vavra, as well as to my fellow fellows A. W. Eaton, Marina Mogilner, Peter Hylton, Roderick Ferguson, and Will Small, who generously engaged with my work and shared their own with me. Astrida Tantillo, Jeff Sklansky, and Tatjana Gajic provided important critical interventions during my research workshop, for which I am grateful. I thank Rachel Zuckert and the members of the Chicago Philosophy Consortium for their gracious reception of my work in the "Philosophy and Literature" seminar. Alice Goff, Sophie Salvo, and the other organizers and participants in the Chicago German Studies Colloquium (now the Newberry German Studies Seminar) gave me the opportunity to receive extensive feedback on my project from brilliant colleagues, and my book is much better for it. Members of the Department of German Studies at the University of Washington generously provided invaluable input on early research on the *tableau*, for which I am truly grateful. My colleagues in the Germanic Studies Department at UIC graciously offered their insights into my research at early stages of this book; I thank them for this and for welcoming me so warmly into their department. And the Goethe Society of North America is not only the organizational home for the wonderful series within which this book appears, it also generously provided funds to support this book's publication.

I have defined kin in this book as a grouping within a frame whose boundaries are porous. Proximity is key, but in our hybrid world of in-person and virtual communication, proximity takes many forms. I have benefited immensely from discussions with intellectual and emotional kin in North America and Europe. When, in March 2020, the pandemic dramatically changed our lives, Horst Lange started a Goethe reading group that included Eleanor ter Horst, Heather Sullivan, Imke Meyer, John Lyon, and Karin Schutjer, the sharpest minds in the business. Our discussions about Goethe, Grillparzer, pandemic life, and music contributed in myriad ways to this project. Christiane Hertel was always ready to share with me her boundless knowledge about Dutch painting and the *tableau vivant*, and her art historian detective skills were invaluable to me in locating images for the book. I cannot thank her enough. Daniel Purdy, Heather Sullivan, and Susan Gustafson provided letters of support for funding applications, and for this thankless work, I am truly grateful. Jane Brown generously gave me feedback on my unwieldy *Wahlverwandtschaften* research, and I thank her not only for this but also for her groundbreaking research on allegory and mimesis, which helped shape this book. Yann Robert discussed Diderot's work with me, and I learned a great deal in the process. Graduate students at UIC likewise cheerfully discussed many of the works that appear in this monograph with me in seminars. In particular, I am grateful to my PhD students, Zach Ramon Fitzpatrick, Erin Gizewski, and Maryann Piel, for our many intersectional discussions about ideas relevant to my research and theirs.

My blood kin and in-law kin near and far have kindly cheered me on throughout this process. I thank my mother, Annie Schlipphacke, and my sister, Eva Kopf, for their love and belief in me. Hilke Meyer, the late Heinrich Meyer, and my favorite Meyers and Germers are always ready to offer supporting words and deeds; I am very lucky. Leila Larson passed away during the book's production phase, leaving a hole that cannot be filled.

Many near and dear to me have supported this project over the past few years through their friendship, reflections on kinship and family, and food (the missing chapter from this book!). I thank Alex Tisman, Colleen McQuillen, Cynthia Bond, Dan Clarenden, Ellen McClure, Emily Carner, Heidi Halbedel, Julia Kölsch, Julia Vaingurt, Katie Arens, Kiki Kefferpütz, Peter Rehberg, Rosi Song, Sally Sedgwick, Sigrid Nieberle, Steve Marsh, Susanne Hochreiter, and Ute Hartmann for their sometimes direct, sometimes indirect roles in the production of this book. Brigitte Prutti has been a champion of my work from the beginning; I will never forget this, and only wish I had her wit and eloquence. Bethany Schneider and Kate Thomas shared with me not only their friendship but the sourdough that "swells" like Goethe's "schwellende Novelle" and keeps me calm. I will write that piece about Goethe and sourdough yet! I have been talking about family and kinship with Frederick Lubich and Susan Wansink since my days in Norfolk, VA, and bits of these conversations have most certainly made their way into this book. To David Perkins I am grateful for his open and sharp mind during lively discussions at his kitchen table, and to the late Jens Rieckmann, too, I owe a debt in this regard. Silke Weineck inspired me with her brilliant book on fatherhood, and I'm grateful for her friendship and wit. Helen Townsend, my very oldest (but not in age!) friend, has supported me cheerfully throughout; I am lucky we started kindergarten together. Jason Jorgensen and Jochen Liesche exemplify the porousness of the terms "kin" and "family," as they are both.

Nanno Marinatos cheered me on from the day I gave my job lecture at UIC, and my intellectual exchanges with her about everything from Nicias and the novella to Weimar cinema have made our friendship deep and lively. Britta Simon brought her brilliant medievalist mind to bear on my project, and it is the better for it. I thank her for her kindness and loyalty. My gratitude to Montanee Wongchinsri is more than I can express: her meditation teachings and retreats have been key to creating the state of mind and body for work and life. I am grateful for her friendship and practice together with our noble friends, Hugh Nicholson, Susanne Rott, and Tatjana Gajic. Gregg Belt sent me the best care package in the history of care packages at the outset of the pandemic, and it is only matched by our decades-long wonderful friendship; he is the most generous person I know. Sangita Gopal, Bish Sen, and Mumu enliven my mind and heart with their friendship. Sangita and I have again shared our struggles while writing second books; she keeps me sharp, and I thank her, even if I can't keep up. I thank one more time Susanne Rott, who wears many hats in this narrative—as my department head, my meditation buddy, and my friend. She is brilliant in all of them; her support of me and this book on so many fronts has meant the world to me.

I cannot thank enough the best librarian in the world, Carl Lehnen, who cheerfully helped me find sources at a time when the library was locked down. Carl Good is the most charming and eloquent editor I can imagine, and his work on this manuscript has improved it manyfold. I am grateful to the New Studies in the Age of Goethe editorial board for carefully reading my sample chapters, to the anonymous readers of the manuscript, to Suzanne Guiod and Pamelia Dailey at Bucknell University Press for their friendly mentorship during the production process, and to Angela Piliouras and Katherine Woodrow for their excellent editorial work. I am particularly thankful to Karin Schutjer for her enthusiasm and generous support throughout the review process. I know this is the last book commissioned by her to appear in the series, and it has been a pleasure and honor to work with her.

Material from chapter 2 was published as an article entitled "Reimagining Diderot's Aesthetics: Lessing's Dramatic *Tableaux*" in *The Lessing Yearbook* 46 (2019). I am grateful to the editor Carl Niekerk for his highly constructive feedback on the essay, for his collegiality, and for permission to reprint it here. I also thank Taylor & Francis for permission to reprint portions of chapter 7 that appeared in the article "Kinship and Aesthetic Depth: The *tableau vivant* in Goethe's *Wahlverwandtschaften*" in *Publications of the English Goethe Society* 87, no. 3 (2018).

My most profound thanks go to my wife and life partner, Imke Meyer, whose brilliant interventions make their mark throughout this monograph, and without whom it would not exist. She is the kindred spirit at the heart of my book.

Introduction

1. Johann Wolfgang von Goethe, "Über Laocoon," FA 1.18, 492; Johann Wolfgang von Goethe, "On the Laocoon Group," in *Goethe: The Collected Works: Vol. 3: Essays on Art and Literature*, ed. John Gearey, trans. Ellen von Nardroff and Ernest H. von Nardroff, (Princeton, NJ: Princeton University Press, 1993), 17.

2. I use "assemblage" with a nod to Deleuze and Guattari, but I engage the concept here in a more literal sense to connote a group that is assembled together, a grouping. See Gilles Deleuze and Félix Guattari, *A Thousand Plateaus: Capitalism and Schizophrenia*, trans. Brian Massumi (Minneapolis: University of Minnesota Press, 1987). The German word "Gruppierung" is often used to refer to premodern kinship groups along these lines. See Claudia Jarzebowski, *Inzest: Verwandtschaft und Sexualität im 18. Jahrhundert* (Cologne: Böhlau, 2006), 146.

3. On this ensemble performance style, see Jane K. Brown, *The Persistence of Allegory: Drama and Neoclassicism from Shakespeare to Wagner* (Philadelphia: University of Pennsylvania Press, 2007), 187.

4. Goethe, "Regeln für Schauspieler," FA 1.18, 881. Unless otherwise noted, all translations in this book are mine.

5. Goethe, "Versuch einer allgemeinen Vergleichungslehre," FA 1.24, 214. See also Astrida Orle Tantillo's analysis of this notion of natural community in *The Will to Create: Goethe's Philosophy of Nature* (Pittsburgh, PA: University of Pittsburgh Press, 2002), 95–103.

6. Erich Auerbach, *Mimesis: The Representation of Reality in Western Literature*, translated by Willard R. Trask (Princeton, NJ: Princeton University Press, 2003), 439–440.

7. Friedrich Schiller, "Kabale und Liebe," NA9, 188.

8. Christian Fürchtegott Gellert, *Leben der schwedischen Gräfin von G****, ed. Jörg-Ulrich Fechner (Stuttgart: Reclam, 1968), 116.

9. Gotthold Ephraim Lessing, *Nathan der Weise*, WB 9, 486.

10. See Niklas Luhmann's theory that "incommunicability" is the hallmark of the eighteenth century: *Love as Passion: The Codification of Intimacy* (Stanford, CA: Stanford University Press, 1982), in particular 121–129.

11. See Charles Taylor on the concept of "unfolding" for the development of the modern self, *Sources of the Self* (Cambridge, MA: Harvard University Press, 1989), especially 211–233.

12. See Luhmann, "Preface to the English Edition," in *Love as Passion*, 2.

13. Luhmann, "Preface to the English Edition," 15.

14. Günter Saße likewise associates modern interiority with the anxiety produced by the new public sphere in the eighteenth-century German territories. See Günter Saße, "Vom 'heimlichen Geist des Widerspruchs': Der Bildungsroman im 18. Jahrhundert. Goethes *Wilhelm Meisters Lehrjahre* im Spannungsfeld von Subjektivität und Intersubjektivität," in *Das 18. Jahrhundert*, ed. Monika Fludernik and Ruth Nestvold (Trier: WTV, 1998), 69.

15. Lawrence Stone places "individualism" at the heart of social and political shifts in the seventeenth and eighteenth centuries in his history of the family, defining it as "first, a growing introspection and interest in the individual personality; and secondly, a demand for personal autonomy and a corresponding respect for the individual's right to privacy, to self-expression, and to the free exercise of his will within limits set by the need for social cohesion." See Lawrence Stone, *The Family, Sex and Marriage in England 1500–1800* (London: Penguin, 1977), 151.

16. Gilles Deleuze and Félix Guattari, *Anti-Oedipus: Capitalism and Schizophrenia*, trans. Robert Hurley, Mark Seem, and Helen R. Lane (Minneapolis: University of Minnesota Press, 1983), 50. Deleuze and Guattari link the nuclear family to the anti-liberational process of psychoanalysis.

17. Immanuel Kant's "Was ist Aufklärung?" ["What is Enlightenment?"] famously opens with the lines: "Aufklärung ist der Ausgang des Menschen aus seiner selbstverschuldeten Unmündigkeit." [Enlightenment is a person's departure from his [*sic*] self-wrought immaturity.] Kant et al., *Was ist Aufklärung? Thesen und Definitionen*, ed. Ehrhard Bahr (Stuttgart: Reclam, 1974), 9.

18. David Warren Sabean and Simon Teuscher, "Kinship in Europe: A New Approach to Long-Term Development," in *Kinship in Europe: Approaches to Long-Term Development (1300–1900)*, ed. D. W. Sabean, S. Teuscher, and Jon Mathieu (New York: Berghahn, 2007), 23.

19. Stone, *The Family, Sex and Marriage*, 149.

20. Ulrich Beck, "Der Konflikt der zwei Modernen," in *Die Modernisierung moderner Gesellschaften: Verhandlungen des 25. Deutschen Soziologentages in Frankfurt am Main 1990*, ed. Wolfgang Zapf, 40–53 (Frankfurt: Campus, 1991), 43.

21. The term "Kernfamilie" has been in circulation since the early nineteenth century, but it only became a widely used concept beginning in the 1950s, presumably in the context of the invention of nuclear power. The "Verlaufskurve" [trend curve] from DWDS (*Digitales Wörterbuch der deutschen Sprache*) shows this clearly: https://www.dwds .de/r/plot/?xrange=1600:1999&window=10&slice=3&q=Kernfamilie&corpus =dta%2Bdwds. The first examples of the use of "Kernfamilie" in sociology handbooks are from the 1950s. Linguistic corpora show that the terms "Kleinfamilie" and "Kernfamilie" are used interchangeably after World War II. See ZDL (*Zentrum für digitale Lexikographie der deutschen Sprache*): https://zdl.org/wb/wortgeschichten/Kernfamilie. A sociology textbook from 1964 emphasizes the "real" (understood as biological) nature of the father and mother in the "Kernfamilie": "Under *Kernfamilie* [nuclear family] is understood that group consisting of the real father, the real mother and their real children." Carl A. Schmitz, *Grundformen der Verwandtschaft* (Basel: Pharos-Verlag, 1964), 33.

22. Gisela Notz, *Kritik des Familismus: Theorie und soziale Realität eines ideologischen Gemäldes* (Stuttgart: Schmetterling, 2015), 19. These statistics are from 2014.

23. Eve Kosofsky Sedgwick, "Tales of the Avunculate: Queer Tutelage in *The Importance of Being Earnest*," in *Tendencies* (Durham, NC: Duke University Press, 1993), 72.

24. Albrecht Koschorke et al., introduction to *Vor der Familie: Grenzbedingungen einer modernen Institution* (Munich: Fink, 2010), 12.

25. Koschorke et al., introduction to *Vor der Familie*, 21.

26. Koschorke et al., introduction to *Vor der Familie*, 14. They characterize the family as "a black hole of norms, (disappointed) expectations, projections of desires, avoidance behaviors."

27. Dieter Schwab, "Familie," in *Geschichtliche Grundbegriffe: Historisches Lexikon zur politisch-sozialen Sprache in Deutschland*, vol. 2, E–G, ed. Otto Brunner, Werner Conze, and Reinhart Koselleck (Stuttgart: Klett-Cotta, 1975), 300.

28. On the long history of the intertwinement of the family and politics, see Adrian Daub and Michael Thomas Taylor, "Introduction: Family Politics," *Republics of Letters: A Journal for the Study of Knowledge, Politics, and the Arts* 3, no. 2 (2013): 1–7.

29. G.W.F. Hegel, *Elements of the Philosophy of Right*, ed. Allen W. Wood, trans. H. B. Nisbet (Cambridge, UK: Cambridge University Press, 1991), 209–210 (my italics).

30. For a compelling counterreading of marriage in Hegel that harnesses the queer potential of the *Grundlinien der Philosophie des Rechts*, see Michael Thomas Taylor, "Right Queer: Hegel's Philosophy of Marriage," *Republic of Letters: A Journal for the Study of Knowledge, Politics, and the Arts* 3, no. 2 (2013): 1–22.

31. See the entry on "Family" in Raymond Williams, *Keywords: A Vocabulary of Culture and Society* (Oxford: Oxford University Press, 1976): "Family, there, combined the strong sense of immediate and positive blood-group relationship and the strong implicit sense of property" (90). The linkage between property and bourgeois marriage is highlighted perhaps most famously by Friedrich Engels in *The Origin of the Family, Private Property and the State* (1884). According to Georg Simmel, "family" was defined by the mother-child bond until the invention of "Privateigentum" [private property]. Only at this point did the father's identity and paternity become important. See Georg Simmel, "Zur Soziologie der Familie," *Individualismus der modernen Zeit und andere soziologische Abhandlungen* (Frankfurt am Main: Suhrkamp, 2008), 127.

32. Edward Shorter, *The Making of the Modern Family* (New York: Basic Books, 1975), 205.

33. Stone, *The Family, Sex and Marriage*, 74. Similarly, Luhmann begins his study of the semantics of love with the assumption that the eighteenth century is the moment when the family begins to be freed from kin. See Luhmann, *Love as Passion*, 2.

34. Stone, *The Family, Sex and Marriage*, 69.

35. Stone, *The Family, Sex and Marriage*, 149. Although Stone's and Shorter's books have frequently served as references for German historians and sociologists, it is important to remember that Britain's middle class was formed much earlier than its German counterpart, and industrialization lagged far behind in the not-yet-nationalized German territories. See also Karin Wurst, who discusses this problem: *Familiale Liebe ist die 'wahre Gewalt': Die Repräsentation der Familie in G.E. Lessings dramatischem Werk* (Amsterdam: Rodopi, 1988), 38.

36. Jürgen Habermas, *Strukturwandel der Öffentlichkeit: Untersuchungen zu einer Kategorie der bürgerlichen Gesellschaft* (1962; repr., Frankfurt am Main: Suhrkamp, 1990), 107.

37. Habermas, *Strukturwandel der Öffentlichkeit*, 110. See in this context Isabel V. Hull, who argues that these spheres only congeal in the nineteenth century. See Isabel V. Hull, *Sexuality, State and Civil Society in Germany, 1700–1815* (Ithaca, NY: Cornell University Press, 1996), 206.

38. Michel Foucault, *The History of Sexuality, Vol. I.*, translated by Robert Hurley (New York: Vintage, 1990), 108–109. Faramerz Dabhoiwala similarly sees the eighteenth century as the point in time when Enlightenment values lead to a release of sexual energies. See Faramerz Dabhoiwala, *The Origins of Sex: A History of the First Sexual Revolution* (Oxford: Oxford University Press, 2012).

39. G.W.F. Hegel, *Phenomenology of Spirit*, trans. A. V. Miller (Oxford: Oxford University Press, 1977), 275.

40. The analogy was famously drawn by Robert Filmer in 1680. See Robert Filmer, *Patriarcha and Other Writings*, ed. Johann Sommerville (Cambridge, UK: Cambridge University Press, 1991). Silke-Maria Weineck writes that "*Patriarcha* may well be the clearest exposition of the logic of the paternal triad ever written." Silke-Maria Weineck, *The Tragedy of Fatherhood: King Laius and the Politics of Paternity in the West* (New York: Bloomsbury, 2014), 118.

41. It is not until the nineteenth century that the ideal family becomes nuclear, organic and "sacred." See Reinhart Koselleck, *Preußen zwischen Reform und Revolution: Allgemeines Landrecht, Verwaltung und soziale Bewegung von 1791 bis 1848* (Stuttgart: Klett, 1967), 63. Raymond Williams likewise locates the origins of the small-kin group "family" not before the nineteenth century. Williams, *Keywords*, 89. It is the Romantics, such as Friedrich Schlegel and Johann Gottlieb Fichte, who fetishize the circumscribed, organic biological family unit: "In der Familie werden die Gemüter organisch eins" [in the family, minds organically meld]. Schlegel, quoted in Schwab, "Familie," 287. Fichte idealized marriage as a purely private, patriarchal space delinked from the state—a "protosociety," as Hull puts it. Hull, *Sexuality*, 295. By the middle of the nineteenth century, the family has retreated to the secluded "Gartenlaube" [garden alcove]. Schwab, "Familie," 294.

42. Sabean and Teuscher, "Kinship in Europe," 23.

43. Sabean and Teuscher, "Kinship in Europe," 23.

44. Leonore Davidoff, *Thicker than Water: Siblings and Their Relations, 1780–1920* (Oxford: Oxford University Press, 2012), 15.

45. Judith Butler, "Is Kinship Always Already Heterosexual?," in *Undoing Gender* (New York: Routledge, 2004), 122.

46. As Stefani Engelstein writes, misogyny and antisemitism merge in policing "female sexuality against miscegenation." See Stefani Engelstein, *Sibling Action: The Genealogical Structure of Modernity* (New York: Columbia University Press, 2017), 224.

47. Butler, "Is Kinship Always Already Heterosexual?," 103. See also Carol Stack's classic study of Black kinship, *All Our Kin: Strategies for Survival in a Black Community* (New York: Harper and Row, 1974), as well as Hortense J. Spillers, "Mama's Baby, Papa's Maybe: An American Grammar Book," *Diacritics* 17, no. 2 (1987): 64–81. Todne Thomas argues that "family normality, and its attendant moral capital, belonged overwhelmingly to people of European descent. The families of people of African descent were essentialized as dysfunctional." Todne Thomas, *Kincraft: The Making of Black Evangelical Society* (Durham, NC: Duke University Press, 2021), 18. Thomas cites Tiffany Lethabo King who

has "provocatively called for the abolition of 'the family' as a framework for black social life," 19.

48. Susanne Zantop argues that eighteenth-century Germany's colonial imaginary was expressed through family romance master-slave narratives. See Susanne Zantop, *Colonial Fantasies: Conquest, Family, and Nation in Precolonial Germany, 1770–1870* (Durham, NC: Duke University Press, 1997).

49. As Christine Lehleiter puts it, these thinkers were torn between a focus on origins/heredity and one of futurity. See Lehleiter, *Romanticism, Origins, and the History of Heredity* (Lewisburg, PA: Bucknell University Press, 2014), 79.

50. See Zantop's discussion of this essay in Zantop, *Colonial Fantasies*, 68–73.

51. Zantop, *Colonial Fantasies*, 77–80. See also Wendy Sutherland, *Staging Blackness and Performing Whiteness in Eighteenth-Century German Drama* (London: Routledge, 2016), 24–40. Kant also famously linked aesthetics to gender and race in *Beobachtungen über das Gefühl des Schönen und Erhabenen* (1764).

52. Étienne Balibar, "Class Racism," in *Race, Nation, Class: Ambiguous Identities* (London: Verso, 1991).

53. See Schwab, "Familie," 298.

54. Hull, *Sexuality*, 204.

55. Ute Frevert, *Women in German History: From Bourgeois Emancipation to Sexual Liberation*, trans. Stuart McKinnon-Evans (Oxford: Berg, 1989), 21. Frevert writes that as late as 1818, "three-quarters of the approximately 30 million inhabitants of the German Confederation lived in rural settlements and only a quarter lived in the 2,500 towns, of which only 70 had more than 10,000 inhabitants" (22).

56. Hull, *Sexuality*, 155.

57. George Mosse likewise relies on the bourgeois family for a theory of the development of the modern nation. See *Nationalism and Sexuality: Middle-Class Morality and Sexual Norms in Modern Europe* (Madison: University of Wisconsin Press, 1997).

58. Max Horkheimer, "Autorität und Familie," in *Traditionelle und kritische Theorie: Fünf Aufsätze* (Frankfurt: Fischer, 1992).

59. Horkheimer and Adorno's *Dialektik der Aufklärung* (1947) similarly revives the family as both a site of the process of internalization of authoritarian/fascist/capitalist structures and of a refuge from oppressive political and economic structures. Horkheimer argues nostalgically that a feeling of community is possible in the family and that the mother's love is an antidote to the "disenchantment of the world" (195), a point taken up by feminist critics of the Frankfurt School theorists. See Robyn Marasco, "There's a Fascist in the Family: Critical Theory and Antiauthoritarianism," *The South Atlantic Quarterly* 117, no. 4 (2018): 791–813. Of Adorno's late work, *Minima Moralia*, Marasco writes: "So many of its images of 'damaged life'—come from the bourgeois household. And so many of his images of freedom are found in escaping it. That's because fascism lives there" (810). See also Barbara Umrath, "A Feminist Reading of the Frankfurt School's Studies on Authoritarianism and Its Relevance for Understanding Authoritarian Tendencies in Germany Today," *The South Atlantic Quarterly* 117, no. 4 (2018): 861–878, and Barbara Becker-Cantarino, "Patriarchy and German Enlightenment Discourse," in *Impure Reason: Dialectic of Enlightenment in Germany*, ed. W. Daniel Wilson and Robert C. Holub (Detroit, MI: Wayne State University Press, 1993), 61.

60. Jarzebowski, *Inzest*, 13.

61. See, for example, Alexander Mitscherlich, *Auf dem Weg zur vaterlosen Gesellschaft: Ideen zur Sozialpsychologie* (Munich: Piper, 1963); Alexander and Margarete Mitscherlich, *Die Unfähigkeit zu trauern: Grundlagen kollektiven Verhaltens* (Munich: Piper, 1967); and Klaus Theweleit, *Männerphantasien*, 2 vols (Frankfurt am Main: Roter Stern, 1977–1978).

62. Ingeborg Bachmann, *Wir müssen wahre Sätze finden: Gespräche und Interviews* (Munich: Piper, 1983), 144.

63. Silvia Bovenschen, *Die imaginierte Weiblichkeit: Exemplarische Untersuchungen zu kulturgeschichtlichen und literarischen Präsentationsformen des Weiblichen* (Frankfurt am Main: Suhrkamp, 1979). Feminist literary scholars have likewise argued that a gender-specific educational system underscores the internalization of gender roles. See, for example, Wurst, *Familiale Liebe*, especially 49–53.

64. See Hausen, Karin. "Die Polarisierung der 'Geschlechtscharaktere'—eine Spiegelung der Dissoziation von Erwerbs—und Familienleben," in *Sozialgeschichte der Familie in der Neuzeit Europas: Neue Forschungen*, 363–393 (Stuttgart: Klett-Cotta, 1976). Hausen follows the narrative laid out by Brunner, Koselleck, and Schwab in arguing that the intense interest in defining the polarized "Geschlechtscharaktere" [gender characteristics] in the late eighteenth century coincided with the transition from the "ganzes Haus" [whole house] to the bourgeois family model around 1780 (370–371), pointing out, however, that gender complementarity did not dictate roles for working-class women who did not have the "luxury" of remaining in the home (382–383). Barbara Becker-Cantarino argues that the increased autonomy given to bourgeois men in the Enlightenment was not extended to women, who continued to serve as caretakers of the "Haus." See Becker-Cantarino, "Vom 'Ganzen Haus' zur Familienidylle: Haushalt als Mikrokosmos in der Literatur der frühen Neuzeit und seine spätere Sentimentalisierung," *Daphnis: Zeitschrift für mittlere deutsche Literatur* 15, nos. 2–3 (1986): 510. See also Thomas Laqueur's theory about the emergence of a "two-sex" system at the end of the eighteenth century, in Laqueur, *Making Sex: Body and Gender from the Greeks to Freud* (Cambridge, MA: Harvard University Press, 1990).

65. Some recent scholarship in German studies has turned toward non-oedipal literary relations. Important examples include Engelstein, *Sibling Action*; Lehleiter, *Romanticism*; Robert Tobin, *Warm Brothers: Queer Theory and the Age of Goethe* (Philadelphia: University of Pennsylvania Press, 2000); and Susan Gustafson, *Goethe's Families of the Heart* (New York: Bloomsbury, 2016). Volker Hoffmann offers a compelling counterreading to the dominant interpretation of eighteenth-century German drama as family drama, arguing that there is a certain "Familienfeindlichkeit" [hostility to family] in the age of Goethe that emerges with the rise of the cult of genius. See Volker Hoffmann, "Tod der Familie und Toleranz: Lessings *Nathan der Weise* (1779. 1783) und Goethes *Iphigenie auf Tauris* (1787) als Programmstücke der Goethezeit," *Deutsche Vierteljahrsschrift* 85, no. 3 (2011): 370.

66. My *Nostalgia after Nazism* explored the post-fascist nuclear family as a literary and filmic space of claustrophobia from which individual members are desperate to escape. See Heidi Schlipphacke, *Nostalgia after Nazism: History, Home and Affect in German and Austrian Literature and Film* (Lewisburg, PA: Bucknell University Press, 2010).

67. Gerhard Kaiser and Friedrich A. Kittler, introduction to *Dichtung als Sozialisationsspiel: Studien zu Goethe und Gottfried Keller* (Göttingen: Vandenhoeck & Ruprecht, 1978), 10.

68. Friedrich A. Kittler, "Über die Sozialisation Wilhelm Meisters," in *Dichtung als Sozialisationsspiel: Studien zu Goethe und Gottfried Keller*, 113.

69. Heidi Schlipphacke, "Die Vaterschaft beruht nur überhaupt auf der Überzeugung: The Displaced Family in Goethe's *Wilhelm Meisters Lehrjahre*," *Journal of English and German Philology* 102, no. 3 (2003): 390–412.

70. Friedrich Kittler, *Aufschreibesysteme 1800/1900* (Munich: Wilhelm Fink, 1985).

71. Kittler, *Aufschreibesysteme*, 43.

72. Georg Lukács, *Die Theorie des Romans: Ein geschichtsphilosophischer Versuch über die Formen der großen Epik* (Munich: Deutscher Taschenbuch Verlag, 1994), 83.

73. See Erich Auerbach, *Mimesis: The Representation of Reality in Western Literature*, trans. Willard R. Trask (Princeton, NJ: Princeton University Press, 1953), especially 443–450.

74. Auerbach, *Mimesis*, 448.

75. Lukács, *Die Theorie des Romans*, 127–128.

76. Martin Luther's "Haus" consisted of "weyb und kind, knecht und magd, vieh und futter" [wife and child, servant and maid, livestock and feed]. Schwab, "Familie," 362.

77. Otto Brunner, "Das 'ganze' Haus und die alteuropäische Ökonomik," in *Neue Wege der Sozialgeschichte* (Göttingen: Vandenhoeck & Ruprecht, 1956). Brunner highlights the idealized peace ("Hausfriede," 39) that prevails in the "Haus" under the benevolent governance of the "Hausvater," revealing a nostalgia for a positive model of patriarchal authority that mirrors the sentiments of Horkheimer and Adorno. In her critique of Brunner, Claudia Opitz points to the important role of the "Hausmutter" in the premodern "Haus," a figure absent from Brunner's narrative. See Claudia Opitz, "Neue Wege der Sozialgeschichte? Ein kritischer Blick auf Otto Brunners Konzept des 'Ganzen Hauses,'" *Geschichte und Gesellschaft* 20, no. 1 (1994): 92.

78. See Reinhart Koselleck, *Preußen zwischen Reform und Revolution: Allgemeines Landrecht, Verwaltung und soziale Bewegung von 1791 bis 1848* (Stuttgart: Klett, 1967), 67.

79. Hull, *Sexuality*, 206.

80. Koselleck, *Preußen*, 62.

81. Through a review of dispensation applications from the period, Claudia Jarzebowski shows that step-relations and in-laws were included under the incest ban. See Jarzebowski, *Inzest*, especially 167–200. Carl Gottlieb Svarez, a leading writer of the 1791 *Allgemeines Landrecht* (*ALR*) argued that a healthy nation-state must be founded on healthy incest laws. Indeed, authors of the *ALR* struggled to delineate family boundaries via laws that legalized and prohibited certain kin marriages: "The word family has many meanings. It can signify the father of the house and those residing in the house, or relations who all share the same name, or maternal relations, or even in-law relatives" (cited in Koselleck, *Preußen*, 62). The *Allgemeines Landrecht* draft of 1794 forbade marriages between first-degree blood relations as well as between siblings, stepparents and stepchildren, parents-in-law and sons—and daughters-in-law. See also Margaret Lanzinger, *Verwaltete Verwandtschaft: Eheverbote, Kirchliche und Staatliche Dispenspraxis im 18. und 19. Jahrhundert* (Vienna: Böhlau, 2015), 44. Indeed, Frederick II had already loosened the incest code in 1740 to allow cousin marriages. See Jarzebowski, *Inzest*, 159. See also Christopher H. Johnson's discussion of the slippage between sibling love and cousin marriages

in light of the deregulation of the family in eighteenth-century France. Christopher H. Johnson, *Becoming Bourgeois: Love, Kinship, and Power in Provincial France, 1670–1880* (Ithaca, NY: Cornell University Press, 2015), 19.

82. Frevert, *Women in German History*, 14.

83. See discussion in Frevert, *Women in German History*, 13. Zedler's *Großes vollständiges Universal-Lexicon* from 1732 included an entry on "Familie" for the first time, but this term is clearly used synonymously with "Haus": "Anzahl Personen, welche der Macht und Gewalt eines Hausvaters unterworfen sind" [a number of people subjected to the might and power of a father of the house]. Schwab, "Familie", 269.

84. See Sabean and Teuscher, "Kinship in Europe"; Lanzinger, *Verwaltete Verwandtschaft*; Davidoff, *Thicker than Water*; and Jarzebowski, *Inzest*. On the shift from vertical (patriarchal) to horizontal (sibling) power structures, see Sabean and Teuscher, 22.

85. Davidoff, *Thicker than Water*, 27, 18.

86. As Stefani Engelstein has forcefully argued, the horizontal structure of sibling relations invites us to focus more on what she calls "differentials" than on dichotomies and to recognize "the subject within networks and vice versa." Engelstein, *Sibling Action*, 56.

87. Lanzinger, *Verwaltete Verwandtschaft*, 41.

88. Davidoff, *Thicker than Water*, 27.

89. On this point, see Jarzebowski, *Inzest*, 159.

90. Davidoff, *Thicker than Water*, 27, my emphasis.

91. Sabean and Teuscher, "Kinship in Europe," 18. Sabean and Teuscher playfully remind us that Max Weber, the modern theorist of bourgeois capitalism par excellence, married his own cousin (23).

92. Consider, for example, Deleuze and Guattari's brilliant reading of Freud's "A Child Is Being Beaten" essay, in which they show how the nuclear family is conjured out of air from an interpretation of the beating fantasies of a child. Deleuze and Guattari, *Anti-Oedipus*, 58.

93. Caroline Levine, *Forms: Whole, Rhythm, Hierarchy, Network* (Princeton, NJ: Princeton University Press, 2015), 6, 7.

94. As Robert Tobin puts it, "With the term 'family' comes a biological bent that had not been so strong with 'house,' which had emphasized actual physical presence rather than blood lines." Tobin, *Warm Brothers*, 9.

95. Judith Butler argues that social transformation occurs when we "refuse, for instance, to allow kinship to become reducible to 'family.'" See Butler, "Is Kinship Always Already Heterosexual?," 129.

96. Stone, *The Family, Sex and Marriage*, 4.

97. Judith Butler, *Antigone's Claim: Kinship between Life and Death* (New York: Columbia University Press, 2000), 23.

98. Jarzebowski points to the "uneindeutige Grenzen" [indistinct boundaries] (*Inzest*, 145) and openness in early modern kinship structures. Kinship, she writes, can be theorized based on its historical lived realities as a "Zusammengehörigkeitsgefühl" [feeling of belonging together] that is produced in the context of small groupings ("kleine Gruppierungen") that arise out of lived social contexts (*Inzest*, 146).

99. Johann Heinrich Zedler, *Grosses vollständiges Universal-lexicon aller Wissenschafften und Künste*, 142, https://www.zedler-lexikon.de/index.html?c=startseite&l=de.

100. Zedler, *Grosses vollständiges Universal-lexicon*, 142.

101. The concept "Blutsfreunde" [friends through an affinity of blood] was used in the late medieval period in a manner that blurs the presumed clear line between blood relations and all other kinds. See Jarzebowski, *Inzest*, 14.

102. Zedler, *Grosses vollständiges Universal-lexicon*, 145.

103. Claude Lévi-Strauss, *The Elementary Structures of Kinship*, trans. James Harle Bell and John Richard von Sturmer (Boston: Eyre & Spottiswoode, 1969), 45.

104. Lévi-Strauss, *The Elementary Structures of Kinship*, 43; emphasis in the original.

105. As summarized by Butler, "Is Kinship Always Already Heterosexual?," 123; emphasis in the original.

106. Quoted in Butler, "Is Kinship Always Already Heterosexual?," 126.

107. Butler, "Is Kinship Always Already Heterosexual?," 126, my emphasis.

108. Donna J. Haraway, *Staying with the Trouble: Making Kin in the Chthulucene* (Durham, NC: Duke University Press, 2016), 2.

109. Engelstein, *Sibling Action*, 8.

110. Sedgwick, "Tales of the Avunculate," 62.

111. Mark Turner, *Death Is the Mother of Beauty: Mind, Metaphor, Criticism* (Chicago: University of Chicago Press, 1987), 11; emphasis in the original.

112. See also Davidoff, who decries the "obsession with genealogy and the normative nuclear family." Davidoff, *Thicker than Water*, 19.

113. Sedgwick, "Tales of the Avunculate," 71.

114. Denis Diderot, *Das Theater des Herrn Diderot*, trans. G. E. Lessing, WB 5.1.

115. Ben Brewster and Lea Jacobs, *Theater to Cinema: Stage Pictorialism and the Early Feature Film* (Oxford: Oxford University Press, 1997), 38.

116. Brewster and Jacobs, *Theater to Cinema*, 48.

117. Suzanne Guerlac, "The Tableau and Authority in Diderot's Aesthetics," *Studies on Voltaire and the Eighteenth Century* 219 (1983): 188.

118. G. E. Lessing, *Hamburgische Dramaturgie*, WB 6, 289.

119. It should be noted that German paintings of the family in the latter half of the eighteenth century are more circumscribed than their literary correlates. Angelika Lorenz details the increasing popularity of family portraits during this period in which the expected nuclear structure is represented. Examples include G. M. Kraus's "Wieland in the Circle of His Family" (1775) and J.F.A. Tischbein's "Family Picture (Self Portrait with Wife and Daughter)" (1788). In both works, the father is pictured alone with his wife and children. In the painting of Wieland's family, he is seated next to a writing desk that connects him metonymically to the public sphere despite his inclusion within the domestic frame. These paintings engage in debates around the private and public sphere in "Kleinfamilie" terms, adhering to the ideological structure of the nuclear family with its complementary gender characteristic. For a detailed discussion of these paintings and other family portraits from the period, see Angelika Lorenz, *Das deutsche Familienbild in der Malerei des 19. Jahrhunderts* (Darmstadt: Wissenschaftliche Buchgesellschaft, 1985); in particular, 42–68.

120. Of course, the argument has frequently been made—not only by Auerbach but also by Lukács and Peter Szondi—that the liberational gesture in eighteenth-century bourgeois German literature failed. See Peter Szondi, *Die Theorie des bürgerlichen Trauerspiels im 18. Jahrhundert* (Frankfurt am Main: Suhrkamp, 1973). But I want to emphasize here that even the nonmimetic, intermedial approach to eighteenth-century bourgeois literature that I take in this book does not produce a clearly liberational narrative.

121. Habermas, *Strukturwandel der Öffentlichkeit*, 68–69.

122. "Suffice it to say that the discursiveness and sentimentality of the epistolary novel emerge as talkiness, much weeping, effusive and often incoherent emotionalism on stage, incoherent or virtually absent plotting in the genres known as bourgeois tragedy, *comédie larmoyante*, and Sturm und Drang (associated with names such as Gotthold Ephraim Lessing, Denis Diderot, Pierre Augustin Caron de Beaumarchais, George Lillo)." Jane K. Brown, *Goethe's Allegories of Identity* (Philadelphia: University of Pennsylvania Press, 2014), 16–17.

123. Denis Diderot contrasts the naturalness of the theatrical *tableau* to the contrived *coup de théâtre*, a point I will take up later. Denis Diderot, *Conversations on the Natural Son*, in *Selected Writings on Art and Literature*, trans. Geoffrey Bremner (London: Penguin, 1994), 4–80, especially 12–16.

124. Eric Méchoulan and Angela Carr, "Intermediality: An Introduction to the Arts of Transmission," *SubStance* 44, no. 3 (2015): 3.

125. John Guillory, "Genesis of the Media Concept," *Critical Inquiry* 36 (2010): 324; emphasis in the original.

126. Eve Kosofsky Sedgwick, "Paranoid Reading and Reparative Reading, Or, You're So Paranoid, You Probably Think This Essay Is about You," in *Touching Feeling: Affect, Pedagogy, Performativity* (Durham, NC: Duke University Press, 2003).

127. Fredric Jameson, *The Political Unconscious: Narrative as a Socially Symbolic Act* (Ithaca, NY: Cornell University Press, 1981), 60. On this critique of Jameson, see Stephen Best and Sharon Marcus, "Surface Reading: An Introduction," *Representations* 108, no. 1 (2009): 1.

128. See Emily Apter and Elaine Freedgood, "Afterword," *Representations* 108, no. 1 (2009): 143.

129. Best and Marcus, "Surface Reading," 2. This kind of reading recalls Paul Ricoeur's "hermeneutics of suspicion." See Ricoeur, *Freud and Philosophy: An Essay on Interpretation*, trans. Denis Savage (New Haven, CT: Yale University Press, 1970).

130. Foucault frames this modern epistemology in terms of sexuality; sex is that which is hidden in the individual: "Our sex harbors what is most true in ourselves." See Michel Foucault, introduction to *Herculine Barbin: Being the Recently Discovered Memoirs of a Nineteenth-Century Hermaphrodite*, trans. Richard McDougall (New York: Pantheon, 1980), xi. Eve Sedgwick's "epistemology of the closet" similarly excavates this point. See Eve Kosofsky Sedgwick, *Epistemology of the Closet* (Berkeley: University of California Press, 1990).

131. Brown, *The Persistence of Allegory*, 9.

132. Judith Butler, *Gender Trouble: Feminism and the Subversion of Identity* (New York: Routledge, 1990), 138.

133. Moe Meyer, "Introduction: Reclaiming the Discourse of Camp," in *The Politics and Poetics of Camp*, ed. Moe Meyer (New York: Routledge, 1994), 2–3

134. Meyer, "Introduction: Reclaiming the Discourse of Camp," 3.

135. Michel Foucault, *Discipline and Punish: The Birth of the Prison*, trans. Alan Sheridan (New York: Vintage, 1979).

136. G.W.F. Hegel, *Hegel's Aesthetics: Lectures on Fine Art*, Vol. 2, trans. T. M. Knox (Oxford: Clarendon, 1975), 703.

137. Hegel, *Hegel's Aesthetics*, 859. G.W.F. Hegel, *Vorlesungen über die Ästhetik III*, ed. Eva Moldenhauer and Karl Markus Michel; Vol. 15 of *Georg Wilhelm Friedrich Hegel Werke*, 20 vols. (Frankfurt am Main: Suhrkamp, 1970), 95.

138. Brown, *The Persistence of Allegory*, 7.

139. Brown, *The Persistence of Allegory*, 6.

140. Brown, *The Persistence of Allegory*, 60.

141. Bengt Algot Sørensen, *Allegorie und Symbol: Texte zur Theorie des dichterischen Bildes im 18. und frühen 19. Jahrhundert* (Frankfurt am Main: Athenäum, 1972), 261. Sørensen's book provides an overview of eighteenth-century discourses on allegory via excerpts from the period.

142. Samuel Taylor Coleridge, "Lectures on Shakespeare" and "Recapitulation, and Summary of the Characteristics of Shakespeare's Dramas," in *Essays and Lectures on Shakespeare and Some Other Old Poets and Dramatists*, edited by S. T. Coleridge (London: Everyman, 1907), 46. The lectures were given in 1810–1811.

143. See Angus Fletcher, *Allegory: The Theory of a Symbolic Mode* (Ithaca, NY: Cornell University Press, 1964), 17–18.

144. Johann Wolfgang von Goethe, *Maximen und Reflexionen*, FA 1.13.

145. Quoted in Fletcher, *Allegory*, 19.

146. Quoted in Paul de Man, "The Rhetoric of Temporality," in *Blindness and Insight: Essays in the Rhetoric of Contemporary Criticism*, trans. Wlad Godzich (Minneapolis: University of Minnesota Press, 1971), 191–192. The renewed interest in allegory in the twentieth century via Walter Benjamin and, later, the deconstructionists is a product of the pastness perceived to be a characteristic of allegory, allegory's "distance in relation to its own origin" (207). This is the sense of Benjamin's return to allegory in *The Origin of German Tragic Drama* (1928), as a signpost for the melancholic relation to history. In this sense, as de Man writes, allegory is an "anachronism" (190). Fredric Jameson's recent engagement with allegory cuts through the nostalgic relation to this older mode of figurality: Jameson argues that allegory purports to be pure form, distanced from ideology, but this apolitical stance is a lie: "Allegory delivers its message by way of concealing it." See Fredric Jameson, *Allegory and Ideology* (London: Verso, 2019), xiv. Jameson's interpretation of the heavily allegorical style of Goethe's *Faust II* is a case in point: Faust's forgetting of his past in the beginning of the play is an allegory of allegory's anti-ideological claims. In fact, Jameson argues, Faust's forgetting is the ideal mental state for the bourgeois capitalist: one can always start anew within capitalism's dominant myth (292).

147. G.W.F. Hegel, *Hegel's Aesthetics: Lectures on Fine Art*, Vol. 2, 703.

148. For sociologists and historians, the year 1750 has stood as the generally accepted temporal marker of the cultural shifts that led to a crystallization of the nuclear family. Otto Brunner locates a "tiefgreifende Strukturwandel seit der Mitte des 18. Jahrhunderts" [significant structural change since the middle of the eighteenth century] in terms of the relationship between the household and the state. Brunner, "Das 'ganze' Haus," 50. See also Dieter Schwab's entry on "Familie." Schwab, "Familie," 254. Niklas Luhmann likewise points to 1750 as the historical moment that brought a radical shift in the semantic terms used to describe society. Luhmann, "Preface to the English Edition," 2. Conversely, Margareth Lanzinger points to 1750 as the transitional point where the vertical power of the father is weakened in favor of horizontal relationships. See Margareth Lanzinger,

"Introduction," *The History of the Family* 17, no. 3 (2012): 279–283. In each instance, 1750 appears as the critical moment in which radical change is realized.

149. See, for example, Lukács's discussion of literary epochs in *Die Theorie des Romans*.

150. Butler, *Antigone's Claim*, 2.

Chapter One   Middle Class/Bourgeois/Bürger

1. August Langen, "Attitüde und Tableau in der Goethezeit," *Jahrbuch der deutschen Schillergesellschaft* 12 (1968): 198.

2. See Willy R. Berger, "Das Tableau: Rührende Schluß-Szenen im Drama," *Arcadia* 24, no. 2 (1989): 139.

3. Friedrich Schiller, *Die Jungfrau von Orleans*, NA 9.2, 315.

4. Friedrich Schiller, *Wilhelm Tell*, NA 10, 219.

5. Walter Benjamin, *Versuche über Brecht*, ed. Rolf Tiedemann (Frankfurt am Main: Suhrkamp, 1967), 20.

6. See Samuel Weber, "Family Scenes: Some Preliminary Remarks on Domesticity and Theatricality," *South Atlantic Quarterly* 98, no. 3 (1999): "The 'family scene' is frozen in place by the glance of a stranger, not a family member—a glance that fixes the aggregate in the process of' disaggregating. Such disaggregation demonstrates that what is heterogeneous about the family is not external to but inherent in it" (358).

7. Louis-Sébastien Mercier, *Merciers Neuer Versuch über die Schauspielkunst*, trans. Heinrich Leopold Wagner (Heidelberg: Lambert Schneider, 1967), 110.

8. Auerbach, *Mimesis*, 406.

9. The *Rührstück* is usually relegated to the "trivial" pile of eighteenth-century literature. Family and marriage in *Rührstück* plays are exposed to external forces of destruction, but in the end, order is reestablished. See Horst Albert Glaser's critical analysis of the genre in Glaser, *Das bürgerliche Rührstück: Dichtung und Erkenntnis* (Stuttgart: Metzler, 1969). Erika Fischer-Lichte reiterates Glaser's critique, relegating the *Rührstück* to a poetics of affirmation in contrast to what she sees as the critical potential of the bourgeois family trope in the plays of Gellert and Lessing. See Erika Fischer-Lichte, *Kurze Geschichte des deutschen Theaters* (Tübingen: Francke, 1993), 98.

10. G.W.F. Hegel, *Vorlesungen über die Ästhetik III*, ed. Eva Moldenhauer and Karl Markus Michel, vol. 15 of *Georg Wilhelm Friedrich Hegel Werke* (Frankfurt: Suhrkamp, 1970), 568.

11. Friedrich Schiller, "Shakespeares Schatten," *Schillers Sämtliche Werke*, 16 vols., ed. Karl Goedeke (Stuttgart: Cotta, 1893), 347–348.

12. See Erika Fischer-Lichte, *Kurze Geschichte des deutschen Theaters*, 143–165.

13. The bourgeois drama is caricatured here as a genre whose content resembles the *Heimatroman* that emerges in the nineteenth century and in which a very narrow bourgeois milieu is represented as the moral center within shifting and chaotic German state constellations. See Celia Applegate, *A Nation of Provincials: The German Idea of Heimat* (Berkeley: University of California Press, 1990). As Applegate shows, a fractured political environment produces a heightened provincialism in the German territories, and provincialism is invariably tied to the family.

14. Karl Guthke has pointed out the bizarre fact that bourgeois tragedy, which we call a "genre" and a standard-bearing one at that, is actually represented by four plays in the German-speaking imagination: *Miß Sara Sampson*, *Emilia Galotti*, Schiller's *Kabale*

und Liebe, and Hebbel's *Maria Magdalena*. See Karl Guthke, *Das deutsche bürgerliche Trauerspiel*, 6th ed. (Heidelberg: J. B. Metzler, 2016), 1. Cornelia Mönch looked at 229 plays categorized as "bourgeois tragedies" in the eighteenth century, revealing that the plays associated with the term by Lessing, Goethe, and Schiller were rather anomalies than clear representatives of the genre. See Cornelia Mönch, "Abschrecken oder Mitleiden: das deutsche bürgerliche Trauerspiel im 18. Jahrhundert, Versuch einer Typologie," *Jahrbuch für internationale Germanistik* 13 (1995): 146. The basis for Mönch's recharacterization of the genre is Johann Gottlob Benjamin Pfeil's *Lucie Woodvil*, which was published one year after Lessing's *Miß Sara Sampson*, in 1756, and functioned as a correction to what Pfeil saw as the weaknesses in Lessing's play: in *Lucie Woodvil*, the virtuous woman Amalia does not die. As Mönch shows, *Lucie Woodvil* and many other popular plays written between 1756 and 1798 presented bourgeois sufferings with a view to *poetic justice* rather than to Lessing's aesthetics of compassion (*Mitleid*).

15. See Paul Fleming, who likewise points to the distinct quality of the German middle class vis-à-vis France and England. Paul Fleming, *Exemplarity and Mediocrity: The Art of the Average from Bourgeois Tragedy to Realism* (Stanford, CA: Stanford University Press, 2009), 9.

16. Szondi's lectures on the bourgeois tragedy follow this literary geneaology, as do more recent analyses of the genre. See, for example, Alex Eric Hernandez, "Prosaic Suffering: Bourgeois Tragedy and the Aesthetics of the Ordinary," *Representations* 138 (2017): 118–141; and Tom McCall, "Liquid Politics: Toward a Theorization of 'Bourgeois' Tragic Drama," *South Atlantic Quarterly* 98, no. 3 (1999): 593–622.

17. Lessing, *Hamburgische Dramaturgie*, WB 6, 559. Lillo's argument for the genre was based on usefulness—more people could be helped through the representation of characters in the middle class. See Szondi, *Die Theorie*, 26.

18. Szondi highlights how the bourgeois tragedy was being theorized as it was being written. Szondi, *Die Theorie*, 15.

19. Diderot read *Miß Sara Sampson* in translation and hired two Germans to write a new translation for a planned collection of translated bourgeois tragedies, since he could not read German himself. See Robert R. Heitner, "Diderot's Own Miss Sara Sampson," *Comparative Literature* 5, no. 1 (1953), 40–49.

20. Lisa A. Freeman, "Tragic Flaws: Genre and Ideology in Lillo's *London Merchant*," *South Atlantic Quarterly* 98, no. 3 (1999): 7. See also Felicity Nussbaum, "The Unaccountable Pleasure of Eighteenth-Century Tragedy," *PMLA* 129, no. 4 (2014): 688–707. Nussbaum likewise highlights the economic mode of gaming that is at the center of Moore's *The Gamester*, a trope that is not a feature in the German context.

21. McCall, "Liquid Politics," 596.

22. McCall, "Liquid Politics," 612.

23. Reinhart Koselleck, "Drei bürgerliche Welten? Zur vergleichenden Semantik der bürgerlichen Gesellschaft in Deutschland, England und Frankreich," in *Begriffsgeschichten: Studien zur Semantik und Pragmatik der politischen und sozialen Sprache* (Frankfurt: Suhrkamp, 2006), 402.

24. Koselleck, "Drei bürgerliche Welten?," 403.

25. Johann Heinrich Zedler, *Grosses vollständiges Universal-Lexicon aller Wissenschaften und Künste* (Leipzig, 1731–1754), cited in Koselleck, "Drei bürgerliche Welten?," 415.

26. Koselleck, "Drei bürgerliche Welten?," 415.

27. Koselleck, "Drei bürgerliche Welten?," 407.

28. Koselleck, "Drei bürgerliche Welten?," 412.

29. Koselleck, "Drei bürgerliche Welten?," 433.

30. Koselleck, "Drei bürgerliche Welten?," 434.

31. Szondi, *Die Theorie*, 110. Lothar Pikulik offers an important counterargument to this kind of Marxist reading of the eighteenth-century German bourgeois tragedy (as a critique of class and rank categories), positing that the category "das Bürgertum" is one of milieu and not class. See Lothar Pikulik, *"Bürgerliches Trauerspiel" und Empfindsamkeit* (Cologne: Böhlau, 1966), 152.

32. Habermas, *Strukturwandel der Öffentlichkeit*, 107.

33. Lessing, *Hamburgische Dramaturgie*, 251: "He believed that the fate of a daughter who is killed by her father, for whom her virtue is more valuable than her life, is already tragic enough and capable of shaking the whole soul, even if no destruction of the whole state constitution follows." Lessing, letter to Friedrich Nicolai, January 21, 1758, WB 11.1, 267.

34. Szondi, *Die Theorie*, 99–100.

35. Paul Fleming argues that "politics sneaks into compassion through the back door" in the bourgeois tragedy; the genre depoliticizes tragedy "by moving it into the domestic interior," but it is repoliticized when Lessing defines compassion as that quality that will improve the larger social order. See Fleming, *Exemplarity and Mediocrity*, 69. Helmut Schneider connects Lessing's aesthetics of compassion with the creation of community within the theater itself. See Helmut Schneider, "Humanity's Imaginary Body: The Concepts of Empathy and Sympathy and the New Theater Experience in the 18th Century," *Deutsche Vierteljahrsschrift für Literaturwissenschaft und Geistesgeschichte* 82, no. 3 (2008): 390. See also Susan Gustafson's intervention into the question of the gender of "Mitleid" in Lessing's works. Susan Gustafson, *Absent Mothers and Orphaned Fathers: Narcissism and Abjection in Lessing's Aesthetic and Dramatic Production* (Detroit, MI: Wayne State University Press, 1995).

36. Georg Lukács, "Zur Soziologie des modernen Dramas," *Schriften zur Soziologie*, ed. Peter Ludz (Neuwied: Luchterhand Verlag, 1961), 277.

37. Lukács calls bourgeois drama the "new" drama, a "Drama des Milieus." Lukács, "Zur Soziologie," 290. In this sense, the bourgeois milieu is always one in which the individual suffers as an unelidable consequence of the abuses and humiliations inherent in class structures.

38. Georg Lukács, "The Sociology of Modern Drama," *The Tulane Drama Review* 9, no. 4 (1965): 166.

39. Peter Demetz, "Defenses of Dutch Painting and the Theory of Realism," *Comparative Literature* 15, no. 2 (1963): 103. Demetz cites F. G. Hotho's *Geschichte der deutschen und niederländischen Malerei* from 1842.

40. Lukács makes the point that the monologue attempts to conceal shame. Lukács, "The Sociology of Modern Drama," 163.

41. Lukács, "The Sociology of Modern Drama," 169.

42. "This is the crux of the paradox: the material of drama consists of the interrelatedness of ethical systems, and the dramatic structure which arises from this relationship is aesthetic-formal." Lukács, "The Sociology of Modern Drama," 169.

43. Lukács, "The Sociology of Modern Drama," 169.

44. See Lisa A. Freeman, "Tragic Flaws: Genre and Ideology in Lillo's *London Merchant*," *South Atlantic Quarterly* 98, no. 3 (1999); and Hernandez, "Prosaic Suffering."

45. Auerbach, *Mimesis*, 437.

46. Auerbach does express a partiality to *Minna von Barnhelm*, and he quotes Goethe's reference to this work as the first play of its time to have a contemporary content. Auerbach, *Mimesis*, 437.

47. Auerbach, *Mimesis*, 438.

48. Auerbach, *Mimesis*, 440.

49. Auerbach, *Mimesis*, 441.

50. Auerbach, *Mimesis*, 442.

51. Auerbach, *Mimesis*, 441. Luise's "failure," as Auerbach calls it (411), is due to her lack of inner freedom, her servile, unenlightened internalization of the rigid and restrictive conflation of power with truth at the court.

52. Auerbach, *Mimesis*, 443, 439.

53. Auerbach, *Mimesis*, 443.

54. Auerbach uses "style" in the way we would use "form."

55. Auerbach, *Mimesis*, 445, italics mine.

56. Auerbach, *Mimesis*, 452. Auerbach quotes Goethe here.

57. Johann Wolfgang von Goethe, letter to Johann Peter Eckermann, May 3, 1827, FA 2.12, 608.

58. Todd Kontje argues, based on his analysis of Schiller's *Wilhelm Tell* and his fragment poem "Deutsche Größe" [German Grandeur], that, in contrast, Schiller saw Germany's political decentralization as a "prerequisite for its cultural renaissance." See Todd Kontje, "Schiller's *Wilhelm Tell*: Weimar Classicism between Empire and Nation," *Monatshefte* 109, no. 4 (2017): 519–538.

59. Norbert Elias, *The Civilizing Process: Sociogenic and Psychogenic Observations*, trans. Edmund Jephcott (Malden, MA: Blackwell, 1982), 20.

60. Elias, *The Civilizing Process*, 26.

61. Eckermann, letter to Goethe, May 3, 1827, FA 2.12, 611. Fleming points to the belatedness of Germany "not only in political terms but also in literary ones," since it is the one major European literary culture in the eighteenth century without a "classical" literature. Fleming, *Exemplarity and Mediocrity*, 9.

62. "For tragedy is not the portrayal of men [as such], but of action, of life . . . dramatists do not employ action in order to achieve character portrayal, but they include character because of its relation to action." See Aristotle, *The Poetics*, trans. Preston H. Epps (Chapel Hill: University of North Carolina Press, 1942), 13.

Chapter Two   Tableau/Tableau Vivant

1. G. E. Lessing, "Vorwort des Übersetzers, zu dieser zweiten Aufgabe," foreword to *Das Theater des Herrn Diderot*, W B 5.1, 15.

2. *Das Theater des Herrn Diderot* contains Lessing's translation of Diderot's two plays (*The Natural Son* of 1757, translated as *Der natürliche Sohn oder die Proben der Tugend*; and *The Father of the Family* of 1758, translated as *Der Hausvater*) along with the theoretical writings that accompany these plays (*Conversations on the Natural Son* and *On Dramatic Poetry*). On Lessing's translations of Diderot's plays and his intention that Germans should cry while watching Diderot's plays, see Nikolas Immer and Olaf Müller, "Lessings Diderot: 'süssere Thränen' zur Läuterung des Nationalgeschmacks," in *"Ihrem Originale nachzudenken": Zu Lessings Übersetzungen*, ed. Helmut Berthold (Tübingen: Niemeyer, 2008), 156.

3. Though he doesn't refer to the *tableau*, Fleming describes Lessing's use of "scenes of admiration" that can serve as a "pause, an intermission to dry one's eyes." See Paul Fleming, *Exemplarity and Mediocrity: The Art of the Average from Bourgeois Tragedy to Realism* (Stanford, CA: Stanford University Press, 2009), 62.

4. On the concluding *tableau* in *Nathan der Weise* see Helmut Schneider, "Der Zufall der Geburt: Lessings *Nathan der Weise* und der imaginäre Körper der Geschichtsphilosophie," in *Körper/Kultur: Kalifornische Studien zur deutschen Moderne*, ed. Thomas W. Kniesche (Würzburg: Königshausen & Neumann, 1995), 121. See also Willy R. Berger, "Das Tableau: Rührende Schluß-Szenen im Drama," *Arcadia* 24, no. 2 (1989): 139–140.

5. According to Neil Flax, "Over twenty painted and engraved versions of the Virginia motif appear[ed] between 1750 and 1815." Neil Flax, "From Portrait to *Tableau Vivant*: The Pictures of *Emilia Galotti*," *Eighteenth Century Studies* 19, no. 1 (1985): 43.

6. Lessing, *Nathan der Weise*, W B 9, 627.

7. Lessing, "Vorwort des Übersetzers," 15.

8. Roland Mortier, *Diderot in Deutschland: 1750–1850*, trans. Hans G. Schürmann (Stuttgart: Metzler, 1967), 71.

9. *The Father of the Family* was not even performed on the French stage until 1771. See F. C. Green, "Editor's Introduction," in *Diderot's Writings on the Theatre* (Cambridge, UK: Cambridge University Press, 1936), 9–10.

10. The play was translated anonymously by members of the Ackermann acting troupe. See Mortier, *Diderot in Deutschland*, 49–50.

11. See Mortier, *Diderot in Deutschland*, 49.

12. Lessing, "Briefe, die neueste Literatur betreffend," W B 4, 700. See in this context Gisela F. Ritchie's argument that Lessing's dramas were, in fact, influenced by French Neoclassicism: Gisela F. Ritchie, "Spuren des französischen Dramas bei Lessing," in *Nation und Gelehrtenrepublik: Lessing im europäischen Zusammenhang* (Detroit, MI: Wayne State University Press, 1984).

13. Lessing's reception of Diderot is not exclusively laudatory. In particular, Lessing quibbled about Diderot's insistence in "Conversations on *The Natural Son*" that drama should focus more on *condition* or milieu than on individual character. See Denis Diderot, "Conversations on *The Natural Son*," in *Selected Writings on Art and Literature*, trans. Geoffrey Bremner (London, Penguin, 1994), 60. In sections 86 through 92 of the *Hamburgische Dramaturgie* (written in February and March of 1768), Lessing presents a one-sided argument with Diderot in which he states that characters in both tragedy and comedy must embody a mixture of particular and general traits in order to stimulate an emotional response from the spectator. See Lessing, *Hamburgische Dramaturgie*, W B 6, 613. See on this point Günter Saße, who argues that Lessing's resistance to Diderot's static sense of character highlights Lessing's more dynamic theater aesthetics. See also, on Lessing's more conflicted characters, Jutta Golawski-Braungart, *Die Schule der Franzosen: Zur Bedeutung von Lessings Übersetzungen aus dem Französischen für die Theorie und Praxis seines Theaters* (Tübingen: Francke, 2005), 174–175.

14. Denis Diderot, "Von der dramatischen Dichtkunst," in *Das Theater des Herrn Diderot*, W B 5.1, 171.

15. Lessing, *Hamburgische Dramaturgie*, 604.

16. Diderot, "Von der dramatischen Dichtkunst," 133.

17. Günther Heeg, "Massive Erhebung: Das französische Theatertableau des 18. Jahrhunderts als Medium der Affektsteuerung und Wahrnehmungslenkung," in *Wahrnehmung und Medialität*, ed. Erika Fischer-Lichte et al. (Tübingen: Francke, 2001), 62.

18. Schneider, "Humanity's Imaginary Body," 348.

19. Heeg, "Massive Erhebung," 54.

20. Emma Barker, "Painting and Reform in Eighteenth-Century France: Greuze's *L'Accordée de Village*," *Oxford Art Journal* 20, no. 2 (1997): 42.

21. In the *Salon* of 1761 Diderot highlights the natural elements of the Greuze painting: "There are twelve figures; each in its place and is doing what it should. How well they are all linked!" Denis Diderot, *On Art and Artists: An Anthology of Diderot's Aesthetic Thought*, ed. Jean Seznec, trans. John S. D. Glaus (London: Springer, 2011), 114.

22. Barker, "Painting and Reform," 46.

23. Barker, "Painting and Reform," 43.

24. It is, however, highly likely that *tableaux vivants* of popular paintings had been performed on Paris stages before 1761, in particular since performance reviews do not reveal the level of shock one might otherwise expect on the part of the audience. See Birgit Jooss, *Lebende Bilder: Körperliche Nachahmung von Kunstwerken in der Goethezeit* (Berlin: Reimer, 1999), 55.

25. Barker, "Painting and Reform," 43.

26. Michael Fried, *Absorption and Theatricality: Painting and Beholder in the Age of Diderot* (Chicago: University of Chicago Press, 1980), 90.

27. Barker, "Painting and Reform," 43.

28. See Walter Benjamin, "Über den Begriff der Geschichte," in *Illuminationen: Ausgewählte Schriften I* (Frankfurt am Main: Suhrkamp, 1955), 260.

29. See Fried, *Absorption and Theatricality*, 167.

30. Fried, *Absorption and Theatricality*, 90.

31. Diderot, "Conversations on *The Natural Son*," 6.

32. Diderot, "Conversations on *The Natural Son*," 96. Suzanne Guerlac argues that the *tableau* and the coup de théâtre are qualitatively linked: the former "takes the place of the '*coup de théâtre*' as a device for producing a moment of extra intensity for the audience." See Guerlac, "The Tableau and Authority in Diderot's Aesthetics," 188.

33. Diderot, "Conversations on *The Natural Son*," 12.

34. Diderot, "Conversations on *The Natural Son*," 12.

35. Diderot, "Conversations on *The Natural Son*," 11.

36. Diderot, "Conversations on *The Natural Son*," 13.

37. Diderot, "Conversations on *The Natural Son*," 20.

38. Anthony Ashley Cooper, Earl of Shaftesbury, *Second Characters, or The Language of Forms*, ed. Benjamin Rand (New York: Greenwood Press, 1969), 30–32; cited in Fried, *Absorption and Theatricality*, 89.

39. Shaftesbury, *Second Characters*, 32.

40. Yann Robert articulates this lack inherent in Diderot's *tableaux* as an "unfinished" quality that stimulates emotional intensity and imagination in the spectator. See Yann Robert, "Mercier's Revolutionary Theater: Reimagining Pantomime, the Aesthetic of the Unfinished, and the Politics of the Stage," *Studies in Eighteenth-Century Culture* 44 (2015): 189.

41. Schneider, "Humanity's Imaginary Body," 397.

42. Cited in Roland Barthes, "Diderot, Brecht, Eisenstein," *Image, Music, Text*, trans. Stephen Heath (New York: Hill and Wang, 1977), 71.

43. Barthes, "Diderot, Brecht, Eisenstein," 71.

44. Barthes, "Diderot, Brecht, Eisenstein," 70.

45. Sigmund Freud, "Fetischismus," in *Psychologie des Unbewußten*, vol. 3 of *Studienausgabe*, ed. Alexander Mitscherlich, Angela Richards, and James Strachey (Frankfurt am Main: Fischer, 1975).

46. See Gilbert J. Jordan, "Lebende Bilder im deutschen Drama des 17. Jahrhunderts," *The South Central Bulletin* 33, no. 4 (1973): 208. For a detailed historical overview of the *tableau vivant* phenomenon see Jooss, *Lebende Bilder*.

47. Alexandra Tacke, "Aus dem Rahmen (ge)fallen: *Tableaux vivants* in Goethes Wahlverwandtschaften und bei Vanessa Beecroft," in *Äpfel und Birnen: Illegitimes Vergleichen in den Kulturwissenschaften*, ed. Helga Lutz, Friedrich Mißfelder, and Tilo Renz (Bielefeld: Transcript, 2006), 85. See also August Langen, *Anschauungsformen in der deutschen Dichtung des 18. Jahrhunderts (Rahmenschau und Rationalismus)* (Jena: Diederichs, 1934).

48. Barthes, "Diderot, Brecht, Eisenstein," 73.

49. Jacques Lacan, "The Mirror Stage as Formative of the Function of the I as Revealed in Psychoanalytic Experience," in *Écrits: A Selection*, trans. Alan Sheridan (New York: W.W. Norton, 1977).

50. Gilles Deleuze, *Cinema 1: The Movement-Image*, trans. Hugh Tomlinson and Barbara Habberjam (Minneapolis: University of Minnesota Press, 1986), 4.

51. Deleuze, *Cinema 1*, 4.

52. Deleuze, *Cinema 1*, 5.

53. Deleuze, *Cinema 1*, 5. On the family and the snapshot, see Suzanne R. Pucci, "Picture Perfect: Snapshots of the Family," *L'Esprit Créateur* 44, no. 1 (2004): 68–82.

54. Benjamin, "Über den Begriff der Geschichte," 261.

55. Deleuze, *Cinema 1*, 6.

56. Heeg, "Massive Erhebung," 56.

57. Heeg, "Massive Erhebung," 57.

58. See, for example, Heeg's articulation of this position. Heeg, "Massive Erhebung," 58.

59. Jay Caplan points out that the subject of Diderot's *tableaux* is always the family and, more specifically, loss in the family. See Jay Caplan, *Framed Narratives: Diderot's Genealogy of the Beholder* (Minneapolis: University of Minnesota Press, 1985), 19.

60. It is curious that Diderot's understanding of a "natural," and hence moral, subject for the dramatic *tableau* is so narrowly centered on the nuclear family. Diderot's works often reveal radically progressive ideas about gender, about the potential "naturalness" of a variety of nontraditional sex acts, including homosexuality and incest, as well as calling into question a rigid notion of procreation based on preformation, offering in its stead an asexual reproduction of polyps in *D'Alembert's Dream*. Andrew S. Curran elucidates the radical nature of Diderot's oeuvre while making the point that Diderot's plays and his art criticism (in the *Salons*) present an anomaly in terms of their curious moral rectitude. See Andrew S. Curran, *Diderot and the Art of Thinking Freely* (New York: Other Press, 2019), 215.

61. Kiki Gounaridou and John Hellweg, introduction to *Two Plays by Denis Diderot: The Illegitimate Son and The Father of the Family*, trans. Kiki Gounaridou and John Hellweg (New York: Peter Lang, 2011), 4.

62. Peter Szondi has argued that Diderot saw the bourgeois family as a space of virtue and retreat in contrast to a threatening public sphere in light of his own imprisonment following the publication of the *Lettre sur les aveugles* in 1749. See Peter Szondi, "Tableau und coup de théâtre: Zur Sozialpsychologie des bürgerlichen Trauerspiels bei Diderot: Mit einem Exkurs über Lessing," in *Erforschung der deutschen Aufklärung*, ed. Peter Pütz (Königstein im Taunus: Athenäum, Hain, Scriptor, Hanstein, 1980), 202.

63. Denis Diderot, *The Illegitimate Son*, in *Two Plays by Denis Diderot*, 53.

64. Deleuze, *Cinema 1*, 7.

65. Szondi argues that for Diderot virtue (*Tugend*) is linked exclusively with the private realm, whereas eighteenth-century English dramas situate virtue in both the private and public spheres. See Szondi, "Tableau und coup de théâtre," 202.

66. Willy R. Berger describes the temporality in Diderot's plays as a "snail's tempo." See Willy R. Berger, "Das Tableau: Rührende Schluß-Szenen im Drama," *Arcadia* 24, no. 2 (1989): 138.

67. Diderot, *The Father of the Family*, in *Two Plays by Denis Diderot*, 174. The original stage directions are not in this translation but are my own from the French.

68. "Walter Benjamin once suggested this affinity between 'Rührung' and *tableau* in this sentence: sentimentality is 'the paralyzing wing of feeling that settles down anywhere because it can't go on.'" Szondi, "Tableau und coup de théâtre," 194.

69. Cited in Barker, "Painting and Reform," 45.

70. Diderot, "Conversations on *The Natural Son*," 61.

71. Szondi, *Die Theorie*, 127.

72. Susan Gustafson shows how Lessing mimics this omission in his own aesthetic project. See Gustafson, *Absent Mothers and Orphaned Fathers*.

73. Denis Jonnes points out that Dorval actually performs the role of the (missing) father in Diderot's play, rendering the father little more than nostalgic fiction. Denis Jonnes, "*Les Pères Victimes*: Diderot and the Socio-Poetics of Bourgeois Drama," *Studies on Voltaire and the Eighteenth Century* 265 (1989): 1367.

74. Szondi, "Tableau und coup de théâtre," 194.

75. Diderot, *The Father of the Family*, 81.

76. Diderot, *The Father of the Family*, 138.

77. Diderot, *The Father of the Family*, 170.

78. Schneider, "Humanity's Imaginary Body," 385.

79. See Albrecht Koschorke, *Körperströme und Schriftverkehr: Mediologie des 18. Jahrhunderts* (Munich: Fink, 2003). See Schneider's discussion of Koschorke in "Humanity's Imaginary Body," 386.

80. Heeg, "Massive Erhebung," 57.

81. G.W.F. Hegel, *Elements of the Philosophy of Right*, ed. Allen W. Wood, trans. H. B. Nisbet (Cambridge, UK: Cambridge University Press, 1991). See, in particular, "The Family," paragraphs 158–181, 199–219.

82. Immanuel Kant, *Über Pädagogik* (Königsberg: Theodor Rink, 1803).

83. Diderot, *The Father of the Family*, 81.

84. See Brown, *The Persistence of Allegory*, and John R. J. Eyck and Katherine Arens, "The Court of Public Opinion: Lessing, Goethe, and Werther's *Emilia Galotti*," *Monatshefte* 96, no. 1 (2004): 40–61.

85. Eyck and Arens, "The Court of Public Opinion," 41.

86. Juliane Vogel offers the compelling interpretation that the space of the inn in *Miß Sara Sampson* is the topos of the "arme[s] Theater" [poor theater], i.e., the traveling theater troupe. The opening scene of the play depicts a foyer with a curtain delineating Mellefont's room that can be seen as a prop associated with the traveling stage. See Juliane Vogel, "Raptus: Eröffnungsfiguren von Drama und Oper des 18. Jahrhunderts," *Deutsche Vierteljahrsschrift für Literaturwissenschaft und Geistesgeschichte* 83, no. 4 (2009): 508–509. See also Volker C. Dörr, who argues that the inn in Lessing's play is distinctly "heimatfern" [far from home]. See Volker C. Dörr, "Elende Wirtshäuser? Zu Lessings *Miß Sara Sampson* und Lillos *The London Merchant*," in *Gastlichkeit und Ökonomie: Wirtschaften im deutschen und englischen Drama des 18. Jahrhunderts*, ed. Sigrid Nieberle and Claudia Nitschke (Berlin: DeGruyter, 2014), 168.

87. Gail Hart argues that William, Waitwell, and Marwood and Mellefont's daughter Arabella produce a new family at the end of the play. See Gail Hart, *Tragedy in Paradise: Family and Gender Politics in German Bourgeois Tragedy 1750–1850* (Rochester, NY: Camden House, 1996). Friedrich Kittler points to the construction of a new family at the end of *Miß Sara Sampson* based on adoption, a trope that shifts the focus from procreation (blood relations) to generation (adoption, production of human family). See Friedrich A. Kittler, "'Erziehung ist Offenbarung': Zur Struktur der Familie in Lessings Dramen," *Jahrbuch der deutschen Schillergesellschaft* 21 (1977): 130.

88. Lessing, *Miß Sara Sampson*, WB 3, 525.

89. Lessing, *Miß Sara Sampson*, WB 3, 525.

90. Brown, *The Persistence of Allegory*, 178. Earlier, Brown notes that, "On the surface bourgeois tragedy is mimetic in its representation of the middle class on the serious stage, but only on the surface" (176).

91. On the dialectic between public and private in *Emilia Galotti*, see Klaus-Detlef Müller, "Das Virginia-Motiv in Lessings *Emilia Galotti*: Anmerkungen zum Strukturwandel der Öffentlichkeit," *Orbis Litterarum* 42 (1987): 305–316.

92. Scholarship on *Emilia Galotti* has historically puzzled over its jarring ending. This scene has been interpreted as a scene of tyranny, of humanism, or of incestuous desires. As an example of the last, see Heidi M. Schlipphacke, "The Dialectic of Female Desire in G.E. Lessing's *Emilia Galotti*," *Lessing Yearbook* 33 (2001): 55–78; and John Poyntner, "The Pearls of Emilia Galotti," *Lessing Yearbook* 9 (1977): 81–95. Brigitte Prutti reads the Emilia-Odoardo relationship as an incestuous one that leads to the spectacular but meaningless coup de théâtre at the end; see Brigitte Prutti, "*Coup de Théâtre—Coup de Femme*, or: What Is Lessing's Emilia Galotti Dying From?" *Lessing Yearbook* 26 (1994): 1–28. Uwe C. Steiner argues that the gendered sacrifice at the end of the play produces not compassion but fear: see Steiner, "Gerechtigkeit für Odoardo Galotti: Ein Theatercoup mit Folgen: Wie Lessing das tragische Opfer geschlechteranthropologisch umwidmet und damit von Bodmer bis zur Gegenwart wirkt," *Deutsche Vierteljahrsschrift für Literaturwissenschaft und Geistesgeschichte* 95 (2021): 43–80. Christopher Wild reads Emilia's virginity via the image of the hymen as the fourth wall. See Christopher Wild, "Der theatralische Schleier des Hymens: Lessings bürgerliches Trauerspiel *Emilia Galotti*," *Deutsche Vierteljahrsschrift für Literaturwissenschaft und Geistesgeschichte* 74 (2000): 189–220. Recent scholarship has moved away from the puzzling ending and tends to focus on the history of criticism on the play. See, for example, Dieter Liewerscheidt, "Lessings *Emilia Galotti*— ein unmögliches Trauerspiel," *Literatur für Leser* 34, no. 4 (2011): 231–246; and Jan

Borkowski, "'Wohin unsre Seelenkräfte uns verleiten können.' Ein Versuch, Lessings *Emilia Galotti* neu zu kontextualisieren," *Text und Kontext* 39, no. 1 (2017): 85–114.

93. Lessing, *Emilia Galotti*, WB 7, 371.

94. Ruth K. Angress highlights the odd fact that in this final scene we watch "three murderers assess one another over a dead body." Ruth K. Angress, "The Generations in *Emilia Galotti*," *Germanic Review* 43 (1968): 22.

95. See also Irene Morris, who ties the rose from the murder scene to baroque drama. Irene Morris, "The Symbol of the Rose: A Baroque Echo in *Emilia Galotti*," *Publications of the English Goethe Society* 64, no. 1 (2016): 53–71.

96. Lessing, *Emilia Galotti*, 371.

97. See Winfried Woesler, "Die beiden Schlüsse von Lessings 'Nathan,'" in *Akten des X. Internationalen Germanistenkongresses Wien 2000: 'Zeitenwende-die Germanistik auf dem Weg vom 20. ins 21. Jahrhundert'-* (Bern: Peter Lang, 2002).

98. Woesler, "Die beiden Schlüsse," 329.

99. Schneider, "Der Zufall der Geburt," 108.

100. Lessing, *Nathan der Weise*, 627.

101. The semiotics of materiality associated with these goods is discussed in chapter 5.

102. Susanne Brüggemann similarly allies Diderot's aesthetic with the *tableau* and Lessing's with action. See Susanne Brüggemann, *Tableau oder Handlung? Zur Dramaturgie Diderots und Lessings* (Würzburg: Königshausen & Neumann, 2017).

103. Carl Niekerk, "Radicalism in Lessing's Domestic Drama (*Miss Sara Sampson, Minna von Barnhelm*, and *Emilia Galotti*)," in *The Radical Enlightenment in German: A Cultural Perspective*, ed. Carl Niekerk (Leiden: Brill, 2018), 162.

104. Günther Heeg, *Das Phantasma der natürlichen Gestalt: Körper, Sprache und Bild im Theater des 18. Jahrhunderts* (Frankfurt am Main: Stroemfeld, 2000), 80.

Chapter Three   The German Dramatic Tableau *beyond Lessing*

1. Lessing translated Gellert's treatise on the "weinerliches Lustspiel" from Latin into German in 1754, in WB 3.

2. Diderot shifts between genre terminologies within his theoretical works on drama, often using the term *"genre sérieux,"* referring to a kind of drama of the middle way. See Diderot, "Conversations on *The Natural Son*," 141.

3. See Winfried Woesler, "Lessing's 'Emilia' und die Virginia-Legende bei Livius," *Zeitschrift für deutsche Philologie* 116, no. 2 (1997): 169–170.

4. Jacques Derrida, "The Law of Genre," trans. Avital Ronell, *Critical Inquiry* 7, no. 1 (1980): 55–57.

5. Derrida cites Gérard Genette on the construction of naturalness within genre theory in which "a factitious symmetry heavily reinforced by fake windows" is constructed; cited in Derrida, "The Law of Genre," 60.

6. Stefano Castelvecchi, *Sentimental Opera: Questions of Genre in the Age of the Bourgeois Drama* (Cambridge, UK: Cambridge University Press, 2013), 6.

7. Cited in Erika Fischer-Lichte, *Kurze Geschichte des deutschen Theaters* (Tübingen: Francke, 1993), 95.

8. See, for example, Karl S. Guthke, *Das deutsche bürgerliche Trauerspiel* (Stuttgart: Metzler, 2006), 104.

9. The substantial critical literature on Schiller's play can be divided into a focus on the topic of love or of politics (class consciousness). The family would seem to bridge these two poles, but readings focused on the family in the work frequently argue for its lack of political relevance. J. M. van der Laan highlights these two poles in *"Kabale und Liebe* Reconsidered," in *A Companion to the Works of Friedrich Schiller*, ed. Steven D. Martinson (Rochester, NY: Boydell & Brewer, 2005). Gerhard Kaiser and Thomas F. Barry read the play as an engagement with paternalism and the patriarchal order within the bourgeois family; see Gerhard Kaiser, "Krise der Familie: Eine Perspektive auf Lessings *Emilia Galotti* und Schillers *Kabale und Liebe*," *Recherches germaniques* 14 (1984): 7–22; and Thomas F. Barry, "Love and the Politics of Paternalism: Images of the Father in Schiller's *Kabale und Liebe*," *Colloquia Germanica* 22 (1989): 21–37. On the fetishization of obedience to the father in the play that conflicts with its message of political disobedience, see Daniel W. Wilson, "Obedience," *PEGS* 77, no. 1 (2008): 52; and Marlene Streeruwitz, *"Kabale und Liebe* oder *Die antiödipale Geste, die da noch möglich war*," in *Friedrich Schiller, Dichter, Denker, Vor- und Gegenbild*, ed. Jan Bürger (Göttingen: Wallstein, 2007), 232. See also Bengt Algot Sørensen, *Herrschaft und Zärtlichkeit: Der Patriarchalismus und das Drama im 18. Jahrhundert* (Munich: Beck, 1984).

10. Friedrich Schiller, *Kabale und Liebe*, NA 5, 8.

11. Reprints of these images can be found in chapter 7.

12. Schiller, *Kabale und Liebe*, NA 5, 8.

13. Some art historians have argued that the young man in the ter Borch painting is holding a coin, indicating his willingness to pay the mother or madam for the services of the young woman who stands in front of them. On the art historical reception of the ter Borch painting see Daniela Hammer-Tugendhat, *The Visible and the Invisible: On Seventeenth-Century Dutch Painting* (Vienna: Böhlau, 2009), 288.

14. Schiller, *Kabale und Liebe*, 12.

15. Lisa A. Freeman, "Tragic Flaws: Genre and Ideology in Lillo's *London Merchant*," *South Atlantic Quarterly* 98, no. 3 (1999): 555.

16. Economic metaphors abound in the play, and Miller frequently refers to his daughter in terms of economic gain. One of many such examples occurs in Act 5, scene 1, when Miller calls Luise his "Haab und Gut" [possessions and goods]. Schiller, *Kabale und Liebe*, 156. On the daughter in the bourgeois tragedy as the father's "ware," see Inge Stephan, "'So ist die Tugend ein Gespenst': Frauenbild und Tugendbegriff bei Lessing und Schiller," in *Inszenierte Weiblichkeit: Codierung der Geschlechter in der Literatur des 18. Jahrhunderts* (Cologne: Böhlau, 2004), 30–31.

17. Critics have complained about what they see as the weak, melodramatic ending in Schiller's play. See, for example, Bernd Fischer, *Kabale und Liebe: Skepsis und Melodrama in Schillers bürgerlichem Trauerspiel* (Frankfurt am Main: Peter Lang, 1987), 130; Walter Pape, "'Ein merkwürdiges Beispiel productiver Kritik': Schillers *Kabale und Liebe* und das zeitgenössische Publikum," *Zeitschrift für deutsche Philologie* 107 (1988): 199. These kinds of frustrations with the play's ending show that scholars have read it as a mimetic, realist drama. On the baroque mixture of tragic and comic within Schiller's play, see Erich Schön, "Schillers *Kabale und Liebe*: (K)ein bürgerliches Trauerspiel—Schiller und Otto von Gemmingens *Der deutsche Hausvater*," in *Bürgerlichkeit im 18. Jahrhundert*, ed. Hans Edwin Friedrich, Fotis Jannidis, and Marianne Willems (Tübingen: Niemeyer, 2006), 389.

18. Schiller, *Kabale und Liebe*, 188.

19. Schiller, *Kabale und Liebe*, 190.

20. Schiller, *Kabale und Liebe*, 386.

21. Schiller, *Kabale und Liebe*, 192.

22. Schiller, *Kabale und Liebe*, 190.

23. Quoted in Monika Fick, *Lessing Handbuch: Leben-Werk-Wirkung*, 4th ed. (Stuttgart: Metzler, 2016), 223. Schiller's use of the term "Familiengemälde" recalls the painting of the sick "Königssohn" from Goethe's *Wilhelm Meisters Lehrjahre* who is in love with his father's bride, a narrative with a direct parallel in Schiller's play and which I discuss in more detail in chapter 6. See Ingrid Haag, "Carlos, der 'kranke Königssohn': Familienroman in einem 'königlichen Hause,'" in *Eros und Literatur: Liebe in Texten von der Antike bis zum Cyberspace: Festschrift für Gert Sautermeister*, ed. Christiane Solte-Gresser, Wolfgang Emmerich, and Hans Wolf Jäger (Bremen: Lumière, 2005). Robert Tobin draws out this connection in his convincing queer reading of the play. See Robert Tobin, *Warm Brothers*, 163.

24. Schiller, *Don Karlos* (letzte Ausgabe), NA 7.1, 644.

25. Several critics have discussed Schiller's use of Diderot's *tableau* in *Don Carlos*. See Zak Easthop, "Adapting Schiller's *Don Karlos*: Verdi, Posa, and the Problem of the 'Familiengemälde,'" *German Life and Letters* 73, no. 2 (2020): 229–245; Helmut Schneider, "Der große Menschheitsaugenblick: Zu Schillers politischer Publikumsdramaturgie in *Don Karlos*," in *Schillers Theaterpraxis*, ed. Peter-André Alt and Stefanie Hundehege (Berlin: De Gruyter, 2020); and Johannes F Lehmann, "Situation, Szene, 'Tableau': Medientheoretische Aspekte der Anfänge von Schillers *Don Karlos*," in *Der Einsatz des Dramas: Dramenanfänge, Wissenschaftspoetik und Gattungspolitik*, ed. Andrea Polaschegg and Claus Haas (Freiburg: Rombach, 2012).

26. Schiller, *Don Karlos*, 645.

27. Schiller, *Don Karlos*, 645.

28. Denis Jonnes sees Schiller's play as an example of the "ultimately futile struggles of the sons against the fathers" who are bolstered by the state in the bourgeois tragedy. See Denis Jonnes, "Pattern of Power: Family and State in Schiller's Early Drama," *Colloquia Germanica* 20, vol. 2/3 (1987): 153.

29. Friedrich Schiller, *Wilhelm Tell*, 219.

30. Friedrich Schiller, *Die Jungfrau von Orleans*, 315.

31. Schiller, *Die Jungfrau von Orleans*, 242.

32. Schiller, *Die Jungfrau von Orleans*, 244.

33. Schiller, *Die Jungfrau von Orleans*, 244.

34. Schiller, *Die Jungfrau von Orleans*, 284.

35. Schiller, *Die Jungfrau von Orleans*, 285.

36. Schiller, *Die Jungfrau von Orleans*, 245.

37. Schiller, *Die Jungfrau von Orleans*, 232.

38. Jane K. Brown, *The Persistence of Allegory*, 176.

39. See Marie-Christin Wilm's essay on the play's generic relation to tragedy: "*Die Jungfrau von Orleans* tragödientheoretisch gelesen: Schillers *Romantische Tragödie* und ihre praktische Theorie," *Jahrbuch der deutschen Schillergesellschaft* 47 (2003): 167.

40. Schiller, *Wilhelm Tell*, 143.

41. Schiller, *Wilhelm Tell*, 177.

42. Schiller, *Wilhelm Tell*, 154.

43. Schiller, *Wilhelm Tell*, 276–277.

44. On the highly performative quality of Schiller's last play, see Peter Utz, "'Hier ist keine Heimat': Zur aktuellen Befremdlichkeit von Schillers *Tell*," *Jahrbuch der deutschen Schillergesellschaft* 48 (2004): 412.

45. G.W.F. Hegel, *Vorlesungen über die Ästhetik III*, 563.

46. Johann Wolfgang von Goethe, *Clavigo*, FA 1.4, 479.

47. Goethe, *Clavigo*, 446.

48. Goethe, *Clavigo*, 479.

49. Goethe, *Clavigo*, 491.

50. Goethe, *Clavigo*, 491.

51. Goethe, *Clavigo*, 491.

52. Goethe, *Clavigo*, 492.

53. Goethe, *Clavigo*, 492.

54. On the signification of the female corpse, see Susan Gustafson, "Goethe's *Clavigo*: The Body as an 'Unorthographic' Sign," in *Body & Text in the Eighteenth Century*, ed. Veronica Kelly and Dorothea von Mücke (Stanford, CA: Stanford University Press, 1994).

55. Goethe, *Clavigo*, 492.

56. Goethe, *Clavigo*, 491.

57. Johann Wolfgang von Goethe, *Stella*, FA 1.4, 558.

58. Goethe, *Stella*, 558–559.

59. Goethe, *Stella*, 572.

60. Goethe, *Stella*, 573.

61. Susan Gustafson maintains that the central relationship in *Stella* is the love bond between Cäcilia and Stella. See Susan Gustafson, *Goethe's Families of the Heart* (New York: Bloomsbury, 2016), especially 45–67. In contrast, Gail Hart argues that the world of women in *Stella* is constructed to reveal the lack of, and hence need for, men. See Gail K. Hart, "Voyeuristic Star-Gazing: Authority, Instinct and the Women's World of Goethe's *Stella*," *Monatshefte* 82, vol. 4 (1990): 409.

62. Goethe, *Stella*, 574.

63. A number of critics have argued that Ferdinand and Clavigo represent Goethe's own thinking about love. See Lothar Pikulik, "*Stella: Ein Schauspiel für Liebende*," in *Goethes Dramen*, ed. Walter Hinderer (Ditzingen: Reclam, 1992), 112; and Ellis Dye, "Substitution, Self-Blame, and Self-Deception in Goethe's *Stella: Ein Schauspiel für Liebende*," *Goethe Yearbook* 12 (2004): 57n50.

64. See Manuel Braun, "Tiefe oder Oberfläche? Zur Lektüre der Schriften des Christian Thomasius über Polygamie und Konkubinat," *Internationales Archiv für Sozialgeschichte der deutschen Literatur* 30, vol. 1 (2005): 28–54. See also Faramerz Dabhoiwala on the questions of polygamy and population, in *The Origins of Sex: A History of the First Sexual Revolution* (New York: Oxford University Press, 2012), especially 215–231.

65. Isabel V. Hull, *Sexuality, State, and Civil Society in Germany, 1700–1815* (Ithaca, NY: Cornell University Press, 1996), 178–179.

66. Hull, *Sexuality, State, and Civil Society*, 178.

67. David Hume, "On Polygamy and Divorce," in *Essays: Moral, Political, Literary*, ed. Eugene F. Miller (Indianapolis, IN: Liberty Classics, 1985).

68. Angela Willey shows how modern sexology defined nonmonogamous sexual activity as "perverse," demonstrating that these categorizations relied on colonial stereotypes. See Angela Willey, *Undoing Monogamy: The Politics of Science and the Possibilities of Biology* (Durham, NC: Duke University Press, 2016), 26–34.

69. Chunjie Zhang argues that non-European characters and locales open up new possibilities for happy endings in Kotzebue's plays, ones that had not been possible in Goethe's play. See Chunjie Zhang, *Transculturality and German Discourse in the Age of European Colonialism* (Evanston, IL: Northwestern University Press, 2017); in particular, see chapter 4: "The New World, Femininity, and Refusal of Tragedy in August von Kotzebue's Melodramas" (87–117).

70. Goethe was grudgingly admiring of Kotzebue's success although critical of what he saw as the fuzzy boundaries between morality and a lack of morals in Kotzebue's plays. See Horst Albert Glaser, *Das bürgerliche Rührstück: Dichtung und Erkenntnis* (Stuttgart: Metzler, 1969), 59. Marion Schmaus and Lothar Fiez trace genealogies from George Lillo to Kotzebue and back to England (via translation), highlighting the transnational character of the melodramatic imagination. See Marion Schmaus, "Zur Genese melodramatischer Imagination: Englisch-deutscher Tauschhandel im Zeichen der Rührung bei George Lillo, Friedrich Ludwig Schröder und August Kotzebue," in *Gastlichkeit und Ökonomie: Wirtschaften im deutschen und englischen Drama des 18. Jahrhunderts*, ed. Sigrid Nieberle and Claudia Nitschke (Berlin: De Gruyter, 2014); and Lothar Fiez, "Zur Genese des englischen Melodramas aus der Tradition der bürgerlichen Tragödie und des Rührstücks: Lillo—Schröder—Kotzebue—Sheridan—Thompson—Jerrold," *Vierteljahrsschrift für Literaturwissenschaft und Geistesgeschichte* 65, no. 1 (1991): 99–116.

71. August von Kotzebue, *La Peyrouse*, in *Schauspiele*, ed. Jürg Mathes (Frankfurt am Main: Athenäum, 1972), 311.

72. Kotzebue, *La Peyrouse*, 318.

73. Kotzebue, *La Peyrouse*, 323.

74. Kotzebue, *La Peyrouse*, 324.

75. Kotzebue, *La Peyrouse*, 324.

76. Kotzebue, *La Peyrouse*, 571.

77. J.M.R. Lenz, *Die Soldaten: Eine Komödie* (Stuttgart: Reclam, 1973), 55–59.

78. Wilfried Wilms connects the final scene in the play to what he sees as Lenz's project of offering an alternative to the private-public split as the bourgeois family becomes a soldier's family. See Wilfried Wilms, "Dismantling the Bourgeois Family: J.M.R. Lenz's 'Soldatenfamilie,'" *Monatshefte* 100, no. 3 (2008): 337–350.

79. August von Kotzebue, *Menschenhaß und Reue* (Berlin: Holzinger, 2013), 75.

80. Erich Schön points out that Gemmingen-Hornberg's play is far more realist than Schiller's *Kabale und Liebe* in its representation of relations between the bourgeoisie and the court. See Erich Schön, "Schillers *Kabale und Liebe*," 383.

81. Otto Heinrich von Gemmingen-Hornberg, *Der deutsche Hausvater oder die Familie* (Berlin: Hofenberg, 2014), 63.

82. Gemmingen-Hornberg, *Der deutsche Hausvater*, 63.

83. Johann Wolfgang von Goethe, *Des Epimenides Erwachen*, FA 1.6, 763.

84. Alex Eric Hernandez, "Prosaic Suffering: Bourgeois Tragedy and the Aesthetics of the Ordinary," *Representations* 138 (2017): 134.

Chapter Four   Against Interiority

1. Jürgen Habermas, *Strukturwandel der Öffentlichkeit*, 113.

2. Habermas, *Strukturwandel*, 113.

3. Georg Steinhausen calls the eighteenth century the "classical century of the letter." See Georg Steinhausen, *Geschichte des deutschen Briefes: Zur Kulturgeschichte des deutschen Volkes*, vol. 1 (Zurich: Weidmann, 1889), 302.

4. Thomas O. Beebee, *Epistolary Fiction in Europe, 1500–1850* (Cambridge, UK: Cambridge University Press, 1999), 33.

5. Habermas, *Strukturwandel*, 113.

6. Habermas, *Strukturwandel*, 112.

7. Habermas, *Strukturwandel*, 113.

8. Habermas, *Strukturwandel*, 114.

9. Simon Richter, "The Ins and Outs of Intimacy: Gender, Epistolary Culture, and the Public Sphere," *German Quarterly* 69, no. 2 (1996): 115.

10. Steinhausen, *Geschichte des deutschen Briefes*, 342.

11. Johann Wolfgang von Goethe, *Dichtung und Wahrheit*, FA 1.14, 607.

12. Rachael Scarborough King, *Writing to the World: Letters and the Origins of Modern Print Genres* (Baltimore, MD: John's Hopkins University Press, 2018).

13. Lessing highlights the importance of hands for actors, advocating for the use of hand gesture that would mimic the natural sign of painting: G. E. Lessing, *Hamburgische Dramaturgie*, WB 6, 203. See also Natalya Baldyga, "Corporeal Eloquence and Sensate Cognition: G. E. Lessing, Acting Theory, and Properly Feeling Bodies in Eighteenth-Century Germany," *Theatre Survey* 58, no. 2 (2017): 161–185.

14. Beebee, *Epistolary Fiction in Europe*, 14.

15. Beebee, *Epistolary Fiction in Europe*, 27.

16. Christian Fürchtegott Gellert, *Roman, Briefsteller*, ed. Bernd Witte, vol. 4 of *Gesammelte Schriften: Kritische, kommentierte Ausgabe* (Berlin: De Gruyter, [1751] 1989), 108.

17. Beebee, *Epistolary Fiction in Europe*, 8.

18. Diderot, "Conversations on *The Natural Son*," 32.

19. Elias, *The Civilizing Process*, 26.

20. On the literary (often queer) "postal plots" that reflect this postal reform, see Kate Thomas, *Postal Pleasures: Sex, Scandal, and Victorian Letters* (Oxford: Oxford University Press, 2012), 2.

21. King, *Writing to the World*, 191.

22. King, *Writing to the World*, 17.

23. We should of course not forget that Habermas likewise emphasizes the public nature of the performance of letter reading.

24. King, *Writing to the World*, 11. King also highlights the public nature of the post office itself. See her discussion of the depiction of rowdy people from all walks of life waiting for the post office to open (8).

25. See Steinhausen, *Geschichte des deutschen Briefes*, 334.

26. Janet G. Altman, *Epistolarity: Approaches to a Form* (Columbus: Ohio State University Press, 1982), 194.

27. Albrecht Koschorke, *Körperströme und Schriftverkehr*.

28. On Gellert's *Briefsteller*, See Wilfried Barner, "'Beredte Empfindungen,' Über die geschichtliche Position der Brieflehre Gellerts," in *'Aus der anmuthigen Gelehrsamkeit.' Tübin-*

gener Studien zum 18. Jahrhundert. Dieter Geyer zum 60. Geburtstag, ed. Eberhard Müller (Tübingen: Attempto, 1988), 11. Laurie Johnson sees Gellert as a "bridge" figure, highlighting his mixing of the rhetorical styles of Classicism and Romanticism in the *Briefsteller*. See Laurie Johnson, "'Wenn man endlich selbst Briefe schreiben will, so vergesse man die Exempel': The Construction of Imitation as Originality in C. F. Gellert's Epistolary Theory," *Wezel-Jahrbuch: Studien zur europäischen Aufklärung* 2 (1999): 97–114.

29. On the proximity-distance dialectic in Gellert's *Briefsteller* see Robert Vellusig, "Aufklärung und Briefkultur: Wie das Herz sprechen lernt, wenn es zu schreiben beginnt," in *Kulturmuster der Aufklärung: ein neues Heuristikum in der Diskussion*, ed. Carsten Zelle (Göttingen: Wallstein, 2011), 166.

30. Steinhausen, *Geschichte des deutschen Briefes*, 216.

31. Beebee, *Epistolary Fiction in Europe*, 1.

32. Gellert, *Roman, Briefsteller*, 150.

33. Gellert, *Roman, Briefsteller*, 104.

34. Steinhausen, *Geschichte des deutschen Briefes*, 55.

35. Steinhausen, *Geschichte des deutschen Briefes*, 100.

36. Steinhausen, *Geschichte des deutschen Briefes*, 100.

37. Steinhausen, *Geschichte des deutschen Briefes*, 101.

38. Steinhausen, *Geschichte des deutschen Briefes*, 102.

39. See Silvia Bovenschen, *Die imaginierte Weiblichkeit*.

40. Steinhausen, *Geschichte des deutschen Briefes*, 348.

41. Gellert, *Roman, Briefsteller*, 113.

42. Gellert, *Roman, Briefsteller*, 115.

43. Review included in Gellert, *Roman, Briefsteller*, 279.

44. Review included in Gellert, *Roman, Briefsteller*, 280. Interestingly, the reception of Gellert's *Briefsteller* after his death in 1769 was far less laudatory, and the "natural" style in Gellert's letters was perceived to be stiff (298).

45. Gellert, *Roman, Briefsteller*, 280.

46. Gellert, *Roman, Briefsteller*, 151.

47. Gellert, *Roman, Briefsteller*, 125.

48. Gellert, *Roman, Briefsteller*, 179.

49. Gellert, *Roman, Briefsteller*, 210. Beebee, who also cites this letter, notes that Gellert's letters reject "business" in favor of "nearly absolute self-reflexivity." Beebee, *Epistolary Fiction*, 38.

50. Gellert, *Roman, Briefsteller*, 219.

51. Gellert, *Roman, Briefsteller*, 219.

52. Bernd Witte highlights the generic fluidity of Gellert's *Briefsteller*, comparing it to Gellert's novel *Das Leben der schwedischen Gräfin von G**** (1747–1748). Witte argues that a liberated, observant narrator emerges in both the *Briefsteller* and the novel, and he calls the *Briefsteller* a "Roman eines Schreibenden" [novel of a writer]. See Bernd Witte, "Die Individualität des Autors: Gellerts Briefsteller als Roman eines Schreibenden," *The German Quarterly* 62, no. 1 (1989): 5–14.

53. The first documented and published German epistolary novel, Johannes Andreas Endte's *Die Neu-Auffgerichtete Liebeskammer*, appeared in 1662. Beebee, *Epistolary Fiction in Europe*, 233. See Beebee's extensive and exceptionally helpful list of European epistolary novels at the end of his book (231–258). I discuss the epistolary novel in more detail in chapter 6.

54. See Denis Diderot, "In Praise of Richardson," *Selected Writings on Art and Literature*, translated by Geoffrey Bremner, 82–97 (London: Penguin, 1994). The essay was published in 1762 after Richardson's death in 1761 and translated into German in 1766.

55. Diderot, "Conversations on *The Natural Son*," 12.

56. Diderot, "Conversations on *The Natural Son*," 12.

57. Diderot, "Conversations on *The Natural Son*," 15.

58. Gellert, *Roman, Briefsteller*, 112.

59. Peter Szondi, "Tableau und coup de théâtre: Zur Sozialpsychologie des bürgerlichen Trauerspiels bei Diderot: Mit einem Exkurs über Lessing," in *Erforschung der deutschen Aufklärung*, ed. Peter Pütz (Königstein im Taunus: Verlagsgruppe Athenäum, Hain, Scriptor, Hanstein, 1980), 196. See, again, in this context, Brigitte Prutti's compelling reading of the spectacular (i.e., unreasonable and unmotivated) ending of *Emilia Galotti* as coup de théâtre in her "*Coup de Théâtre—Coup de Femme*."

60. Aristotle, *Poetics*, quoted in Andrew Sofer, *The Stage Life of Props* (Ann Arbor: University of Michigan Press, 2003). Cited from *Aristotle's Poetics*, trans. S. H. Butcher (New York: Hill and Wang, 1961), 64.

61. Sofer emphasizes that props are not only interesting in the early modern period: "For example, W.B. Worthen finds complicity between the 'transparent' objects of the contemporary stage and realism's fetishization of bourgeois interiority." Sofer, *The Stage Life*, 17. See also Suzanne R. Pucci on Diderot's excessive use of props in *The Natural Son*: Pucci, "The Nature of Domestic Intimacy and Sibling Incest in Diderot's *Fils Naturel*," *Eighteenth-Century Studies* 30, no. 3 (1997): 276.

62. Sofer, *The Stage Life*, ix.

63. Sofer, *The Stage Life*, xii.

64. Sofer, *The Stage Life*, 20.

65. Sofer, *The Stage Life*, ix.

66. Erika Fischer-Lichte, *The Semiotics of Theater*, trans. Jeremy Gaines and Doris L. Jones (Bloomington: Indiana University Press, 1992), 110.

67. Fischer-Lichte, *The Semiotics of Theater*, 109.

68. Elaine Freedgood, *The Ideas in Things: Fugitive Meaning in the Victorian Novel* (Chicago: University of Chicago Press, 2006), 4.

69. On this point see Steven R. Cerf, "*Miss Sara Sampson* and *Clarissa*: The Use of Epistolary Devices in Lessing's Drama," in *Theatrum Mundi: Essays on German Drama and German Literature, dedicated to Harold Lenz on his Seventieth Birthday, September 11, 1978*, ed. Edward Haymes (Munich: Wilhelm Fink, 1980), 26. See also Theresa Homm, "'Ich muß doch schreiben—': Briefe und Empfindungen in Richardsons Briefroman *Clarissa* und Lessings Trauerspiel *Miß Sara Sampson*," *Lessing Yearbook* 42 (2015): 94; Edgar Landgraf, "Romantic Love and the Enlightenment: From Gallantry and Seduction to Authenticity and Self-Validation," *The German Quarterly* 77, no. 1 (2004): 29–46; and Johannes Anderegg, *Schreibe mir oft! Das Medium Brief von 1750–1830* (Göttingen: Wallstein, 2001), 29.

70. G. E. Lessing, *Miß Sara Sampson*, WB 3, 467.

71. Lessing, *Miß Sara Sampson*, 468.

72. Lessing, *Miß Sara Sampson*, 472.

73. Lessing, *Miß Sara Sampson*, 473.

74. Lessing, *Miß Sara Sampson*, 451.

75. Lessing, *Miß Sara Sampson*, 479.

76. Romira Wovill points to this scene as illustrative of how characters of the period utilize the declamatory language of the neoclassical French theater. See Romira Worvill, "Lessing and the French Enlightenment," in *Lessing and the German Enlightenment*, ed. Ritchie Robertson (Oxford: Oxford University Press, 2018), 34.

77. Lessing, *Miß Sara Sampson*, 483.

78. Lessing, *Miß Sara Sampson*, 518.

79. Lessing, *Miß Sara Sampson*, 518.

80. Lessing, *Miß Sara Sampson*, 487.

81. Friedrich Schiller, *Kabale und Liebe*, vol. 5 of *Schillers Werke, Nationalausgabe*, ed. Heinz Otto Burger and Walter Höllerer (Weimar: Hermannn Böhlaus Nachfolger, 1957), 118.

82. Schiller, *Kabale und Liebe*, 158.

83. Schiller, *Kabale und Liebe*, 186.

84. Kotzebue, *Menschenhaß und Reue* (Berlin: Christian Friedrich Himburg, 1790), 32.

85. Johann Wolfgang von Goethe, *Faust: Der Tragödie zweiter Teil*, FA 7.1, part 1, 250.

86. See Catherine M. Soussloff, *The Subject in Art: Portraiture and the Birth of the Modern* (Durham, NC: Duke University Press, 2006), 7.

87. Soussloff, *The Subject in Art*, 13.

88. Soussloff, *The Subject in Art*, 19.

89. Laura R. Bass, *The Drama of the Portrait: Theater and Visual Culture in Early Modern Spain* (University Park, PA: Penn State University Press, 2008), 63. On the concept of "visual genealogies," see also Joanna Woodall, "An Exemplary Consort: Antonis Mor's Portrait of Mary Tudor," *Art History* 14 (1991): 192–224.

90. Bass, *The Drama of the Portrait*, 62–63.

91. Soussloff, *The Subject in Art*, 5–6.

92. Soussloff, *The Subject in Art*, 11.

93. Aristotle, *Poetics*, 18–19.

94. Hegel, *Aesthetics: Lectures on Fine Art*, vol. 2, 866.

95. Hegel, *Aesthetics*, 866.

96. Hegel, *Aesthetics*, 868.

97. Hegel, *Aesthetics*, 868–869.

98. Gellert, *Roman, Briefsteller*.

99. Gellert, *Roman, Briefsteller*.

100. As Gregory Racz notes, "*Life is a Dream* was by far the most popular play in Germany for practically the entire first half of the nineteenth century, and such influential German poets and critics as A.W. Schlegel, Friedrich von Schiller, and Johann Wolfgang von Goethe enthusiastically hailed a figure they considered to be the most 'aristocratic' of playwrights." See Gregory J. Racz, introduction to *Life Is a Dream*, by Pedro Calderón de la Barca, trans. Gregory J. Racz (London: Penguin, 2006), xviii.

101. G. E. Lessing, *Emilia Galotti*, WB 7, 294.

102. Lessing, *Emilia Galotti*, 345.

103. Lessing, *Emilia Galotti*, 293.

104. On the prince's desire vis-à-vis the portrait, see Brigitte Prutti, "Das Bild des Weiblichen und die Phantasie des Künstlers: Das Begehren des Prinzen in Lessings *Emilia Galotti*," *Zeitschrift für deutsche Philologie* 110 (1991): 481–505.

105. Lessing, *Emilia Galotti*, 296.

106. Lessing, *Emilia Galotti*, 297.

107. See Ellwood Wiggins on Marwood's alternating sentimental and baroque performances. Ellwood Wiggins, "Pity Play: Sympathy and Spectatorship in Lessing's *Miss Sara Sampson* and Adam Smith's *Theory of Moral Sentiments*," in *Performing Knowledge, 1750–1850*, ed. Mary Helen Dupree and Sean Franzel (Berlin: De Gruyter, 2015), 93.

108. Lessing, *Emilia Galotti*, 297, 298.

109. Lessing, *Emilia Galotti*, 300. On this scene as one of "absorption," see Christopher Wild, "Der theatralische Schleier des Hymens. Lessings bürgerliches Trauerspiel *Emilia Galotti*," *Deutsche Vierteljahrsschrift für Literaturwissenschaft und Geistesgeschichte* 74 (2000): 208.

110. Lessing, *Emilia Galotti*, 298.

111. Lessing, *Emilia Galotti*, 299.

112. Lessing, *Emilia Galotti*, 299.

113. Lessing, *Emilia Galotti*, 297.

114. Lessing, *Emilia Galotti*, 297.

115. The father's interpellation into this scene resituates Odoardo within the political sphere. See Wilfried Wilms, "Im Griff des Politischen: Konfliktfähigkeit und Vaterwerdung in *Emilia Galotti*," *Deutsche Vierteljahrsschrift für Literaturwissenschaft und Geistesgeschichte* 76 (2002): 50–73. See also Denis Jonnes's seminal essay on private and public spheres in Lessing's play. Denis Jonnes, "*Solche Väter*: The Sentimental Family Paradigm in Lessing's Dramas," *Lessing Yearbook* 12 (1981): 157–174.

116. Inge Stephan reminds us that Emilia functions via the portrait as an object of exchange between men. See Stephan, "'So ist die Tugend ein Gespenst': Frauenbild und Tugendbegriff bei Lessing und Schiller," in *Inszenierte Weiblichkeit: Codierung der Geschlechter in der Literatur des 18. Jahrhunderts* (Cologne: Böhlau, 2004), 17.

117. Kati Röttger observes that the prince turns the portrait toward the wall before Marinelli enters in Act 1, scene 5, thereby "focusing the audience's gaze on the back of the painting, the *medium of the empty space*," so that the intermedial force of the painting comes to the fore. See Kati Röttger, "'What Do I See?' The Order of Looking in Lessing's *Emilia Galotti*," *Art History* 33, no. 2 (2010): 386.

118. Lessing, *Emilia Galotti*, 298–299.

119. Lessing, *Emilia Galotti*, 300.

120. Johann Wolfgang von Goethe, *Stella*, FA 1.4, 548–549.

121. Goethe, *Stella*, 550.

122. Goethe, *Stella*, 550.

123. Goethe, *Stella*, 568.

124. Goethe, *Stella*, 568.

125. Goethe, *Stella*, 569.

126. Kai Sina interprets *Stella* as a play that reflects a secularized nihilism, an interpretation that resonates with this scene. See Kai Sina, "Nihilismusgefahr: *Stella*, Goethe und das Unerträgliche," *Goethe-Jahrbuch* 136 (2019): 142–156.

127. Goethe, *Stella*, 569.

128. In Goethe's *Götz von Berlichingen* (1773) the portrait is similarly reduced to its material qualities and serves as a residue of the past. When Weißlingen professes to contain Adelheid's "image" in his heart, she responds, "In some corner next to the portraits of extinct families" (168). Johann Wolfgang von Goethe, *Götz von Berlichingen*, FA 1.4.

129. Gemmingen-Hornberg makes an error here, as it is not Madame Sommer but Stella who paces at her child's grave.

130. Otto Heinrich von Gemmingen-Hornberg, *Der deutsche Hausvater oder die Familie* (Berlin: Hofenberg, 2014), 44.

131. Gemmingen-Hornberg, *Der deutsche Hausvater*, 44.

132. Gemmingen-Hornberg, *Der deutsche Hausvater*, 45.

133. Murray Krieger, "*Ekphrasis* and the Still Movement of Poetry, or *Laokoön Revisited*," in *Ekphrasis: The Illusion of the Natural Sign* (Baltimore, MD: Johns Hopkins University Press 1992), 266. Krieger originally published the essay in 1967.

134. See W.T.J. Mitchell, *Picture Theory* (Chicago: University of Chicago Press, 1994), 156.

Chapter Five   Material Kinship

1. Lessing wrote *Nathan der Weise* at a time when he was involved in a highly public theological debate whose content is reiterated in the play's plot. See Lessing, *Fragmentenstreit II*, in *Werke 1778–1780*, ed. Klaus Bohnen and Arno Schilson, vol. 9 of *Gotthold Ephraim Lessing: Werke und Briefe*, 12 vols. (Frankfurt am Main: Deutscher Klassiker, 1993), 9.

2. Elfriede Jelinek, *Abraumhalde*, "Zum Theater/Theatertexte," accessed May 18, 2021, https://www.elfriedejelinek.com/.

3. The first performance of *Nathan der Weise* in 1783 occurred after Lessing's death and was met with mixed reviews, as some spectators found it to be cold and dull. See Jo-Jacqueline Eckardt, *Lessing's* Nathan the Wise *and the Critics: 1779–1991* (Columbia, SC: Camden House, 1993), 24–25. Lessing himself had expressed doubts as to whether *Nathan der Weise* would be effective when performed on stage. See G. E. Lessing, letter to Karl Gotthelf Lessing, April 18, 1779, *Briefe 1776–1781*, ed. Wilfried Barner, vol. 12 of *Gotthold Ephraim Lessing: Werke und Briefe*, 12 vols. (Frankfurt am Main: Deutscher Klassiker, 1994), 247.

4. Johann Wolfgang von Goethe, "Zu Lessings *Nathan der Weise*," in *Gotthold Ephraim Lessing, Nathan der Weise* (Stuttgart: Reclam, 1987), 142.

5. See Eckardt, *Lessing's* Nathan the Wise, 55–63.

6. Eckardt, *Lessing's* Nathan the Wise, 6.

7. This was the line of thought taken by Friedrich Schlegel. See Friedrich Schlegel, "Über Lessing," in *Charakteristiken und Kritiken I, 1796–1801*, ed. Hans Eichner; vol. 2 of *Kritische Friedrich Schlegel Ausgabe* (Munich: Ferdinand Schöningh, 1967), 100–126.

8. See Stefani Engelstein, *Sibling Action*, 188.

9. Helmut Schneider, "Der Ring, die Statue, der Krug und seine Scherben: Eine Skizze zum Symbol und symbolischen Darstellungsverfahren im klassischen Humanitätsdrama (Lessing, Goethe, Kleist)," *Zeitschrift für deutsche Philologie* 4 (2004): 45–61. The dialectic between material and its transcendence in *Nathan der Weise* is analyzed by Sascha Nawrocki and Winfried Woesler as they trace the source of Saladin's famous line delivered to his treasurer Ali Hafi to the *Bibliothèque orientale* of 1697: "Ein Kleid, Ein Schwert, Ein Pferd,—und Einen Gott! Was brauch' ich mehr?" Nawrocki and Woesler show that Lessing added "Einen Gott!" to the historical source. See Sascha Nawrocki and Winfried Woesler, "Ein Kleid, Ein Schwert, Ein Pferd: Miszelle zu Lessings *Nathan*," *Euphorion* 97 (2003): 131–133.

10. See Eva Urban, "Lessing's *Nathan the Wise*: From the Enlightenment to the Berliner Ensemble," *New Theatre Quarterly* 30, no. 2 (2014): 194.

11. F. H. Jacobi admitted to being "in fact not entirely satisfied" with the ending. See Winfried Woesler, "Die beiden Schlüsse von Lessings 'Nathan,'" in *Akten des X. Internationalen Germanistenkongresses Wien 2000: 'Zeitenwende-die Germanistik auf dem Weg vom 20. ins 21. Jahrhundert'* (Bern: Peter Lang, 2002), 328. Likewise, a reviewer in the "Baierische Beyträge zur schönen und nützlichen Literatur" (1779) complained about what he saw as a lack of resolution and character development at the end of the drama; cited in Woesler, "Die beiden Schlüsse," 329.

12. Cited in Woesler, "Die beiden Schlüsse," 329.

13. See Woesler, "Die beiden Schlüsse."

14. Helmut Schneider writes of "Lessing's utopian human family" in Schneider, "Der Zufall der Geburt," 108.

15. Willi Goetschel, "Negotiating Truth: On Nathan's Business," *Lessing Yearbook* 28 (1996): 106.

16. Gotthold Ephraim Lessing, *Nathan der Weise*, in *Werke 1778–1780*, ed. Klaus Bohnen and Arno Schilson; vol. 9 of *Gotthold Ephraim Lessing: Werke und Briefe*, 12 vols. (Frankfurt am Main: Deutscher Klassiker Verlag, 1993), 486.

17. Lessing, *Nathan der Weise*, 497.

18. Lessing, *Nathan der Weise*, 554.

19. Richard T. Gray, "Buying into Signs: Money and Semiosis in Eighteenth-Century German Language Theory," *The German Quarterly* 69, no. 1 (1996): 5.

20. Friedrich Nietzsche, "On Truth and Lies in an Extramoral Sense," in *The Nietzsche Reader*, ed. Keith Ansell Pearson and Duncan Large (Malden, MA: Blackwell, 2006), 117. Nietzsche makes a poignant direct reference to Lessing at the beginning of the essay when he compares the fleetingness of life to the untimely departure of Lessing's infant son (114).

21. Lessing, *Nathan der Weise*, 516.

22. Mark Lehrer, "Lessing's Economic Comedy," *Seminar* 20, no. 2 (1984): 84.

23. For Seeba the utopian victory of human relations over commerce situates the play as a critique of modern capitalism. See Hinrich C. Seeba, *Die Liebe zur Sache: Öffentliches und privates Interesse in Lessings Dramen* (Tübingen: Niemeyer, 1973), 81.

24. Karl Marx, "Geld," in *Ökonomisch-philosophische Manuskripte* (Berlin: Berliner Ausgabe, 2007), 106.

25. Marx, "Geld," 107. Italics in the original.

26. Marx, "Geld," 107. Italics in the original.

27. Brown, *The Persistence of Allegory*, 6.

28. Brown, *The Persistence of Allegory*, 60.

29. Further clear instances of allegory in the play are the roles taken on by Recha and the Templar in the course of the fire that burns Nathan's house and threatens Recha's life. Recha is coded here as a victim of dark forces, and the Templar, her rescuer, as an angel (literally, in Recha's imagination).

30. G. A. Lester, ed., *Three Late Medieval Morality Plays: Mankind, Everyman, Mundus et Infans* (New York: W.W. Norton, 1981), 80.

31. Lessing, *Nathan der Weise*, 485.

32. Similarly, in Lessing's early play *Der Schatz* (1750) [*The Treasure*], the wealthy Anselmo returns home with a suitcase full of money, and the short play focuses for a considerable amount of time on the logistics of how the suitcase will be carried inside the

house. See G. E. Lessing, *Der Schatz*, in *Werke 1743–1750*, ed. Jürgen Stenzel, vol. 1 of *Werke und Briefe* (Frankfurt am Main: Deutscher Klassiker Verlag, 1989), 588. Ilse Appelbaum Graham points to the purse full of gold that similarly functions as a prop that signifies wealth and its potential loss in *Kabale und Liebe*. See Ilse Appelbaum Graham, "Passions and Possessions in Schiller's 'Kabale und Liebe,'" *German Life and Letters* 6, no. 1 (1952): 14.

33. Lessing, *Nathan der Weise*, 580.

34. Lessing, *Nathan der Weise*, 580.

35. Lessing, *Nathan der Weise*, 590.

36. Lessing, *Nathan der Weise*, 590.

37. Lessing, *Nathan der Weise*, 600.

38. Lessing, *Nathan der Weise*, 621.

39. Lessing, *Nathan der Weise*, 525.

40. Marx, "Geld," 105. Marx also quotes Mephisto's celebration of possession and riches from *Faust* in this essay.

41. Marx, "Geld," 105.

42. Lessing, *Nathan der Weise*, 526.

43. Brown, *The Persistence of Allegory*, 136.

44. Lehrer, "Lessing's Economic Comedy," 84.

45. See Helga Slessarev, "Nathan der Weise und Adam Smith," in *Nation und Gelehrtenrepublik: Lessing im europäischen Zusammenhang*, ed. Wilfried Barner and Albert M. Reh (Munich: text + kritik, 1984), 253. See also Heiner Weidmann, "Ökonomie der 'Großmuth': Geldwirtschaft in Lessings *Minna von Barnhelm* und *Nathan der Weise*," *Deutsche Vierteljahrsschrift für Literaturwissenschaft und Geistesgeschichte* 68, no. 3 (1994): 452.

46. Slessarev, "Nathan der Weise und Adam Smith," 248.

47. Max Weber, "Die protestantische Ethik und der 'Geist' des Kapitalismus," in *Archiv für Sozialwissenschaft und Sozialpolitik*, vols. 20–21 (Tübingen: Mohr, 1904–1905), 20: 41–43.

48. Goetschel, "Negotiating Truth," 111.

49. Daniel Fulda, "'Er hat Verstand, Er weiß/Zu leben; Spielt gut Schach': Nathan der Weise als Politicus," in *Aufklärung und Weimarer Klassik im Dialog*, eds. Andre Rudolph and Ernst Stöckmann (Tübingen: Niemeyer, 2009): 55–78.

50. Jörg Schönert, "Der Kaufmann von Jerusalem: Zum Handel mit Kapitalien und Ideen in Lessings *Nathan der Weise*," *Scientia Poetica* 12 (2009): 97. During the last third of the eighteenth century, the power of the nobility began to weaken via their loss of property and debts to the middle class (in some cases comprising up to 50 percent of a particular noble's net worth). Hence, although the bourgeoisie did not possess tangible political power, it accumulated authority via its slow takeover of the properties of the nobility. Within the bourgeois family itself, money was likewise linked to authority as well as to independence and virtue. See Reinhart Koselleck, *Preußen zwischen Reform und Revolution: Allgemeines Landrecht, Verwaltung und soziale Bewegung von 1791 bis 1848* (Stuttgart: Ernst Klett, 1967), 83. See also Fritz Martiny, *Die Adelsfrage in Preußen vor 1806 als politisches und soziales Problem (Beiheft 35 zur Vierteljahrsschrift für Sozial—und Wirtschaftsgeschichte)* (Stuttgart: Kohlhammer, 1938).

51. Schönert, "Der Kaufmann von Jerusalem," 100.

52. Lessing, *Nathan der Weise*, 518.

53. Lessing, *Nathan der Weise*, 549.

54. Elaine Freedgood, *The Ideas in Things*, 14.

55. Freedgood, *The Ideas in Things*, 15.

56. Angus Fletcher, *Allegory*.

57. Lessing, *Nathan der Weise*, 584.

58. Lessing, *Nathan der Weise*, 534–535.

59. Lessing, *Nathan der Weise*, 486.

60. Lessing, *Nathan der Weise*, 621. Ellipses in the original.

61. Thomas Hobbes, *De Cive*, ed. Howard Warrender (Oxford: Oxford University Press, 1987), 181.

62. Silke-Maria Weineck, *The Tragedy of Fatherhood: King Laius and the Politics of Paternity in the West* (New York: Bloomsbury, 2014), 112.

63. Lessing, *Nathan der Weise*, 555–556.

64. Lessing, *Nathan der Weise*, 559.

65. Lessing, *Nathan der Weise*, 483.

66. Lessing, *Nathan der Weise*, 559.

67. Lessing, *Nathan der Weise*, 499.

68. See Eva Urban's discussion of Al-Hafi's identity. Urban, "Lessing's *Nathan the Wise*, 193. On Lessing's engagement with Islam, see Nina Berman, *German Literature of the Middle East: Discourses and Practices, 1000–1989* (Ann Arbor: University of Michigan Press, 2013), especially 104–144.

69. Lessing, *Nathan der Weise*, 620.

70. Søren Kierkegaard, *Either/Or: A Fragment of Life*, trans. Alastair Hannay, ed. Victor Eremita (London: Penguin, 1992).

71. Karl Marx, *Das Kapital: Kritik der politischen Ökonomie, Buch 1*, in Karl Marx and Friedrich Engels, *Werke*, vol. 23 (Berlin: Karl Dietz, 1962), 97.

72. Wendy Sutherland, *Staging Blackness and Performing Whiteness in Eighteenth-Century German Drama* (London: Routledge, 2016), 97–98. On Blackness on the eighteenth-century stage, see also Birgit Tautz, "Bodies on Stage: Late Eighteenth-Century Aesthetics of Blackness," in *Reading and Seeing Ethnic Differences in the Enlightenment: From China to Africa* (New York: Palgrave McMillan, 2007), 137–173.

73. Diderot, *The Illegitimate Son*, 44.

74. Diderot, *The Illegitimate Son*, 52.

75. Diderot, *The Illegitimate Son*, 42.

76. Caroline Weber, "The Sins of the Father: Colonialism and Family History in Diderot's 'Le fils naturel,'" *PMLA* 118, no. 3 (2003): 488–501. Andrea Schatz contrasts Diderot's critique of colonialism in his historical and encyclopedic writings with his failure to translate this critique into drama. See Andrea Schatz, "Interrupted Games: Lessing and Mendelssohn on Religion, Intermarriage and Integration," *Lessing Yearbook* 39 (2012): 51–72. Aamir R. Mufti points to the uncanny return of repressed colonial endeavors abroad in *Nathan der Weise*. See Aamir R. Mufti, "Jewishness as Minority: Postcolonial Perspectives on the Limits of Enlightenment," *Lessing Yearbook* 39 (2012): 27–36.

77. Schatz, "Interrupted Games," 63. Uta Degner cites Schiller's elegy *Der Spazier-gang* (1795) in her analysis of the links between economics and morality within the works of Lillo and Schiller, and it is striking to see how enthusiastically the poet embraces colonialism as a driver of the free market:

Auf den Stapel schüttet die Ernten der Kaufmann,
Was dem glühenden Strahl Afrikas Boden gebiert,
Hoch mit erfreuendem Gut füllt Amalthea das Horn.
[The merchant shakes out the bounty onto the pile,
What is yielded to the fiery radiance by Africa's earth,
Amalthea fills the horn high with the pleasing goods.]

Cited in Uta Degner, "Interessendramen: Zur Rivalität von Ökonomie, Moral und Ästhetik bei Friedrich Schiller und 'Intertexten' von Richard Glover und George Lillo," in *Gastlichkeit und Ökonomie: Wirtschaften im deutschen und englischen Drama des 18. Jahrhunderts*, ed. Sigrid Nieberle and Claudia Nitschke (Berlin: De Gruyter, 2014), 243.

78. Diderot, *The Father of the Family*, 123.

79. Hegel, *Elements of the Philosophy of Right*, 215.

80. Peter Szondi, "Tableau und coup de théâtre, 196.

81. See also Peter Szondi, *Die Theorie*, 67. Horst Albert Glaser points out that money is the "measure of bourgeois morality" in late eighteenth-century *Rührstücke*. See Horst Albert Glaser, *Das bürgerliche Rührstück*, 31.

82. Lessing, *Nathan der Weise*, 620.

83. Lessing, *Nathan der Weise*, 614.

84. Lessing, *Nathan der Weise*, 625.

85. Lessing, *Nathan der Weise*, 627.

86. Jane Brown points out that there were still plenty of examples of mumming and pageantry in the period. See Jane Brown, *The Persistence of Allegory*, 119–120.

87. Lessing, *Nathan der Weise*, 625. Ellipses in the original.

88. This scene offers an interesting contrast to some of Lessing's other major plays in which men are eager to be named "son" by a chosen father figure (i.e., *Emilia Galotti* and *Miß Sara Sampson*).

89. "In the ordinary meaning of the word *harem* usually refers to the extended household and may or may not refer to a polygamous household. Ruling-class harems, however, were usually polygamous and contained several servants and slaves in addition to close relatives." Fariba Zarinebaf, "Harem," in *Europe, 1450–1789: Encyclopedia of the Early Modern World*, vol. 3, ed. Jonathan Dewald (New York: Scribner, 2004), 132.

90. See Zarinebaf, "Harem," 132.

91. Schneider, "Der Zufall der Geburt."

92. Quoted in Schönert, "Der Kaufmann von Jerusalem," 97.

93. Butler, *Antigone's Claim*. See especially Butler's argument that there can be "no distinction between symbolic and social law" and, hence, that a change in kinship structures will affect the social and symbolic spheres (19).

94. Volker Hoffmann, Friedrich Kittler, and Helmut Schneider all point to the centrality of adoption and nonbiological notions of family within *Nathan der Weise*, although they do not draw a connection between kinship and props/property within the play. See Volker Hoffmann, "Tod der Familie und Toleranz: Lessings *Nathan der Weise* (1779. 1783) und Goethes *Iphigenie auf Tauris* (1787) als Programmstücke der Goethezeit," *Deutsche Vierteljahrsschrift* 85, no. 3 (2011): 367–379; Kittler, "'Erziehung ist Offenbarung'"; and

Helmut J. Schneider, "Geburt und Adoption bei Lessing und Kleist," *Kleist-Jahrbuch* (2002): 21–41.

95. Alice Kuzniar, *The Queer German Cinema* (Stanford, CA: Stanford University Press, 2000), 8–9.

96. Kuzniar, *The Queer German Cinema*, 14.

97. Lee Edelman, *No Future: Queer Theory and the Death Drive* (Durham, NC: Duke University Press, 2004), 2.

98. Lessing, *Nathan der Weise*, 618.

99. The use of ruins here recalls Ernest Renan's 1882 lecture "What Is a Nation?," a reflection on national sentiment that, in stark contrast to Lessing's play, locates the source of national feeling in the past, in a community of shared losses and traumas. See Ernest Renan, "What Is a Nation?," in *Nation and Narration*, ed. Homi K. Bhabha, trans. Martin Thom (London: Routledge, 1990).

100. Gotthold Ephraim Lessing, *Die Erziehung des Menschengeschlechts*, in *Werke 1778–1781*, ed. Arno Schilson and Axel Schmitt; vol. 10 of *Werke und Briefe* (Frankfurt am Main: Deutscher Klassiker Verlag, 2001), 97.

101. Lessing, *Die Erziehung des Menschengeschlechts*, 302.

102. Lessing, *Die Erziehung des Menschengeschlechts*, 98.

103. Lessing, *Die Erziehung des Menschengeschlechts*, 98.

104. Eva Urban writes that the ecstatic hug between Nathan and Al-Hafi in the Berliner Ensemble production, "one lifting up the other and turning him around, suggests not only loving brotherhood but also the possibility of an erotic relationship." Urban, "Lessing's *Nathan the Wise*," 194.

105. Lessing, *Nathan der Weise*, 540.

106. I have argued elsewhere that in *Emilia Galotti* the father Odoardo is desperate to escape the impossible role of patriarch. See Schlipphacke, "The Dialectics of Female Desire in G. E. Lessing's *Emilia Galotti*." See also Silke-Maria Weineck, who argues that Lessing's fathers cannot embody the impossible role of "paternal, royal and divine" father. Weineck, *The Tragedy of Fatherhood*, 143.

Chapter Six   The Tableau *of Relations*

1. Denis Diderot, *Diderot on Art. Vol. I: The Salon of 1765* and *Notes on Painting*, trans. and ed. John Goodman (New Haven: Yale University Press, 1995), 96.

2. Thomas Beebee highlights the aesthetics of wholeness that characterizes the letter in eighteenth-century Germany: "The letter itself became a cultural object surcharged with an aura, and invested with the task of uniting the fragmented German intellectual community." Thomas Beebee, *Epistolary Fiction in Europe 1500–1850* (Cambridge, UK: Cambridge University Press, 1999), 17.

3. Cited in Dieter Kimpel, *Der Roman der Aufklärung (1670–1774)* (Stuttgart: Metzler, 1967), 98. Italics mine.

4. Quoted in Bruno Hillebrand, *Theorie des Romans: Erzählstrategien der Neuzeit* (Stuttgart: Metzler, 1993), 94.

5. Elsaesser describes "tableau-like static compositions which by their very symmetry 'cite' an invisible observer" and "shots where another spectator perspective is constructed within the action, through a character or characters whose main function it is to

observe and who 'anchor' the scene by their presence and gaze." Elsaesser, *Fassbinder's Germany*, 86.

6. Elsaesser, *Fassbinder's Germany*, 86.

7. August Langen cites additional novels from the period, including Wilhelm Heinse's *Ardinghello* (1787) and Tieck's *Franz Sternbalds Wanderungen* (1798), that focus on the figure of the painter and include descriptive scenes that call forth paintings, sometimes explicitly. See Langen, "Attitüde und Tableau in der Goethezeit," 238.

8. Manuel Frey, "Tugendspiele: Zur Bedeutung der 'Tableaux vivants' in der bürgerlichen Gesellschaft des 19. Jahrhunderts," *Historische Anthropologie* 6 (1998): 406. Frey locates the eighteenth-century literary *tableau* primarily in the "trivial" tendencies in drama and novels (a position with which I take issue in this book).

9. Anna Kornbluh, *The Order of Forms: Realism, Formalism, and Social Space* (Chicago: University of Chicago Press, 2019).

10. Karl Marx and Friedrich Engels, *The German Ideology, Including Theses on Feuerbach* (Amherst, NY: Prometheus, 1998), 37.

11. Johann Wolfgang von Goethe, "*Wilhelm Meisters Lehrjahre* im Urteil Goethes und seiner Zeitgenossen" (Kommentarteil), *Romane und Novellen II*, ed. Erich Trunz, vol. 7 of *Goethes Werke* (Munich: Deutscher Taschenbuch, 2000), 613.

12. "Briefwechsel zwischen Goethe und Schiller," in Goethe, *Werke*, vol. 7, *Romane und Novellen II* (Munich: Deutscher Taschenbuch Verlag, 2000), 630.

13. "Briefwechsel zwischen Goethe und Schiller," 641.

14. Cited in Wilfried Barner, "'Die Verschiedenheit unserer Naturen': Zu Goethes und Schillers Briefwechsel über *Wilhelm Meisters Lehrjahre*," in *Unser Commercium: Goethes und Schillers Literaturpolitik*, ed. Wilfried Barner, Eberhard Lämmert, and Norbert Oellers (Stuttgart: Cotta, 1984), 390.

15. See Mark M. Anderson, "Die Aufgabe der Familie/das Ende der Moderne: Eine kleine Geschichte des Familienromans," in *Deutsche Familienromane: Literarische Genealogien und internationaler Kontext*, ed. Simone Costagli and Matteo Galli (Munich: Fink, 2010), 23. Goethe refers to the canonicity of *Das Leben der schwedischen Gräfin von G**** in *Dichtung und Wahrheit*, despite Gellert's loss of popularity by the latter part of the eighteenth century: "Gellerts Schriften waren so lange schon das Fundament der deutschen sittlichen Kultur" [Gellert's writings were for a long time the fundament of German moral culture]. Cited in Kimpel, *Der Roman der Aufklärung*, 96–97.

16. Matteo Galli and Simone Costagli, "Chronotopoi: Vom Familienroman zum Generationenroman," in *Deutsche Familienromane: Literarische Genealogien und internationaler Kontext*, ed. Costagli and Galli (Munich: Fink, 2010), 7.

17. Erich Schmidt points to Goethe's expression of debt to Richardson in *Dichtung und Wahrheit* for the concept of what Goethe calls "eines dichterischen Ganzen" [a poetic unity] and traces the immense importance of Richardson's novels for Gellert, Goethe, Wieland, and numerous other authors of the period. See Erich Schmidt, *Richardson, Rousseau und Goethe: Ein Beitrag zur Geschichte des Romans im 18. Jahrhundert* (Jena: Eduard Frommann, 1875).

18. Johann David Michaelis, a professor at Göttingen University, translated *Clarissa* between 1749 and 1751, with a supplemental volume based on Richardson's revisions appearing in 1753. See Thomas O. Beebee, Clarissa *on the Continent: Translation and Seduction* (State College, PA: Penn State University Press, 1990), 21.

19. Beebee, Clarissa *on the Continent*, 17.

20. See Kimpel, *Der Roman der Aufklärung*, 94.

21. Ian Watt, *The Rise of the Novel: Studies in Defoe, Richardson and Fielding* (Berkeley: University of California Press, 1957). See, in particular, chapter 2, "The Reading Public and the Rise of the Novel," 35–60.

22. Watt, *The Rise of the Novel*, 13.

23. Watt, *The Rise of the Novel*, 177.

24. Michael McKeon, *The Origins of the English Novel 1600–1740* (Baltimore, MD: Johns Hopkins University Press, 1987), 22.

25. Watt maintains that literary realism of the period is analogous to the Dutch School in painting. Watt, *The Rise of the Novel*, 17.

26. Watt, *The Rise of the Novel*, 19.

27. Watt, *The Rise of the Novel*, 29.

28. Watt, *The Rise of the Novel*, 30.

29. Watt, *The Rise of the Novel*, 13.

30. See also Lisa Freeman's discussion of theories of the English novel that highlight interiority and the emergence of the subject (two concepts that should be kept separate), in Freeman, *Character's Theater: Genre and Identity on the Eighteenth-Century English Stage* (Philadelphia: University of Pennsylvania Press, 2002), in particular 6–7.

31. Brown, *Allegories of Identity*, 13.

32. Brown, *Allegories of Identity*, 14.

33. In *The Order of Things*, Michel Foucault writes that the eighteenth century is the period during which we begin to see truth under the surface. See Foucault, *The Order of Things: An Archeology of the Human Sciences* (New York: Vintage, 1994).

34. In his discussion of Herculine Barbin, Foucault writes: "The idea that there exist complex, obscure, and essential relationships between sex and truth is to be found—at least in a diffused state—not only in psychiatry, psychoanalysis, and psychology, but also in current opinion." Michel Foucault, introduction to *Herculine Barbin: Being the Recently Discovered Memoirs of a Nineteenth-Century Hermaphrodite*, trans. Richard McDougall (New York: Pantheon, 1980), x.

35. On the derisive views on the novel form in the eighteenth century, see Claire Baldwin, *The Emergence of the Modern German Novel: Christoph Martin Wieland, Sophie von La Roche, and Maria Anna Sagar* (Columbia, SC: Camden House, 2002), 2. See also Hillebrand, *Theorie des Romans*, 121.

36. Friedrich von Blanckenburg, *Versuch über den Roman. Faksimiledruck der Originalausgabe von 1774* (Stuttgart: Metzlersche, 1965), 355. Quoted in Hillebrand, *Theorie des Romans*, 113.

37. Quoted in Kimpel, *Der Roman der Aufklärung*, 140.

38. Quoted in Kimpel, *Der Roman der Aufklärung*, 114.

39. See George Mosse's discussion of Herder's *Bildung* model as central to modern notions of masculinity and nation: Mosse, *The Image of Man: The Creation of Modern Masculinity* (New York: Oxford University Press, 1996), 8. See also Todd Kontje, *The German Bildungsroman: History of a National Genre* (Columbia, SC: Camden House, 1993), especially 2–4. See also Hillebrand, *Theorie des Romans*, 113.

40. The term appeared in the preface to Wezel's own novel *Herrmann und Ulrike*. See Hillebrand, *Theorie des Romans*, 125.

41. Hegel, *Vorlesungen über die Ästhetik III*, 392.

42. Hegel, *Aesthetics: Lectures on Fine Art*, 1109.

43. See Beebee, *Clarissa on the Continent*, 19.

44. See, for example, Bruno Hillebrand, who in his standard volume *Theorie des Romans* often remarks on the inferiority of German letters to their French and English counterparts. Hillebrand, *Theorie des Romans*, 95.

45. As Bernd Witte points out, the derisive response to Gellert's novel began around 1771 after the birth of the genius cult. Gellert's writing was considered to be both unnatural and immoral (with the inclusion of the incest narrative), and Gellert was deemed an author "without a spark of genius." Quoted in Witte, "Christian Fürchtegott Gellert: *Leben der schwedischen Gräfin von G****: Die Frau, die Schrift, der Tod," in *Romane des 17. und 18. Jahrhunderts (Interpretationen)* (Stuttgart: Reclam, 1996), 116. On the flatness of Gellert's characters and the "failure" of the novel, see Anna Richards, "Forgetting the Dead in Gellert's *Leben der schwedischen Gräfin von G****(1747/8)," *Oxford German Studies* 35, no. 2 (2006): 175; and Norbert Miller, *Der empfindsame Erzähler. Untersuchungen zur erzähltechnischen Verwendung des Briefes im deutschen Roman des 18. Jahrhunderts* (Munich: C. Hanser, 1968), 88.

46. On the generic hybridity of Gellert's novel, see Ferdinand Josef Schneider, *Die deutsche Dichtung vom Ausgang des Barock bis zum Beginn des Klassizismus 1700–1785* (Stuttgart: Metzler, 1924), 263. See also Helmut Schmiedt, *Liebe, Ehe, Ehebruch: Ein Spannungsfeld in deutscher Prosa von Christian Fürchtegott Gellert bis Elfriede Jelinek* (Opladen: Westdeutscher Verlag, 1993), 32; and Eckhardt Meyer-Krentler, *Der andere Roman: Gellerts 'Schwedische Gräfin': Von der aufklärerischen Propaganda gegen den 'Roman' zur empfindsamen Erlebnisdichtung* (Göppingen: Kümmerle, 1974).

47. Schmidt, *Richardson, Rousseau und Goethe*, 41.

48. Cited in Schmidt, *Richardson, Rousseau und Goethe*, 19.

49. For an analysis of the didactic function of the novel beginning around 1800, see Sarah Vandegrift Eldridge, who utilizes the concept of "imaginative didacticism" to describe the novel's pedagogical work: Eldridge, *Novel Affinities: Composing the Family in the German Novel, 1795–1830* (Rochester, NY: Camden House, 2016).

50. See Beebee, *Clarissa on the Continent*, 12. Beebee argues for a Clarissa vs. Lovelace reception of Richardson's novel; German readers, via Michaelis's translation, were wont to take the side of Clarissa and focus on the preservation of virtue, whereas readers of Prévost's French translation of the novel frequently sided with Lovelace.

51. The reception of La Roche's novel turned from laudatory to cool and offers a fascinating picture of gendered models for reading and writing. See Becker-Cantarino, "Dokumente zur Wirkungsgeschichte," in *Die Geschichte des Fräuleins von Sternheim*, ed. Barbara Becker-Cantarino (Stuttgart: Reclam, 1983); and Silvia Bovenschen, *Die imaginierte Weiblichkeit: Exemplarische Untersuchungen zu kulturgeschichtlichen und literarischen Präsentationsformen des Weiblichen* (Frankfurt: Suhrkamp, 1979). See also Helga Meise's argument that La Roche's hybrid and "moral-didactic" writing style led to the more negative reception of La Roche's writings later in her life: Helga Meise, "Die Schreibweisen der Sophie von La Roche," *German Life and Letters* 67, no. 4 (2014): 530–541. Claire Baldwin astutely critiques the artificial scholarly divide between novels written by men and "women's novels" in the eighteenth century. Baldwin, *The Emergence of the Modern German Novel*.

52. On the relationship between class and "Empfindsamkeit" [sentimentality] in Richardson's and La Roche's novels, Peter Uwe Hohendahl shows that the virtue of having compassion for those who suffer is not an exclusively bourgeois trait. See Hohendahl, "Empfindsamkeit und gesellschaftliches Bewußtsein: Zur Soziologie des empfindsamen Romans am Beispiel von *La Vie de Marianne, Clarissa, Fräulein von Sternheim* und *Werther*," *Jahrbuch der deutschen Schillergesellschaft* 16 (1972): 198.

53. Sophie has a double class status (as an aristocrat with a middle-class father), and the class problem's "solution" can only be realized in England. See, on this point, Hohendahl, "Empfindsamkeit und gesellschaftliches Bewußtsein," 197.

54. Christoph Martin Wieland, "(An D.F.G.R.V.*******)," in *Geschichte des Fräuleins von Sternheim*, by Sophie von La Roche, (Stuttgart: Reclam, 1983), 10. Wieland nevertheless express in the same preface his frustration with both La Roche's and her heroine's fixation on England.

55. Wieland, "(An D.F.G.R.V.*******)," 14.

56. "Rezension von Merck [mit Einschub von Goethe?] in den *Frankfurter gelehrten Anzeigen* vom 14. Februar 1772," *Dokumente zur Wirkunggeschichte, Geschichte des Fräuleins von Sternheim*, in *Die Geschichte des Fräuleins von Sternheim*, by Sophie von La Roche (Stuttgart: Reclam, 1983), 367. It is perhaps no surprise that in 1774, Friedrich von Blanckenburg finds Richardson's characters too stiffly moral and wooden. See Hohendahl, "Empfindsamkeit und gesellschaftliches Bewußtsein," 189.

57. Jean-Jacques Rousseau, *La Nouvelle Héloïse: Julie, or the New Eloise. Letters of Two Lovers, Inhabitants of a Small Town at the Foot of the Alps*, trans. Judith H. McDowell (University Park, PA: Penn State University Press, 1968), 124.

58. Sophie von La Roche, *Die Geschichte des Fräuleins von Sternheim*, ed. Barbara Becker-Cantarino (Stuttgart: Reclam, 1983), 222.

59. Brown shows that, despite some biographical similarities, Goethe disdained what he saw as Rousseau's serious moral shortcomings in rejecting his own children by placing them in an orphanage. Hence, Brown surmises that Goethe became ever more repelled by Rousseau. Jane K. Brown, "Goethe, Rousseau, the Novel, and the Origins of Psychoanalysis," *Goethe Yearbook* 12 (2004): 111–128.

60. Brown argues that Goethe's allegorical language was developed in response to Rousseau's writings, as a way to exteriorize interior subjectivity. See Brown, *Allegories of Identity*.

61. Brown, "Goethe, Rousseau," 114.

62. Niklas Luhmann, *Liebe als Passion* (Frankfurt: Suhrkamp, 1982), 168.

63. Luhmann, *Love as Passion*, 133.

64. Georg Lukács, "Erzählen oder beschreiben? Zur Diskussion über den Naturalismus und Formalismus," in *Probleme des Realismus I: Essays über Realismus*, vol. 4 of *Georg Lukács Werke* (Neuwied and Berlin: Luchterhand, 1971), 198.

65. Lukács, "Erzählen oder beschreiben?," 198.

66. Lukács, "Erzählen oder beschreiben?," 216.

67. Lukács, "Erzählen oder beschreiben?," 217.

68. Lukács, "Erzählen oder beschreiben?," 220.

69. Lukács, "Erzählen oder beschreiben?," 209. Italics mine.

70. On the historical context for Schlegel's novel (her marriage to Friedrich Schlegel, conversion from Judaism to Christianity, and so on), see Liliane Weissberg, "The Master's

Theme, and Some Variations: Dorothea Schlegel's *Florentin* as *Bildungsroman*," *Michigan German Studies* 13, no. 2 (1987): 169–181. On *Florentin* as a successful parody of the male *Bildungsroman*, see Barbara Becker-Cantarino, "'Die wärmste Liebe zu unsrer literarischen Ehe': Friedrich Schlegels *Lucinde* und Dorothea Veits *Florentin*," in *Bi-Textualität: Insṛenierungen des Paares: ein Buch für Ina Schabert*, ed. Annegret Heitmann (Berlin: Erich Schmidt Verlag, 2001), 136.

71. Dorothea Schlegel was famously enamored of and puzzled by *Wilhelm Meisters Lehrjahre*: see Weissberg, "The Master's Theme," 172. Schlegel wrote to Clemens Brentano on February 27, 1801, that *Florentin* was "stolen" "from Goethe's *Meister*, from *Sternbald*, and from *Woldemar*." Cited in J. M. Raich, ed., *Dorothea v. Schlegel geb. Mendelssohn und deren Söhne Johannes und Phillipp Veit. Briefwechsel* (Mainz: Franz Kirchheim, 1988), 19–20.

72. Dorothea Schlegel, *Florentin: Roman, Fragmente, Varianten* (Frankfurt: Ullstein, 1986), 161–162. Inge Stephan likewise notes the discrete nature of the pictures in the "Bildergalerie" that cannot be organically connected to create a unified whole, attributing this style to Dorothea Schlegel's self-proclaimed insecurity. See Stephan, "Weibliche und männliche Autorschaft: Zum *Florentin* von Dorothea Schlegel und zur *Lucinde* von Friedrich Schlegel," in *Insṛenierte Weiblichkeit: Codierung der Geschlechter in der Literatur des 18. Jahrhunderts*, ed. Claudia Benthien and Inge Stephan (Cologne: Böhlau, 2004), 247–250.

73. Adrian Daub intriguingly looks to the family gallery in order to trace residues of the "dynastic imagination" in the nineteenth-century family. See, in particular, Daub, "Into the Family Gallery," in *The Dynastic Imagination: Family and Modernity in Nineteenth-Century Germany* (Chicago: University of Chicago Press, 2021).

74. Schlegel's notion of the family portrait gallery differs in important ways from the family portrait in Oliver Goldsmith's *The Vicar of Wakefield* (1766), a novel that Goethe's Lotte is reading in *Die Leiden des jungen Werthers*. Christopher Flint begins his book on the family and narrative in eighteenth-century British fiction with the family portrait chapter in Goldsmith's novel. In chapter 16, the Primrose family decides to have a portrait made in which they will be "drawn together, in one large historical family piece . . . in which one frame would serve for all." Oliver Goldsmith, *The Vicar of Wakefield*, ed. Stephen Coote (London, Penguin, 1982), 99. Flint points to the fact that the resultant painting, which is cheaper than individual portraits, is nevertheless too large to actually fit into the Primrose home, and that the contradictions within the concept of the family of the period are beautifully pictured in this scene. See Christopher Flint, *Family Fictions: Narrative and Domestic Relations in Britain, 1688–1798* (Stanford, CA: Stanford University Press, 1998), 1–2. Flint is critical of the smooth narrative of the "so-called rise of the nuclear family" in the eighteenth century (10). It is nevertheless important to note that the Primrose family is thoroughly middle class, and that Goldsmith depicts the creation of a nuclear family portrait, two elements that are difficult to find in the eighteenth-century German novel and drama.

75. Martha Helfer makes a compelling case that *Florentin* reflects a unique feminist Romantic aesthetic characterized by "entropy, alterity, absence, and exclusion." See Martha Helfer, "Dorothea Veit-Schlegel's *Florentin*: Constructing a Feminist Romantic Aesthetic," *The German Quarterly* 69, no. 2 (1996): 156.

76. Schlegel, *Florentin*, 15. Ellipses in the original.

77. Schlegel, *Florentin*, 17. Italics mine.

78. And the family castle, we learn, itself contains both old *and* modern elements. Schlegel, *Florentin*, 27.

79. Schlegel, *Florentin*, 162.

80. Paul Fischer, *Goethe-Wortschatz: Ein sprachgeschichtliches Wörterbuch zu Goethes Sämtlichen Werken* (Leipzig: Rohmkopf, 1929), 699.

81. Johann Wolfgang von Goethe, *Faust: Der Trägodie zweiter Teil*, FA 7.1, pt. 1, 309.

82. Johann Wolfgang von Goethe, *Faust: Texte*, FA 7, pt. 1, 62.

83. Goethe, *Faust: Texte*, 74.

84. Goethe, *Faust: Texte*, 74–75.

85. Fischer, *Goethe-Wortschatz*, 699.

86. Johann Wolfgang von Goethe, "Der Versuch als Vermittler," *Schriften zur Allgemeinen Naturlehre, Physik und zur Farbenlehre nach 1810*, FA 1.25, 30.

87. Norbert Puszkar, "Verwandtschaft und Wahlverwandtschaft," *Goethe Yearbook* 4 (1988): 164.

88. Goethe, *Die Wahlverwandtschaften*, 482.

89. Eve Sedgwick, "Queer and Now," in *Tendencies* (Durham, NC: Duke University Press, 1994), 7n6.

90. Goethe, *Faust: Texte*, 64.

91. Bernd Witte points to the radical inclusivity of the community represented within Gellert's novel, calling it a "community of outsiders." See Witte, "Christian Fürchtegott Gellert," 133. With a view to the children in the novel, Stephan K. Schindler likewise argues that Gellert's work, despite its "Familienroman" moniker, consistently deconstructs constellations that would produce a stable nuclear family. See Stephan K. Schindler, *Das Subjekt als Kind: Die Erfindung der Kindheit im Roman des 18. Jahrhunderts* (Berlin: Erich Schmidt, 1994), 39. See also Heidi Schlipphacke, "Eros and Community: C. F. Gellert's *Das Leben der schwedischen Gräfin von G***,*" *The Germanic Review* 76, no. 1 (2001): 70–90.

92. Christian Fürchtegott Gellert, *Das Leben der schwedischen Gräfin von G****, ed. Jörg-Ulrich Fechner (Stuttgart: Reclam, 1968), 64.

93. Wolfgang Bunzel argues that the novel's shift between first-person narrative and letters teaches the reader to experience emotions and then subsequently to distance themselves from them. Bunzel, "Gellerts Roman *Leben*," 387.

94. Gellert, *Leben der schwedischen Gräfin*, 64.

95. Bernd Witte notes that the repeated dialectic of pairs and their demise in the novel reflects the bumpy shift to a bourgeois nuclear family model. See Bernd Witte, "Der Roman als moralische Anstalt: Gellerts *Leben der schwedischen Gräfin von G . . .* und die Literatur des achtzehnten Jahrhunderts," *Germanisch-Romanische Monatsschrift* 63 (1980): 162.

96. Gellert, *Leben der schwedischen Gräfin*, 46.

97. Gayle S. Rubin's diagrams "The Sex Hierarchy: The Charmed Circle vs. The Outer Limits" and "The Sex Hierarchy: The Struggle over Where to Draw the Line" picture the ways in which determinations about which kinds of sexual acts are acceptable and which are not are motivated by shifting political discourses. See Gayle S. Rubin, "Thinking Sex: Notes for a Radical Theory of the Politics of Sexuality," in *Deviations: A Gayle Rubin Reader* (Durham, NC: Duke University Press, 2011), 152–153.

98. Witte also points to the quick shifts between life partners in Gellert's novel, a quality he connects to the baroque novel form. See Bernd Witte, "Die andere Gesellschaft: Der Ursprung des bürgerlichen Romans in Gellerts "Leben der Schwedischen Gräfin von G***,*" in *"Ein Lehrer der ganzen Nation": Leben und Werk Christian Fürchtegott Gellerts*, ed.

Bernd Witte (Munich: Fink, 1990), 70. Witte cites Paul Kluckhohn's well-known 1922 study, *Die Auffassung der Liebe in der Literatur des achtzehnten Jahrhunderts*, in which Kluckhohn marvels at the easy transferability of love between objects within the novel. Witte, "Die andere Gesellschaft," 117.

99. Gellert, *Leben der schwedischen Gräfin*, 37.

100. Gellert, *Leben der schwedischen Gräfin*, 37.

101. Gellert, *Leben der schwedischen Gräfin*, 53.

102. Gellert, *Leben der schwedischen Gräfin*, 109.

103. Gellert, *Leben der schwedischen Gräfin*, 116.

104. Gellert, *Leben der schwedischen Gräfin*, 116. Anna Richards claims—correctly, I think—that "the relationship between the Count and Steeley is the most passionate in the book." See Richards, "Forgetting the Dead," 173.

105. Diderot, "Conversations on *The Natural Son*," 21.

106. See Luhmann, *Love as Passion*, 121–128.

107. Gellert, *Leben der schwedischen Gräfin*, 116. Italics mine.

108. La Roche, *Geschichte des Fräuleins*, 58.

109. La Roche, *Geschichte des Fräuleins*, 58.

110. La Roche, *Geschichte des Fräuleins*, 89. Interestingly, the canoness always wears a veil (89). Here we have a self-conscious articulation of the beginnings of an epistemology of truth as depth.

111. La Roche, *Geschichte des Fräuleins*, 88.

112. Barbara Becker-Cantarino sees this idyllic ending as a "feminine utopia." See Becker-Cantarino, "Sophie La Roche, der Beginn der 'Frauenliteratur' und der weiblichen Tradition," in *Der lange Weg zur Mündigkeit* (Stuttgart: Metzler, 1987), 300.

113. La Roche, *Geschichte des Fräuleins*, 347–348.

114. La Roche, *Geschichte des Fräuleins*, 348. Italics mine.

115. La Roche, *Geschichte des Fräuleins*, 348. Italics mine.

116. La Roche, *Geschichte des Fräuleins*, 348. Italics mine.

117. La Roche, *Geschichte des Fräuleins*, 349. Italics mine.

118. Scholars have noted Werther's shifting relationship to notions of family within the novel. Bengt Algot Sørensen shows how in *Werther* the natural family is good, whereas the family connected to society is bad. See Bengt Algot Sørensen, "Über die Familie in Goethes 'Werther' und 'Wilhelm Meister,'" *Orbis Litterarum* 42 (1987): 118–140. W. Daniel Wilson notes a shift from Werther's desire to be part of Lotte's family in part 1 to his sexual passion for Lotte alone in part 2; see W. Daniel Wilson, "'Ein Glied der liebenswürdigen Familie auszumachen': Labor, Family, and Werther's Search for Nature," in *Zerreissproben/Double Bind: Familie und Geschlecht in der deutschen Literatur des 18. und 19. Jahrhunderts*, ed. Christine Kanz (Bern: eFeF, 2007).

119. Johann Wolfgang von Goethe, *Die Leiden des jungen Werthers*, FA 1.8, 41–42.

120. Goethe, *Die Leiden*, 91.

121. In the satirical play "Pandämonium Germanikum" (1775), Jakob M. R. Lenz links the two figures, Goethe and La Roche, via the figures of Sternheim and Werther. Jakob M. R. Lenz, "Dokumente zur Wirkungsgeschichte," in *Die Geschichte des Fräuleins von Sternheim*, 373.

122. There are a number of parallels between these two novels. Goethe was initially enthusiastic about La Roche's novel but later criticized her writing for its "mediocrity."

Becker-Cantarino, "Dokumente zur Wirkungsgeschichte," 391. Yet Maryann Piel makes the convincing case that Goethe borrowed significantly from La Roche's *Sternheim* in his creation of *Werther*. See Maryann Piel, "La Roche and Goethe: Gender, Genre, and Influence," in *Goethe Yearbook 30*, forthcoming. Monika Nenon shows how La Roche served as a kind of mentor for the younger Goethe. See Monika Nenon, "A Dynamic Interplay: Cooperation between Sophie von La Roche, Christoph Martin Wieland, and Goethe on Their Way to Authorship," in *Gender, Collaboration, and Authorship in German Culture*, ed. Laura Deiulio and John B. Lyon (New York: Bloomsbury, 2019).

123. Goethe, *Die Leiden*, 249.

124. Jane K. Brown points out that Goethe is generally hostile to "the tight family." Brown, *Allegories of Identity*, 4.

125. As Marc Redfield writes, "The more this genre [*Bildungsroman*] is cast into question, the more it flourishes." See Redfield, *Bildungsroman: Phantom Formations: Aesthetic Ideology and the* Bildungsroman (Ithaca, NY: Cornell University Press, 1996), 42. On the contours of the traditional *Bildungsroman*, see Fritz Martini, "Der Bildungsroman: Zur Geschichte des Wortes und der Theorie," *Deutsche Vierteljahrsschrift* 35 (1961): 44–63; and Wilhelm Dilthey, *Das Erlebnis und die Dichtung: Lessing, Goethe, Novalis, Hölderlin* (Göttingen: Vandenhoeck & Ruprecht, 1965). Dilthey writes paradigmatically that the *Bildungsroman* represents the regular and logical development of the individual (272). As Günter Saße puts it, the return home in the *Bildungsroman* is a turn inward: Günter Saße, "Von 'heimlichen Geist des Widerspruchs': Der Bildungsroman im 18. Jahrhundert. Goethes *Wilhelm Meisters Lehrjahre* im Spannungsfeld von Subjektivität und Intersubjektivität," in *Das 18. Jahrhundert*, ed. Monika Fludernik and Ruth Nestvold (Trier: WTV, 1998), 72. Kittler points out that a *Bildungsroman* should present the hero's continuous development from childhood to his integration into bourgeois society. See Kittler, "Über die Sozialisation Wilhelm Meisters." Important gendered, postmodern, and ecocritical critiques of this teleological notion of development and individuality inherent in the *Bildungsroman* form have been offered by Baldwin, *The Emergence of the Modern German Novel*; Marianne Hirsch, "Spiritual *Bildung*: The Beautiful Soul as Paradigm," in *The Voyage In: Fictions of Female Development* (Lebanon, NH: University Press of New England, 1983); Elisabeth Krimmer, "Abortive *Bildung*: Women Writers, Male Bonds, and Would-Be Fathers," in *Challenging Separate Spheres: Female Bildung in Eighteenth- and Nineteenth-Century Germany*, ed. Marjanne Goozé (Oxford: Peter Lang, 2007); Christine Lehleiter, "Sophie von La Roche's *Die Geschichte des Fräuleins von Sternheim* (1771): Conceptualizing Female Selfhood around 1800," *Women in German Yearbook* 29 (2013): 33; and Heather Sullivan, "Nature and the 'Dark Pastoral' in Goethe's *Werther*," *Goethe Yearbook* 21 (2015): 116–117.

126. Stuart Atkins points to the "wealth of motifs" and episodes in *Wilhelm Meisters Lehrjahre* and compares it to a "Trivialroman." See Atkins, "*Wilhelm Meisters Lehrjahre: Novel or Romance?*," in *Essays on Goethe*, ed. Jane K. Brown and Thomas P. Saine (Columbia, SC: Camden House, 1995).

127. See my article, Schlipphacke, "Die Vaterschaft beruht nur überhaupt auf der Überzeugung: The Displaced Family in Goethe's *Wilhelm Meisters Lehrjahre*," *Journal of English and Germanic Philology* 102, no. 3 (2003): 390–412.

128. Kirk Wetters likewise points to the transitoriness of human societies in *Wilhelm Meisters Lehrjahre*. See Wetters, "Who Cares about Society? *Sorge* and Reification in

Goethe's *Wilhelm Meisters Lehrjahre,*" *Colloquia Germanica* 47, no. 3 (2014): 243–262. Stefan Hajduk writes of Wilhelm's "Beziehungsbegabung" and ability to substitute in relationships; see Hajduk, "Identität und Verlust: Der Wandei des Familienbildes und die Dynamik der Geniuspsychologie in *Wilhelm Meisters Lehrjahre,*" *Weimarer Beiträge* 55, no. 2 (2009): 197.

129. Goethe, *Wilhelm Meisters Lehrjahre*, FA 1.9, 547.

130. Goethe, *Wilhelm Meisters Lehrjahre*, 553.

131. Scholars have noted how the narrators of *Wilhelm Meisters Lehrjahre* and, even more pronouncedly, of *Wilhelm Meisters Theatralische Sendung* switch pronouns when referring to Mignon, opening up the question as to Mignon's biological sex. See Christine Lehleiter, *Romanticism, Origins, and the History of Heredity*, 124–125. Lehleiter posits that Mignon is an intersex figure (144–150). Catriona MacLeod, Eleanor ter Horst, and Robert Tobin likewise analyze Mignon's function in the novel in light of Mignon's shifting roles as "hermaphrodite" and cross-dresser. See Eleanor E. ter Horst, *Lessing, Goethe, Kleist, and the Transformation of Gender: From Hermaphrodite to Amazon* (New York: Peter Lang, 2003), especially 69–120; Robert Tobin, *Warm Brothers*, especially 124–131; and Catriona MacLeod, *Embodying Ambiguity: Androgyny and Aesthetics from Winckelmann to Keller* (Detroit, MI: Wayne State University Press, 1998), especially 91–139.

132. Along these lines, Barbara N. Nagel reads Philine as an allegory of sexual metaphor. See Barbara N. Nagel, "Slut-Shaming Metaphorologies: On Sexual Metaphor in Goethe's *Wilhelm Meister,*" *Critical Inquiry* 46 (2020): 304–324.

133. Goethe, *Wilhelm Meisters Lehrjahre*, 565.

134. For a discussion of the queer aunt, see Kate Thomas, "Eternal Gardens and the Queer Uncanny in Frances Hodgson Burnett's 'In the Closed Room' (1902)," *Pacific Coast Philology* 50, no. 2 (2015): 173–183.

135. Goethe, *Wilhelm Meisters Lehrjahre*, 754. Friedrich Schlegel, interestingly, is critical of the Beautiful Soul for her theatrical and superficial life: see Friedrich Schlegel, "Über Goethes Meister," in *Friedrich Schlegel: Charakteristiken & Kritiken I (1796–1801)*, ed. Ernst Behler et al. (Munich: Schöningh, 1967).

136. See Susan Gustafson's masterful chapter in which she sketches the elective affinities within *Wilhelm Meisters Lehrjahre*. Gustafson, "Learning What Family and Love Can Be in *Wilhelm Meisters Lehrjahre,*" in *Goethe's Families of the Heart*, 67–139.

137. Goethe, *Wilhelm Meisters Lehrjahre*, 940. Elisabeth Krimmer and Stefani Engelstein likewise question the veracity of the Tower Society's pronouncement that Felix is Wilhelm's biological son. See Elisabeth Krimmer, "Mama's Baby, Papa's Maybe: Paternity and *Bildung* in Goethe's *Wilhelm Meisters Lehrjahre,*" *The German Quarterly* 77, no. 3 (2004): 257–277; Engelstein, *Sibling Action*, 99–106.

138. Barbara Becker-Cantarino, in contrast, interprets this moment as reconfirming the patriarchal power of the Tower Society. See Barbara Becker-Cantarino, "Patriarchy and German Enlightenment Discourse: From Goethe's *Wilhelm Meister* to Horkheimer and Adorno's *Dialectic of Enlightenment,*" in *Impure Reason; Dialectic of Enlightenment in Germany*, ed. W. Daniel Wilson and Robert C. Holub (Detroit, MI: Wayne State University Press, 1999), 51.

139. Johann Wolfgang von Goethe, *Wilhelm Meisters Wanderjahre*, FA 1.10, 26.

140. On the elective affinities in *Wilhelm Meisters Wanderjahre*, see Gustafson, *Families of the Heart*, 139–185.

141. Goethe, *Wilhelm Meisters Lehrjahre*, 950.

142. Goethe, *Wilhelm Meisters Lehrjahre*, 950.

143. Goethe, *Wilhelm Meisters Lehrjahre*, 601. Natalie's aunt, the "schöne Seele," remarks on Natalie's uniqueness, calling her "unnachahmlich" [inimitable] (418). The half-aristocratic Sophie Sternheim is frequently described similarly as "unnachahmlich" in La Roche's novel. See, for example, La Roche, *Geschichte des Fräuleins*, 71 and 169.

144. Goethe, *Wilhelm Meisters Lehrjahre*, 806.

145. Goethe, *Wilhelm Meisters Lehrjahre*, 899–900.

146. Goethe, *Wilhelm Meisters Lehrjahre*, 899.

147. Goethe, *Wilhelm Meisters Lehrjahre*.

148. Goethe, *Wilhelm Meisters Lehrjahre*, 979–980.

149. My reading deviates not only from Kittler's in this regard ("Über die Sozialisation Wilhelm Meisters") but also from that of Bengt Algot Sørensen, who sees the novel's ending as a moment when the family circle has closed with Wilhelm at its center. Sørensen, "Über die Familie in Goethe's *Werther* und *Wilhelm Meister*," 132.

150. Goethe, *Wilhelm Meisters Lehrjahre*, 990.

151. As a correlate to the expanding and shifting representations of kinship in the novel that blur the *Verwandtschaft/Bekanntschaft* divide, expanding communities correspond to more wealth, as in Gellert's novel. The rakish yet charitable Lothario expresses his desire to use his increasing wealth (the cause of this increase is unnamed) to expand his community via his serfs and friends. Goethe, *Wilhelm Meisters Lehrjahre*, 807.

152. Hans Eichner makes this attempt (unsuccessfully) in Eichner, "'Camilla': Eine unbekannte Fortsetzung von Dorothea Schlegels *Florentin*," *Jahrbuch des Freien Deutschen Hochstifts* (1965): 314–368.

153. Despite the slipperiness of biological ties in the novel, it is important to note, as Elisabeth Krimmer does, that Florentin is fixated on paternity. Krimmer, "Abortive *Bildung*, 249. When asked early in the novel where he is from, he answers that his fatherland will be that place where he first hears himself called "father." Schlegel, *Florentin*, 16. Importantly, the only moment in the novel that offers up the potential for Florentin to become a father is vanquished when his Roman wife has an abortion.

154. Schlegel, *Florentin*, 28.

155. Schlegel, *Florentin*, 80.

156. Schlegel, *Florentin*, 116.

157. Lukács, "Erzählen oder beschreiben?," 209. Italics mine.

158. Lukács, *Die Theorie des Romans*, 57.

159. Lukács, *Die Theorie des Romans*, 78.

160. Lukács, *Die Theorie des Romans*, 62.

161. Lukács, *Die Theorie des Romans*, 61.

162. Lukács, *Die Theorie des Romans*, 127.

163. Lukács, *Die Theorie des Romans*, 128.

164. Lukács, *Die Theorie des Romans*, 128.

165. Deleuze, *Cinema 1*, 4.

166. *Goethe-Wörterbuch*, *Wörterbuchnetz*, http://woerterbuchnetz.de/cgi-bin/WBNetz/wbgui_py?sigle=GWB&mode=Vernetzung&lemid=JA02716#XJA02716.

167. *Goethe-Wörterbuch*.

168. Elsaesser, *Fassbinder's Germany*, 86.

169. La Roche, *Geschichte des Fräuleins*, 104. Italics mine.

170. La Roche, *Geschichte des Fräuleins*, 188.

171. La Roche, *Geschichte des Fräuleins*, 220.

172. On the questionable relationship between rape and *Bildung* in *Clarissa* and *Sternheim*, see Peter Arnds, "Sophie von La Roche's *Geschichte des Fräuleins von Sternheim* as an Answer to Samuel Richardson's *Clarissa*," *Lessing Yearbook* 29 (1997): 87–105.

173. La Roche, *Geschichte des Fräuleins*, 225.

174. La Roche, *Geschichte des Fräuleins*, 69.

175. Scholars have discussed this and other similar passages from *Werther*, utilizing the notion of the *tableau*, the idyll, and the pastoral. On this passage and "absorption," see Martin Wagner, "'. . . So ganz in dem Gefühl vom ruhigen Daseyn versunken, dass meine Kunst darunter leidet . . .': Michael Frieds *Absorption and Theatricality* und Goethes *Die Leiden des jungen Werthers*," *Jahrbuch der Grillparzer-Gesellschaft* 24 (2011–2012): 183–226. Peter Morgan argues that the idyll cannot be realized within *Werther*. See Peter Morgan, "The Spirit of the Place: Idyll as 'Imagined Community' in Goethe's *Werther*," *AUMLA: Journal of the Australasian Universities Modern Language Association* (2003): 42–54. Heather Sullivan argues forcefully that Goethe's use of the pastoral in *Werther* is deeply critical; Goethe's hyperbolic pastoral creates the scene for "critique through artifice": Sullivan, "Nature and the 'Dark Pastoral' in Goethe's *Werther*," 115.

176. Goethe, *Die Leiden*, 27.

177. See Lauren Nossett's analysis of Lotte as an archetypical virgin mother in German literature: Lauren Nossett, "Impossible Ideals: Reconciling Virginity and Materiality in Goethe's *Werther*," *Goethe Yearbook* 23 (2016): 77–93.

178. Goethe, *Die Leiden*, 41.

179. Goethe, *Die Leiden*, 247. Astrida Orle Tantillo intriguingly compares this scene to a confession. See Tantillo, *Goethe's Modernisms* (New York: Bloomsbury, 2010), 99.

180. Both Astrida Orle Tantillo and Heather Sullivan draw the connection between *Werther* and Goethe's farcical play *Triumph der Empfindsamkeit* (1777), in which sentimentality is mocked as the protagonist carries a doll around that is stuffed with sentimental novels, including *Werther* and Rousseau's *La nouvelle Heloise*. Both Sullivan and Tantillo show how this intertext underscores the ironic and critical stance Goethe takes vis-à-vis Werther's sentimental indulgences in the novel. See Heather Sullivan, "Nature and the 'Dark Pastoral'"; and Astrida Orle Tantillo, "A New Reading of *Werther* as Goethe's Critique of Rousseau," *Orbis Litterarum* 56 (2001): 443–465.

181. Along these lines, Erwin Liebfried interprets Werther's suicide as a sign of the impotence of the individual when confronted with the material world. See Erwin Liebfried, "Goethes Werther als Leser von Lessings 'Emilia Galotti,'" in *Text—Leser—Bedeutung: Untersuchungen zur Interaktion von Text und Leser*, ed. Herbert Grabes (Grossen-Linden: Hoffmann, 1977). Alice Kuzniar interprets Werther's failure as a failure to read, comparing Werther's to Goethe's semiotics: "The Misrepresentation of Self: Werther versus Goethe," *Mosaic* 22, no. 2 (Spring 1989): 15–28.

182. Goethe, *Die Leiden*, 265.

183. Edgar Landgraf writes that Werther "stages his suicide" and "turns it into an artistic act." See Landgraf, "Romantic Love and the Enlightenment: From Gallantry and Seduction to Authenticity and Self-Validation," *The German Quarterly* 77, no. 1 (2004): 40.

184. Goethe, *Die Leiden*, 265–267.

185. Evelyn Moore interestingly sees the scene in which Wilhelm wears the clothes of the count as a *tableau vivant* that becomes a mirror, pointing likewise to movement in Goethe's novel. See Moore, "Erlebendes Schauen: Goethes Tableaux vivants in Erzähl-werken, Theater und Politik," in *Transactions of the Ninth International Congress on the Enlightenment*, vol. 1, ed. Anthony Strugnell and Werner Schneiders (Oxford: Voltaire Foundation, 1996), 467.

186. Goethe, *Wilhelm Meisters Lehrjahre*, 463. Italics mine.

187. Goethe, *Wilhelm Meisters Lehrjahre*, 497–498.

188. Goethe, *Wilhelm Meisters Lehrjahre*, 498. Italics mine.

189. See Lehleiter, who reads this as an ejaculation. Lehleiter, *Romanticism, Origins and the History of Heredity*, 132.

190. Goethe, *Wilhelm Meisters Lehrjahre*, 498.

191. Goethe, *Wilhelm Meisters Lehrjahre*, 498.

192. Goethe, *Wilhelm Meisters Lehrjahre*, 499.

193. Goethe, *Wilhelm Meisters Lehrjahre*, 574.

194. Goethe, *Wilhelm Meisters Lehrjahre*, 574.

195. Goethe, *Wilhelm Meisters Lehrjahre*, 626.

196. Goethe, *Wilhelm Meisters Lehrjahre*, 626. Italics mine.

197. Goethe, *Wilhelm Meisters Lehrjahre*, 955.

198. Goethe, *Wilhelm Meisters Lehrjahre*, 958.

199. Goethe, "Über Laokoon," FA 1.18, 493.

200. Goethe, *Wilhelm Meisters Lehrjahre*, 924.

201. Ingrid Broszeit-Rieger posits the intriguing thesis that characters in *Wilhelm Meisters Lehrjahre* channel their unacceptable, deviant desires into acts of nurturing. See Broszeit-Rieger, "Transgressions of Gender and Generation in the Families of Goethe's *Meister*," in *Romantic Border Crossings*, ed. Jeffrey Cass and Larry Peer (Burlington, VT: Ashgate, 2008), 76.

202. Goethe, *Wilhelm Meisters Lehrjahre*, 985. Italics mine.

203. Erich Trunz, "Nachwort," afterword to *Wilhelm Meisters Lehrjahre*, in *Romane und Novellen*, ed. Erich Trunz, vol. 6 of *Johann Wolfgang Goethe Werke: Hamburger Ausgabe*, 14 vols. (Munich: Deutscher Taschenbuch Verlag, 1999), 684, 685. Although the early Romantics generally responded enthusiastically to *Wilhelm Meisters Lehrjahre*, the novel was initially only popular in Germany, in contrast to *Die Leiden des jungen Werthers*, a novel that quickly became an international hit and was translated into multiple languages. See Trunz, "Nachwort," 706. Friedrich Schlegel, of course, celebrated Goethe's novel and his character, Wilhelm, as embodying a "grenzenlose Bildsamkeit" [boundary-less capacity for development]: Friedrich Schlegel, "Über Goethes Meister," 129.

204. For a close reading and analysis of Goethe and Schiller's correspondence about *Wilhelm Meisters Lehrjahre*, see Wilfried Barner and Günter Saße. Each follows the shift in discourse, as Schiller's reception moves from laudatory to critical. See Barner, "'Die Verschiedenheit unserer Naturen'"; and Saße, "'Gerade seine Unvollkommenheit hat mir am meisten Mühe gemacht': Schillers Briefwechsel mit Goethe über *Wilhelm Meisters Lehrjahre*," *Goethe-Jahrbuch* 122 (2005): 88.

205. "Briefwechsel zwischen Goethe und Schiller," 630.

206. "Briefwechsel zwischen Goethe und Schiller," 640.

207. "Briefwechsel zwischen Goethe und Schiller," 640.

208. "Briefwechsel zwischen Goethe und Schiller," 641.
209. "Briefwechsel zwischen Goethe und Schiller," 650.
210. "Briefwechsel zwischen Goethe und Schiller," 629.
211. "Briefwechsel zwischen Goethe und Schiller," 648.
212. Goethe, *Wilhelm Meisters Lehrjahre*, 422.
213. See Trunz, "Nachwort," 721.
214. Goethe, *Wilhelm Meisters Lehrjahre*, 422.
215. Goethe, *Wilhelm Meisters Lehrjahre*, 872.
216. Goethe, *Wilhelm Meisters Lehrjahre*, 896.
217. Goethe, *Wilhelm Meisters Lehrjahre*, 987.
218. Goethe, *Wilhelm Meisters Lehrjahre*, 988.
219. In contrast, Christoph E. Schweitzer argues that the final scene in *Wilhelm Meisters Wanderjahre* is the realization of the painting's meaning, as Wilhelm becomes both father and doctor to Felix, moving from the role of the sick son to a melding of the adult male roles in the painting. See Christoph E. Schweitzer, "Wilhelm Meister und das Bild des kranken Königssohns," *PMLA* 2, no. 3 (1957): 419–432. Katerina Karakassi comes to a similar interpretation, pointing out that paintings are used in novels to slow time and therefore function to model roles for the characters that they will take on in the future. See Katerina Karakassi, "Der kranke Königssohn oder das zeitlose Bild im Sog der Zeit: Notizen zu Goethes *Wilhelm Meisters Lehr- und Wanderjahre*," *Estudios Filológicos Alemanes* 18 (2009): 251–262.

Chapter Seven   Kinship and Aesthetic Depth

1. Astrida Tantillo details the many ways in which *Die Wahlverwandtschaften* has stimulated "from the time of its publication to today, . . . a storm of interpretive confusion" in terms of content, themes, and form. Astrida Orle Tantillo, *Goethe's* Elective Affinities *and the Critics* (Rochester, NY: Camden House, 2001), xiii.

2. G.W.F. Hegel, *Ästhetik I/II: Vorlesungen über die Ästhetik: Erster und Zweiter Teil*, ed. Rüdiger Bubner (Stuttgart: Reclam, 1971), 413.

3. Hegel, *Aesthetics: Lectures on Fine Art*, vol. 1, 297–298.

4. Hegel, *Aesthetics: Lectures on Fine Art*, vol. 1, 295.

5. Johann Wolfgang von Goethe, *Die Wahlverwandtschaften*, FA 1.8. Page number references for *Die Wahlverwandtschaften* are hereafter provided parenthetically in the text.

6. Gertrude Brude-Firnau, "Lebende Bilder in den *Wahlverwandtschaften*: Goethes *Journal intime* vom Oktober 1806," *Euphorion* 74 (1980): 403–416. Nils Reschke also offers a compelling political reading of the Borzone and Poussin paintings in light of the French Revolution; see Nils Reschke, "'Die Wirklichkeit als Bild': Lebende Bilder in Goethes *Wahlverwandtschaften*," in *Medien der Präsenz: Museum, Bildung und Wissenschaft im 19. Jahrhundert*, ed. Jürgen Fohrmann, Andrea Schütte, and Wilhelm Voßkamp (Cologne: Dumont, 2001). See also Nicholas Boyle, "What Really Happens in *Die Wahlverwandtschaften*," *The German Quarterly* 89, no. 3 (2016): 298–312. Boyle argues that the novel not only reflects Goethe's feelings about the Napoleonic Wars but that it directly refers to the political events of 1806. In proposing that Eduard fights on the side of Napoleon, Boyle shows that Eduard represents a "self-destructive" aristocratic tendency that speeds up the fall of the Holy Roman Empire (305).

7. Hegel, *Aesthetics: Lectures on Fine Art*, vol. 1, 155–156.

8. Nicholas Boyle highlights the novel's unique combination of verisimilitude and unspecificity. See Boyle, "What Really Happens," 298.

9. Brown, *The Persistence of Allegory*.

10. Brown, *The Persistence of Allegory*, 60.

11. Langen, "Attitüde und Tableau in der Goethezeit"; Frey, "Tugendspiele."

12. Jordan, "Lebende Bilder im deutschen Drama des 17. Jahrhunderts," 208.

13. Along these lines, J. Hillis Miller applauds Goethe's gift for "reconciling allegorical emblem and obedience to the stylistic decorums of realism." See Miller, "Interlude as Anastomosis in *Die Wahlverwandtschaften*," *Goethe Yearbook* 6 (1992): 117.

14. MacLeod points out that the Romantic novel has often been understood as a hybrid form, citing Schiller's comments to Goethe in 1797 that the novel is an "impure medium." See Catriona MacLeod, "Sculptural Blockages: Wilhelm Heinse's *Ardinghello*, Clemens Brentano's *Godwi*, and the Early Romantic Novel," *Seminar* 49, no. 2 (2013): 232–247.

15. Levine, *Forms: Whole, Rhythm, Hierarchy, Network*, 16.

16. Frey, "Tugendspiele," 419. As Frey points out, the *tableau vivant* represents the family as "Gemälde" (405).

17. Birgit Jooss, *Lebende Bilder: Körperliche Nachahmungen von Kunstwerken in der Goethezeit* (Berlin: Reimer, 1999), 93. Jooss's monograph contains an extremely useful catalog of *tableau vivant* performances and reviews of these performances between 1760 (the year of the first documented performance of a *tableau vivant* in the theater) and 1820.

18. Frey, "Tugendspiele," 412.

19. Benjamin refers here to R. M. Meyer's comment to this effect. Walter Benjamin, "Goethes Wahlverwandtschaften," *Illuminationen: Ausgewählte Schriften*, vol. 1 (Frankfurt am Main: Suhrkamp, 1955), 103.

20. Cited in Jooss, *Lebende Bilder*, 378.

21. G. E. Lessing, "Laocoön, oder Über die Grenzen der Malerei und Poesie," WB 5.2, 60.

22. Lessing, "Laocoön, oder Über die Grenzen, 81.

23. G. E. Lessing, *Laocoon: An Essay upon the Limits of Painting and Poetry*, trans. Ellen Frothingham (Mineola, NY: Dover, 2005), 59.

24. Catriona MacLeod, *Fugitive Objects: Sculpture and Literature in the German Nineteenth Century* (Evanston, IL: Northwestern University Press, 2014), 35.

25. Hegel, *Aesthetics: Lectures on Fine Art*, vol. 2, 703.

26. This polarity also hinges on the dichotomy color vs. colorlessness—painting is color; sculpture is colorlessness/white. Of course, this distinction became untenable once scholars began to learn that Greek sculpture was generally not white.

27. Hegel, *Aesthetics: Lectures on Fine Art*, vol. 2, 859.

28. Hegel, *Aesthetics: Lectures on Fine Art*, vol. 2, 859.

29. In "Notes on Painting" (1765)—an essay Hegel knew well via Goethe's 1799 translation—Denis Diderot likewise complains about the persistence of allegory in modern painting, what he calls the mixing of "allegory and the real": "The mixture of allegorical and real beings makes history seem like a fairy tale, and, to make myself clear, this flaw disfigures most of Rubens' compositions for me. I can't make any sense of them. What is this figure holding a bird's nest, this Mercury, this rainbow, this zodiac, this Sagittarius doing in a bedroom, around the bed of a woman in labor? Texts should be made to emerge

from the mouths of each of these figures, stating their purpose, as in the old tapestries in our châteaux." See Diderot, *Diderot on Art, Volume I: The Salon of 1765 and Notes on Painting*, 223.

30. Hegel, *Aesthetics: Lectures on Fine Art*, vol. 2, 805.

31. Hegel, *Aesthetics: Lectures on Fine Art*, vol. 1, 518–519.

32. Hegel, *Aesthetics: Lectures on Fine Art*, vol. 1, 527.

33. The resistance to art forms perceived as overly naturalist and material extended to wax figures, which were deemed too material to count as real art. As Birgit Jooss reminds us, Diderot, Schlegel, Herder, and Kant were also dismissive of painted statues. Jooss, *Lebende Bilder*, 249.

34. Benjamin famously states that the novel is not about marriage—in contrast to Hebbel's understanding of the novel as a reflection on marriage and the state. Benjamin, "Goethes Wahlverwandtschaften," 124.

35. Indeed, Hegel gives Goethe's *Elective Affinities* as an example of a "genuine" work of art whose moral reception is contingent: "e.g. for one reader the moral of Goethe's *Elective Affinities* is approval of marriage, while for another reader it is disapproval. . . . In a work of art, as in life, the greater a man's character, the more are different interpretations put on it by different people." Hegel, *Aesthetics: Lectures on Fine Art*, vol. 1, 52.

36. J. Hillis Miller highlights the power of erotic desire in the novel. See Miller, *Ariadne's Thread* (New Haven, CT: Yale University Press, 1992), 207. Tantillo likewise provides a fascinating overview of the moral debates around the novel's representation of marriage and extramarital erotic desire. See, in particular, chapter 1 of Tantillo, *Goethe's Elective Affinities*, 1–45.

37. See the chapter titled "Same-Sex, Nonexclusive, and Adoptive Affinities" in Gustafson, *Goethe's Families of the Heart*, 9–45.

38. The famous passage from Goethe's novel reads: "Diejenigen Naturen, die sich beim Zusammentreffen einander schnell ergreifen und wechselseitig bestimmen, nennen wir verwandt. An den Alkalien und Säuren, die, obgleich einander entgegengesetzt und vielleicht eben deswegen, weil sie einander entgegengesetzt sind, sich am entschiedensten suchen und fassen, sich modifizieren und zusammen einen neuen Körper bilden, ist diese Verwandtschaft auffallend genug." Johann Wolfgang von Goethe, *Die Wahlverwandtschaften*, FA 1.8, 302–303. Page number references for *Die Wahlverwandtschaften* are hereafter provided parenthetically in the text. The translation of the above text is as follows: [Those kinds of substances that rapidly combine and interact when brought together are what we call "related." It is easy to see this relatedness, or "affinity," with alkalis and bases, which, though opposites (and perhaps even because of this), most determinedly seek each other out, combine, modify each other and form through their interaction a new compound.] Johann Wolfgang von Goethe, *Elective Affinities*, in *The Sorrows of Young Werther; Elective Affinities; Novella*, trans. Judith Ryan (New York: Suhrkamp, 1988), 114. All translations of the novel in this chapter not attributed to this edition are mine.

39. Norbert Puszkar sees the dialectic between "Verwandtschaft" and "Wahlverwandtschaft" in the novel as informed by the categories of the natural and the unnatural, a dialectic that cannot be sublated within the work. See Norbert Puszkar, "Verwandtschaft und Wahlverwandtschaft," *Goethe Yearbook* 4 (1988): 164.

40. Hegel, *Elements of the Philosophy of Right*, 215.

41. Goethe, *Elective Affinities*, 233–234.

42. Boyle makes the case that the Captain is the biological father of Otto; see Boyle, "What Really Happens," 309. Puszkar points out that Ottilie is very likely not Charlotte's niece; see Puszkar, "Verwandtschaft und Wahlverwandtschaft," 176.

43. Paul Stöcklein, "Nachwort," afterword to Johann Wolfgang Goethe, *Die Wahlverwandtschaften* (Munich: DTV, 1963), 226.

44. Goethe, *Elective Affinities*, 126.

45. Friedrich Jacobi, "Friedrich Jacobi an Köppen, 12. Jan. 1810." Letter from Jacobi to Köppen, January 12, 1810, in *"Die Wahlverwandtschaften* im Urteil Goethes und seiner Zeitgenossen," in Johann Wolfgang von Goethe, *Romane und Novellen*, ed. Erich Trunz, vol. 6 of *Johann Wolfgang Goethe Werke: Hamburger Ausgabe*, 14 vols. (Munich: Deutscher Taschenbuch Verlag, 1999), 663.

46. See Paul Stöcklein's "Nachwort" for a discussion of these early plans.

47. Benjamin, "Goethes *Wahlverwandtschaften*," 104.

48. Quoted in Jooss, *Lebende Bilder*, 319. Karl August Böttinger's distaste for the *tableau vivant* is likewise based on the form's hybridity and excess materiality. His 1810 review of *Die Wahlverwandtschaften* in the *Allgemeine Literatur-Zeitung* compares the incongruent collision of art forms in a *tableau vivant* performance to baking a Haydn symphony into a pastry: "Da man sich nun zu der Kunst malerische Ideen darzustellen, die lange genug mit todten Farben und Pinseln getrieben ist, nunmehr lebender Menschen bedient; so hoffen wir auch nächstens zu hören, daß die flüchtigen Töne einer Haydnschen Symphonie fixirt, und etwas in eine Pastete gebacken werden, um sie mit der Zunge zu genießen." [Since one now uses living people in order to represent painterly ideas that have long been created with dead colors and brushes; so we hope soon to hear that the fleeting tones of a Haydn symphony have been fixed and for instance baked into a pastry so that one can enjoy them with the tongue.] Quoted in Jooss, *Lebende Bilder*, 296. On this topic of the *tableau vivant* and hybridity, see also Kerstin Gram Holmström, *Monodrama, Attitudes, Tableaux Vivants* (Stockholm: Almqvist and Wiksell, 1967), 216–217.

49. See Giuliana Bruno, *Surface: Matters of Aesthetics, Materiality, and Media* (Chicago: University of Chicago Press, 2014). Bruno posits a link between intermediality and materiality: "aesthetic encounters are actually 'mediated' on the surface and . . . such mediated encounters engage forms of projection, transmission, and transmutation" (3).

50. Brigitte Peucker discusses Goethe's prohibition on exact copies as a reminder of death. See Brigitte Peucker, "The Material Image in Goethe's *Wahlverwandtschaften*," *The Germanic Review* 74, no. 3 (1999): 202. Walter Benjamin also refers to Goethe's fear of death, asserting that he never came near the deathbed of his wife, Christiane. See Benjamin, "Goethes *Wahlverwandtschaften*," 88.

51. Johanna Schopenhauer, *Gabriele: Ein Roman in drei Teilen* (Berlin: Berliner Ausgabe, 2015), 60.

52. Published in the *Journal für Literatur, Kunst, Luxus und Mode*. Cited in Jooss, *Lebende Bilder*, 335–336.

53. Martin Meisel, *Realizations: Narrative, Pictorial, and Theatrical Arts in Nineteenth-Century England* (Princeton, NJ: Princeton University Press, 1983), 47.

54. In Johanna Schopenhauer's *Gabriele*, the curtain falls and is raised three times on the characters who perform a *tableau vivant* of Cleopatra. Schopenhauer, *Gabriele*, 34.

55. A review of the February 1813 *tableau vivant* performances at the Weimar court published in the *Journal für Luxus, Mode und Gegenstände der Kunst* likewise mentions that performances are repeated so that spectators can take in both the whole and the parts of the representation. Jooss, *Lebende Bilder*, 320.

56. Birgit Jooss, "Lebende Bilder als Charakterbeschreibungen in Goethes Roman *Die Wahlverwandtschaften*," in *Erzählen und Wissen: Paradigmen und Aporien ihrer Inszenierung in Goethes "Wahlverwandtschaften"*, ed. Gabriele Brandstetter (Freiburg im Breisgau: Rombach, 2003), 132. See also Peucker, who links the wax figure in Goethe's "Der Sammler und die Seinigen" to Goethe's fear of death. Peucker, "The Material Image," 196.

57. Meisel, *Realizations*, 29.

58. See Erich Trunz, "Die Kupferstiche zu den 'Lebenden Bildern' in den *Wahlverwandtschaften*," in *Weimarer Goethe-Studien* (Weimar: Böhlau, 1980). Truntz provides reproductions of the etchings as well as a detailed overview of *tableau vivant* performances at the Weimar court (212–214).

59. Trunz, "Die Kupferstiche," 215–217.

60. Hammer-Tugendhat, *The Visible and the Invisible*, 288.

61. Trunz, "Die Kupferstiche," 215.

62. Jooss points to the discourse of "real feeling" on the part of spectators who viewed Belisarius. See Jooss, *Lebende Bilder*, 199.

63. For a critical discussion of attitude performances, see Gabrielle Bersier, "'Hamiltonian-Hendelian' Mimoplastics and Tableau of the Underworld: The Visual Aesthetics of Goethe's 1815 *Proserpina* Production," *Goethe Yearbook* 22 (2016): 171–194. See also Jooss, who shows that young girls were taught to perform "Attitüden" as part of their education for acquiring "natural" femininity." Jooss, *Lebende Bilder*, 98.

64. As Dagmar von Hoff and Helga Meise point out, attitude performances were overcoded, pointing away from a representation of interiority. See Dagmar von Hoff and Helga Meise, "*Tableaux vivants*—Die Kunst—und Kultform der Attitüden und lebenden Bilder," in *Weiblichkeit und Tod in der Literatur*, ed. Renate Berger and Inge Stephan (Cologne: Böhlau, 1987), 78.

65. See Jooss, *Lebende Bilder*, 100. See also Holmström's discussion of performances of attitudes in the late eighteenth century, in Holmström, *Monodrama*, 110–209.

66. Goethe, *Elective Affinities*, 189.

67. For a contextualization and close analysis of Poussin's painting, see Jonathan Unglaub, "'Esther before Ahasuerus': Beauty, Majesty, Bondage," *The Art Bulletin* 85, no. 1 (2003): 114–136.

68. Eve Kosofsky Sedgwick, *Epistemology of the Closet* (Berkeley: University of California Press, 1990), 67. D. A. Miller observes that "the phenomenon of the 'open secret' does not, as one might think, bring about the collapse of those binarisms and their ideological effects, but rather attests to their fantasmatic recovery." See D. A. Miller, "Secret Subjects, Open Secrets," *The Novel and the Police* (Berkeley: University of California Press, 1989), 207.

69. The case of Esther, as Sedgwick points out, is both parallel and tangential to that of a queer "open secret," insofar as Esther's secret, as devastating as it is, need not be revealed repeatedly. Sedgewick, *Epistemology*, 78–83.

70. Johann Wolfgang von Goethe, "Goethe an Karl Friedrich Zelter," FA 1.8, 979. A few months later, on August 26, 1809, Goethe returns to the metaphor of the open

secret via the veil in another letter to Zelter about his novel: "Ich bin überzeugt, daß Sie der durchsichtige und undurchsichtige Schleier nicht verhindern wird bis auf die eigentlich intentionierte Gestalt hineinzusehen" [I am convinced that the transparent and opaque veil will not stop you from seeing into the truly intended form]. Goethe, FA 1.8, 980.

71. Benjamin, "Goethes *Wahlverwandtschaften*," 83.

72. Walter Benjamin, "Goethe's *Elective Affinities*," in *Selected Writings I: 1913–1926*, trans. Stanley Corngold (Cambridge, MA: Harvard University Press, 2004), 335.

73. Benjamin, "Goethe's *Elective Affinities*," 351.

74. Jooss, *Lebende Bilder*, 126. A number of literary works from the nineteenth century depict *tableau vivant* scenes: George Eliot's *Daniel Deronda* (1876), Fanny Lewald's *Jenny* (1842), E.T.A. Hoffmann's "Nachricht von den neuesten Schicksalen des Hundes Berganza" (1814), and Johanna Schopenhauer's *Gabriele* (1819).

75. Fürst Metternich is even purported to have taken part in *tableaux vivants*, not only as a spectator but also as a performer. See Jooss, *Lebende Bilder*, 130.

76. The *Oxford English Dictionary* locates the etymology of *tableau vivant* in "1799 or earlier."

77. Jooss, *Lebende Bilder*, 155.

78. Jooss, *Lebende Bilder*, 157.

79. Jooss, *Lebende Bilder*, 169.

80. The most popular motifs for *tableaux vivants* in the *Goethezeit* were *Achilles unter den Töchtern des Lykomedes*, *Die väterliche Ermahnung*, *Die Mutter der Gracchen*, *Esther vor Ahasuerus*, *Die heilige Cäcilia*, and *Der geblendete Belisarius*. Jooss, *Lebende Bilder*, 204.

81. Jooss, *Lebende Bilder*, 352.

82. Edmund Wallner, *Eintausend Sujets zu lebenden Bildern* (Erfurt: Bartholomäus, 1876–1881), 147.

83. The example from the Florence performance of 1819 is Andrea del Sarto's self-portrait with his wife that served as a secondary piece. See Jooss, *Lebende Bilder*, 377–378. In this sense, the *tableaux vivants* sometimes functioned like a triptych. At the Vienna Congress, five *tableaux vivants* were simultaneously performed in the same room. Jooss, *Lebende Bilder*, 219.

84. Letter from Julie von Egloffstein to her mother Henriette, February 4, 1817, cited in Jooss, *Lebende Bilder*, 355.

85. A critic of the *tableau vivant* performance on the first Easter day at the Leipzig theater in 1818 similarly calls it "an artistic ragout of declamation, music and picture"; cited in Jooss, *Lebende Bilder*, 365.

86. Johann Wolfgang von Goethe, "Einleitung in die Propyläen," FA 1.18, 468.

87. Goethe, *Die Wahverwandtschaften*, 302.

88. See Brude-Firnau, "Lebende Bilder," 410. This performance took place in the Weimar court on February 16, 1813, and was based on Jacques-Louis David's 1781 "Belisarius Begging for Alms." Jooss, *Lebende Bilder*, 314 and 317. David's paintings self-consciously engaged in a dialectical conversation between painting and theater at the time. See Jooss, *Lebende Bilder*, 187.

89. Jooss, *Lebende Bilder*, 367.

90. *Proserpina* was first published as an oddly disjointed insert within the 1777 comedic play *Triumph der Empfindsamkeit*.

91. See Holmström, *Monodrama*, 88–92; see also Bersier, who points to Goethe's "continued allegiance to the performance aesthetics." Bersier, "'Hamiltonian-Hendelian,'" 181.

92. Johann Wolfgang von Goethe, *Proserpina: Melodram von Goethe, Musik von Eberwein*, FA 1.19, 715.

93. Goethe, *Proserpina*, 712. Jooss also mentions Goethe's creation of an "Arcadia" *tableau vivant* for the Weimar court that was a product of his own imagination. Jooss, *Lebende Bilder*, 220.

94. Goethe's enthusiasm about the "Vollendung" [accomplishment] of the final *tableau vivant* of the *Proserpina* performance is mirrored in Julie von Egloffstein's letter to her mother detailing her experience as a performer in the role of "die Poesie" in Goethe's *tableaux vivants* for the court festival on the birthday of the grand duke Prinz Carl Friedrich von Sachsen-Weimar-Eisenach on February 2, 1817, at the Weimar court. During a draping crisis "the old Goethe had pity with poor 'Poesie' . . . and pulled and tugged and plucked for so long on my coat until he finally—delighted over his own work—cried out, 'lovely, lovely—beautiful' and assured me that it was truly unfortunate that I couldn't see and draw myself." Jooss, *Lebende Bilder*, 355. The image of the "old Goethe" fussing with Julie's dress in order to create the impression he desires provides a picture of the immense pleasure Goethe took in the art form of the *tableau vivant*.

95. Goethe, "Regeln für Schauspieler," FA 1.18, 881.

96. Goethe, "Regeln für Schauspieler," 880.

97. Christiane Hertel highlights class shifts ("from the landed gentry and educated middle class . . . to the urban middle class") that correspond to the shift from an interest in historical paintings of an "elevated style" to Dutch genre painting. See Christiane Hertel, "Centennials, Sculptures, and *Tableaux Vivants* in the Nineteenth-Century Schiller Cult," *Yearbook of German-American Studies* 38 (2003): 167.

98. Peter Demetz, "Defenses of Dutch Painting and the Theory of Realism," *Comparative Literature* 15, no. 2 (1963): 103.

99. Demetz, "Defenses of Dutch Painting," 114.

100. See Christiane Hertel's discussion of Hegel's reception of the Dutch painters in *Vermeer: Reception and Interpretation* (Cambridge, UK: Cambridge University Press, 1996), 22–30.

101. Hegel, *Vorlesungen über die Ästhetik II*, 26–27.

102. Hegel, *Vorlesungen über die Ästhetik II*, 129.

103. Along these lines, Michael Fried interprets this scene in Goethe's novel as showing us that "there can be no such thing as an absolutely antitheatrical work of art." Michael Fried, *Absorption and Theatricality: Painting and Beholder in the Age of Diderot* (Chicago: University of Chicago Press, 1980), 173.

104. According to Friedrich Kittler, for example, Luciane stands for feudal representation and Ottilie stands for bourgeois interiority. See Friedrich A. Kittler, "Ottilie Hauptmann," in *Goethes* Wahlverwandtschaften: *Kritische Modelle und Diskursanalysen zum Mythos Literatur*, ed. Norbert W. Bolz (Hildesheim: Gerstenberg, 1981), 263. Wolf Kittler makes the interesting argument that Ottilie and the Hauptmann represent the future as "civil servant" and "mother" or, in psychoanalytic terms, "compulsive neurotic" and "hysteric." See Wolf Kittler, "Goethe's *Wahlverwandtschaften*: Soziale Verhältnisse symbolisch dargestellt," in *Goethes* Wahlverwandtschaften, 254–255.

105. Jane Brown demonstrates that in *Die Wahlverwandtschaften*, Goethe reverses allegory, revealing both the surface and double underneath. See Jane K. Brown, *Goethe's Allegories of Identity* (Philadelphia: University of Pennsylvania Press, 2014), 170.

106. William J. Lillyman sees this repeated gesture as Ottilie's prayer, a sign of her monasticism. See William J. Lillyman, "'Tableau Vivant,' and Romanticism: Ottilie in Goethe's *Die Wahlverwandtschaften*," *Journal of English and Germanic Philology* 81 no. 3 (1982): 356. See also Jochen Hörisch, who argues that Ottilie and Eduard represent a pre-modern mode of socialization, as represented in the "Abendmahl," in Jochen Hörisch, "Die Dekonstruktion der Sprache und der Advent neuer Medien in Goethes *Wahlver-wandtschaften*," *Merkur* 52, no. 9 (1998): 826–839.

107. Goethe, *Elective Affinities*, 119.

108. Goethe, *Elective Affinities*, 251.

109. Giorgio Agamben, "Notes on Gesture," in *Means without Ends: Notes on Politics*, trans. Vincenzo Binetti and Cesare Casarino (Minneapolis: University of Minnesota Press, 2000), 52.

110. A similar use of gesture as immediately visible sign that conveys unambiguous meaning is used by Ottilie in part 1, chapter 8, when she first arrives at the castle: "Charlotte ging ihr entgegen; das liebe Kind eilte sich ihr zu nähern, warf sich ihr zu Füßen und umfaßte ihre Kniee" (311) [Charlotte walked up to her; the dear child hurried to come near her, threw herself at Charlotte's feet and embraced her knees]. But Charlotte pulls her up and hugs her. The gestural language Ottilie uses is ceremonial, and Charlotte interrupts it with a gesture indicating intimacy.

111. Goethe, *Elective Affinities*, 190.

112. Goethe, *Elective Affinities*, 219.

113. Goethe, *Elective Affinities*, 197.

114. Norbert Miller points to the anticipatory function of *tableaux vivants*, one that surprisingly dovetails with the narrative goals of the novel. See Norbert Miller, "Mutmaßungen über lebende Bilder: Attitüde und *tableau vivant* als Anschauungsformen des 19. Jahrhunderts," in *Das Triviale in Literatur, Musik und Bildender Kunst*, ed. Helga de la Motte-Haber (Frankfurt: Vittorio Klostermann, 1972), 113.

115. Rita Lennartz suggests that Goethe might be offering a critique of Diderot's "natural truth" here, as Diderot cautions against actors turning their backs to the audience in the tableau. Rita Lennartz, "'Von Angesicht zu Angesicht': Lebende Bilder und tote Buchstaben in Goethes *Wahlverwandtschaften*," in *Bildersturm und Bilderflut um 1800: Zur schwierigen Anschaulichkeit der Moderne*, ed. Helmut J. Schneider, Ralf Simon, and Thomas Wirtz (Bielefeld: Aisthesis, 2001), 150.

116. The almost hysterical reaction of the impatient "Vogel" [clown] is mirrored in E.T.A. Hoffmann's "Nachricht von den neuesten Schicksalen des Hundes Berganza" [News of the Newest Fates of the Dog Berganza] of 1814, in which a *tableau vivant* performance of Rafael's "Cecilia" unleashes hysteria in the audience. E.T.A. Hoffmann, "Nachricht von den neuesten Schicksalen des Hundes Berganza," in *Fantasiestücke in Callot's Manier. Werke* 1814, vol 2.1 (Frankfurt am Main: Surhkamp, 1993), 150.

117. See Peter McIsaac, "Rethinking *Tableaux Vivants* and Triviality in the Writings of Johann Wolfgang von Goethe, Johanna Schopenhauer, and Fanny Lewald," *Monatshefte* 99, no. 2 (2007): 152–176.

118. See Sabine Folie and Michael Glasmeier, "Atmende Bilder: Tableau vivant und Attitüde zwischen 'Wirklichkeit und Imagination,'" in *Tableaux Vivants: Lebende Bilder und Attitüden in Fotografie, Film und Video* (exhibition catalogue) (Vienna: Kunsthalle Wien, 2002), 15–16.

119. "Zum Denken gehört nicht nur die Bewegung der Gedanken sondern ebenso ihre Stillstellung" [Not only movement of thoughts but also their arrest is part of thinking]: Walter Benjamin, "Über den Begriff der Geschichte," in *Illuminationen: Ausgewählte Schriften I* (Frankfurt am Main: Suhrkamp, 1955), 260.

120. In temporal terms, the *tableau vivant* enacts transitoriness, something that frustrates Fräulein Silberhain in Johanna Schopenhauer's *Gabriele*: "'Ich begreife nicht, wie man um so nichtigen Zweck seine Identität zu opfern vermag,' fuhr Fräulein Silberhain in ihrer Rede fort, 'wie kann ein in seinen tiefsten Tiefen vom Höchsten erfülltes Gemüth so ganz diese vergessen und dem prunkenden Schimmer irdischer Vergänglichkeit huldigen!'" ["I don't understand how one can sacrifice one's identity for such a negligible goal," continued Fräulein Silberhain in her lecture, "how can a mind that is filled with the highest ideas in its deepest depth forget this so completely and pay homage to the false shimmer of earthly transitoriness!"] Schopenhauer, *Gabriele*, 58.

121. Manfred Frey, *Tugendspiele*, 410. See also Daniel Wiegland, *Gebannte Bewegung: Tableaux vivants und früher Film in der Kultur der Moderne* (Marburg: Schüren, 2016). Wiegland argues that the *tableau vivant* holds a tension between a disciplinary action ("festsetzen") and a revolutionary effect ("umkippen").

122. For Foucault, "the law" constructs both conscience and desire, and Judith Butler shows us that "reality is fabricated as an interior essence . . . ; acts and gestures, articulated and enacted desires create the illusion of an interior and organizing gender core, an illusion discursively maintained for the purposes of the regulation of sexuality within the obligatory frame of reproductive heterosexuality. The displacement of a political and discursive origin of gender identity onto a psychological 'core' precludes an analysis of the political constitution of the gendered subject and its fabricated notions about the ineffable interiority of its sex or of its true identity." Judith Butler, *Gender Trouble: Feminism and the Subversion of Identity* (New York: Routledge, 1990), 136.

123. See Jack Halberstam, *The Queer Art of Failure* (Durham, NC: Duke University Press, 2011).

124. Nobert Puszkar suggests that in laying Eduard and Ottilie to rest together, Charlotte tries to stabilize the world by transforming "Wahlverwandtschaft" into "Verwandtschaft." But as he rightly points out, there is no future to this "family." See Puszkar, "Verwandtschaft und Wahlverwandtschaft," 180.

125. An additional scene in which the semiotics of the *tableau* slows the narrative and potentially flattens interiority is presented during Charlotte's birthday celebrations in part 1, chapter 9. The group is invited to take a walk through the village, and the Captain has constructed groupings of villagers in a *tableau* that pictures domesticity as spectacle:

> "Dort hatten sich, auf des Hauptmanns Veranlassung, die Bewohner vor ihren Häusern versammelt; sie standen nicht in Reihen, sondern Familienweise natürlich gruppiert, teils wie es der Abend forderte beschäftigt, teils auf neuen Bänken ausruhend. Es ward ihnen zur angenehmen Pflicht gemacht,

wenigstens jeden Sonntag und Festtag, diese Reinlichkeit, diese Ordnung zu erneuen." (335)

[The Captain had ordered the inhabitants to gather in front of their houses; they were standing, now in rows, but grouped naturally in families, partly occupied with their evening's work, partly resting on the new benches. It had been made their pleasant duty to take up this neat and orderly pose at least on Sundays and holidays.] (Goethe, *Elective Affinities*, 135–136)

The tension between the "natural" familial groupings and the "Ordnung" of this choreographed picture highlights yet again the *tableau vivant*'s tendency to bring to the fore the ways in which materiality and interiority are conceived as conceptually oppositional.

Concluding Reflections

1. See Patricia White, who shows how the pleasure of viewing and reading retroactively has the potential to open alternative futures, in *Uninvited: Classical Hollywood Cinema and Lesbian Representability* (Bloomington: Indiana University Press, 1999).

2. A prime example of this slippage is a press conference with Chancellor Angela Merkel on November 2, 2020, in which she articulated the coronavirus pandemic gathering rules as follows: "Der Aufenthalt im öffentlichen Raum ist beschränkt auf zwei *Hausstände*. Sollten diese *Haushalte* größer sein als je fünf Personen in einer *Familie*, dann ist das noch einmal auf maximal zehn Personen beschränkt. Das eigentlich Wichtige sind aber die zwei *Hausstände*, die zwei *Haushalte*." [The shared habitation in a public space is reduced to two households (*Hausstände*). If these households (*Haushalte*) are larger than five people per family, then capacity is reduced to a maximum of ten people. The actually important thing is the two households (*Hausstände*), the two housholds (*Haushalte*).] The flurry of terms for family and households is dizzying. Merkel utilizes "Hausstand" to indicate a household, shifts to "Haushalt," and then falls back to the more comfortable term "Familie," only to realize her slip and repeat each of the alternative terms back-to-back as a bolstering device ("die zwei Hausstände, die zwei Haushalte"). "Familie" will not go away, no matter how ill-defined or imprecise its use. Indeed, Merkel cannot resist using "Kernfamilie" in her discussion about pandemic gathering guidelines for New Year's Eve 2020: "Dass es die großen, rauschenden Silvesterpartys geben wird, glaube ich nicht, aber ich glaube, dass sich *Kernfamilien, wie man so schön sagt,* auch besuchen können, vielleicht mit Vorsichtsmaßnahmen" (my italics). [I don't believe that there will be the big ecstatic New Year's parties, but I believe that nuclear families, in a manner of speaking, can visit, maybe with precautions.] Despite the plethora of alternative terms, it is seemingly not possible to speak around the vaguely defined yet crystal clear concept of the nuclear family. "Pressekonferenz von Bundeskanzlerin Merkel zur Corona-Pandemie (Berlin, 2. November 2020)," Die Bundesregierung, accessed May 15, 2021, https://www.bundesregierung .de/breg-de/suche/pressekonferenz-von-bundeskanzlerin-merkel-zur-corona-pandemie -1807048; my italics.

3. In 2020, a lesbian and gay organization ("Lesben- und Schwulenverband") articulated this preference as follows: "The rules of exception for limiting personal contacts

should not only refer to the narrowest family circle, so that no one has to celebrate alone, even if they have broken ties with their family. Other important people should be allowed, too. One should follow the rules in Berlin. There a maximum of five people from any number of households plus children are allowed to meet," in "Lesben- und Schwulenverband zu Corona-Lockerungen an Weihnachten," *Deutschlandfunk*, accessed December 17, 2020, https://www.deutschlandfunk.de/covid-19-lesben-und-schwulenverband-corona -lockerungen-an.1939.de.html?drn:news_id=1206296.

BIBLIOGRAPHY

Agamben, Giorgio. "Notes on Gesture." In *Means without Ends: Notes on Politics*, translated by Vincenzo Binetti and Cesare Casarino, 49–59. Minneapolis: University of Minnesota Press, 2000.

Altman, Janet G. *Epistolarity: Approaches to a Form*. Columbus: Ohio State University Press, 1982.

Anderegg, Johannes. *Schreibe mir oft! Das Medium Brief von 1750–1830*. Göttingen: Wallstein, 2001.

Anderson, Mark M. "Die Aufgabe der Familie/das Ende der Moderne: Eine kleine Geschichte des Familienromans." In *Deutsche Familienromane: Literarische Genealogien und internationaler Kontext*, edited by Simone Costagli and Matteo Galli, 23–46. Munich: Fink, 2010.

Angress, Ruth K. "The Generations in *Emilia Galotti*." *Germanic Review* 43 (1968): 15–23.

Applegate, Celia. *A Nation of Provincials: The German Idea of Heimat*. Berkeley: University of California Press, 1990.

Apter, Emily, and Elaine Freedgood. "Afterword." *Representations* 108, no. 1 (2009): 139–146.

Aristotle. *The Poetics*. Translated by Preston H. Epps. Chapel Hill: University of North Carolina Press, 1942.

Arnds, Peter. "Sophie von La Roche's *Geschichte des Fräuleins von Sternheim* as an Answer to Samuel Richardson's *Clarissa*." *Lessing Yearbook* 29 (1997): 87–105.

Atkins, Stuart. "*Wilhelm Meisters Lehrjahre*: Novel or Romance?" in *Essays on Goethe*, edited by Jane K. Brown and Thomas P. Saine, 130–137. Columbia, SC: Camden House, 1995.

Auerbach, Erich. *Mimesis: Dargestellte Wirklichkeit in der abendländischen Literatur*. Bern: Francke, 1946.

———. *Mimesis: The Representation of Reality in Western Literature*. Translated by Willard R. Trask. Princeton, NJ: Princeton University Press, 1953.

Bachmann, Ingeborg. *Wir müssen wahre Sätze finden: Gespräche und Interviews*. Munich: Piper, 1983.

Baldwin, Claire. *The Emergence of the Modern German Novel: Christoph Martin Wieland, Sophie von La Roche, and Maria Anna Sagar*. Columbia, SC: Camden House, 2002.

Baldyga, Natalya. "Corporeal Eloquence and Sensate Cognition: G. E. Lessing, Acting Theory, and Properly Feeling Bodies in Eighteenth-Century Germany." *Theatre Survey* 58, no. 2 (2017): 161–185.

Balibar, Étienne. "Class Racism." In *Race, Nation, Class: Ambiguous Identities*, 204–217. London: Verso, 1991.

Barker, Emma. "Painting and Reform in Eighteenth-Century France: Greuze's *L'Accordée de Village*." *Oxford Art Journal* 20, no. 2. (1997): 42–52.

Barner, Wilfried. "'Beredte Empfindungen,' Über die geschichtliche Position der Brieflehre Gellerts." In *Aus der anmuthigen Gelehrsamkeit.' Tübingener Studien zum 18. Jahrhundert. Dieter Geyer zum 60. Geburtstag*, edited by Eberhard Müller, 7–23. Tübingen: Attempto, 1988.

———. "'Die Verschiedenheit unserer Naturen': Zu Goethes und Schillers Briefwechsel über *Wilhelm Meisters Lehrjahre*." In *Unser Commercium: Goethes und Schillers Literaturpolitik*, edited by Wilfried Barner, Eberhard Lämmert, and Norbert Oellers, 379–404. Stuttgart: Cotta, 1984.

Barry, Thomas F. "Love and the Politics of Paternalism: Images of the Father in Schiller's *Kabale und Liebe*." *Colloquia Germanica* 22 (1989): 21–37.

Barthes, Roland. "Diderot, Brecht, Eisenstein." In *Image, Music, Text*, translated by Stephen Heath, 69–79. New York: Hill and Wang, 1977.

Bass, Laura R. *The Drama of the Portrait: Theater and Visual Culture in Early Modern Spain*. University Park, PA: Penn State University Press, 2008.

Beck, Ulrich. "Der Konflikt der zwei Modernen." In *Die Modernisierung moderner Gesellschaften: Verhandlungen des 25. Deutschen Soziologentages in Frankfurt am Main 1990*, edited by Wolfgang Zapf, 40–53. Frankfurt: Campus, 1991.

Becker-Cantarino, Barbara. "Freundschaftsutopie: Die Fiktionen der Sophie La Roche." In *Untersuchungen zum Roman von Frauen um 1800*, edited by Helga Gallas and Magdalene Heuser, 92–113. Tübingen: Niemeyer, 1990.

———. Nachwort to *Die Geschichte des Fräuleins von Sternheim*, by Sophie von La Roche, edited by Barbara Becker-Cantarino, 381–415. Stuttgart: Reclam, 1983.

———. "Patriarchy and German Enlightenment Discourse." In *Impure Reason: Dialectic of Enlightenment in Germany*, edited by W. Daniel Wilson and Robert C. Holub, 48–65. Detroit, MI: Wayne State University Press, 1993.

———. "Sophie La Roche, der Beginn der 'Frauenliteratur' und der weiblichen Tradition." In *Der lange Weg zur Mündigkeit*, 278–302. Stuttgart: Metzler, 1987.

———. "Vom 'Ganzen Haus' zur Familienidylle: Haushalt als Mikrokosmos in der Literatur der frühen Neuzeit und seine spätere Sentimentalisierung." *Daphnis: Zeitschrift für mittlere deutsche Literatur* 15, nos. 2–3 (1986): 509–534.

———. "'Die wärmste Liebe zu unsrer literarischen Ehe': Friedrich Schlegels *Lucinde* und Dorothea Veits *Florentin*." In *Bi-Textualität: Inszenierungen des Paares: Ein Buch für Ina Schabert*, edited by Annegret Heitmann, 131–141. Berlin: Erich Schmidt, 2001.

Beebee, Thomas O. *Clarissa on the Continent: Translation and Seduction*. State College, PA: Penn State University Press, 1990.

———. *Epistolary Fiction in Europe, 1500–1850*. Cambridge, UK: Cambridge University Press, 1999.

Benjamin, Jessica. "The End of Internalization: Adorno's Social Psychology." *Telos* 32 (1977): 42–64.

Benjamin, Walter. "Goethe's *Elective Affinities*." In *Selected Writings I: 1913–1926*, translated by Stanley Corngold. Cambridge, MA: Harvard University Press, 2004.

————. "Goethes Wahlverwandtschaften." In *Illuminationen: Ausgewählte Schriften*. Vol. 1, 63–136. Frankfurt am Main: Suhrkamp, 1955.

————. "Über den Begriff der Geschichte." In *Illuminationen: Ausgewählte Schriften*. Vol. 1, 251–262. Frankfurt am Main: Suhrkamp, 1955.

————. *Versuche über Brecht*. Edited by Rolf Tiedemann. Frankfurt am Main: Suhrkamp, 1967.

Berger, Willy R. "Das Tableau: Rührende Schluß-Szenen im Drama." *Arcadia* 24, no. 2 (1989): 131–147.

Berman, Nina. *German Literature of the Middle East: Discourses and Practices, 1000–1989*. Ann Arbor: University of Michigan Press, 2013.

Bersier, Gabrielle. "'Hamiltonian-Hendelian' Mimoplastics and Tableau of the Underworld: The Visual Aesthetics of Goethe's 1815 *Proserpina* Production." *Goethe Yearbook* 22 (2016): 171–194.

Best, Stephen, and Sharon Marcus. "Surface Reading: An Introduction." *Representations* 108, no. 1 (2009): 1–21.

Borkowski, Jan. "'Wohin unsre Seelenkräfte uns verleiten können.' Ein Versuch, Lessings *Emilia Galotti* neu zu kontextualisieren." *Text und Kontext* 39, no. 1 (2017): 85–114.

Bovenschen, Silvia. *Die imaginierte Weiblichkeit: Exemplarische Untersuchungen ʒu kulturge-schichtlichen und literarischen Präsentationsformen des Weiblichen*. Frankfurt am Main: Suhrkamp, 1979.

Boyle, Nicholas. "What Really Happens in *Die Wahlverwandtschaften*." *The German Quarterly* 89, no. 3 (2016): 298–312.

Braun, Manuel. "Tiefe oder Oberfläche? Zur Lektüre der Schriften des Christian Thomasius über Polygamie und Konkubinat." *Internationales Archiv für Soʒialgeschichte der deutschen Literatur* 30, no. 1 (2005): 28–54.

Brewster, Ben, and Lea Jacobs. *Theater to Cinema: Stage Pictorialism and the Early Feature Film*. Oxford: Oxford University Press, 1997.

Broszeit-Rieger, Ingrid. "Transgressions of Gender and Generation in the Families of Goethe's *Meister*." In *Romantic Border Crossings*, edited by Jeffrey Cass and Larry Peer, 75–85. Burlington, VT: Ashgate, 2008.

Brown, Jane K. "Goethe, Rousseau, the Novel, and the Origins of Psychoanalysis." *Goethe Yearbook* 12 (2004): 111–128.

————. *Goethe's Allegories of Identity*. Philadelphia: University of Pennsylvania Press, 2014.

————. *The Persistence of Allegory: Drama and Neoclassicism from Shakespeare to Wagner*. Philadelphia: University of Pennsylvania Press, 2007.

Brude-Firnau, Gertrude. "Lebende Bilder in den *Wahlverwandtschaften*: Goethes *Journal intime* vom Oktober 1806." *Euphorion* 74 (1980): 403–416.

Brüggemann, Susanne. *Tableau oder Handlung? Zur Dramaturgie Diderots und Lessings*. Würzburg: Königshausen & Neumann, 2017.

Brunner, Otto. "Das 'ganze' Haus und die alteuropäische Ökonomik." In *Neue Wege der Soʒialgeschichte*, 33–61. Göttingen: Vandenhoeck & Ruprecht, 1956.

Bruno, Giuliana. *Surface: Matters of Aesthetics, Materiality, and Media*. Chicago: University of Chicago Press, 2014.

Bunzel, Wolfgang. "Gellerts Roman *Das Leben der schwedischen Gräfin von G****. Erzählstruktur und Wirkungsabsicht." *Wirkendes Wort* 45, no. 3 (1995): 377–395.

Butler, Judith. *Antigone's Claim: Kinship between Life and Death.* New York: Columbia University Press, 2000.

————. *Gender Trouble: Feminism and the Subversion of Identity.* New York: Routledge, 1990.

————. "Is Kinship Always Already Heterosexual?" In *Undoing Gender*, 102–131. New York: Routledge, 2004.

Caplan, Jay. *Framed Narratives: Diderot's Genealogy of the Beholder.* Minneapolis: University of Minnesota Press, 1985.

Castelvecchi, Stefano. *Sentimental Opera: Questions of Genre in the Age of the Bourgeois Drama.* Cambridge, UK: Cambridge University Press, 2013.

Cerf, Steven R. *"Miss Sara Sampson* and *Clarissa*: The Use of Epistolary Devices in Lessing's Drama." In *Theatrum Mundi: Essays on German Drama and German Literature, Dedicated to Harold Lenz on His Seventieth Birthday, September 11, 1978*, edited by Edward Haymes, 22–30. Munich: Wilhelm Fink, 1980.

Coleridge, Samuel Taylor. "Lectures on Shakespeare" and "Recapitulation, and Summary of the Characteristics of Shakespeare's Dramas." In *Essays and Lectures on Shakespeare and Some Other Old Poets and Dramatists.* London: Everyman, 1907.

Cooper, Anthony Ashley, Earl of Shaftesbury. *Second Characters, or The Language of Forms.* Edited by Benjamin Rand. New York: Greenwood Press, 1969.

Crane, Mary Thomas. "Surface, Depth, and the Spatial Imaginary: A Cognitive Reading of *The Political Unconscious." Representations* 108, no. 1 (2009): 76–97.

Curran, Andrew S. *Diderot and the Art of Thinking Freely.* New York: Other Press, 2019.

Dabhoiwala, Faramerz. *The Origins of Sex: A History of the First Sexual Revolution.* New York: Oxford University Press, 2012.

Daub, Adrian. *The Dynastic Imagination: Family and Modernity in Nineteenth-Century Germany.* Chicago: University of Chicago Press, 2021.

Daub, Adrian, and Michael Thomas Taylor. "Introduction: Family Politics." *Republics of Letters: A Journal for the Study of Knowledge, Politics, and the Arts* 3, no. 2 (2013): 1–7.

Davidoff, Leonore. *Thicker than Water: Siblings and Their Relations, 1780–1920.* Oxford: Oxford University Press, 2012.

Degner, Uta. "Interessendramen: Zur Rivalität von Ökonomie, Moral und Ästhetik bei Friedrich Schiller und 'Intertexten' von Richard Glover und George Lillo." In *Gastlichkeit und Ökonomie: Wirtschaften im deutschen und englischen Drama des 18. Jahrhunderts*, edited by Sigrid Nieberle and Claudia Nitschke, 223–245. Berlin: De Gruyter, 2014.

Deleuze, Gilles. *Cinema 1: The Movement-Image.* Translated by Hugh Tomlinson and Barbara Habberjam. Minneapolis: University of Minnesota Press, 1986.

Deleuze, Gilles, and Félix Guattari. *A Thousand Plateaus: Capitalism and Schizophrenia.* Translated by Brian Massumi. Minneapolis: University of Minnesota Press, 1987.

————. *Anti-Oedipus: Capitalism and Schizophrenia.* Translated by Robert Hurley, Mark Seem, and Helen R. Lane. Minneapolis: University of Minnesota Press, 1983.

de Man, Paul. "The Rhetoric of Temporality." In *Blindness and Insight: Essays in the Rhetoric of Contemporary Criticism*, translated by Wlad Godzich. Minneapolis: University of Minnesota Press, 1971.

Demetz, Peter. "Defenses of Dutch Painting and the Theory of Realism." *Comparative Literature* 15, no. 2 (1963): 97–115.

Derrida, Jacques. "The Law of Genre." Translated by Avital Ronell. *Critical Inquiry* 7, no. 1 (1980): 55–81.

Deutschlandfunk. "Lesben- und Schwulenverband zu Corona-Lockerungen an Weihnachten." Accessed December 17, 2020. https://www.deutschlandfunk.de/covid-19 -lesben-und-schwulenverband-corona-lockerungen-an.1939.de.html?drn:news_id =1206296.

Diderot, Denis. *Diderot on Art, Volume I:* The Salon of 1765 *and* Notes on Painting. Translated and edited by John Goodman. New Haven, CT: Yale University Press, 1995.

———. *Der Hausvater*. In *Das Theater des Herrn Diderot*, translated by G. E. Lessing, in *Werke 1760–1766*. Vol. 5.1 of *Gotthold Ephraim Lessing: Werke und Briefe*. 12 vols. Frankfurt am Main: Deutscher Klassiker Verlag, 1990.

———. "In Praise of Richardson." In *Selected Writings on Art and Literature*, translated by Geoffrey Bremner, 82–97. London: Penguin, 1994.

———. *Der natürliche Sohn*. In Lessing, *Das Theater des Herrn Diderot*. Stuttgart: Reclam, 1986.

———. *On Art and Artists: An Anthology of Diderot's Aesthetic Thought*. Edited by Jean Seznec, translated by John S. D. Glaus. London: Springer, 2011.

———. *Selected Writings on Art and Literature*. Translated by Geoffrey Bremner. London: Penguin, 1994.

———. *Das Theater des Herrn Diderot*. Translated by G. E. Lessing. Stuttgart: Reclam, 1986.

———. *Das Theater des Herrn Diderot*. Translated by G. E. Lessing. In *Werke 1760–1766*, edited by Wilfried Barner. Vol. 5.1 of *Gotthold Ephraim Lessing: Werke und Briefe*. 12 vols. Frankfurt am Main: Deutscher Klassiker Verlag, 1990.

———. *Two Plays by Denis Diderot*. The Illegitimate Son *and* The Father of the Family. Translated by Kiki Gounaridou and John Hellweg. New York: Peter Lang, 2011.

———. *Unterredungen über den 'Natürlichen Sohn.'* In Lessing, *Das Theater des Herrn Diderot*. Stuttgart: Reclam, 1986.

———. "Von der dramatischen Dichtkunst." In *Das Theater des Herrn Diderot*, translated by G. E. Lessing. In *Werke 1760–1766*, edited by Wilfried Barner. Vol. 5.1 of *Gotthold Ephraim Lessing: Werke und Briefe*. 12 vols. Frankfurt am Main: Deutscher Klassiker Verlag, 1990.

Die Bundesregierung. "Corona-Regeln: Das gilt an Weihnachten und Silvester." Accessed December 17, 2020. https://www.bundesregierung.de/breg-de/themen /coronavirus/corona-weihnachten-1825108Corona-Regeln Das gilt an Weihnachten und Silvester.

Die Bundesregierung. "Pressekonferenz von Bundeskanzlerin Merkel zur Corona-Pandemie (Berlin, 2. November 2020)." Accessed May 15, 2021. https://www.bundesregierung .de/breg-de/suche/pressekonferenz-von-bundeskanzlerin-merkel-zur-corona -pandemie-1807048.

Digitales Wörterbuch der deutschen Sprache. Accessed July 15, 2020. https://www.dwds.de/.

Dilthey, Wilhelm. *Das Erlebnis und die Dichtung: Lessing, Goethe, Novalis, Hölderlin*. Göttingen: Vandenhoeck & Ruprecht, 1965.

Dörr, Volker C. "Elende Wirtshäuser? Zu Lessings *Miß Sara Sampson* und Lillos *The London Merchant.*" In *Gastlichkeit und Ökonomie: Wirtschaften im deutschen und englischen Drama des 18. Jahrhunderts*, edited by Sigrid Nieberle and Claudia Nitschke, 163–176. Berlin: De Gruyter, 2014.

Dye, Ellis. "Substitution, Self-Blame, and Self-Deception in Goethe's *Stella: Ein Schauspiel für Liebende.*" *Goethe Yearbook* 12 (2004): 41–57.

Easthop, Zak. "Adapting Schiller's *Don Karlos*: Verdi, Posa, and the Problem of the 'Familiengemälde.'" *German Life and Letters* 73, no. 2 (2020): 229–245.

Eckardt, Jo-Jacqueline. *Lessing's Nathan the Wise and the Critics: 1779–1991.* Columbia, SC: Camden House, 1993.

Eckermann, Johann Peter. Letter to Goethe, May 3, 1827, in *Johann Peter Eckermann, Gespräche mit Goethe*, edited by Christoph Michel. Vol. 2.12 of *Sämtliche Werke: Briefe, Tagebücher, Gespräche.* 40 vols. Frankfurt am Main: Deutscher Klassiker Verlag, 1999.

Edelman, Lee. *No Future: Queer Theory and the Death Drive.* Durham, NC: Duke University Press, 2004.

Eichner, Hans. "'Camilla': Eine unbekannte Fortsetzung von Dorothea Schlegels *Florentin.*" *Jahrbuch des Freien Deutschen Hochstifts* (1965): 314–368.

Eldridge, Sarah Vandegrift. *Novel Affinities: Composing the Family in the German Novel, 1795–1830.* Rochester, NY: Camden House, 2016.

Elias, Norbert. *The Civilizing Process: Sociogenetic and Psychogenetic Investigations.* Translated by Edmund Jephcott. Oxford: Blackwell, 2000.

———. *The Court Society.* Translated by Edmund Jephcott. New York: Pantheon, 1983.

———. *Über den Prozess der Zivilisation: Soziogenetische und psychogenetische Untersuchungen.* Munich: Francke, 1969.

Elsaesser, Thomas. *Fassbinder's Germany: History, Identity, Subject.* Amsterdam: Amsterdam University Press, 1996.

Engelstein, Stefani. *Sibling Action: The Genealogical Structure of Modernity.* New York: Columbia University Press, 2017.

Eyck, John R. J., and Katherine Arens. "The Court of Public Opinion: Lessing, Goethe, and Werther's *Emilia Galotti.*" *Monatshefte*, 96, no. 1 (2004): 40–61.

Fick, Monika. *Lessing Handbuch: Leben-Werk-Wirkung.* 4th ed. Stuttgart: Metzler, 2016.

Fiez, Lothar. "Zur Genese des englischen Melodramas aus der Tradition der bürgerlichen Tragödie und des Rührstücks: Lillo—Schröder—Kotzebue—Sheridan—Thompson—Jerrold." *Deutsche Vierteljahrsschrift für Literaturwissenschaft und Geistesgeschichte* 65, no. 1 (1991): 99–116.

Filmer, Robert. *Patriarcha and Other Writings.* Edited by Johann Sommerville. Cambridge, UK: Cambridge University Press, 1991.

Fischer, Bernd. *Kabale und Liebe: Skepsis und Melodrama in Schillers bürgerlichem Trauerspiel.* Frankfurt am Main: Peter Lang, 1987.

Fischer, Paul. *Goethe-Wortschatz: Ein sprachgeschichtliches Wörterbuch zu Goethes Sämtlichen Werken.* Leipzig: Rohmkopf, 1929.

Fischer-Lichte, Erika. *Kurze Geschichte des deutschen Theaters.* Tübingen: Francke, 1993.

———. *The Semiotics of Theater.* Translated by Jeremy Gaines and Doris L. Jones. Bloomington: Indiana University Press, 1992.

———. "Das Weimarer Hoftheater." In *Kurze Geschichte des deutschen Theaters*, 143–164. Tübingen: Francke, 1993.

Flax, Neil. "From Portrait to *Tableau Vivant*: The Pictures of *Emilia Galotti*." *Eighteenth-Century Studies* 19, no. 1 (1985): 39–55.

Fleming, Paul. *Exemplarity and Mediocrity: The Art of the Average from Bourgeois Tragedy to Realism.* Stanford, CA: Stanford University Press, 2009.

Fletcher, Angus. *Allegory: The Theory of a Symbolic Mode.* Ithaca, NY: Cornell University Press, 1964.

Flint, Christopher. *Family Fictions: Narrative and Domestic Relations in Britain, 1688–1798.* Stanford, CA: Stanford University Press, 1998.

Folie, Sabine, and Michael Glasmeier. "Atmende Bilder: Tableau vivant und Attitüde zwischen 'Wirklichkeit und Imagination.'" In *Tableaux Vivants: Lebende Bilder und Attitüden in Fotografie, Film und Video* (exhibition catalogue), 9–52. Vienna: Kunsthalle Wien, 2002.

Foucault, Michel. *The History of Sexuality, Vol. I.* Translated by Robert Hurley. New York: Vintage, 1990.

———. Introduction to *Herculine Barbin: Being the Recently Discovered Memoirs of a Nineteenth-Century Hermaphrodite*, translated by Richard McDougall, vii–xvii. New York: Pantheon, 1980.

———. *The Order of Things: An Archeology of the Human Sciences.* New York: Vintage, 1994.

Freedgood, Elaine. *The Ideas in Things: Fugitive Meaning in the Victorian Novel.* Chicago: University of Chicago Press, 2006.

Freeman, Lisa. *Character's Theater: Genre and Identity on the Eighteenth-Century English Stage.* Philadelphia: University of Pennsylvania Press, 2002.

———. "Tragic Flaws: Genre and Ideology in Lillo's *London Merchant*." *South Atlantic Quarterly* 98, no. 3 (1999): 539–556.

Freud, Sigmund. "Fetischismus." In *Psychologie des Unbewußten*, vol. 3 of *Studienausgabe*, 11 vols., edited by Alexander Mitscherlich, Angela Richards, and James Strachey, 379–389. Frankfurt am Main: Fischer, 1975.

———. "Das ökonomische Problem des Masochismus." *Gesammelte Werke*, vol. 13, 371–387. Frankfurt: Fischer, 2001.

Frevert, Ute. *Women in German History: From Bourgeois Emancipation to Sexual Liberation.* Translated by Stuart McKinnon-Evans. Oxford: Berg, 1989.

Frey, Manuel. "Tugendspiele: Zur Bedeutung der 'Tableaux vivants' in der bürgerlichen Gesellschaft des 19. Jahrhunderts." *Historische Anthropologie* 6 (1998): 401–430.

Fried, Michael. *Absorption and Theatricality: Painting and Beholder in the Age of Diderot.* Chicago: University of Chicago Press, 1980.

Fulda, Daniel. "'Er hat Verstand, Er weiß/Zu leben; Spielt gut Schach': Nathan der Weise als Politicus." In *Aufklärung und Weimarer Klassik im Dialog*, edited by Andre Rudolph and Ernst Stöckmann, 55–78. Tübingen: Niemeyer, 2009.

Galli, Matteo, and Simone Costagli. "Chronotopoi. Vom Familienroman zum Generationenroman." In *Deutsche Familienromane: Literarische Genealogien und internationaler Kontext*, edited by Simone Costagli and Matteo Galli, 23–46. Munich: Fink, 2010.

Gellert, Christian Fürchtegott. *Abhandlungen von dem weinerlichen oder rührenden Lustspiele.* Translated by Lessing, in Lessing, *Werke 1754–1757*, edited by Wilfried Barner. Vol. 3 of *Gotthold Ephraim Lessing: Werke und Briefe*. 12 vols. Frankfurt am Main: Deutscher Klassiker Verlag, 2003.

———. *Leben der schwedischen Gräfin von G****. Edited by Jörg-Ulrich Fechner. Stuttgart: Reclam, 1968.

———. *Roman, Briefsteller*. Edited by Bernd Witte. Vol. 4 of *Gesammelte Schriften: Kritische, kommentierte Ausgabe*. Berlin: De Gruyter, [1751] 1989.

Gemmingen-Hornberg, Otto Heinrich von. *Der deutsche Hausvater oder die Familie*. Berlin: Hofenberg, 2014.

Glaser, Horst Albert. *Das bürgerliche Rührstück: Anelekten zum Zusammenhang von Sentimentalität mit Autorität in der trivialen Dramatik Schröders, Ifflands, Kotzebues und anderer Autoren am Ende des achtzehnten Jahrhunderts*. Stuttgart: Metzler, 1969.

Goethe, Johann Wolfgang von. *Clavigo*. In *Dramen 1765–1775*, edited by Dieter Borchmeyer. Vol. 1.4 of *Sämtliche Werke: Briefe, Tagebücher und Gespräche*. 40 vols. Frankfurt am Main: Deutscher Klassiker Verlag, 1985.

———. *Dichtung und Wahrheit*. Edited by Klaus-Detlef Müller. Vol. 1.14 of *Sämtliche Werke: Briefe, Tagebücher und Gespräche*. 40 vols. Frankfurt am Main: Deutscher Klassiker Verlag, 1986.

———. "Einleitung in die Propyläen." In *Ästhetische Schriften, 1771–1805*, edited by Friedmar Apel, 457–475. Vol. 1.18 of *Sämtliche Werke: Briefe, Tagebücher und Gespräche*. Frankfurt am Main: Deutscher Klassiker Verlag, 1998.

———. *Elective Affinities*. In *The Sorrows of Young Werther; Elective Affinities; Novella*, translated by Judith Ryan. New York: Suhrkamp, 1988.

———. *Des Epimenides Erwachen*. In *Dramen 1791–1832*, edited by Dieter Borchmeyer and Peter Huber. Vol. 1.6 of *Sämtliche Werke: Briefe, Tagebücher und Gespräche*. 40 vols. Frankfurt am Main: Deutscher Klassiker Verlag, 1993.

———. *Egmont*. In *Dramen 1776–1790*, edited by Dieter Borchmeyer. Vol. 1.5 of *Sämtliche Werke. Briefe, Tagebücher und Gespräche*. 40 vols. Frankfurt am Main: Deutscher Klassiker Verlag, 1985.

———. *Götz von Berlichingen*. In *Dramen 1765–1775*, edited by Dieter Borchmeyer. Vol. 4 of *Sämtliche Werke: Briefe, Tagebücher und Gespräche*. 40 vols. Frankfurt am Main: Deutscher Klassiker Verlag, 1985.

———. *Faust: Der Trägodie zweiter Teil*. In *Faust*, edited by Albrecht Schöne. Vol. 7.1 of *Sämtliche Werke: Briefe, Tagebücher und Gespräche*. 40 vols. Frankfurt am Main: Deutscher Klassiker Verlag, 1999.

———. *Faust: Texte*. Edited by Albrecht Friedmar Schöne and Hendrik Birus. Vol. 7 of *Sämtliche Werke: Briefe, Tagebücher und Gespräche*. 40 vols. Frankfurt am Main: Deutscher Klassiker Verlag, 1996.

———. *Die Leiden des jungen Werthers*. In *Werther/Wahlverwandtschaften*, edited by Waltraud Wiethölter. Vol. 1.8 of *Sämtliche Werke: Briefe, Tagebücher und Gespräche*. Frankfurt: Deutscher Klassiker Verlag, 1994.

———. Letter to Johann Peter Eckermann, May 3, 1827. In *Johann Peter Eckermann, Gespräche mit Goethe*, edited by Christoph Michel. Vol. 2.12 of *Sämtliche Werke: Briefe, Tagebücher und Gespräche*. 40 vols. Frankfurt am Main: Deutscher Klassiker Verlag, 1999.

———. "On the Laocoon Group." In *Goethe: The Collected Works: Vol. 3: Essays on Art and Literature*, edited by John Gearey, translated by Ellen von Nardroff and Ernest H. von Nardroff, 15–23. Princeton, NJ: Princeton University Press, 1993.

————. *Proserpina: Melodram von Goethe, Musik von Eberwein.* In *Ästhetische Schriften 1806–1815*, edited by Friedmar Apel, 714–715. Vol. 1.19 of *Sämtliche Werke: Briefe, Tagebücher und Gespräche.* Frankfurt am Main: Deutscher Klassiker Verlag, 1998.

————. "Regeln für Schauspieler." In *Ästhetische Schriften, 1771–1805*, edited by Friedmar Apel, 857–883. Vol. 1.18 of *Sämtliche Werke: Briefe, Tagebücher und Gespräche.* Frankfurt am Main: Deutscher Klassiker Verlag, 1998.

————. *Stella* (zweite Fassung). In *Dramen 1791–1832*, edited by Dieter Borchmeyer and Peter Huber. Vol. 1.6 of *Goethes Sämtliche Werke: Briefe, Tagebücher und Gespräche.* 40 vols. Frankfurt am Main: Deutscher Klassiker Verlag, 1993.

————. *Stella.* In *Dramen 1765–1775*, edited by Dieter Borchmeyer, 531–575. Vol. 1.4 of *Sämtliche Werke: Briefe, Tagebücher und Gespräche.* 40 vols. Frankfurt am Main: Deutscher Klassiker Verlag, 1994.

————. "Über Laocoon." In *Ästhetische Schriften 1771–1805*, edited by Friedmar Apel, et al., 489–500. Vol. 1.18 of *Sämtliche Werke: Briefe, Tagebücher und Gespräche.* 40 vols. Frankfurt am Main: Deutscher Klassiker Verlag, 1998.

————. "Der Versuch als Vermittler." In *Schriften zur Allgemeinen Naturlehre, Physik und zur Farbenlehre nach 1810*, edited by Wolf von Engelhardt and Manfred Wenzel, 26–36. Vol. 1.25 of *Sämtliche Werke: Briefe, Tagebücher und Gespräche.* 40 vols. Frankfurt am Main: Deutscher Klassiker Verlag, 1998.

————. "Versuch einer allgemeinen Vergleichungslehre." In *Schriften zur Morphologie*, edited by Dorothea Kuhn, 209–214. Vol. 1.24 of *Sämtliche Werke: Briefe, Tagebücher und Gespräche.* Frankfurt am Main: Deutscher Klassiker Verlag, 1987.

————. *Die Wahlverwandtschaften.* In *Die Leiden des jungen Werthers, Die Wahlverwandtschaften, Kleine Prosa, Epen*, edited by Waltraud Wiethölter, 269–557. Vol. 1.8 of *Sämtliche Werke: Briefe, Tagebücher und Gespräche.* 40 vols. Frankfurt am Main: Deutscher Klassiker Verlag, 1999.

————. *Wilhelm Meisters Lehrjahre.* Edited by Wilhelm Voßkamp and Herbert Jaumann. Vol. 1.9 of *Sämtliche Werke: Briefe, Tagebücher und Gespräche.* 40 vols. Frankfurt am Main: Deutscher Klassiker Verlag, 1992.

————. "*Wilhelm Meisters Lehrjahre* im Urteil Goethes und seiner Zeitgenossen" (Kommentarteil), *Romane und Novellen II.* Edited by Erich Trunz. Vol. 7 of *Goethes Werke.* Munich: Deutscher Taschenbuch Verlag, 2000.

————. *Wilhelm Meisters Wanderjahre.* Edited by Gerhard Neumann and Hans-Georg Drewitz. Vol. 1.10 of *Sämtliche Werke: Briefe, Tagebücher und Gespräche.* 40 vols. Frankfurt am Main: Deutscher Klassiker Verlag, 1989.

————. "Zu Lessings *Nathan der Weise.*" In *Gotthold Ephraim Lessing*, Nathan der Weise. Stuttgart: Reclam, 1987.

Goetschel, Willi. "Negotiating Truth: On Nathan's Business." *Lessing Yearbook* 28 (1996): 105–123.

Golawski-Braungart, Jutta. *Die Schule der Franzosen: Zur Bedeutung von Lessings Übersetzungen aus dem Französischen für die Theorie und Praxis seines Theaters.* Tübingen: Francke, 2005.

Goldsmith, Oliver. *The Vicar of Wakefield.* Edited by Stephen Coote. London: Penguin, 1982.

Gounaridou, Kiki, and John Hellweg. Introduction to *Two Plays by Denis Diderot:* The Illegitimate Son *and* The Father of the Family, translated by Kiki Gounaridou and John Hellweg, 1–6. New York: Peter Lang, 2011.

Graham, Ilse Appelbaum. "Passions and Possessions in Schiller's 'Kabale und Liebe.'" *German Life and Letters* 6, no. 1 (1952): 12–20.

Gray, Richard T. "Buying into Signs: Money and Semiosis in Eighteenth-Century German Language Theory." *The German Quarterly* 69, no. 1 (1996): 1–14.

————. *Money Matters: Economics and the German Cultural Imagination, 1770–1850*. Seattle: University of Washington Press, 2008.

Green, F. C. "Editor's Introduction." In *Diderot's Writings on the Theatre*, 1–17. Cambridge, UK: Cambridge University Press, 1936.

Guerlac, Suzanne. "The Tableau and Authority in Diderot's Aesthetics." *Studies on Voltaire and the Eighteenth Century* 219 (1983): 183–194.

Guillory, John. "Genesis of the Media Concept." *Critical Inquiry* 36 (2010): 321–362.

Gustafson, Susan. *Absent Mothers and Orphaned Fathers: Narcissism and Abjection in Lessing's Aesthetic and Dramatic Production*. Detroit, MI: Wayne State University Press, 1995.

————. "Goethe's *Clavigo*: The Body as an 'Unorthographic' Sign." In *Body & Text in the Eighteenth Century*, edited by Veronica Kelly and Dorothea von Mücke, 229–247. Stanford, CA: Stanford University Press, 1994.

————. *Goethe's Families of the Heart*. New York: Bloomsbury, 2016.

Guthke, Karl S. *Das deutsche bürgerliche Trauerspiel*. 6th ed. Heidelberg: J.B. Metzler, 2016.

Haag, Ingrid. "Carlos, der 'kranke Königsohn': Familienroman in einem 'königlichen Hause.'" In *Eros und Literatur: Liebe in Texten von der Antike bis zum Cyberspace: Festschrift für Gert Sautermeister*, edited by Christiane Solte-Gresser, Wolfgang Emmerich, and Hans Wolf Jäger, 117–127. Bremen: Lumière, 2005.

Habermas, Jürgen. *Strukturwandel der Öffentlichkeit: Untersuchungen zu einer Kategorie der bürgerlichen Gesellschaft*. Frankfurt am Main: Suhrkamp [1962], 1990.

Hajduk, Stefan. "Identität und Verlust: Der Wandel des Familienbildes und die Dynamik der Geniuspsychologie in *Wilhelm Meisters Lehrjahre*." *Weimarer Beiträge* 55, no. 2 (2009): 196–220.

Halberstam, Jack. *The Queer Art of Failure*. Durham, NC: Duke University Press, 2011.

Hammer-Tugendhat, Daniela. *The Visible and the Invisible: On Seventeenth-Century Dutch Painting*. Vienna: Böhlau, 2009.

Haraway, Donna J. *Staying with the Trouble: Making Kin in the Chthulucene*. Durham, NC: Duke University Press, 2016.

Hart, Gail K. *Tragedy in Paradise: Family and Gender Politics in German Bourgeois Tragedy 1750–1850*. Rochester, NY: Camden House, 1996.

————. "Voyeuristic Star-Gazing: Authority, Instinct and the Women's World of Goethe's *Stella*." *Monatshefte* 82, vol. 4 (1990): 408–420.

Hausen, Karin. "Die Polarisierung der 'Geschlechtscharaktere'—eine Spiegelung der Dissoziation von Erwerbs—und Familienleben." In *Sozialgeschichte der Familie in der Neuzeit Europas: Neue Forschungen*, 363–393. Stuttgart: Klett-Cotta, 1976.

Heeg, Günther. "Massive Erhebung: Das französische Theatertableau des 18. Jahrhunderts als Medium der Affektsteuerung und Wahrnehmungslenkung." In *Wahrnehmung und Medialität*, edited by Erika Fischer-Lichte et al., 52–66. Tübingen: Francke, 2001.

———. *Das Phantasma der natürlichen Gestalt: Körper, Sprache und Bild im Theater des 18. Jahrhunderts*. Frankfurt am Main: Stroemfeld, 2000.

Hegel, Georg Wilhelm Friedrich. *Aesthetics: Lectures on Fine Art*. Vol. 1, translated by T. M. Knox. Oxford: Oxford University Press, 1975.

———. *Ästhetik I/II: Vorlesungen über die Ästhetik: Erster und Zweiter Teil*. Edited by Rüdiger Bubner. Stuttgart: Reclam, 1971.

———. *Grundlinien der Philosophie des Rechts oder Naturrecht und Staatswissenschaft im Grundrisse*. Vol. 7 of *Werke*. 20 vols. Frankfurt: Suhrkamp, 1986.

———. *Phänomenologie des Geistes*. Vol. 3 of *Werke*. Frankfurt am Main: Suhrkamp, 1970.

———. *Phenomenology of Spirit*. Translated by A. V. Miller. Oxford: Oxford University Press, 1977.

———. *Vorlesungen über die Ästhetik II*. Edited by Eva Moldenhauer and Karl Markus Michel. Vol. 14 of *Georg Wilhelm Friedrich Hegel: Werke in 20 Bänden*. Frankfurt am Main: Suhrkamp, 1970.

———. *Vorlesungen über die Ästhetik III*. Edited by Eva Moldenhauer and Karl Markus Michel. Vol. 15 of *Georg Wilhelm Friedrich Hegel Werke*. 20 vols. Frankfurt: Suhrkamp, 1970.

Heitner, Robert R. "Diderot's Own Miss Sara Sampson." *Comparative Literature* 5, no. 1 (1953): 40–49.

Helfer, Martha. "Dorothea Veit-Schlegel's *Florentin*: Constructing a Feminist Romantic Aesthetic." *The German Quarterly* 69, no. 2 (1996): 144–160.

Hernandez, Alex Eric. "Prosaic Suffering: Bourgeois Tragedy and the Aesthetics of the Ordinary." *Representations* 138 (2017): 118–141.

Hertel, Christiane. "Centennials, Sculptures, and *Tableaux Vivants* in the Nineteenth-Century Schiller Cult." *Yearbook of German-American Studies* 38 (2003): 155–204.

———. *Vermeer: Reception and Interpretation*. Cambridge, UK: Cambridge University Press, 1996.

Hillebrand, Bruno. *Theorie des Romans: Erzählstrategien der Neuzeit*. Stuttgart: Metzler, 1993.

Hirsch, Marianne. "Spiritual *Bildung*: The Beautiful Soul as Paradigm." In *The Voyage in: Fictions of Female Development*, 23–48. Lebanon, NH: University Press of New England, 1983.

Hobbes, Thomas. *De Cive*. Edited by Howard Warrender. Oxford: Oxford University Press, 1987.

Hoff, Dagmar von, and Helga Meise. "*Tableaux vivants*. Die Kunst- und Kultform der Attitüden und lebenden Bilder." In *Weiblichkeit und Tod in der Literatur*, edited by Renate Berger and Inge Stephan, 69–87. Cologne: Böhlau, 1987.

Hoffmann, E.T.A. "Nachricht von den neuesten Schicksalen des Hundes Berganza." In *Fantasiestücke in Callot's Manier*. Vol 2.1 of *Werke*, 1814. Frankfurt am Main: Surhkamp, 1993.

Hoffmann, Volker. "Tod der Familie und Toleranz: Lessings *Nathan der Weise* (1779. 1783) und Goethes *Iphigenia auf Tauris* (1787) als Programmstücke der Goethezeit." *Deutsche Vierteljahrsschrift* 85, no. 3 (2011): 367–379.

Hohendahl, Peter Uwe. "Empfindsamkeit und gesellschaftliches Bewußtsein: Zur Soziologie des empfindsamen Romans am Beispiel von *La Vie de Marianne, Clarissa, Fräulein von Sternheim* und *Werther*." *Jahrbuch der deutschen Schillergesellschaft* 16 (1972): 176–207.

Holmström, Kerstin Gram. *Monodrama, Attitudes, Tableaux Vivants.* Stockholm: Almqvist and Wiksell, 1967.

Homm, Theresa. "'Ich muß doch schreiben—': Briefe und Empfindungen in Richardsons Briefroman *Clarissa* und Lessings Trauerspiel *Miß Sara Sampson.*" *Lessing Yearbook* 42 (2015): 87–102.

Hörisch, Jochen. "Die Dekonstruktion der Sprache und der Advent neuer Medien in Goethes *Wahlverwandtschaften.*" *Merkur* 52, no. 9 (1998): 826–839.

Horkheimer, Max. "Allgemeiner Teil." In *Studien über Autorität und Familie*, edited by Max Horkheimer, 3–77. Paris: Librairie Félix Alcan, 1936.

———. "Autorität und Familie." In *Traditionelle und kritische Theorie: Fünf Aufsätze*, 123–204. Frankfurt: Fischer, 1992.

Hull, Isabel V. *Sexuality, State and Civil Society in Germany, 1700–1815.* Ithaca, NY: Cornell University Press, 1996.

Hume, David. "On Polygamy and Divorce." In *Essays: Moral, Political, Literary*, edited by Eugene F. Miller. Indianapolis, IN: Liberty Classics, 1985.

Immer, Nikolas, and Olaf Müller. "Lessings Diderot: 'süssere Thränen' zur Läuterung des Nationalgeschmacks." In *"ihrem Originale nachzudenken": Zu Lessings Übersetzungen*, edited by Helmut Berthold, 147–165. Tübingen: Niemeyer, 2008.

Jacobi, Friedrich. "Friedrich Jacobi an Köppen, 12. Jan. 1810." Letter from Jacobi to Köppen, Jan. 12, 1810, in *"Die Wahlverwandtschaften* im Urteil Goethes und seiner Zeitgenossen,"* in Johann Wolfgang von Goethe, *Romane und Novellen*, edited by Erich Trunz, 638–672. Vol. 6 of *Johann Wolfgang Goethe Werke: Hamburger Ausgabe.* 14 vols. Munich: Deutscher Taschenbuch Verlag, 1999.

Jameson, Fredric. *Allegory and Ideology.* London: Verso, 2019.

———. *The Political Unconscious: Narrative as a Socially Symbolic Act.* Ithaca, NY: Cornell University Press, 1981.

Jarzebowski, Claudia. *Inzest: Verwandtschaft und Sexualität im 18. Jahrhundert.* Cologne: Böhlau, 2006.

Jelinek, Elfriede. "Abraumhalde." Zum Theater/Theatertexte, *Elfriedesfotoalbum*, https:// www.elfriedejelinek.com/.

Johnson, Christopher H. *Becoming Bourgeois: Love, Kinship, and Power in Provincial France, 1670–1880.* Ithaca, NY: Cornell University Press, 2015.

Johnson, Laurie. "'Wenn man endlich selbst Briefe schreiben will, so vergesse man die Exempel': The Construction of Imitation as Originality in C. F. Gellert's Epistolary Theory." *Wezel-Jahrbuch: Studien zur europäischen Aufklärung* 2 (1999): 97–114.

Jonnes, Denis. "Pattern of Power: Family and State in Schiller's Early Drama." *Colloquia Germanica* 20, vols. 2/3 (1987): 138–162.

———. *"Les Pères Victimes:* Diderot and the Socio-Poetics of Bourgeois Drama." *Studies on Voltaire and the Eighteenth Century* 265 (1989): 1365–1367.

———. *"Solche Väter:* The Sentimental Family Paradigm in Lessing's Dramas." *Lessing Yearbook* 12 (1981): 157–174.

Jooss, Birgit. *Lebende Bilder: Körperliche Nachahmung von Kunstwerken in der Goethezeit.* Berlin: Reimer, 1999.

———. "Lebende Bilder als Charakterbeschreibungen in Goethes Roman *Die Wahlver-wandtschaften.*" In *Erzählen und Wissen: Paradigmen und Aporien ihrer Inszenierung in*

Goethes "Wahlverwandtschaften," edited by Gabriele Brandstetter, 111–136. Freiburg im Breisgau: Rombach, 2003.

Jordan, Gilbert J. "Lebende Bilder im deutschen Drama des 17. Jahrhunderts." *The South Central Bulletin* 33, no. 4 (1973): 207–210.

Kaiser, Gerhard. "Krise der Familie: Eine Perspektive auf Lessings *Emilia Galotti* und Schillers *Kabale und Liebe.*" *Recherches germaniques* 14 (1984): 7–22.

Kaiser, Gerhard, and Friedrich A. Kittler. Introduction to *Dichtung als Sozialisationsspiel: Studien zu Goethe und Gottfried Keller.* Göttingen: Vandenhoeck & Ruprecht, 1978.

Kant, Immanuel. *Über Pädagogik.* Königsberg: Theodor Rink, 1803.

———. "Was ist Aufklärung?" In *Was ist Aufklärung? Thesen und Definitionen*, edited by Ehrhard Bahr, 9–17. Stuttgart: Reclam, 1974.

Karakassi, Katerina. "Der kranke Königssohn oder das zeitlose Bild im Sog der Zeit: Notizen zu Goethes *Wilhelm Meisters Lehr—und Wanderjahre.*" *Estudios Filológicos Alemanes* 18 (2009): 251–262.

Kierkegaard, Søren. *Either/Or: A Fragment of Life.* Translated by Alastair Hannay, edited by Victor Eremita. London: Penguin, 1992.

Kimpel, Dieter. *Der Roman der Aufklärung (1670–1774).* Stuttgart: Metzler, 1967.

King, Rachael Scarborough. *Writing to the World: Letters and the Origins of Modern Print Genres.* Baltimore, MD: Johns Hopkins University Press, 2018.

Kittler, Friedrich A. *Aufschreibesysteme 1800/1900.* Munich: Wilhelm Fink, 1985.

———. "'Erziehung ist Offenbarung': Zur Struktur der Familie in Lessings Dramen." *Jahrbuch der deutschen Schillergesellschaft* 21 (1977): 111–137.

———. "Ottilie Hauptmann." In *Goethes* Wahlverwandtschaften: *Kritische Modelle und Diskursanalysen zum Mythos Literatur*, edited by Norbert W. Bolz, 260–276. Hildesheim: Gerstenberg, 1981.

———. "Über die Sozialisation Wilhelm Meisters." In *Dichtung als Sozialisationsspiel: Studien zu Goethe und Gottfried Keller*, edited by Gerhard Kaiser and Friedrich A. Kittler, 13–125. Göttingen: Vandenhoeck & Ruprecht, 1978.

Kittler, Wolf. "Goethes *Wahlverwandtschaften*: Soziale Verhältnisse symbolisch dargestellt." In *Goethes* Wahlverwandtschaften: *Kritische Modelle und Diskursanalysen zum Mythos Literatur*, edited by Norbert W. Bolz, 230–260. Hildesheim: Gerstenberg, 1981.

Kontje, Todd. *The German* Bildungsroman: *History of a National Genre.* Columbia, SC: Camden House, 1993.

———. "Schiller's *Wilhelm Tell*: Weimar Classicism between Empire and Nation." *Monatshefte* 109, no. 4 (2017): 519–538.

Kornbluh, Anna. *The Order of Forms: Realism, Formalism, and Social Space.* Chicago: University of Chicago Press, 2019.

Koschorke, Albrecht. *Körperströme und Schriftverkehr: Mediologie des 18. Jahrhunderts.* Munich: Fink, 1999.

Koschorke, Albrecht, et al. Introduction to *Vor der Familie: Grenzbedingungen einer modernen Institution*, 1–48. Munich: Fink, 2010.

Koselleck, Reinhart. "Drei bürgerliche Welten? Zur vergleichenden Semantik der bürgerlichen Gesellschaft in Deutschland, England und Frankreich." In *Begriffsgeschichten: Studien zur Semantik und Pragmatik der politischen und sozialen Sprache*, 402–461. Frankfurt: Suhrkamp, 2006.

————. *Preußen zwischen Reform und Revolution: Allgemeines Landrecht, Verwaltung und soziale Bewegung von 1791 bis 1848*. Stuttgart: Klett, 1967.

Kotzebue, August von. *Menschenhaß und Reue*. Berlin: Holzinger, 2013.

————. *La Peyrouse*. In *Schauspiele*, edited by Jürg Mathes, 291–325. Frankfurt am Main: Athenäum, 1972.

Krieger, Murray. "*Ekphrasis* and the Still Movement of Poetry, or *Laokoön Revisited*." In *Ekphrasis: The Illusion of the Natural Sign*, 263–289. Baltimore, MD: Johns Hopkins University Press, 1992.

Krimmer, Elisabeth. "Abortive *Bildung*: Women Writers, Male Bonds, and Would-Be Fathers." In *Challenging Separate Spheres: Female Bildung in Eighteenth- and Nineteenth-Century Germany*, edited by Marjanne Goozé, 235–259. Oxford: Peter Lang, 2007.

————. "Mama's Baby, Papa's Maybe: Paternity and *Bildung* in Goethe's *Wilhelm Meisters Lehrjahre*." *The German Quarterly* 77, no. 3 (2004): 257–277.

Kuzniar, Alice. "The Misrepresentation of Self: Werther versus Goethe." *Mosaic* 22, no. 2 (Spring 1989): 15–28.

————. *The Queer German Cinema*. Stanford, CA: Stanford University Press, 2000.

Lacan, Jacques. "The Mirror Stage as Formative of the Function of the I as Revealed in Psychoanalytic Experience." In *Écrits: A Selection*, translated by Alan Sheridan, 1–8. New York: W.W. Norton, 1977.

Landgraf, Edgar. "Romantic Love and the Enlightenment: From Gallantry and Seduction to Authenticity and Self-Validation." *The German Quarterly* 77, no. 1 (2004): 29–46.

Langen, August. *Anschauungsformen in der deutschen Dichtung des 18. Jahrhunderts (Rahmenschau und Rationalismus)*. Jena: Diederichs, 1934.

————. "Attitüde und Tableau in der Goethezeit." *Jahrbuch der deutschen Schillergesellschaft* 12 (1968): 194–258.

Lanzinger, Margareth. "Introduction." *The History of the Family* 17, no. 3 (2012): 279–283.

————. *Verwaltete Verwandtschaft: Eheverbote, kirchliche und staatliche Dispenspraxis im 18. und 19. Jahrhundert*. Vienna: Böhlau, 2015.

Laqueur, Thomas. *Making Sex: Body and Gender from the Greeks to Freud*. Cambridge, MA: Harvard University Press, 1990.

La Roche, Sophie von. *Geschichte des Fräuleins von Sternheim*. Edited by Barbara Becker-Cantarino. Stuttgart: Reclam, 1983.

Lehleiter, Christine. *Romanticism, Origins, and the History of Heredity*. Lewisburg, PA: Bucknell University Press, 2014.

————. "Sophie von La Roche's *Die Geschichte des Fräuleins von Sternheim* (1771): Conceptualizing Female Selfhood around 1800." *Women in German Yearbook* 29 (2013): 21–40.

Lehmann, Johannes F. "Situation, Szene, 'Tableau': Medientheoretische Aspekte der Anfänge von Schillers *Don Karlos*." In *Der Einsatz des Dramas: Dramenanfänge, Wissenschaftspoetik und Gattungspolitik*, edited by Andrea Polaschegg and Claus Haas, 215–232. Freiburg: Rombach, 2012.

Lehrer, Mark. "Lessing's Economic Comedy." *Seminar* 20, no. 2 (1984): 79–94.

Lennartz, Rita. "'Von Angesicht zu Angesicht': Lebende Bilder und tote Buchstaben in Goethes *Wahlverwandtschaften*." In *Bildersturm und Bilderflut um 1800: Zur schwierigen Anschaulichkeit der Moderne*, edited by Helmut J. Schneider, Ralf Simon, and Thomas Wirtz, 145–183. Bielefeld: Aisthesis, 2001.

Lenz, J.M.R. *Die Soldaten: eine Komödie*. Stuttgart: Reclam, 1973.

Lessing, Gotthold Ephraim. "Briefe, die neueste Literatur betreffend." In *Werke 1758–1759*, edited by Gunter E. Grimm. Vol. 4 of *Gotthold Ephraim Lessing: Werke und Briefe*. 12 vols. Frankfurt am Main: Deutscher Klassiker Verlag, 1997.

———. *Emilia Galotti*. In *Werke 1770–1773*, edited by Klaus Bohnen, 291–371. Vol. 7 of *Werke und Briefe*. 12 vols. Frankfurt am Main: Deutscher Klassiker Verlag, 2000.

———. *Die Erziehung des Menschengeschlechts*. In *Werke 1778–1781*, edited by Arno Schilson and Axel Schmitt. Vol. 10 of *Werke und Briefe*. Frankfurt am Main: Deutscher Klassiker Verlag, 2001.

———. *Fragmentenstreit II*. In *Werke 1778–1780*, edited by Klaus Bohnen and Arno Schilson. Vol. 9 of *Gotthold Ephraim Lessing: Werke und Briefe*. 12 vols. Frankfurt am Main: Deutscher Klassiker Verlag, 1993.

———. *Hamburgische Dramaturgie*. In *Werke 1767–1769*, edited by Klaus Bohnen. Vol. 6 of *Gotthold Ephraim Lessing: Werke und Briefe*. 12 vols. Frankfurt am Main: Deutscher Klassiker Verlag, 1985.

———. "Laocoön, oder Über die Grenzen der Malerei und Poesie." In *Laocoön: Werke 1766–1769*, edited by Wilfried Barner. Vol. 5.2 of *Gotthold Ephraim Lessing Werke und Briefe*. 12 vols. Frankfurt am Main: Deutscher Klassiker Verlag, 1990.

———. Letter to Friedrich Nicolai, January 21, 1758. In *Briefe 1743–1770*, edited by Helmuth Kiesel, Georg Braungart, and Klaus Fischer. Vol. 11.1 of *Gotthold Ephraim Lessing: Werke und Briefe*. 12 vols. Frankfurt am Main: Deutscher Klassiker Verlag, 1987.

———. Letter to Karl Gotthelf Lessing, April 18, 1779. In *Briefe 1776–1781*, edited by Wilfried Barner. Vol. 12 of *Gotthold Ephraim Lessing: Werke und Briefe*. 12 vols. Frankfurt am Main: Deutscher Klassiker Verlag, 1994.

———. *Miß Sara Sampson*. In *Werke 1754–1757*, edited by Conrad Wiedemann et al., 431–526. Vol. 3 of *Werke und Briefe*. 12 vols. Frankfurt am Main: Deutscher Klassiker Verlag, 2003.

———. *Nathan der Weise*. In *Werke 1778–1780*, edited by Klaus Bohnen and Arno Schilson. Vol. 9 of *Gotthold Ephraim Lessing: Werke und Briefe*. 12 vols. Frankfurt am Main: Deutscher Klassiker Verlag, 1993.

———. *Der Schatz*. In *Werke 1743–1750*, edited by Jürgen Stenzel. Vol. 1 of *Werke und Briefe*. Frankfurt am Main: Deutscher Klassiker Verlag, 1989.

———. "Vorwort des Übersetzers, zu dieser zweiten Ausgabe." Foreword to *Das Theater des Herrn Diderot*, translated by G. E. Lessing, in *Werke 1760–1766*, edited by Wilfried Barner. Vol. 5.1 of *Gotthold Ephraim Lessing: Werke und Briefe*. 12 vols. Frankfurt am Main: Deutscher Klassiker Verlag, 1990.

Lester, G. A., ed. *Three Late Medieval Morality Plays: Mankind, Everyman, Mundus et Infans*. New York: W.W. Norton, 1981.

Levine, Caroline. *Forms: Whole, Rhythm, Hierarchy, Network*. Princeton, NJ: Princeton University Press, 2015.

Lévi-Strauss, Claude. *The Elementary Structures of Kinship*. Translated by James Harle Bell and John Richard von Sturmer. Boston: Eyre & Spottiswoode, 1969.

Liebfried, Erwin. "Goethes Werther als Leser von Lessings 'Emilia Galotti.'" In *Text—Leser—Bedeutung: Untersuchungen zur Interaktion von Text und Leser*, edited by Herbert Grabes, 145–156. Grossen-Linden: Hoffmann, 1977.

Liewerscheidt, Dieter. "Lessings *Emilia Galotti*—ein unmögliches Trauerspiel." *Literatur für Leser* 34, no. 4 (2011): 231–246.

Lillyman, William J. "'Tableau Vivant,' and Romanticism: Ottilie in Goethe's *Die Wahlver-wandtschaften.*" *JEGP* 81 no. 3 (1982): 347–366.

Lorenz, Angelika. *Das deutsche Familienbild in der Malerei des 19. Jahrhunderts.* Darmstadt: Wissenschaftliche Buchgesellschaft, 1985.

Luhmann, Niklas. *Liebe als Passion: Zur Codierung von Intimität.* Frankfurt am Main: Suhrkamp, 1982.

———. "Preface to the English Edition." *Love as Passion: The Codification of Intimacy,* 1–7. Stanford, CA: Stanford University Press, 1998.

Lukács, Georg. "Erzählen oder beschreiben? Zur Diskussion über den Naturalismus und Formalismus." In *Probleme des Realismus I: Essays über Realismus,* 197–243. Vol. 4 of *Georg Lukács Werke.* Neuwied and Berlin: Luchterhand, 1971.

———. "The Sociology of Modern Drama." *The Tulane Drama Review* 9, no. 4 (1965): 146–170.

———. *Die Theorie des Romans: Ein geschichtsphilosophischer Versuch über die Formen der großen Epik.* Munich: Deutscher Taschenbuch Verlag, 1994.

———. "Zur Soziologie des modernen Dramas." In *Schriften zur Soziologie,* edited by Peter Ludz, 261–295. Neuwied: Luchterhand, 1961.

MacLeod, Catriona. *Embodying Ambiguity: Androgyny and Aesthetics from Winckelmann to Keller.* Detroit, MI: Wayne State University Press, 1998.

———. *Fugitive Objects: Sculpture and Literature in the German Nineteenth Century.* Evanston, IL: Northwestern University Press, 2014.

———. "Sculptural Blockages: Wilhelm Heinse's *Ardinghello,* Clemens Brentano's *Godwi,* and the Early Romantic Novel." *Seminar* 49, no. 2 (2013): 232–247.

Marasco, Robyn. "There's a Fascist in the Family: Critical Theory and Antiauthoritarianism." *The South Atlantic Quarterly* 117, no. 4 (2018): 791–813.

Martini, Fritz. "Der Bildungsroman: Zur Geschichte des Wortes und der Theorie." *Deutsche Vierteljahrsschrift* 35 (1961): 44–63.

Martiny, Fritz. *Die Adelsfrage in Preußen vor 1806 als politisches und soziales Problem (Beiheft 35 zur Vierteljahrsschrift für Sozial—und Wirtschaftsgeschichte).* Stuttgart: Kohlhammer, 1938.

Marx, Karl. "Geld." In *Ökonomisch-philosophische Manuskripte.* Berlin: Berliner Ausgabe, 2007.

———. *Das Kapital: Kritik der politischen Ökonomie, Buch 1.* In *Werke,* by Karl Marx and Friedrich Engels. Vol. 23. Berlin: Karl Dietz, 1962.

Marx, Karl, and Friedrich Engels. *The German Ideology, Including Theses on Feuerbach.* Amherst, NY: Prometheus, 1998.

McCall, Tom. "Liquid Politics: Toward a Theorization of 'Bourgeois' Tragic Drama." *The South Atlantic Quarterly* 98, no. 3 (1999): 593–622.

McIsaac, Peter. "Rethinking *Tableaux Vivants* and Triviality in the Writings of Johann Wolfgang von Goethe, Johanna Schopenhauer, and Fanny Lewald." *Monatshefte* 99, no. 2 (2007): 152–176.

McKeon, Michael. *The Origins of the English Novel 1600–1740.* Baltimore, MD: Johns Hopkins University Press, 1987.

Méchoulan, Eric, and Angela Carr. "Intermediality: An Introduction to the Arts of Transmission." *SubStance* 44, no. 3 (2015): 3–18.

Meise, Helga. "Die Schreibweisen der Sophie von La Roche." *German Life and Letters* 67, no. 4 (2014): 530–541.

Meisel, Martin. *Realizations: Narrative, Pictorial, and Theatrical Arts in Nineteenth-Century England*. Princeton, NJ: Princeton University Press, 1983.

Mercier, Louis-Sébastian. *Merciers Neuer Versuch über die Schauspielkunst*. Translated by Heinrich Leopold Wagner. Heidelberg: Lambert Schneider, 1967.

Meyer, Moe. "Introduction: Reclaiming the Discourse of Camp." In *The Politics and Poetics of Camp*, edited by Moe Meyer, 1–22. New York: Routledge, 1994.

Meyer-Krentler, Eckhardt. *Der andere Roman: Gellerts 'Schwedische Gräfin': Von der aufklärerischen Propaganda gegen den 'Roman' zur empfindsamen Erlebnisdichtung*. Göppingen: Kümmerle, 1974.

Miller, D. A. "Secret Subjects, Open Secrets." In *The Novel and the Police*. Berkeley: University of California Press, 1989.

Miller, J. Hillis. *Ariadne's Thread*. New Haven, CT: Yale University Press, 1992.

———. "Interlude as Anastomosis in *Die Wahlverwandtschaften*." *Goethe Yearbook* 6 (1992): 115–122.

Miller, Norbert. "Mutmaßungen über lebende Bilder: Attitüde und *tableau vivant* als Anschauungsformen des 19. Jahrhunderts." In *Das Triviale in Literatur, Musik und bildender Kunst*, edited by Helga de la Motte-Haber, 106–130. Frankfurt: Vittorio Klostermann, 1972.

———. *Der empfindsame Erzähler. Untersuchungen zur erzähltechnischen Verwendung des Briefes im deutschen Roman des 18. Jahrhunderts*. Munich: C. Hanser, 1968.

Mitchell, W.T.J. *Picture Theory*. Chicago: University of Chicago Press, 1994.

Mitscherlich, Alexander. *Auf dem Weg zur vaterlosen Gesellschaft: Ideen zur Sozialpsychologie*. Munich: Piper, 1963.

Mitscherlich, Alexander, and Margarete Mitscherlich. *Die Unfähigkeit zu trauern: Grundlagen kollektiven Verhaltens*. Munich: Piper, 1967.

Mönch, Cornelia. "Abschrecken oder Mitleiden: Das deutsche bürgerliche Trauerspiel im 18. Jahrhundert, Versuch einer Typologie." *Jahrbuch für internationale Germanistik* 13 (1995): 142–150.

Moore, Evelyn. "Erlebendes Schauen: Goethes Tableaux vivants in Erzählwerken, Theater und Politik." In *Transactions of the Ninth International Congress on the Enlightenment*, vol. 1, edited by Anthony Strugnell and Werner Schneiders, 466–468. Oxford: Voltaire Foundation, 1996.

Morgan, Peter. "The Spirit of the Place: Idyll as 'Imagined Community' in Goethe's *Werther*." *AUMLA: Journal of the Australasian Universities Modern Language Association* (2003): 42–54.

Morris, Irene. "The Symbol of the Rose: A Baroque Echo in *Emilia Galotti*." *Publications of the English Goethe Society* 64, no. 1 (2016): 53–71.

Mortier, Roland. *Diderot in Deutschland: 1750–1850*. Translated by Hans G. Schürmann. Stuttgart: Metzler, 1967.

Mosse, George. *The Image of Man: The Creation of Modern Masculinity*. New York: Oxford University Press, 1996.

———. *Nationalism and Sexuality: Middle-Class Morality and Sexual Norms in Modern Europe*. Madison: University of Wisconsin Press, 1997.

Mufti, Aamir R. "Jewishness as Minority: Postcolonial Perspectives on the Limits of Enlightenment." *Lessing Yearbook* 39 (2012): 27–36.

Müller, Klaus-Detlef. "Das Virginia-Motiv in Lessings *Emilia Galotti*: Anmerkungen zum Strukturwandel der Öffentlichkeit." *Orbis Litterarum* 42 (1987): 305–316.

Nagel, Barbara N. "Slut-Shaming Metaphorologies: On Sexual Metaphor in Goethe's *Wilhelm Meister.*" *Critical Inquiry* 46 (2020): 304–324.

Nawrocki, Sascha, and Winfried Woesler. "Ein Kleid, Ein Schwert, Ein Pferd: Miszelle zu Lessings *Nathan.*" *Euphorion* 97 (2003): 131–133.

Nenon, Monika. "A Dynamic Interplay: Cooperation between Sophie von La Roche, Christoph Martin Wieland, and Goethe on Their Way to Authorship." In *Gender, Collaboration, and Authorship in German Culture*, edited by Laura Deiulio and John B. Lyon, 45–75. New York: Bloomsbury, 2019.

Niekerk, Carl. "Radicalism in Lessing's Domestic Drama (*Miss Sara Sampson, Minna von Barnhelm*, and *Emilia Galotti*)." In *The Radical Enlightenment in German: A Cultural Perspective*, edited by Carl Niekerk, 131–163. Leiden: Brill, 2018.

Nietzsche, Friedrich. "Über Wahrheit und Lüge im außermoralischen Sinne." In *Unzeitgemässe Betrachtungen*, 373–389. Munich: Wilhelm Goldmann, 1964.

Nossett, Lauren. "Impossible Ideals: Reconciling Virginity and Materiality in Goethe's *Werther.*" *Goethe Yearbook* 23 (2016): 77–93.

Notz, Gisela. *Kritik des Familismus: Theorie und soziale Realität eines ideologischen Gemäldes.* Stuttgart: Schmetterling, 2015.

Nussbaum, Felicity. "The Unaccountable Pleasure of Eighteenth-Century Tragedy." *PMLA* 129, no. 4 (2014): 688–707.

Opitz, Claudia. "Neue Wege der Sozialgeschichte? Ein kritischer Blick auf Otto Brunners Konzept des 'Ganzen Hauses.'" *Geschichte und Gesellschaft* 20, no. 1 (1994): 88–98.

Pape, Walter. "'Ein merkwürdiges Beispiel productiver Kritik': Schillers *Kabale und Liebe* und das zeitgenössische Publikum." *Zeitschrift für deutsche Philologie* 107 (1988): 190–211.

Peucker, Brigitte. "The Material Image in Goethe's *Wahlverwandtschaften.*" *The Germanic Review* 74, no. 3 (1999): 195–213.

Piel, Maryann. "La Roche and Goethe: Gender, Genre, and Influence." *Goethe Yearbook* 30, forthcoming.

Pikulik, Lothar. *"Bürgerliches Trauerspiel" und Empfindsamkeit.* Cologne: Böhlau, 1966.

———. "*Stella*: Ein Schauspiel für Liebende." In *Goethes Dramen*, edited by Walter Hinderer, 88–116. Ditzingen: Reclam, 1992.

Poyntner, John. "The Pearls of Emilia Galotti." *Lessing Yearbook* 9 (1977): 81–95.

Prutti, Brigitte. "Das Bild des Weiblichen und die Phantasie des Künstlers: Das Begehren des Prinzen in Lessings *Emilia Galotti.*" *Zeitschrift für deutsche Philologie* 110 (1991): 481–505.

———. *Bild und Körper: Weibliche Präsenz und Geschlechterbeziehungen in Lessings Dramen* Emilia Galotti *und* Minna von Barnhelm. Würzburg: Königshausen & Neumann, 1996.

———. "Coup de Théâtre—Coup de Femme, or: What Is Lessing's Emilia Galotti Dying From?" *Lessing Yearbook* 26 (1994): 1–28.

Pucci, Suzanne R. "The Nature of Domestic Intimacy and Sibling Incest in Diderot's *Fils Naturel.*" *Eighteenth-Century Studies* 30, no. 3 (1997): 271–287.

————. "Picture Perfect: Snapshots of the Family." *L'Esprit Créatur* 44, no. 1 (2004): 68–82.

Puszkar, Norbert. "Verwandtschaft und Wahlverwandtschaft." *Goethe Yearbook* 4 (1988): 161–183.

Racz, Gregory J. Introduction to *Life is a Dream*, by Pedro Calderón de la Barca, translated by Gregory J. Racz, vii–xxi. London: Penguin, 2006.

Raich. J. M., ed. *Dorothea v. Schlegel geb. Mendelssohn und deren Söhne Johannes und Phillipp Veit. Briefwechsel.* Mainz: Franz Kirchheim, 1988.

Redfield, Marc. *Bildungsroman: Phantom Formations: Aesthetic Ideology and the* Bildungsroman. Ithaca, NY: Cornell University Press, 1996.

Renan, Ernest. "What Is a Nation?" In *Nation and Narration*, translated by Martin Thom, edited by Homi K. Bhabha, 8–22. London: Routledge, 1990.

Reschke, Nils. "'Die Wirklichkeit als Bild': Lebende Bilder in Goethes *Wahlverwandtschaften.*" In *Medien der Präsenz: Museum, Bildung und Wissenschaft im 19. Jahrhundert*, edited by Jürgen Fohrmann, Andrea Schütte, and Wilhelm Voßkamp, 42–69. Cologne: Dumont, 2001.

Richards, Anna. "Forgetting the Dead in Gellert's *Leben der schwedischen Gräfin von G**** (1747/8)." *Oxford German Studies* 35, no. 2 (2006): 165–175.

Richter, Simon. "The Ins and Outs of Intimacy: Gender, Epistolary Culture, and the Public Sphere," *German Quarterly* 69, no. 2 (1996): 111–24.

Ricoeur, Paul. *Freud and Philosophy: An Essay on Interpretation.* Translated by Denis Savage. New Haven, CT: Yale University Press, 1970.

Ritchie, Gisela F. "Spuren des französischen Dramas bei Lessing." In *Nation und Gelehrtenrepublik: Lessing im europäischen Zusammenhang*, 120–138. Detroit, MI: Wayne State University Press, 1984.

Robert, Yann. "Mercier's Revolutionary Theater: Reimagining Pantomime, the Aesthetic of the Unfinished, and the Politics of the Stage." *Studies in Eighteenth-Century Culture* 44 (2015): 185–206.

Röttger, Kati. "'What Do I See?' The Order of Looking in Lessing's *Emilia Galotti.*" *Art History* 33, no. 2 (2010): 378–387.

Rousseau, Jean-Jacques. *La Nouvelle Héloïse: Julie, or the New Eloise. Letters of Two Lovers, Inhabitants of a Small Town at the Foot of the Alps.* Translated by Judith H. McDowell. University Park, PA: Penn State University Press, 1968.

Rubin, Gayle S. "Thinking Sex: Notes for a Radical Theory of the Politics of Sexuality." *Deviations: A Gayle Rubin Reader*, 137–182. Durham, NC: Duke University Press, 2011.

Sabean, David Warren, and Simon Teuscher. "Kinship in Europe: A New Approach to Long-Term Development." In *Kinship in Europe: Approaches to Long-Term Development (1300–1900)*, edited by D. W. Sabean, S. Teuscher, and Jon Mathieu, 1–32. New York: Berghahn, 2007.

Saße, Günter. "Das Besondere und das Allgemeine: Lessings Auseinandersetzung mit Diderot über Wahrheit und Wirkung des Dramas." In *Gesellige Vernunft: Zur Kultur der literarischen Aufklärung*, edited by Ortrud Gutjahr, Wilhelm Kühlmann, and Wolf Wucherpfennig, 263–277. Würzburg: Königshausen & Neumann, 1993.

————. "'Gerade seine Unvollkommenheit hat mir am meisten Mühe gemacht': Schillers Briefwechsel mit Goethe über *Wilhelm Meisters Lehrjahre.*" *Goethe-Jahrbuch* 122 (2005): 76–91.

————. "Vom 'heimlichen Geist des Widerspruchs': Der Bildungsroman im 18. Jahrhundert. Goethes *Wilhelm Meisters Lehrjahre* im Spannungsfeld von Subjektivität und Intersubjektivität." *Das 18. Jahrhundert*, edited by Monika Fludernik and Ruth Nestvold, 69–89. Trier: Wissenschaftlicher, 1998.

Schatz, Andrea. "Interrupted Games: Lessing and Mendelssohn on Religion, Intermarriage and Integration." *Lessing Yearbook* 39 (2012): 51–72.

Schiller, Friedrich. *Die Jungfrau von Orleans*. In *Maria Stuart; die Jungfrau von Orleans*, edited by Benno von Wiese and Lieselotte Blumenthal. Vol. 9 of *Schillers Werke, Nationalausgabe*. Weimar: Hermannn Böhlaus Nachfolger, 1948.

————. *Die Jungfrau von Orleans*. Edited by Winfried Woesler. Vol. 9.2 of *Schillers Werke, Nationalausgabe*. Weimar: Hermannn Böhlaus Nachfolger, 2012.

————. *Don Karlos* (letzte Ausgabe). Vol. 7.1 of *Schillers Werke, Nationalausgabe*, edited by Paul Böckmann and Gerhard Kluge. Weimar: Hermannn Böhlaus Nachfolger, 1974.

————. *Kabale und Liebe*. Vol. 5 of *Schillers Werke, Nationalausgabe*, edited by Herbert Kraft, Claudia Pilling and Gert Vonhoff. Weimar: Hermannn Böhlaus Nachfolger, 2000.

————. "Shakespeares Schatten." In *Schillers Sämtliche Werke*, edited by Karl Goedeke. 16 vols. Stuttgart: Cotta, 1893, 347–348.

————. *Wilhelm Tell*. In *Maria Stuart; die Jungfrau von Orleans*, edited by Benno von Wiese and Lieselotte Blumenthal. Vol. 9 of *Schillers Werke, Nationalausgabe*. Weimar: Hermannn Böhlaus Nachfolger, 1948.

Schindler, Stephan K. *Das Subjekt als Kind: Die Erfindung der Kindheit im Roman des 18. Jahrhunderts*. Berlin: Erich Schmidt, 1994.

Schlegel, Dorothea. *Florentin: Roman, Fragmente, Varianten*. Frankfurt: Ullstein, 1986.

Schlegel, Friedrich. "Über Goethes Meister." In *Friedrich Schlegel: Charakteristiken & Kritiken I (1796–1801)*, edited by Ernst Behler, Jean Jacques Anstett, and Hans Eichner, 126–146. Munich: Schöningh, 1967.

————. "Über Lessing." *Charakteristiken und Kritiken I, 1796–1801*, edited by Hans Eichner, 100–126. Vol. 2 of *Kritische Friedrich Schlegel Ausgabe*. Munich: Ferdinand Schöningh, 1967.

Schlipphacke, Heidi M. "The Dialectics of Female Desire in G.E. Lessing's *Emilia Galotti*." *The Lessing Yearbook* 33 (2001): 55–78.

————. "Eros and Community: C.F. Gellert's *Das Leben der schwedischen Gräfin von G****.*" *The Germanic Review* 76, no. 1 (2001): 70–90.

————. *Nostalgia after Nazism: History, Home and Affect in German and Austrian Literature and Film*. Lewisburg, PA: Bucknell University Press, 2010.

————. "Die Vaterschaft beruht nur überhaupt auf der Überzeugung: The Displaced Family in Goethe's *Wilhelm Meisters Lehrjahre*." *Journal of English and Germanic Philology* 102, no. 3 (2003): 390–412.

Schmaus, Marion. "Zur Genese melodramatischer Imagination: Englisch-deutscher Tauschhandel im Zeichen der Rührung bei George Lillo, Friedrich Ludwig Schröder und August Kotzebue." In *Gastlichkeit und Ökonomie: Wirtschaften im deutschen und englischen Drama des 18. Jahrhunderts*, edited by Sigrid Nieberle and Claudia Nitschke, 89–108. Berlin: De Gruyter, 2014.

Schmidt, Erich. *Richardson, Rousseau und Goethe: Ein Beitrag zur Geschichte des Romans im 18. Jahrhundert*. Jena: Eduard Frommann, 1875.

Schmiedt, Helmut. *Liebe, Ehe, Ehebruch: Ein Spannungsfeld in deutscher Prosa von Christian Fürchtegott Gellert bis Elfriede Jelinek.* Opladen: Westdeutscher Verlag, 1993.

Schmitz, Carl A. *Grundformen der Verwandtschaft.* Basel: Pharos, 1964.

Schneider, Helmut J. "Geburt und Adoption bei Lessing und Kleist." *Kleist-Jahrbuch* (2002): 21–41.

———. "Der große Menschheitsaugenblick: Zu Schillers politischer Publikumsdramaturgie in *Don Karlos.*" In *Schillers Theaterpraxis,* edited by Peter-André Alt and Stefanie Hundehege, 9–38. Berlin: De Gruyter, 2020.

———. "Humanity's Imaginary Body: The Concepts of Empathy and Sympathy in the New Theater Experience in the 18th Century." *Deutsche Vierteljahrsschrift für Literaturwissenschaft und Geistesgeschichte* 82, no. 3 (2008): 382–399.

———. "Der Ring, die Statue, der Krug und seine Scherben: Eine Skizze zum Symbol und symbolischen Darstellungsverfahren im klassischen Humanitätsdrama (Lessing, Goethe, Kleist)." *Zeitschrift für deutsche Philologie* 4 (2004): 45–61.

———. "Der Zufall der Geburt: Lessings *Nathan der Weise* und der imaginäre Körper der Geschichtsphilosophie." In *Körper/Kultur: Kalifornische Studien zur deutschen Moderne,* edited by Thomas W. Kniesche, 100–125. Würzburg: Königshausen & Neumann, 1995.

Schneider, Josef. *Die deutsche Dichtung vom Ausgang des Barock bis zum Beginn des Klassizismus 1700–1785.* Stuttgart: Metzler, 1924.

Schön, Erich. "Schillers *Kabale und Liebe*: (K)ein bürgerliches Trauerspiel—Schiller und Otto von Gemmingens *Der deutsche Hausvater.*" In *Bürgerlichkeit im 18. Jahrhundert,* edited by Hans Edwin Friedrich, Fotis Jannidis, and Marianne Willems, 377–403. Tübingen: Niemeyer, 2006.

Schönert, Jörg. "Der Kaufmann von Jerusalem: Zum Handel mit Kapitalien und Ideen in Lessings *Nathan der Weise.*" *Scientia poetica* 12 (2009): 89–113.

Schopenhauer, Johanna. *Gabriele: Ein Roman in drei Teilen.* Berlin: Berliner Ausgabe, 2015.

Schwab, Dieter. "Familie." In *Geschichtliche Grundbegriffe: Historisches Lexikon zur politisch-sozialen Sprache in Deutschland,* vol. 2, E–G, edited by Otto Brunner, Werner Conze, and Reinhart Koselleck, 253–301. Stuttgart: Klett-Cotta, 1975.

Schweitzer, Christoph E. "Wilhelm Meister und das Bild des kranken Königssohns." *PMLA* 2, no. 3 (1957): 419–432.

Sedgwick, Eve Kosofsky. *Epistemology of the Closet.* Berkeley: University of California Press, 1990.

———. "Paranoid Reading and Reparative Reading, Or, You're So Paranoid, You Probably Think This Essay Is about You." In *Touching Feeling: Affect, Pedagogy, Performativity,* 123–151. Durham, NC: Duke University Press, 2003.

———. "Queer and Now." In *Tendencies,* 1–20. Durham, NC: Duke University Press, 1994.

———. "Tales of the Avunculate: Queer Tutelage in *The Importance of Being Earnest.*" In *Tendencies,* 52–73. Durham, NC: Duke University Press, 1993.

Seeba, Hinrich C. *Die Liebe zur Sache: Öffentliches und privates Interesse in Lessings Dramen.* Tübingen: Niemeyer, 1973.

Shorter, Edward. *The Making of the Modern Family.* New York: Basic Books, 1975.

Simmel, Georg. "Zur Soziologie der Familie." In *Individualismus der modernen Zeit und andere soziologische Abhandlungen,* 119–132. Frankfurt am Main: Suhrkamp, 2008.

Sina, Kai. "Nihilismusgefahr. *Stella*, Goethe und das Unerträgliche." *Goethe-Jahrbuch* 136 (2019): 142–156.

Slessarev, Helga. "Nathan der Weise und Adam Smith." In "Nation und Gelehrtenrepublik: Lessing im europäischen Zusammenhang," edited by Wilfried Barner and Albert M. Reh, special issue, *Lessing Yearbook* (1984): 248–256.

Sofer, Andrew. *The Stage Life of Props*. Ann Arbor: University of Michigan Press, 2003.

Soloman, Andrew. *Far from the Tree: Parents, Children, and the Search for Identity*. New York: Scribner, 2012.

Sørensen, Bengt Algot. *Allegorie und Symbol: Texte zur Theorie des dichterischen Bildes im 18. und frühen 19. Jahrhundert*. Frankfurt am Main: Athenäum, 1972.

———. *Herrschaft und Zärtlichkeit: Der Patriarchalismus und das Drama im 18. Jahrhundert*. Munich: Beck, 1984.

———. "Über die Familie in Goethes 'Werther' und 'Wilhelm Meister.'" *Orbis Litterarum* 42 (1987): 118–140.

Soussloff, Catherine M. *The Subject in Art: Portraiture and the Birth of the Modern*. Durham, NC: Duke University Press, 2006.

Spillers, Hortense J. "Mama's Baby, Papa's Maybe: An American Grammar Book." *Diacritics* 17, no. 2 (1987): 64–81.

Stack, Carol. *All Our Kin: Strategies for Survival in a Black Community*. New York: Harper and Row, 1974.

Steiner, Uwe C. "Gerechtigkeit für Odoardo Galotti: Ein Theatercoup mit Folgen: Wie Lessing das tragische Opfer geschlechteranthropologisch unwidmet und damit von Bodmer bis zur Gegenwart wirkt." *Deutsche Vierteljahrsschrift für Literaturwissenschaft und Geistesgeschichte* 95 (2021): 43–80.

Steinhausen, Georg. *Geschichte des deutschen Briefes: Zur Kulturgeschichte des deutschen Volkes*. Vol. 1. Zurich: Weidmann, 1889.

Stephan, Inge. "'So ist die Tugend ein Gespenst': Frauenbild und Tugendbegriff bei Lessing und Schiller." In *Inszenierte Weiblichkeit: Codierung der Geschlechter in der Literatur des 18. Jahrhunderts*, 13–41. Cologne: Böhlau, 2004.

———. "Weibliche und männliche Autorschaft: Zum *Florentin* von Dorothea Schlegel und zur *Lucinde* von Friedrich Schlegel." In *Inszenierte Weiblichkeit: Codierung der Geschlechter in der Literatur des 18. Jahrhunderts*, edited by Claudia Benthien and Inge Stephan, 233–253. Cologne: Böhlau, 2004,

Stöcklein, Paul. "Nachwort." Afterword to *Die Wahlverwandtschaften*, by Johann Wolfgang Goethe. Munich: DTV, 1963.

Stone, Lawrence. *The Family, Sex and Marriage in England 1500–1800*. London: Penguin, 1977.

Streeruwitz, Marlene. "*Kabale und Liebe* oder *Die antiödipale Geste, die da noch möglich war*." In *Friedrich Schiller, Dichter, Denker, Vor- und Gegenbild*, edited by Jan Bürger, 225–234. Göttingen: Wallstein, 2007.

Sullivan, Heather. "Nature and the 'Dark Pastoral' in Goethe's *Werther*." *Goethe Yearbook* 21 (2015): 115–132.

Sutherland, Wendy. *Staging Blackness and Performing Whiteness in Eighteenth-Century German Drama*. London: Routledge, 2016.

Szondi, Peter. "Tableau und coup de théâtre: Zur Sozialpsychologie des bürgerlichen Trauerspiels bei Diderot: Mit einem Exkurs über Lessing." In *Erforschung der deutschen*

Aufklärung, edited by Peter Pütz, 192–208. Königstein im Taunus: Athenäum, Hain, Scriptor, Hanstein, 1980.

———. *Die Theorie des bürgerlichen Trauerspiels im 18. Jahrhundert*. Frankfurt am Main: Suhrkamp, 1973.

Tacke, Alexandra. "Aus dem Rahmen (ge)fallen: *Tableaux vivants* in Goethes Wahlverwandtschaften und bei Vanessa Beecroft." In *Äpfel und Birnen: Illegitimes Vergleichen in den Kulturwissenschaften*, edited by Helga Lutz, Friedrich Mißfelder, and Tilo Renz, 73–93. Bielefeld: Transcript, 2006.

tagesschau. "Bund-Länder Treffen: Corona-Maßnahmen ab Dezember. Pressekonferenz mit Merkel, Müller und Söder (Berlin, 25. November 2020)." Accessed May 15, 2021. https://www.youtube.com/watch?v=2Vd0ZDXem74.

Tantillo, Astrida Orle. *Goethe's Elective Affinities and the Critics*. Rochester, NY: Camden House, 2001.

———. *Goethe's Modernisms*. New York: Bloomsbury, 2010.

———. "A New Reading of *Werther* as Goethe's Critique of Rousseau." *Orbis Litterarum* 56 (2001): 443–465.

———. *The Will to Create: Goethe's Philosophy of Nature*. Pittsburgh, PA: University of Pittsburgh Press, 2002.

Tautz, Birgit. *Reading and Seeing Ethnic Differences in the Enlightenment: From China to Africa*. New York: Palgrave McMillan, 2007.

Taylor, Charles. *Sources of the Self*. Cambridge, MA: Harvard University Press, 1989.

Taylor, Michael Thomas. "Right Queer: Hegel's Philosophy of Marriage." *Republic of Letters: A Journal for the Study of Knowledge, Politics, and the Arts* 3, no. 2 (2013): 1–22.

ter Horst, Eleanor E. *Lessing, Goethe, Kleist, and the Transformation of Gender: From Hermaphrodite to Amazon*. New York: Peter Lang, 2003.

Theweleit, Klaus. *Männerphantasien*. 2 vols. Frankfurt am Main: Roter Stern, 1977–1978.

Thomas, Kate. "Eternal Gardens and the Queer Uncanny in Frances Hodgson Burnett's 'In the Closed Room' (1902)." *Pacific Coast Philology* 50, no. 2 (2015): 173–183.

———. *Postal Pleasures: Sex, Scandal, and Victorian Letters*. Oxford: Oxford University Press, 2012.

Thomas, Todne. *Kincraft: The Making of Black Evangelical Society*. Durham, NC: Duke University Press, 2021.

Tobin, Robert. *Warm Brothers: Queer Theory and the Age of Goethe*. Philadelphia: University of Pennsylvania Press, 2000.

Trunz, Erich. "Die Kupferstiche zu den 'Lebenden Bildern' in den *Wahlverwandtschaften*." In *Weimarer Goethe-Studien*, 203–218. Weimar: Böhlau, 1980.

———. "Nachwort." Afterword to *Romane und Novellen*, by Johann Wolfgang von Goethe, edited by Erich Trunz, 689–711. Vol. 6 of *Johann Wolfgang Goethe Werke: Hamburger Ausgabe*. 14 vols. Munich: Deutscher Taschenbuch Verlag, 1999.

Turner, Mark. *Death Is the Mother of Beauty: Mind, Metaphor, Criticism*. Chicago: University of Chicago Press, 1987.

Umrath, Barbara. "A Feminist Reading of the Frankfurt School's Studies on Authoritarianism and Its Relevance for Understanding Authoritarian Tendencies in Germany Today." *The South Atlantic Quarterly* 117, no. 4 (2018): 861–878.

Unglaub, Jonathan. "'Esther before Ahasuerus': Beauty, Majesty, Bondage." *The Art Bulletin* 85, no. 1 (2003): 114–136.

Urban, Eva. "Lessing's *Nathan the Wise*: From the Enlightenment to the Berliner Ensemble." *New Theatre Quarterly* 30, no. 2 (2014): 183–196.

Utz, Peter. "'Hier ist keine Heimat': Zur aktuellen Befremdlichkeit von Schillers *Tell*." *Jahrbuch der deutschen Schillergesellschaft* 48 (2004): 409–413.

Van der Laan, J. M. "*Kabale und Liebe* Reconsidered." In *A Companion to the Works of Friedrich Schiller*, edited by Steven D. Martinson, 115–135. Rochester, NY: Boydell & Brewer, 2005.

Vellusig, Robert. "Aufklärung und Briefkultur: Wie das Herz sprechen lernt, wenn es zu schreiben beginnt." In *Kulturmuster der Aufklärung: Ein neues Heuristikum in der Diskussion*, edited by Carsten Zelle, 154–171. Göttingen: Wallstein, 2011.

Vogel, Juliane. "Raptus: Eröffnungsfiguren von Drama und Oper des 18. Jahrhunderts." *Deutsche Vierteljahrsschrift für Literaturwissenschaft und Geistesgeschichte* 83, no. 4. (2009): 507–521.

Wagner, Martin. "'. . . So ganz in dem Gefühl vom ruhigen Daseyn versunken, dass meine Kunst darunter leidet . . .': Michael Frieds *Absorption and Theatricality* und Goethes *Die Leiden des jungen Werthers*." *Jahrbuch der Grillparzer-Gesellschaft* 24 (2011–2012): 183–226.

Wallner, Edmund. *Eintausend Sujets zu lebenden Bildern*. Erfurt: Bartholomäus, 1876–1881.

Watt, Ian. *The Rise of the Novel: Studies in Defoe, Richardson and Fielding*. Berkeley: University of California Press, 1957.

Weber, Caroline. "The Sins of the Father: Colonialism and Family History in Diderot's 'Le fils naturel.'" *PMLA* 118, no. 3 (2003): 488–501.

Weber, Max. "Die protestantische Ethik und der 'Geist' des Kapitalismus." In *Archiv für Sozialwissenschaft und Sozialpolitik*, 41–43. Vol. 20. Tübingen: Mohr, 1904–1905.

Weber, Samuel. "Family Scenes: Some Preliminary Remarks on Domesticity and Theatricality." *South Atlantic Quarterly* 98, no. 3 (1999): 355–364.

Weidmann, Heiner. "Ökonomie der 'Großmuth': Geldwirtschaft in Lessings *Minna von Barnhelm* und *Nathan der Weise*." *Deutsche Vierteljahrsschrift für Literaturwissenschaft und Geistesgeschichte* 68, no. 3 (1994): 447–461.

Weineck, Silke-Maria. *The Tragedy of Fatherhood: King Laius and the Politics of Paternity in the West*. New York: Bloomsbury, 2014.

Weissberg, Liliane. "The Master's Theme, and Some Variations: Dorothea Schlegel's *Florentin* as *Bildungsroman*." *Michigan German Studies* 13, no. 2 (1987): 169–181.

Wellbery, David E. *Lessing's Laocoon: Semiotics and Aesthetics in the Age of Reason*. Cambridge, UK: Cambridge University Press, 1984.

Wetters, Kirk. "Who Cares about Society? *Sorge* and Reification in Goethe's *Wilhelm Meisters Lehrjahre*." *Colloquia Germanica* 47, no. 3 (2014): 243–262.

White, Patricia. *Uninvited: Classical Hollywood Cinema and Lesbian Representability*. Bloomington: Indiana University Press, 1999.

Wiegland, Daniel. *Gebannte Bewegung: Tableaux vivants und früher Film in der Kultur der Moderne*. Marburg: Schüren, 2016.

Wiggins, Ellwood. "Pity Play: Sympathy and Spectatorship in Lessing's *Miss Sara Sampson* and Adam Smith's *Theory of Moral Sentiments*." In *Performing Knowledge, 1750–1850*, edited by Mary Helen Dupree and Sean Franzel, 85–111. Berlin: De Gruyter, 2015.

Wild, Christopher. "Der theatralische Schleier des Hymens. Lessings bürgerliches Trauerspiel *Emilia Galotti*." *Deutsche Vierteljahrsschrift für Literaturwissenschaft und Geistesgeschichte* 74 (2000): 189–220.

Willey, Angela. *Undoing Monogamy: The Politics of Science and the Possibilities of Biology*. Durham, NC: Duke University Press, 2016.

Williams, Raymond. *Keywords: A Vocabulary of Culture and Society*. Oxford: Oxford University Press, 1976.

Wilm, Marie-Christin. "*Die Jungfrau von Orleans* tragödientheoretisch gelesen: Schillers *Romantische Tragödie* und ihre praktische Theorie." *Jahrbuch der deutschen Schillergesellschaft* 47 (2003): 141–170.

Wilms, Wilfried. "Dismantling the Bourgeois Family: J.M.R. Lenz's 'Soldatenfamilie.'" *Monatshefte* 100, no. 3 (2008): 337–350.

———. "Im Griff des Politischen: Konfliktfähigkeit und Vaterwerdung in *Emilia Galotti*." *Deutsche Vierteljahrsschrift für Literaturwissenschaft und Geistesgeschichte* 76 (2002): 50–73.

Wilson, W. Daniel. "'Ein Glied der liebenswürdigen Familie auszumachen': Labor, Family, and Werther's Search for Nature." In *Zereissproben/Double Bind: Familie und Geschlecht in der deutschen Literatur des 18. und 19. Jahrhunderts*, edited by Christine Kanz, 85–112. Bern: eFeF, 2007.

———. "Obedience." *PEGS* 77, no. 1 (2008): 47–59.

Witte, Bernd: "Die andere Gesellschaft: Der Ursprung des bürgerlichen Romans in Gellerts 'Leben der Schwedischen Gräfin von G***.'" In *"Ein Lehrer der ganzen Nation": Leben und Werk Christian Fürchtegott Gellerts*, edited by Bernd Witte, 66–85. Munich: Fink, 1990.

———. "Christian Fürchtegott Gellert: *Leben der schwedischen Gräfin von G****: Die Frau, die Schrift, der Tod." In *Romane des 17. und 18. Jahrhunderts (Interpretationen)*, 112–149. Stuttgart: Reclam, 1996.

———. "Die Individualität des Autors: Gellerts Briefsteller als Roman eines Schreibenden." *The German Quarterly* 62, no. 1 (1989): 5–14.

———. "Der Roman als moralische Anstalt: Gellerts *Leben der schwedischen Gräfin von G*** und die Literatur des achtzehnten Jahrhunderts." *Germanisch-Romanische Monatsschrift* 63 (1980): 150–168.

Woesler, Winfried. "Die beiden Schlüsse von Lessings 'Nathan.'" In *Akten des X. Internationalen Germanistenkongresses Wien 2000: 'Zeitenwende-die Germanistik auf dem Weg vom 20. ins 21. Jahrhundert*, 323–330. Bern: Peter Lang, 2002.

———. "Lessing's 'Emilia' und die Virginia-Legende bei Livius." *Zeitschrift für deutsche Philologie* 116, no. 2 (1997): 161–171.

Woodall, Joanna. "An Exemplary Consort: Antonis Mor's Portrait of Mary Tudor." *Art History* 14 (1991): 192–224.

Worvill, Romira. "Lessing and the French Enlightenment." In *Lessing and the German Enlightenment*, edited by Ritchie Robertson, 15–38. Oxford: Oxford University Press, 2018.

Wurst, Karin. *Familiale Liebe ist die 'wahre Gewalt': Die Repräsentation der Familie in G.E. Lessings dramatischem Werk*. Amsterdam: Rodopi, 1988.

Zantop, Susanne. *Colonial Fantasies: Conquest, Family, and Nation in Precolonial Germany, 1770–1870*. Durham, NC: Duke University Press, 1997.

Zarinebaf, Fariba. "Harem." In *Europe, 1450–1789: Encyclopedia of the Early Modern World*, vol. 3, edited by Jonathan Dewald, 132–135. New York: Scribner, 2004.

Zedler, Johann Heinrich. *Grosses vollständiges Universal-Lexicon aller Wissenschaften und Künste*. Leipzig, 1731–1754.

Zentrum für digitale Lexikographie der deutschen Sprache. Accessed July 15, 2020. https:// zdl.org/.

Zhang, Chunjie. *Transculturality and German Discourse in the Age of European Colonialism*. Evanston, IL: Northwestern University Press, 2017.

INDEX

❦

ABOUT THE AUTHOR

HEIDI SCHLIPPHACKE is a professor of Germanic studies at the University of Illinois, Chicago. Her research explores the intersections of aesthetics, gender, sexuality, and social forms in the European Enlightenment and in post-WWII German-language literature, thought, and film. Her monograph *Nostalgia after Nazism: History, Home, and Affect in German and Austrian Literature and Film* (Bucknell University Press) was published in 2010.